Intercepted

Intercepted

The Rise and Fall of NFL Cornerback Darryl Henley

MICHAEL MCKNIGHT

University of Nebraska Press | Lincoln & London

© 2012 by Michael McKnight
Map courtesy of Shawn Ryan.

All rights reserved
Manufactured in the United States of America

Library of Congress Cataloging-in-Publication Data

McKnight, Michael.
Intercepted: the rise and fall of NFL cornerback
Darryl Henley / Michael McKnight.
p. cm.
Includes bibliographical references.
ISBN 978-0-8032-3849-7 (cloth: alk. paper)
1. Henley, Darryl, 1966– 2. Drug dealers—United
States—Biography. 3. Prisoners—United States—
Biography. 4. Football players—United States—
Biography. I. Title.
HV5805.H39M35 2012
364.1'77092—dc23
[B]
2012012169

Set in Scala by Bob Reitz.

For Kelly
words cannot express

Author's Note

Speech or writing that appears between quotation marks was taken from a document, an interview, or a recording, or was verified as accurate by more than one source. Rare exceptions are specifically noted as one person's recollection. In these cases, the veracity of the source was taken into account, and the general tone and content of the statement (if not the precise words) were verified by other informed sources.

Speech that appears without quotation marks is the recollection of a single source who was not the speaker but was privy to the conversation. Quotation marks are not used in such cases because I cannot be certain that the words written were precisely the words spoken.

This is a true story, not one based on real events.

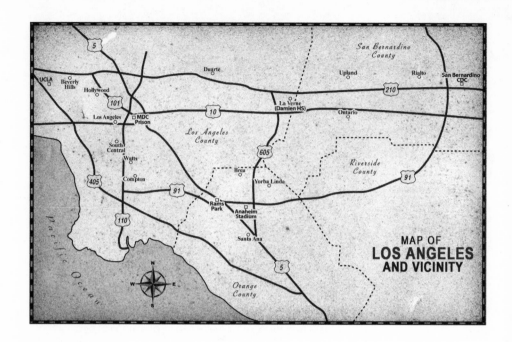

MAP OF
LOS ANGELES
AND VICINITY

"What has happened to me?" he thought.
It was no dream.

—FRANZ KAFKA, *The Metamorphosis*

Introduction

The black box was designed by a prisoner. Darryl Henley would not find this out until later, but it was true. The unwieldy block of steel that bound his shackles to his belly chain was the invention of a nameless inmate who had devised a better way to restrain himself. This irony would not have mattered to Henley had he known just then, as he stood staring at a hot tarmac stretching beyond an airplane emblazoned "Federal Bureau of Prisons." It was the same runway where he'd boarded over thirty flights destined for NFL road games, "dressed to impress and smelling like new money," as he liked to say. But on this day he was wearing a plain white T-shirt, pocketless khaki pants, prison-issue plastic slippers, handcuffs, a belly chain, leg irons, and the black box. Always the black box. He had recently been sentenced to forty-one years at the U.S. penitentiary in Marion, Illinois, the worst federal prison in the

1

Darryl Henley, age nine. (Courtesy of the Henley family)

country, with no possibility of parole. Darryl Henley did not smell like new money anymore. He smelled like fear.

At his sentencing a month earlier, he'd been ordered to serve a little more than twenty-one years for cocaine trafficking, plus nineteen years for the heroin deal and double murder plot he'd tried to pull off from behind bars. This second set of crimes happened when Henley paid a prison guard at the Metropolitan Detention Center in Los Angeles to bring a mobile phone to his cell each night. He then used that phone to arrange a million-dollar shipment of heroin from LA to Detroit. His newfound supplier, a Mafia soldier named Joey Gambino whom Henley had never met, had presented Henley with the heroin deal over the phone and followed it up by offering to do away with the young woman who had been the star witness at Henley's trial, Rams cheerleader Tracy Donaho, and the presiding judge, too. Two hits in exchange for a portion of Henley's imminent heroin profits.

Henley accepted Gambino's offer. Only Joey Gambino wasn't a Mafiosi. He was an undercover DEA agent named Mike Bansmer who recorded all of his conversations with Henley.

Once a jovial, popular, articulate NFL player with a clean criminal record, Henley found himself in court a few days later pleading guilty to soliciting two murders, including the assassination of a federal judge.

And now Henley was waiting to board the plane that would take him to Marion, the end of the line for American criminals. No one could explain how or why a man who made $600,000 a year playing pro football had sunk to such depths, especially this exceptionally bright young man who had been raised by a close-knit Christian family in the LA suburbs, excelled in parochial schools throughout his youth, and graduated from UCLA as a B-average history student. As perplexed as they all were, though, no one stood more confused by the events of the previous four years than Henley himself.

Standing there on that hot runway at LAX, he saw a mirage in the shimmering heat distorting the asphalt. It was an image of himself, wearing a tailored Armani suit bearing just the right sheen, a $400 tie, $300 sunglasses, and Italian loafers that cost more than the tie and shades combined. His friends, fellow Rams defensive backs Todd Lyght and Keith Lyle, were standing with him, diamond studs in their earlobes, all three men eager to board the jet droning next to them so they could slide on their headphones and catch a nap on the way to Atlanta. Or New York. Or Miami. Only this time it would be to Marion, a secluded collection of cages built in 1983 to replace Alcatraz. This was the prison that Henley's sentencing judge had referred to as "the highest level of security known to the federal prison system."

"This defendant should be locked down in the Marion facility," the judge had said, "because it is obvious that he is even more dangerous in custody than out of custody."

One of usp Marion's greatest security advantages is its location in a vast, desolate swamp in southern Illinois — much closer to Arkansas than Chicago. An escaped inmate would be easy to find because the only thing around for miles would be him. The hills around the prison were grayish-green the day Henley arrived, the grass just starting to breathe again after a long winter. Tall guard towers jutted from the meadow like gray flowers; atop the nearest one Darryl saw a darkened window slide open and a guard lean out and aim his rifle down at the van like a hunter tracking a deer. The brakes groaned, the door slid open, and Darryl saw the man he would later refer to as the Thin Man.

He was a caricature of himself, a prison boss straight out of *Cool Hand Luke*. Wearing black boots, black sunglasses, a black jacket, and a black bop baseball cap, he stood atop the stairway that led inside the penitentiary. As Darryl was led up the stairs, he noticed that the Thin Man was chewing tobacco and that his teeth were the color of candy caramels. The Thin Man's slight build accentuated the immensity of the prison behind him — the silence of its exterior hiding the ugliness that Henley knew breathed inside. For only the second time in his life — the first being the announcement of his trial verdict — Henley's legs nearly failed him. As he reached the top of the stairs, the Thin Man, his ring of keys glinting in the sun, knowing full well that the inmate before him was the pro ballplayer everybody in the compound had been talking about, gestured like a game show host revealing what's behind door number three and said to Henley and his fellow inmates, "Welcome to Marion, ladies."

Chapter 1

The Rams lost the day Darryl Henley was born. It was October 30, 1966, and the Rams' "Fearsome Foursome" defensive line could not stop Johnny Unitas on what the history books show was a cold, blustery day in Baltimore. Twenty-five hundred miles west, in the Jungle section of South Los Angeles, it got up to ninety-six degrees that day, and no one gave much of a damn about the Rams and the Colts. By then, gangs had begun sowing their seed in the Jungle, an area that over the next twenty years would spawn the most violent urban culture in American history. Only a few people called it the Jungle back in the mid-1960s, when the man who would become Darryl Henley's father, Thomas Henley Jr., stepped off a Greyhound bus from rural Texas onto the cracked asphalt of Crenshaw Boulevard. Back then people called it Baldwin Village. Populated almost exclusively by young black families cramped into small houses that would soon be converted into smaller apartments, its residents spent many nights watching televised images of the civil rights struggles in the Deep South, a region from which a healthy number of Jungle dwellers had come, seeking a brighter future for their children.

Thomas Henley had left Texas for Los Angeles on the Fourth of July, 1965, in search of the American Dream. A four-year football letterman at West High School, just outside Waco, he'd discovered shortly after graduation that his girlfriend, Dorothy, was pregnant, so he did what he thought a real man should do: he by-passed his shot at a football scholarship to Prairie View A&M, married Dot, and like thousands of other southern black men at the time, headed for California in search of work. His aunt Idella let him sleep in the extra room in her house in Baldwin Village until he earned enough money to bring Dot and their newborn son, Thomas III, out from Texas.

The Henleys arrived in LA, coincidentally, at the same time as *Newsweek* reporter Karl Fleming, who had covered the civil rights movement in the South since 1960 and discovered upon arriving in Los Angeles that it "was in real senses more segregated than Mississippi." Thomas Henley discovered this as well, but he was an optimist by nature, and he held tight to his dreams of giving Thomas III all the things *he'd* never had. Little Thomas came into the world two weeks before the Watts rebellion erupted down the street. Thirty-four people died, most of them the same age and skin color as the Jungle's newest father. That fall, Henley took the money he'd saved from his work as a day laborer and moved his wife and son into a two-room apartment on Wall Street, about twenty blocks south of Baldwin Village. The Henleys were closer to the smoldering tension in Watts, but they were on their own, and that mattered to Thomas Henley.

This is the world into which Darryl Keith Henley was born. By all accounts there was something unique about him from the beginning. He was precocious, always up to something, but he was so joyous—"always smiling" is the phrase used most often to describe him as a child—that he was hard to scold. Darryl was his mother's favorite and by far the most emotional member of a family that would soon add a third son, Eric. Darryl was quick to lash out and quick to cry, with skin that seemed too thin for his environs. Fortunately for him and his brothers, their parents had skins of iron.

His father's new job at Western Union was the rope that pulled the Henleys out of the cauldron of South Los Angeles and into the suburbs. Thomas and Dot chose Duarte, a working-class town in the San Gabriel Valley—an hour north of Watts by freeway—and moved their family into a two-bedroom house on Wesleygrove Avenue, a mostly black enclave where folks still washed clothes by hand and hung them on shared clotheslines that dangled over their yards like the power lines drooping over the street. "Everybody on that whole street, man, they liked each other," Darryl's father recalled. "And everybody in that neighborhood knew T.H. And T.H.'s sons had to succeed."

Darryl's father was rarely called Thomas in Duarte. "Thomas Henley was a man's name," said Chris Hale, who was coached by him in Pop Warner and would later play in two Super Bowls. "T.H. was a legend." As coach of the nine- and ten-year-old Duarte Gorillas, T.H. earned a reputation for being strong-willed and stern, "the consummate coach that you didn't want to play for," Hale said. "I shouldn't say didn't want to play for—it was more like you were *scared* to play for him. You knew he was a good coach, you knew he was a good man, but you were scared of him *because* he was a good man." Henley's reputation was combined with a sturdy 5'11" frame that conjured a longshoreman, and a facial expression that usually lingered closer to scowl than smirk. When someone broke into his car one night and stole his radio, T.H. found out who did it and knocked on his door. His radio was back in his dash and playing the Isley Brothers again by nightfall.

T.H.'s neighbors pitied his sons for what he and Dot demanded of them, while simultaneously envying the Henleys for raising their boys so fiercely. It seemed as if Darryl and Thomas were always doing chores or reading books. T.H.'s sons, after all, had to succeed, and succeeding meant private school. Private school meant that T.H. and Dot worked overtime to pay tuition. Money was tight for the Henleys even before Eric was born in 1969. The three Henley brothers would sleep in the same bed for most of the next four years, until the glorious day when T.H. came home with three-story bunk beds, a gift whose luster wore off the night Darryl discovered that Eric, who slept up top, was not completely potty-trained.

The two older boys were like night and day. Thomas was docile and obedient, and everyone liked him for it. Darryl was brash and confident, and everyone loved him for it. Darryl was the Henley child to whom grownups gravitated, taking an extra second to crack a joke with him or poke fun at him because they knew he could crack and poke right back. And, boy, could he play ball. All three Henley boys were fast and strong—traits that were like currency in their sports-mad neighborhood—and all three had exceptional college football careers ahead of them, but Darryl was the most gifted, the purest athlete, one of the rare few born to compete with his body. A number of famous champions throughout history have had their first competitive fires stoked by older siblings, perhaps the most notable being Michael Jordan, whose older brother Larry bullied him in their one-on-one basketball games until Michael became both tall and famously averse to losing. Michael had been considered the laziest of the five Jordan kids; so it was with Darryl Henley. He excelled without trying. By age seven, he was the best football player in the Arcadia youth league, where his father had sent him, two towns away, so he could get the best coaching and equipment possible. That same year, Darryl's older brother, Thomas, was cut from his Pop Warner team. Thomas was no slouch on the football field, as he would soon prove, but that day left him humiliated.

Darryl wasn't sure how *he* felt about Thomas's failure. He'd always looked up to his older brother, but his hero worship back then was reserved for only one kid.

Willie McGowan, who would later have a dramatic impact on Darryl's life, was three years older than Darryl and the undisputed star of T.H.'s Pop Warner team, for which Darryl served as water boy. A swift running back, Willie wore number 45 on his jersey, and white athletic tape wrapped just so around his wrists and cleats. Darryl mimicked this "spatted" look in his own pee-wee games and copied Willie's running style as well, leading his team to the championship game against Pasadena, the best pee-wee team in the valley. Just before the opening kick, Darryl's mother came out of the stands and reminded him of what he'd learned in *The Power of Positive Thinking*—the Norman Vincent Peale book she made her sons read as soon as they were able. After repeating Peale's mantra with his mother—"I can do all things through Christ who strengthens me"—Darryl scored a touchdown on the first play from scrimmage and added three more before the game was over. An opposing coach came up to him afterward and said something that Henley would never forget: "Man, you are *good*."

Willie McGowan's approval meant more to Darryl than that of any adult, though. Decades later Henley would remember spending time with Willie after practice, learning his feints and cuts and stutter-steps. Darryl felt on top of the world, hanging with the neighborhood's golden boy, the young man everyone in town smiled upon, knowing that if Willie kept his priorities straight he'd end up in the pros. "Willie was a good kid back then," Darryl's father recalled. "His mother was an upstanding woman. . . . Everything with Willie back then was 'Yes sir' and 'No sir.'"

The Henleys' dual incomes and penny-pinching allowed them to buy a home in Ontario, a nearby community that—with its neighbor Upland—was known as "The Model Colony." It was a step up in real estate terms and in the quality of its high school football programs, which began paying close attention to Thomas and Darryl Henley, in that order. Thomas had always been bigger and stronger than Darryl, but he'd also been a step slower. That changed around 1979, when Thomas suddenly became the Henley everyone expected to see playing on TV someday. And just as suddenly, Darryl became "just a little tiny thing," recalled Chris Hale. As for all the high school recruiters, T.H. told them to save their time. He'd already decided that Thomas was going to Damien High, an elite parochial boys' school in nearby Laverne.

With its distinction of having sent more boys to West Point than any school west of the Mississippi, Damien was a place that emphasized life after graduation, in stark contrast to the public schools just down the street, where a diploma often meant that school was out for life. Thomas Henley III aced Damien's challenging entrance requirements and never looked back, embarking on a quest for academic achievement that would earn him degrees from the West Coast's finest universities. "Thomas caught on early," his father said. "He knew what we wanted out of life for him at an early age." "And everybody expected Darryl to be the same way," their mother added.

Instead, Darryl seemed committed to becoming Thomas's opposite. Darryl was always polite, and he had no trouble with the law, but he owned a rebellious streak. At the end of his eighth-grade year, Darryl decided he wanted to go to Chaffey High, a minority-heavy public school where most of his church friends went. Surprisingly, his father agreed to it. It was the happiest moment of Darryl's young life until his father added: "But you can't compete against Thomas." It was a simple condition, but a harsh one: when Chaffey played Damien, Darryl would have to sit out. And so, very much against his will, Darryl became a Damien Spartan, too.

The rivalry between the two brothers would deepen over the years as Thomas and Darryl competed to become the first of T.H.'s sons to succeed. More often than not, Darryl finished second in this race. "Darryl was a good athlete," said Willie Abston, one of Darryl's best friends at both Damien and UCLA, "but Thomas was a *great* athlete. Darryl was a good student, but Thomas was a *great* student. Thomas was always more, and Eric was looked at as the next Thomas, not the next Darryl."

The only thing Darryl had that Thomas did not have was a natural strut in his walk, a hipness that Thomas would have looked goofy trying to pull off. Darryl may not have been smarter than Thomas, or even a better athlete, but he was by all accounts cooler.

T.H. was working as a supervisor at Lockheed Aircraft by this time, and Dot Henley was a grade-school teacher. Their combined salaries were not enough to bankroll two private tuitions, so Thomas and Darryl helped pay their way at Damien by working as campus groundskeepers during the summer. That fall, on the same field they had seeded and watered in summer, Thomas and Darryl unleashed a level of football talent that their small school opponents were ill-prepared to handle. In 1981 Thomas Henley became a football star, setting a career rushing record at Damien that stood for more than twenty years (until it was broken by college All-American and NFL player Ian Johnson). Protecting the football as securely as he guarded his perfect grade point average, number 25 rumbled up and down high school fields in the San Gabriel Valley in the autumns of 1981 and 1982 with a humility that belied his age. After each of the school-record twenty-nine touchdowns Thomas scored as a senior, the first teammate to greet him was a smaller kid who, fittingly, wore number 24, for Darryl always seemed one less, one back.

Thomas Henley III was captain of the football team, president of the student body, a 4.0 student, league champion in the triple jump, and was named the second-best Catholic school athlete in all of California.[1] Most important to his parents, however, Thomas was someone T.H. and Dot could point to, right across the dinner table, as the perfect example for Darryl and Eric to follow. Many of the college coaches who came to visit Thomas that fall winked at Darryl as they left the Henley home in Ontario. "See you next year," they'd say, just as they'd done with the younger brothers of other recruits. Except Darryl winked back and whispered to himself: "Damn right you will."

He never claimed to be an angel. Darryl tried to steal a bike from outside Kmart when he was eleven. In high school, he became the first and only Henley son to come home drunk. It did not happen again. He tried to turn in a paper he had copied from a football buddy—an act of plagiarism that inflamed Damien's headmaster, Father Travers, and resulted in an F on Darryl's report card. Incensed by what he saw as over-punishment, T.H. drove Darryl the next morning to Ontario High School and enrolled him there as a transfer. As the story goes, Darryl, who had been groomed as Thomas's replacement at running back for the Spartans, returned to Damien two days later, after Damien's Father acquiesced to Darryl's father.

Despite their promises, usc and Nebraska did not see Darryl next year. The consensus was that he was too small. But to everyone's surprise, Tom Hayes, the defensive backs coach at ucla, began driving to Damien twice a week to watch practice. Damien's athletic director, an amiable bear of a man named Tom Carroll, couldn't figure out why. Darryl was a good kid, but he was no Thomas. He was fast enough, but he needed rocks in his pockets to weigh 150. "What do you see in him?" Carroll asked Hayes on the sideline. "One of those big Pac Ten fullbacks will come around the corner and you'll have to scoop Darryl up with a damn shovel."

"No, no, no," replied Hayes. "We're not recruiting him so he can take on fullbacks. We want him to cover all these track stars in our conference who are dressed up as wideouts. This kid has the quickest feet of anyone we're looking at this year. And from what I've seen, he's not afraid of anything."

Chapter 2

The call came at 10 a.m. on July 15, 1993. Awaking next to Jennifer in his condo outside Atlanta, Darryl picked up the phone and muttered a groggy hello.

Come get your truck, man. I'm in the wind. See you in the next life.

It was Willie's voice. He sounded nervous. Willie never sounded nervous.

What? Darryl said.

The keys are under the front left fender, Willie said. They got her. She got popped.

Where is she?

Feds got her.

Darryl's heart sank. Jennifer stirred next to him. What's going on, baby? she asked.

So you're just gonna leave her? Darryl said into the phone.

Hell, yeah, I'm gonna leave her. I ain't trying to be no hero. Yo, if she pages you, do not call her back.

You gotta come over here, man.

Darryl Henley, 1993. (Courtesy of the St. Louis Rams)

I'm the last person you should be near right now.

You're really going to leave her, Darryl repeated. You're just gonna leave her in jail.

Silence. Darryl could hear Willie thinking on the other end. He knew Willie had a heart.

I'll be over in a minute, Willie said. *Click.*

"It started with Tracy," Darryl said inside the visiting room of the United States Penitentiary. "This whole chain of events started when I met Tracy Donaho."

"I met Darryl Henley on Super Bowl Sunday, January of '93," Tracy Donaho wrote in her DEA statement in December 1993. It was the Cowboys versus the Bills at the Rose Bowl in Pasadena, where Darryl, who had just completed his fourth season with the NFL's Los Angeles Rams, had played his college games.[1] Darryl and Tracy, a Rams cheerleader, were "in a tent out front," Tracy wrote.

"There were about seven cheerleaders and about five football players. We were scheduled to sign autographs for about four hours. The first hour the cheerleaders sat and talked and ate lunch. The players were at the table next to us. I noticed Darryl because he kept looking over at our table, and because he was wearing Karl Kani (menswear). Some of my girlfriends and I had wanted to find out where to get it for along [sic] time."[2]

Tracy was a nineteen-year-old from suburban Orange County with a round, pretty face framed by long, fluffy blonde hair. Darryl recognized her from somewhere. The player seated next to him, fellow Rams cornerback Steve Israel, reminded him. "She was with me that night at Todd's," Israel said, referring to the end-of-the-season party hosted by their teammate Todd Lyght a month earlier. Darryl and his girlfriend Alisa—also a Rams cheerleader—had been there that night, along with several other players and cheerleaders, including the blonde Darryl was now exchanging glances with outside the Rose Bowl. "Her name's Tracy," Israel said.

"Finally Darryl came over to our table," Tracy wrote. "None of the other football players followed. Darryl introduced himself to every girl personally. When he got to me and my girlfriend Alli we asked him about where to get the [Karl Kani] clothes."

Darryl told Tracy about a clothing retailer he knew at the Fox

Hills Mall, and asked her and Alli if they wanted to go shopping sometime. They said sure, so Darryl pulled out his walkie-talkie-size cell phone and called his friend and told him he'd be by in a few days with a couple of Rams cheerleaders.

"We talked a little longer," Tracy wrote. "But Darryl was mainly asking me questions about myself. I was feeling nervous and excited at the same time. I knew that the cheerleaders and football players are not supposed to associate, but he was paying so much attention to me I was taken aback."

In the weeks following, Israel would make fun of Henley for lavishing so much attention on Tracy that day. It was certainly not uncommon for Henley to pay attention to women, though. The lifestyle of—as he described it—"non-stop, fun, casual sex" he'd enjoyed at UCLA had developed into an almost constant juggling of women by his fourth year in the NFL, and he'd learned the hard way that it wasn't all it was cracked up to be. First there was Terri, the pristine churchgoer Darryl found out had been intercepting letters to him from other women and hiding them at her parents' house. Then came Carra, Tonya, Jamie, Nina, Yvette, Gina, Adrianne, and Nicole, in rapid succession, and mixed in there somewhere was a Jamaican girl whose name Darryl couldn't remember, and countless others whose names he wished he could forget. There was that curious string of five or six women who screamed during their most intimate moments with him—each woman louder than the one before—until he couldn't take it anymore. "What's up with all the screaming?" he finally asked, laughing.

"Sherelle said you like it like that."

Sherelle had been the first woman in the string. She was also the woman who had convinced Darryl to let her stay in a spare bedroom at his house so she could save money for cancer surgery. Sherelle later conspired with another woman in the string to rip a check from Darryl's checkbook, cash it for $5,000, and split the money. It was one of the oldest ploys in the gold digger handbook, and Sherelle might have gotten away with it had she known about the most important woman in Darryl's life. Every month, Darryl's bank statement was sent to D. Henley—as in Dorothy. When Darryl's mother scolded him for exceeding his monthly budget and showed him a $5,000 check as an example, he immediately smelled a rat and suspected that it was living with him and claiming it had cancer. Darryl did not press charges, but Sherelle's tenancy at his home in Orange County was over.

It was one of the more colorful episodes in his increasingly reckless personal life. Since his freshman year at UCLA, his pregame ritual had included donning headphones and listening to a song by funk-rap band Cameo called "Single Life," whose lyrics reflected his unapologetic commitment to playing the field. Or as he described it later in a memo to his attorneys: "I don't feel that I'm untruthful to women. I've always had a hard time being faithful. I just really like women. It's always been a weakness for me."

Darryl called Tracy the night of the Super Bowl, just a few hours after she passed him her number outside the stadium. She didn't answer the phone, so Darryl left a message asking when she wanted to go shopping. When Tracy heard the message, "I called Alli, since she was supposed to [go] shopping with us. . . . She said she couldn't go until Wed. When I hung up the phone it rang again immediately afterwards. It was Darryl. I got real nervous. Though he was so nice and funny. . . .

"Before we got off the phone he asked me to go to dinner with him. Luckily I had to work so I could say no. He said that he would call my [sic] the following day. . . .

"When I got home from school on Wednesday he had already called. When I returned his phone call we talked for awhile and made our plans to go shopping. He lived about ten minutes from me. I was to drive to his house and then we would pick Alli up."

When Tracy arrived, she and Darryl hugged hello in his living room. "I had never really been attracted to black guys before," she wrote, "but I remember thinking he was kind of cute. Plus being who he was didn't hurt either. I loved the way he dressed and [he] had a great body."

She would later describe the "shock" she felt upon seeing Henley's three gleaming cars parked in his garage—a Pathfinder, a Mercedes, and a new Lexus. For the trip to the mall Darryl chose the Lexus, a creme 300-SE coupe that would later become a crucial pawn in the drug trafficking madness yet to begin. "We had a great time trying on the clothes," Tracy recalled. "Every time we walked out of the dressing rooms, someone was there to mark for alterations."

The girls didn't buy much. They were both pretty broke. Darryl had heard his main girl, Alisa, complain about how she made just $40 per game, and somewhere between $20 and $50 per promotion. All told, it was possible for a Rams cheerleader to make $3,000 a year *if* she cheered at all twenty games (including exhibitions) and *if* she earned the maximum promo rate at every event. Not likely. They usually made less than a grand. Some cheerleaders gave dance lessons to kids to make ends meet. Alisa worked at a law office in downtown LA. Tracy waited tables and lived with her mom in Yorba Linda while taking classes at Orange Coast Community College.

Tracy and Alli bought an item or two each, just to be nice, then Darryl treated them to dinner. Just as he was about to start his Lexus, he stole a second alone with Tracy as she plopped into the back seat. He asked if she wanted to see a movie. Before Tracy could answer, Alli sat in the passenger seat. When Darryl dropped Alli off, Tracy told him that she had plans with her family, so instead of a movie she and Darryl had ice cream at Baskin-Robbins. They ended up back at his house. Tracy sat demurely on one of his sofas. Darryl asked if he could sit by her. "All right," Tracy said.

"He then asked me if it was okay to hold my hand," Tracy recounted at trial. "I said, 'Yes, it's okay. You can hold my hand.' And then I said, 'It's time for me to go. It's 10:00.' And then he asked me if he could kiss me, and I said yes. And he kissed me." Then he drove her home.

They flirted over the phone for the next few days, discussing how he'd never dated a white girl before and how she'd never dated a black guy. When Darryl told her he was moving to Atlanta in a few days, it confirmed Tracy's belief that any fling with Darryl Henley would be a short-lived one.

Henley went to Las Vegas that weekend. He called Tracy when he returned home. "It was a rainy day around noon," Tracy wrote in her statement. "He wanted me to come over. . . . Before I left for his house, he called back. He just wanted to tell me to drive safe in the rain. When I got there he said something sarcastic. I hit him just joking around. We ended up wrestling on the floor. He was so much fun. He was like a little kid."

A few nights later she dropped by his house after having dinner with another guy she was dating—a white college student named Travis. She and Darryl watched TV together. He taught her how to shoot craps on the new table he'd bought in Vegas. "Before I left, by my car, we had a talk about how he was leaving in a few days to move to Atlanta. We had discussed this several times. He asked me to spend the day with him the next day. . . . This would be the last time that I would see him. So I agreed."

She skipped class and accompanied Darryl to his realtor's office, then to a bank near the Rams' headquarters. Tracy stayed in the car because "it was too close to the Rams [headquarters] to be seen together." They went to a Thai restaurant for lunch, then returned to Darryl's house, where Tracy got behind the wheel of the Lexus and followed him to the car wash. Darryl drove the Mercedes. They watched TV in Darryl's bedroom as night fell. They kissed a little. It was the first week in February. Knowing he'd be on the other side of the continent by the time the fourteenth rolled around, Darryl asked Tracy to be his Valentine. She said yes.

Though he hadn't had sex with Tracy at that point, Darryl moved to Atlanta with a soft spot in his heart for her. He had three good reasons for taking things slowly, however, aside from the 2,000-mile distance. The first reason was Alisa, who'd captivated him and his family in a way no woman ever had; Alisa was also the leader of Tracy's cheerleading "line" — a squad within the squad that conducted gossip the way copper conducts electricity. His second reason was the vague, loosely enforced NFL rule about players dating cheerleaders. Darryl was now romantically linked with two. Third, and most obstructive, he was black. Tracy was candid with him about her mother's distaste for interracial relationships, and she feared what might happen if her mom found out about the African American cornerback in her life.

Darryl was willing to accept these risks, though, and for reasons that went deeper than Tracy's physical appeal, which was considerable. He liked her sense of humor. She wasn't afraid to make fun of people, including herself, and she enjoyed wrestling with him on the floor, where, to Darryl's surprise, her subtle dancer's strength helped her hold her own. Tracy's dancing had also given her an appreciation for hip-hop. She knew most of the songs Darryl liked and a surprising number of the lyrics. Their initial icebreaker — his Karl Kani clothing — was a cue that Tracy had tastes that ran surprisingly black. Tracy Ann Donaho, Darryl had discovered, was not your usual Orange County white girl.

Chapter 3

For a young man unafraid of attention, UCLA made sense as Darryl's choice to play college football. For the next five years he would practice amid the sound of traffic on Sunset Boulevard, where students made money selling Star Maps on the corner where campus met Bel Air. It was quite a departure from the nondescript, suburban setting of his sheltered upbringing. "I remember Henley on his recruiting trip," recalled former UCLA safety and two-time Super Bowl champion James Washington, who was raised in Watts. "Darryl was green. He was definitely green." Said sportswriter Bob Keisser: "When I think of Darryl Henley, I don't think of everything they said about him in the mid-nineties. I think of an eighteen-year-old kid with braces who always had a lollipop in his mouth, running around laughing."

Henley and the other redshirt freshmen were not allowed to dress for UCLA's home

Darryl Henley, 1987. (Courtesy of UCLA Athletics)

games that fall. Instead, they lifted weights every morning and mimicked the Bruins' upcoming opponent in practice every afternoon, which gave Darryl the opportunity not only to add muscle to his 140-pound frame (there were chuckles when that embarrassing number appeared at his first weigh-in) but to compete against what was probably the best receiving corps in the country — a group that included future NFL starters Mike Sherrard and Flipper Anderson. "Darryl was very, very bright," said Karl Dorrell, who led the Bruins in receptions in 1985 and later became head coach at UCLA. "He really understood how to play corner. He could quick-jam you and then start running out of his backpedal, and if you broke it off to a shorter route—" Dorrell paused and shook his head, smiling at days long gone. "He was just so good with his feet. He could plant and drive on the ball as well as anyone in college at that time." Chris Hale, Henley's childhood friend who played cornerback at USC during those years, agreed: "At the college level Darryl was as good as anybody in the country. At the pro level, he was just smarter than the average guy. That's where most of his development was, in my opinion. Early on he saw the importance of knowing his opponent. He realized he was smarter than most people, and he built a career on that."

Most of the upperclassmen on the UCLA team drove new Mopeds, but Darryl's father stayed true to his rural roots and bought Darryl a secondhand scooter with some miles on it. From time to time a few players cruised West LA together; Darryl struggled to keep up with the others until a red light afforded him a chance to time things so he could breeze past them on green. This herd of athletes, white and black, a laughing gang of clean-cut Hells Angels in UCLA football shorts, took their time rolling past the voluptuous homes of Bel Air. As he sat in the prison visiting room some twenty years later, Henley remembered sitting on his sputtering scooter, dreaming of buying a house like that for his mother one day.

In 1985 Darryl's redshirt came off and he was invited to choose his real jersey number. Darryl wanted to uphold the tradition of Bruin All-Americans Don Rogers and Kenny Easley, who'd worn single-digit numbers in the defensive backfield. Head coach Terry Donahue didn't allow anyone to wear number 1, so Darryl seized the next best thing.

Early on during spring practice, it became clear that number 2 was gifted in the art of man-to-man coverage—the skill that would earn him millions. The upperclassman who started ahead of Henley at cornerback injured his shoulder ten days before the season opener, forcing eighteen-year-old Darryl into the starting lineup. It would prove to be a busy semester. Henley was also pledging Alpha Phi Alpha, one of the "Original Eight" black fraternities, which meant he was sent on strenuous, meaningless errands almost nightly, and had to perform endless push-ups in moonlit public parks while Alpha Men sat astride his back commanding him and his fellow pledges to recite Paul Laurence Dunbar poems by heart.[1] UCLA safety James Washington was pledging Phi Beta Sigma, the Alphas' top rivals, which made his new friendship with Henley even more unlikely. Washington wore number 3, so his locker was right next to Henley's, although "J-Dub" and "D-Hen" had traveled much different paths to get there.

Raised in Watts, Washington provided a look at how Darryl might have turned out had his parents succumbed to their early pressures and stranded their kids in South Central. An interesting part of Darryl's character sometimes wished that were the case. After all, Run-DMC didn't rhyme about places like Ontario or Laverne. They wrote raps like "Hard Times," and James Washington had seen the hardest. In high school, he watched his best friend take a fatal bullet to the head in a Church's Fried Chicken on 103rd Street. Most of the few relatives he knew of were either on drugs, in jail, or both. "I always told Darryl the one thing I envied about him was his mother," recalled Washington, who had been abandoned by both parents by age four. "Darryl Henley had the most wonderful parents in the world."

Washington broke into a story that would foretell later events: "I remember one day Darryl walked into the locker room with a garage door opener on his hip. This is back when beepers first came out. Nobody on the team had any damn money, including Henley, and he comes in there with a damn garage door opener on his hip, trying to act like it was a beeper. *Garage fucking door opener*

26

on his hip! I was like, 'What are you trying to do, man? Dude, just be *you.*' I used to always tell him that. 'Just be you. You're fine! I'm fucking dying to have half of what you have—a mama and daddy and everybody in the same house. You're trying to be like you came from the streets. Just be you.'" Washington sat back in his posh office in Century City, shaking his head. "If we were to walk down the street together when we first started out," he said, "you would have thought that I would be where he is today and he would be the one with his own business, doing what I'm doing."

Henley played well enough as a freshman that during his sophomore year the *Times* ran a story about him titled "Colorful and Daring, on Football Field and Off." Henley had arrived for the interview wearing white Italian loafers, no socks, and a belt that matched his leather briefcase. His outfit was mentioned in the story as evidence of his flashiness, which was fine, but the moment Darryl read the reference to his gold earring, he nearly choked. His father had no idea he'd gotten his ear pierced. As longtime UCLA Sports Information director Marc Dellins recalled: "I remember Darryl pacing around the football building with that newspaper in his hand, saying, 'My dad's going to kill me. My dad's going to kill me.'"

T.H. did not kill his son. Instead, less than a month after the earring article, Darryl helped provide his dad with the proudest day of his life.

It was November 8, 1986, Homecoming at the Rose Bowl. UCLA was playing Stanford, and Darryl was facing his brother Thomas, a Stanford senior who had been moved to receiver to make room for star running back Brad Muster. Darryl had been excelling at cornerback for UCLA, returning a fumble fifty yards for a score against Arizona ("If Carl Lewis had come out of the stands he couldn't have caught me," he said afterward) and tying a UCLA record with three interceptions in one game versus Oregon State.

Having shelved his rule about sibling competition, T.H. offered Darryl advice about facing Thomas. "He told me that if I'm ever covering my brother," Darryl told the *Times*, "to take his head off if I get the chance." That remark led to a last-minute request from Dot to Darryl just before the game. "She told me not to hit him," Darryl said with a laugh, "to let him catch some passes and to look like I'm trying, but fall down. I'm going to have to tell my mom to chill out."

Thomas, true to form, was more judicious with his pregame comments. "I'll be glad when it's over," he said.

"The brothers may be from the same household," wrote one reporter, ". . . but their personalities are a football field apart. Put a tape recorder in front of Darryl and all you need to do is come back in a half hour to change the tape. The polite, mild-mannered Thomas needs more prodding."

The Pac Ten championship was on the line, and Muster played like it, leading Stanford to a 21–13 halftime lead. The battle of the Henleys was a standoff until the third quarter, when Thomas took off on what looked like a deep route, only to hit the brakes as soon as Darryl turned into a downfield sprint. Thomas made a tiptoe catch near the sideline before falling out of bounds. First down. His brother was a good twelve yards away. It was their only real confrontation of the game, which Stanford won in an upset, 28–23, after coming in as two-touchdown underdogs. As the clock hit 00:00, the Henley brothers embraced at midfield, where a nearby TV camera caught them smiling and where a good lip reader might have caught Darryl saying, "I should have had that."

Darryl was named the Bruins' most improved player that season. In the opening game the next fall, he became the first Bruin to score on a punt return in over twenty years—a feat he would soon make commonplace. His senior year—with Troy Aikman at quarterback and future NFL greats Carnell Lake and Eric Turner lining up with him on defense—Henley and the Bruins were expected to contend for the national championship.

Henley, who would later call the 1988 Bruins the closest team he ever played on, had gone from a 140-pound redshirt with a bad knee to captain of the Pac Ten's best defense. Within weeks of his arrival on campus in 1984, a defensive coach had called him "a wasted scholarship" to his face, prompting Darryl to call his dad from the nearest payphone and tearfully ask if he could come home. "It's about time someone challenged you," T.H. had said. And now, in 1988, three minutes into the first game of his senior season, Darryl was weaving through tacklers, returning yet another punt for a score, this one covering eighty-nine yards. The following week, against powerful Nebraska, he sped virtually untouched down the sideline for another punt return TD as ABC's Keith Jackson bellowed, "Touchdown!" to a national TV audience. It was the first time Nebraska had allowed such a score in twenty-four years, a span of nearly three hundred games. On the sideline, TV cameras caught Henley, his braces glinting in the sun, yelling, "Hi Mom!" beneath the still roaring fans. "Hi Dad! Hi Eric!"

Prior to the Nebraska game Henley had been considering a job in either business or law after graduation. He had asked local sportswriter Bob Keisser if he could list him as a reference on his resume. After the Nebraska win, however—after *Sports Illustrated*'s Rick Telander called Henley "the little return man with braces on his teeth and skates on his feet"—pro scouts became more willing to disregard Henley's lack of size and focus instead on his game-breaking speed and open-field playmaking.

Ranked number one in the country and undefeated at 8-0, UCLA saw its national title hopes dashed when they were upset by mediocre Washington State, then dismantled by crosstown rival USC. Darryl played one of his more forgettable games against the Trojans, while USC's Chris Hale, his childhood friend from Duarte, played the game of his life—including a hit on Henley that forced a critical fumble. As the final seconds ticked away, ABC's cameras found former USC star O.J. Simpson celebrating with the victors at midfield while signing autographs. Six weeks later, on New Year's night, Simpson would give his wife Nicole a bloody lip and a black eye before throwing her out of their home in her underwear. Nicole Simpson would make a breathless call to 911 that night, a call that would later become famous because it resulted in only a token visit from the LAPD—their ninth such visit to the Simpson home. Simpson avoided arrest by fleeing in his Bentley. A few hours after that incident, the countdown to Darryl Henley's own grim future ticked forward when Henley, who would one day stand trial at the same time as Simpson, played his last game in a UCLA uniform—his last under the protective blanket of college football.

An avalanche of postseason awards carried Henley toward the NFL draft. He earned first-team All Pac Ten honors at two positions (cornerback and punt returner), and was named a finalist for the Jim Thorpe Award, given to the nation's best defensive back. He was one of just three Bruins to receive the Wellman Award for All-Around Excellence and one of two to receive the Sugarman Award for leadership—an honor voted upon by his teammates. As proud as he was of these accolades, however, they did not compare to his being named a consensus, first-team All-American. The football world was in agreement—Darryl Henley was one of the two best cornerbacks in college football. The other was Deion Sanders.

"Not bad for a wasted scholarship," his father told him.

Chapter 4

Within days of his move to Atlanta in 1993, Darryl felt lonelier than he'd ever felt in his life. The Rams' fifth-year cornerback had never lived outside Southern California, and thus he found himself calling his parents every day from his bachelor pad in the tony Buckhead section of town, speaking with his mom as often as three times a day.

He had moved to Atlanta for two reasons. First, Atlanta had become the place to be among the country's young, gifted, and black; the early nineties brought an influx of popular African American artists and athletes, and Henley always liked being where the action was. Second, he wanted to build a home for himself and the family he dreamed of creating one day, and he knew he could get more for his money in Atlanta's real estate market than in Orange County's.

But now he missed Tracy.

"He called on Valentines Day," Tracy wrote.

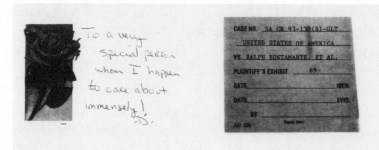

Plaintiff's exhibit 69, *United States v. Rafael Bustamante, et al.*

". . . Wished me a Happy Valentines Day and told me something to the effect of remember your my Valentine. From this point we started to talk every day and if I wasn't home, he would leave a message on my voice mail. My mom at this point was not very nice to him on the phone so he would hang up if she answered."

Darryl was officially regretting his decision to leave California when he ran into Ant Williams. Everything changed then.

An old friend from Pomona whom Darryl had played against in high school, Ant instantly became Darryl's wingman and un-official Atlanta tour guide. Most nights found them inside Magic City, one of the most renowned strip clubs in a city full of them. Because the Atlanta Falcons were in the Rams' division, Darryl had visited Atlanta at least once a year since turning pro, so he was well acquainted with the city's reputation for gentlemen's en-tertainment. But Atlanta's strip clubs had changed since his rook-ie year. The city's population boom and the international gossip about its flesh trade had made for more strippers — and more cus-tomers. The girls were more attractive, their outfits skimpier and removed quicker. The clientele was different, too — more afflu-ent and not as racially diverse. One of the many things Magic City and Club Nikki's did not hide was the fact that they catered to Af-rican American men. Wealthy black athletes were treated like roy-alty there. Broke white guys could come, too, if they could afford the cover charge, but they could not go where Darryl Henley went.

A layperson might have assumed that the men sitting in the recesses of the clubs' VIP areas were pro athletes. Many of them looked the part—young, fit, and well dressed—but Darryl knew better. These were quiet men, with gold ropes around their necks, diamonds in their ears, and imported sweaters on their backs, and they were usually surrounded by two groups of people striking in their dissimilarity: 300-pound bodyguards wearing trench coats; nubile dancers wearing nothing. The men were drug dealers. More specifically, they were drug suppliers, traffickers, and street salesmen, and they dealt mostly in cocaine.

Darryl steered clear of them. He'd always enjoyed running with the fast crowd—the James Washingtons of the world—and had even hung out with LA Ram-turned-rap mogul Suge Knight on occasion. But he knew where the line was. During his first weeks in Atlanta, when Henley spent as many nights in strip clubs as elsewhere, this line between Darryl's world and the world of drug trafficking shrank gradually, imperceptibly, until it was gone.

It began to fade when the dealers recognized the NFL starter across the room and strolled over to give Henley some "dap"—a cool handshake. Darryl felt flattered by the attention and grateful for its brevity. He didn't know at the time that it was common in the drug game to ask anyone from California if they knew about "them thangs"—code for kilos of cocaine—which often entered the United States in California before being distributed elsewhere. One would have been hard pressed to find anyone in the club who knew less about them thangs than Darryl Henley. But he kept going back. To the clubs. Behind the velvet ropes. Closer to the line.

All the hustler types at the clubs saw him as Mr. Bigtime LA, and Darryl didn't go out of his way to deny it. Years later he would recall the night Ant introduced him to a guy called G, a tall Californian who greeted him like a long lost brother.

You remember me? G implored of Henley. I played basketball at Montclair High. Me and you were All-Valley the same year. We met at the banquet.

G said his real name was Garey West. For real, you don't remember me? he asked.

That's how Henley remembered that fateful meeting, anyway. At a federal prison in Kentucky in 2010, Garey West recalled that his relationship with Henley started much earlier. "Growing up, I was one of the top athletes in the area," West said. "I was playing football back then, and we made it to the championship game against the junior high that Darryl went to. No one in our area knew Darryl Henley. . . .

"The game was close, and I remember running a post route and being wide open, and this little dude comes out of nowhere and leaps up and snatches it and runs it back the whole way. Ball game. I'm crushed. I was the best athlete in the area. I was like, 'Who is this little dude?' . . .

"In high school we'd see each other through sports. I wouldn't say friends. Knew each other, though. Coming out of high school he had his scholarship to UCLA. I had a basketball scholarship to Wyoming. This was '85, '86. That's when drugs got introduced to the United States. I had a friend of mine ask me, 'Why haven't you left for school?' And I was like, 'Man, there's snow up there, and I don't even got money for a coat.' He said, 'Come see me and I'll see what I can do. . . .'

"He ended up giving me cocaine. . . . I started moving it. I got caught, I went to prison — three years in state prison. My mind, in prison, it got tarnished, like, by the criminal element in there. Then when I got out I ran into the same guy. He said he's got another drug proposal for me. He wanted me to set up shop in Memphis. That's when I blew up in the drug game. Around '93 I was real large. . . .

"I went to Freaknik [an annual Atlanta street party] and I'm riding in my [Mercedes] 560 SEC, I pull up next to a black Benz with California tags, so I tap the horn. Dude looks over, and it's Darryl. I hadn't seen him in four or five years. . . . I knew he was playing football for the Rams. In the back of my mind I was thinking,

I need to get someone like Darryl Henley on my team. Because I was getting burnt out on the drug game. I was looking to get out. I thought he could give me experience on investing. Legitimate stuff. So that's how we hooked up."

However it happened — meeting in the strip club or at a red light — within a matter of days Darryl had immersed himself in an entirely new world. He mentioned to G that he had an old friend named Willie McGowan who'd played ball in Duarte growing up. G said he knew about Will, yes indeed. From there, things began moving fast.

"Darryl was like a kid in a candy store," West recalled. "He was always curious about what was going on. I tried to tell him all that glitters isn't gold. There's more to this lifestyle. There's risk."

Jennifer Wilson was attractive enough to be a dancer at Magic City, but she'd chosen modeling and nightclub management instead — jobs better suited for the mother of a five-year-old girl. Darryl's mind contained a Rolodex of women's names and faces, but as soon as he met Jennifer, her card rose above the others. She was physically beautiful, certainly, but she also had an easygoing manner, a confident calm that Henley had never experienced before. Jennifer explained right off the bat that she didn't want to date someone who was paid to be physically violent. She'd been hit a few times in her life, including by her most recent boyfriend. Darryl's persistence and gentle nature persuaded her.

Rams running back David Lang was another important cast member in Henley's evolving drama. A muscular athlete with a reputation as one of the league's fastest players, Lang, like Henley, knew that a helmet to the knee could bring the life they were leading to an end, *so we better live it up now*. They brought that mindset with them to Mardi Gras that March.

Like the Falcons, the Saints were in the Rams' division, so Henley and Lang had visited New Orleans at least once a year since they became Rams. They knew the French Quarter well and re-acquainted themselves with it in a manner befitting the middle of their off-season. Henley's personal account of his stay in New Orleans (provided later to his lawyers) read:

02/21 Sunday: Party in New Orleans
02/22 Monday: Party in New Orleans
02/23 Tuesday: Party in New Orleans

The moment Darryl walked into his Atlanta apartment, his phone rang. It was another friend from California.

Christopher Leggio had taken over his father's successful car dealership after he and Henley graduated from Damien High together in 1984. Darryl had since become something of a figure-head for Leggio's business — serving as host for the "Dare to Say No to Drugs" event held there each year, and providing Leggio with a charming athlete to show off as an example of his connection to the big-money world of pro sports. Leggio called Henley that February to invite him to a promotional golf tournament in Las Vegas. Darryl agreed to make the trip before Leggio could even offer to pay for his flight. And when Leggio asked Darryl to bring a girl along, one name rose above Jennifer's in Henley's mind.

When Darryl called Tracy and asked her to run by his house and pick up his golf clubs on her way to the airport, he gave her the code to his garage door so she could get in. It seemed a small gesture at the time, a matter of convenience, but it would later have dire consequences.

"It all started to work out perfectly," Tracy wrote, "because my mom and her boyfriend were driving to Vegas that same weekend, because of my mom's business."

Leggio actually asked Darryl to bring two girls — one for Darryl and one for an older client of Leggio's named Al. When Tracy and her girlfriend Wendy Long landed in Vegas, they were whisked by limousine to the San Remo hotel. "I was real nervous," Tracy wrote, "because I just figured, with my luck I would run into my mom somewhere. . . . When I got to my room I found that it was Darryl's also. He never told me it would be any different."

Tracy and Wendy found Darryl playing craps in the casino. Tracy introduced him to Wendy, and Darryl handed the girls $300 in chips, which they readily dumped into the slot machines. Tracy and Wendy joined Henley, Leggio, and Al that night for dinner at Michael's, one of the most exclusive restaurants on the Strip. "Darryl informed me later that dinner was over a thousand dollars," Tracy wrote. "Never in my life had I ever eaten in such a fancy restaurant. We went back to the hotel and Al and Wendy sat down at a Black Jack table. Al was teaching her and gave her some money. Darryl and I watched for awhile. I was getting nervous and scared because Darryl wanted to go upstairs because he was tired. Wendy could tell and tried to get me to stay and gamble [with] her and Al. Darryl wouldn't go for it. He wanted to spend sometime alone with me. That was the first night I had sex with him. I knew I wasn't ready, but wasn't sure how to tell him.

"The next morning he was getting ready for the [golf] tournament. He was saying so many nice things to me. How he was nervous to see me again. But he was glad I came and how impressed his friends were by me."

Chris Leggio wasn't impressed. He later told Henley's lawyers that he considered Darryl out of Tracy's league and Tracy out of her element. Leggio could tell Darryl wasn't serious about Tracy by the way he acted around her, as if she were just a friend.

The morning after Tracy and Darryl first had sex, "It seemed as if he really liked and cared about me," Tracy wrote. "Until he was walking out the door. He was telling me he'd be back around four o'clock. He threw me a $500 chip. Told me to go shopping or gambling. I threw it back. I didn't want his money. He made me feel used . . . we fought for awhile about it. He said have fun and try to be back by the time he was. Wendy and I cashed the chip and took a cab to the mall.

"I used the money to buy us lunch, taxi, and we both got sweat outfits."

Darryl and Tracy spent that evening "wrestling . . . laughing and joking around" in their hotel room.

"Tracy was real cool and the first white girl I had ever dated," Darryl wrote to his lawyers in preparation for trial. "I thought she was as close to being hip as any black woman I'd ever dated. We did not have a wild romance, but instead it was a friendly relationship that included sex sometimes (not regularly)."

They loved playfighting. The night after their first Vegas wrestling match, "I was trying to beat him up," Tracy wrote. "Wendy just sat and watched. I remember her hysterically laughing. After meeting Darryl, Wendy really liked him. She thought he was perfect for me."

When Darryl and Tracy flew back to Los Angeles, "We said goodbye and discussed maybe seeing each again that night or the next day," Tracy wrote.

"He didn't call the rest of that day. All day thursday and friday he would call and acted like he wanted to see me. He supposedly had all these things to take care of. I sat home both of those days and nights. Friday night the last call was about 9:00 p.m. He would call when he was done so we could see each other. He never called. The next day which was Saturday and he was going back to Atlanta.

"I was getting ready for work when he called. At this point I was very hurt and mad. After I slept with him in Vegas, I felt used. He knew I was mad. He kept saying that he was coming into my work to say goodbye."

That afternoon, a boy entered the restaurant where Tracy worked and presented her with a dozen roses, a balloon, and a card handwritten in Henley's loopy cursive that read, "To a very special person whom I happen to care about immensely! — D." Darryl walked in and thanked the boy — a little league ballplayer he'd just met in the parking lot — for helping him surprise the pretty waitress, then he hugged Tracy and sat and talked with her for a few minutes. Tracy's anger eased. Darryl stayed for lunch. He told her he was stopping by a family barbecue later, then flying to Atlanta that evening. He said he wouldn't be back in California until the Rams' minicamp, but he wanted to stay in touch by phone. They left the restaurant on good terms. Darryl gave autographs to the little leaguers outside before driving to his parents' house. That was March 6, 1993.

The timeline that Darryl would write a year or two later, while preparing for trial, showed the same entry for March 7 through March 13, 1993:

"Spent the days with Candice [another woman he was seeing]. At night, went to strip clubs; [Club] Nikki's and Magic [City]; eating at Hooters; generally loafing and hanging out." He was waking each day at "around 1300 hours."

Darryl and Ant drove Henley's Mercedes from Atlanta to Black Beach Weekend in Daytona, which was basically Mardi Gras with sand. Soon after his return to Atlanta, Darryl invited Jennifer and her daughter to move in with him, into a larger apartment at his current complex. Jennifer's daughter took the downstairs bedroom while Darryl and Jennifer shared the master upstairs. Henley laid down a few ground rules, including a rule that Jennifer should not expect him to come home every night. Darryl would respect Jennifer, he said — and more important, her daughter — by not bringing other women into the apartment. He would be leaving for training camp in July anyway, so if the arrangement became uncomfortable, it would only be temporary. They agreed that during the season the place would be Jennifer's. The best part of the deal as far as Jennifer was concerned was that it allowed her to save money for her daughter's future while living in a safe environment, far from the abusive ex-boyfriend she was still trying to elude.[1]

"I kept two [phone] lines in the condo because I still had people (women) calling me from California and other places," Darryl wrote to his attorneys. Tracy was one of many women who called Darryl on his private line. At one point they were speaking almost every day. But with Jennifer's emergence, the length of his conversations with Tracy and his eagerness to have them shriveled. In a short time, Jennifer Wilson and her daughter became two of Darryl's top priorities.

The girls had the apartment to themselves the weekend of April 11, when Darryl flew home to California for his father's fiftieth birthday. After a surprise party at the family home in Upland, Darryl drove down to Brea to check on his own house, which he hadn't seen in five weeks — since the day he surprised Tracy with flowers. His uncle, Rex Henley, was crashing there because he was having problems with his wife.

Before he became embroiled in the criminal fiasco to come, Rex Henley was often assumed to be Darryl's brother, not his uncle, because they were only three years apart. Darryl's real brother, Thomas, was closer to Rex than anyone, having become best friends during a string of boyhood summers spent together in Texas.

Darryl's father was twenty years older than Rex, with seven siblings in between, so T.H. didn't know his youngest brother very well. When Rex was two, T.H. was fighting to move his wife and sons from South LA to the suburbs. T.H.'s success in that fight had inspired a number of Henleys to follow him out west, including Rex, who moved to California during Darryl's freshman year at UCLA. Rex stayed with T.H. and Dot until he could afford a place of his own. Then he got married, had a child, got separated, and now he was staying at Darryl's house.

Rex was quiet, good-hearted, well-intentioned. His deep voice resonated from a pear-shaped, 220-pound frame that had once excelled in high school football in Texas. Most of his relatives called him "Chubby." His failing marriage and his layoff from Lockheed (where he'd worked for nearly eight years), while difficult, had at least afforded him a welcome measure of independence as he tried to piece his life back together at Darryl's house. Sadly, Darryl's house would become the place where Rex's life fell apart.

Two of the four crucial convergences in Darryl Henley's life were now complete. The first had been meeting Tracy Donaho at the Super Bowl; the second had been meeting Garey "G" West in Atlanta. The third and fourth events happened the week after his father's birthday, when he returned to Atlanta and got a phone call from Rams equipment manager Todd Hewitt, who also organized the Rams' charity basketball team.

Hewitt asked Henley if he could play that Saturday.

"I just got back from California," Darryl said.

"We really need you. We won't have enough guys if you don't show up."

"I could always count on Darryl," Hewitt said eleven years later. "If I ever needed anyone on short notice, he's the guy I would call. And I knew if he said yes, he'd be there and he'd be on time."

It actually worked out well. Henley's U-turn back to California enabled him to attend the grand opening of his parents' new southern-style fish market — an enterprise hatched from T.H.'s mind and financed by Darryl's wallet — where members of both of his extended families, the Henleys and the Rams, ate catfish and shrimp and marveled at the line of customers stretching out to the street.

After the grand opening, Darryl and a few NFL friends — including former Bruins Carnell Lake of the Steelers and Marvcus Patton of the Bills — headed to the Mount SAC Relays, a renowned track meet at nearby Mount San Antonio College that Darryl's father had been bringing his sons to since they were kids. At the previous year's Relays, Darryl had watched fifteen eventual gold medalists in the Barcelona Olympics compete. The 1993 Mount SAC Relays were not as star-studded, but they did feature Carl Lewis and Michael Johnson and were therefore hard to pass up. Plus, the event had become a place to see and be seen among Southern California athletes and celebrities. This year it was the setting where, like the sprinters who dug their toes into the blocks that day, Darryl Henley's life abruptly gained speed.

Chapter 5

In July 1989, after graduating from UCLA with a history degree and a 2.8 grade point average, Darryl Henley signed a four-year, $1.2 million contract with the Los Angeles Rams, who had selected him in the second round of the NFL draft. He'd attained the rare privilege of not just playing in the NFL but of doing so in his hometown.

The Rams also signed Thomas Henley that summer. The Saints had drafted Thomas in 1987 before leg injuries struck and he was left to drift in and out of the 49ers' plans for two years. There was sadness in realizing as the Rams' 1989 training camp progressed that whatever time Thomas spent playing football with Darryl on the Cal State Fullerton campus that summer would probably be the last time they played together, and the last time Thomas played at all. The number of backyard wars they had fought over the years numbered well into the thousands.

Thomas Henley III, Eric Henley, Darryl Henley (*left to right*), 1990. (Courtesy of the Henley family)

Two weeks before Darryl and Thomas suited up for the Rams' first preseason game, the NFL suspended Rams cornerback LeRoy Irvin for violating the league's substance abuse policy.[1] The same week, President George H. W. Bush delivered his first televised address from the Oval Office — the speech in which he famously declared his "war on drugs" and vowed to "enlarge our criminal justice system across the board. . . . We need more prisons, more jails, more courts, more prosecutors." Darryl Henley, whose life would be directly impacted by both of these events, replaced Irvin in the Rams' starting lineup and did not relinquish that position for four years, until he became engaged far deeper than Irvin in America's drug war.

Henley helped the 1989 Rams achieve a 9-4 record headed into a crucial December game against the 49ers. Joe Montana passed for a team-record 458 yards that day, leading the Rams' rivals to a come-from-behind win, and afterward Rams head coach John Robinson boldly predicted that his battered team would win four in a row and meet the Niners again in the NFC championship game. That's exactly what happened. But when the Rams met Montana again, this time with a trip to the Super Bowl on the line, they were blown out, 30–3.

Henley was voted the Rams' defensive rookie of the year—ahead, he liked to note, of the three defenders the Rams had picked ahead of him. It was his last happy moment in what would prove to be the Los Angeles Rams' last winning season.

The early 1990s were the best of times for the Henley family. In the off-season after his rookie year, Darryl bought his parents a home in Upland. Eric had just finished his sophomore season at Rice University, in which he set the school record for single-season receptions. Academically Eric appeared to be following in the footsteps of Thomas, who had responded to being cut by the Rams by starting his own real estate firm. When Eric came home to LA that summer and the three Henley brothers worked out together, Thomas, who was still in great shape, suggested they begin with an old-fashioned foot race: forty yards, with Eric's first step acting as the starting gun.

Eric was still in the lead at the halfway mark ("And I know that stunned them," he remembered), but Darryl passed him at about twenty-five yards—just as Thomas was surging past Darryl. "And that's how it came in," Eric recalled. "Thomas, Darryl, and then me. Thomas would've done whatever it took to beat us."

"Especially Darryl," added their father.

The home Darryl bought for himself—the house where he would allow his uncle Rex to crash three years later—was in Brea, a quiet bedroom community in the heart of Orange County. An angular, two-story house near the end of a cul-de-sac, the home was not grandiose. Darryl didn't plan on growing old there; it was merely a place to hang his hat until his big NFL payday arrived in three years. Then he would build his dream home. When the 57 Freeway was clear, he had about a fifteen-minute commute to Rams Park.

He worked harder than ever that summer to prepare for his first full season as an NFL starter. Then he noticed a shooting pain in his lower abdomen during training camp. The team doctors thought it was a hernia. It was eventually discovered that Henley had torn a hip muscle and chipped a bone at the point where the muscle attached to his pelvis (an injury similar to the one that would end Bo Jackson's football career a year later). Henley was declared out of action for at least three weeks. "At times I want to say, 'Cut this thing out, whatever it is,'" he told reporters as he slogged through rehab. He spent his days either nudging his ailing limb back toward health or appearing at charity events like the fund-raiser for the Boys & Girls Club where he met a Rams cheerleader named Alisa Denmon.

He had already been introduced to Alisa once, in passing, but he'd been with another woman at the time, and Alisa didn't strike him as the type to get involved with a taken man. Darryl had become unattached just before the Boys & Girls Club event, though, so he asked Alisa out. Their first date was a jazz concert at the Redondo Beach pier, where they listened to Najee play saxophone against the crashing waves. In the weeks that followed, Alisa provided comfort to Darryl during the most trying time of his life to that point. The healing of his hip was painful and behind schedule; his teammates were moving on without him, and he was not his usual fun self. Alisa cooked for him almost every day and massaged his leg each night.

Jerry Gray, the veteran cornerback who had been moved to safety in the off-season, reluctantly moved back to corner to replace the injured Henley. "I want to get to the Super Bowl just like everyone else," Gray grumbled, but the Rams would get nowhere near the Super Bowl in 1990. In fact, they would not make the playoffs again until 1999, a stretch of ten barren years that contrasted starkly with their run of fourteen playoff appearances over the previous seventeen seasons.

Henley fought through his hip injury to play nine games in 1990. "My most vivid memory of Darryl was when we were out there playing them in 1990 in Anaheim," said his former college teammate Troy Aikman, who went on to stardom as the Cowboys' quarterback. "That was the year we started turning things around in Dallas, and I remember we were able to take advantage of Michael Irvin's height advantage over Darryl — basically just throwing it up high for him in the end zone like a jump ball. We got a touchdown or two that way, but Darryl, he was the kind of competitor that even after the touchdown, he would line up against Michael like he was seven feet tall."

That observation was made often about Henley by those who knew him — that he possessed the ideal psychological makeup for a cornerback. He was confident, smart, and courageous — willing to take risks and take on any challenge, even challenges that, like Michael Irvin or Jerry Rice, often proved more than he could handle. Most important, when the inevitable happened and he was beaten for a touchdown, Henley had the rare ability to delete it from his mind and move forward as if it had never happened, maintaining the required fearlessness. They were traits that came in handy in 1990, when the Rams' defense allowed the most touchdowns in the NFL.

The upcoming draft offered a ray of hope for the team. The Rams used the fifth overall pick to draft Todd Lyght, a swift cornerback from Notre Dame. Displeased with what the pick insinuated — that the Rams needed young help at his position — Henley then watched the Rams select another corner, Robert Bailey, in the fourth round. By choosing two cornerbacks within the draft's first 150 picks, the Rams had all but advertised their intention to replace Henley in the lineup.

The issue, as usual, was his size. At 5'9" and 170 pounds, he was among the smallest defensive players in a league obsessed with size and appearance. The tall, rangy Lyght was named the starter at one cornerback spot, while Henley, Bailey, and four others were left to fight for backup roles. Henley responded with the best training camp of his young career. He beat out the others and started fourteen games that season. In week two, he ended Giants quarterback Jeff Hostetler's streak of 183 passes without an interception, the pick setting up a field goal that helped the Rams—for the second straight year—defeat the defending Super Bowl champions on the road. Three weeks later Henley intercepted a pass against the Packers, contributing to a two-point Rams win. But neither Henley nor Lyght, who showed tremendous potential his rookie season, could prevent 1991 from becoming the worst season in Rams history. The Rams surrendered more points than any team in the NFC. They won three games and lost thirteen—including their last ten of the season—setting the franchise record for single-season losses. For the first time in franchise history, not a single Ram made the Pro Bowl, an ugly accomplishment that the team would duplicate in 1992.

Head coach John Robinson would not be around in 1992. Owner Georgia Frontiere fired him following the '91 season, twenty-three months after she had hugged him following a playoff win and called him "the best coach in the world." Apathy had infected the locker room since that watershed moment, and this in turn had infected the fan base, making Rams games, once a popular way to spend a Sunday in LA, an afterthought in a city where there were plenty of other things to do. "Rams Park was right beside a golf course," Robert Bailey recalled. "The beach was twenty minutes away. Hollywood was a huge magnet, of course. I mean, it was *Los Angeles*. We lost ten in a row my rookie year, and I remember guys going out to the clubs after most of those losses. Most of the guys didn't seem too concerned [about losing]."

To no one's surprise, Jerry Gray signed with the Oilers that off-season for less money than the Rams offered. He wasn't the only one who wanted out. The vibe around Rams Park was stale. "They stunk," said radio reporter Joe McDonnell. "They were awful. A lot of people thought they didn't have much talent. I think that's part of it, but I also think they were just a horribly mismanaged organization from the top. They had no marketing at all during their last five years here."

Mike Sherrard, who played for the 49ers while living in Los Angeles, said that "the difference between us and the Rams was like night and day. We got a lot of respect. We were a class organization. The Rams weren't. And it all starts with the management. . . . The [Rams] organization was just known for being tightwads. They didn't want to pay players, and if you don't have the right leaders in place, that kind of mentality can trickle down into the locker room."

As the losses mounted, the Rams—no longer a team as much as a fractious group of employees—faced the weekly task of, as Robert Bailey put it, "trying to come up with some kind of motivation as to why the next game was important."

"At a certain point, I hated going to the stadium," Henley told author Don Yeager in 1997 for the book *Pros and Cons*. "I hated getting in my car and going to practice. I hated it. Everyone started pointing fingers. People said, 'Well, the coach was this . . .' That wasn't it at all. It wasn't management. . . . It was the dudes on the team. They didn't have the desire and the commitment. They didn't have the attitude to win. They weren't staying around practice, working out. You get beat by deep balls, you should be staying after practice, showing up on Tuesday, on a day off. Nobody was doing that. My rookie year when I was screwing up, on Tuesday mornings, on my day off they had me up there with the coaching staff. I was up there and I loved it. They had my ass working out, going over mistakes I made to the point where I started doing it on my own. And then in '91 and '92, we didn't have that anymore. . . . [A]t the end of every practice, the discussion was, 'What are we doing afterward?' After a while it starts to have a real effect on you. A real effect. To the point where I lost my love for football. I allowed myself to become bored with something that I had always wanted to do all my life. How can you get bored with money, women, football, cameras, TV? How can you get bored with that? It's everybody's dream. How can you get bored with that?"

Despite this malaise, Henley's teammates presented him with the Carl Ekern Spirit of the Game Award, "given annually to the Rams player who best exemplifies sportsmanship, ethics, and commitment to his teammates." His reputation as a positive locker room presence was unassailable. "We used to ask Darryl to come over and watch our house," said Todd Hewitt, the Rams' longtime equipment manager. "After games sometimes, a few of the guys would go somewhere for pizza and we'd meet them there, and Darryl would drive my six-year-old in his Mercedes. You think that doesn't mean something to a little kid? Darryl was the kind of guy you could call and say, 'Hey, Darryl, my wife and I are going out of town for the weekend. Could you watch our kids?' And he'd be right over, and you'd have no qualms about asking him. A lot of players you could never say that to because half of them can't take care of themselves. Darryl was a responsible person."

Responsible, but naïve.

"I used to always get on him about trusting people," said Donna Henson, a white mother of two who lived two houses down from Henley in Brea. "I would tell him, 'There are too many people around your house.' This is a guy that kept a framed photo of his mom in his entry way. That was the only picture in his foyer. He was a mama's boy. . . . He gave my daughter rides to work. He babysat my son."

"I used to fly home for Christmas," said Eric Henley, "and Darryl would always let me use one of his cars. One time I flew home and I said, 'Come up here and bring me the car and I'll take you back home.' He said one of his buddies had his car. I'm thinking, 'What do you mean? They've got their *own* cars!' Darryl never learned how to say no to people."

As for the maelstrom of crime that still lay ahead of Henley, his former teammate Steve Israel said, "I can see how his middle-class upbringing might make him want to break out of that [middle-class] mold. The usual example is the sheltered Catholic school girl who goes off to college and starts lifting her skirt more than the public school girls do."

Louis Oliver, a safety for the Dolphins and one of Henley's closest friends at the time, theorized: "Maybe he wanted to take on some kind of street persona because of his size, to let guys know that, 'Yo, I ain't no joke, I ain't nobody to be fucked with,' you know? 'I'll get you guys up off me.' There was no need for all that, though. Nobody was going to mess with him anyway. He had the NFL shield on. . . . So I don't know why he needed street credibility. For what?"

"One guy in college called him 'the Chameleon,'" said Willie Abston, a close friend of Henley's at both Damien High and UCLA. "Darryl could talk politics, then run down the lyrics to the latest rap song. He fit in anywhere. People who say he's two-faced — I always saw it as Darryl trying to make everyone around him feel comfortable."

"I remember Darryl wanting to go to law school," said Troy Aikman, the quarterback who was inducted into the Pro Football Hall of Fame during Henley's eleventh year in prison. "I can't sit here and say he thought he was more streetwise than he really was, but looking back, maybe there was a side of him that thought he was smarter than the next guy. I can see how that might lead to what happened later."

"Darryl is not a street guy," Darryl's father said resolutely. "None of my three sons were involved in the streets. Darryl was a wannabe. He always wanted to be 'on the scene.'"

Whatever conflicts may have been roiling inside him, in 1993 Henley appeared on the surface to have it all: a bright future, a nice home, a Mercedes-Benz, a Lexus, a Pathfinder, his choice of beautiful young women in most every NFL city, a college degree, and a mind as quick as the feet that had gotten him to NFL

starterhood. He had loving parents, an older brother he respected, a younger brother who idolized him. He was the funniest guy
most of his friends knew. He had financial security and every as-
surance that his next football contract would be worth three times
his current one.

"I'd watch him play on Sundays," remembered Karl Dorrell,
"and I'd remember the skills I saw back when we were teammates
at UCLA, and I'd say, 'Look at him now. Boy, he's one of the best in
the game.' . . . I admired Darryl because he reached the goal that
he wanted to reach. He fought his way there. But he couldn't fight
himself out of what happened next."

The Moor is of a free and open nature
that thinks men honest that but seem to be so
and will as tenderly be led by the nose
as asses are.

—WILLIAM SHAKESPEARE, *Othello*

Chapter 6

On April 16, 1993, as Darryl strolled through the stands at Mount SAC's track stadium looking for a seat, he heard a familiar voice calling his name. He turned to find Willie McGowan, his childhood football hero, smiling at him from a few rows away. They hadn't seen each other in fifteen years, not counting a brief encounter at a UCLA track meet two or three years earlier when Darryl had approached Willie, only to be shunned with the backhanded compliment: "I should be where you are." That slight was the first thing Darryl mentioned to Willie in the bleachers at Mount SAC.

Man, I wasn't in a place where I could do anything good for you back then, Willie said by way of apology. He'd been deeply embedded in sports gambling at the time, he explained, and keeping in touch with Darryl might have brought the NFL athlete more harm than good. With a nod Willie confirmed

1978 Duarte High School freshman football team: Willie McGowan (*second row, second from left*); T.H. Henley (*third row, first from left*). (Duarte High School)

the rumors Darryl had heard about his transition from gambling to the drug game, but Willie said he was done with all that now. "Did you know I've been to every Rams home game since you got drafted?" he asked.

"Why didn't you holler at me?" Darryl said.

Within minutes, their friendship was like new again.

Though he was nearing thirty, Willie McGowan's face still looked like that of teenage Bob Marley, with a long, thin nose, high cheekbones, and a smile of perfectly aligned teeth that had defused more than a few dicey situations over the years. Since the days when Darryl had brought him water during his storied Pop Warner career, McGowan had gone on to achieve local legend status as a three-sport high school athlete, then infamy after a sad decline toward petty crime, and eventually drug dealing.

The slide began sometime after his freshman year at Duarte High School—the last year T.H. Henley coached him—and it probably cost him a college scholarship. Willie landed at Pasadena City College, but he played only sparingly due to the same obstacle that would later hinder Darryl: his size. Listed at 5'8" and 160 pounds, Willie fizzled at PCC, then dropped out of school, and in 1982, at age nineteen, was convicted of vandalism and sentenced to sixty days in jail. A year later, he had a burglary and grand theft case dismissed due to mistrial. In November 1989 he was convicted of carrying a concealed weapon in a vehicle and given probation and a fine. By the early 1990s, McGowan was under DEA investigation for selling cocaine, having ascended from moving packets on the corner to packages over the phone. "I've known Willie since I was ten years old," said Chris Hale, the former USC and NFL defensive back. "He used to come over to our house. I would go places with Willie, hang out with him, the whole thing. I never had a clue he would get mixed up in all that. . . . Incredible athlete. Incredible. But every neighborhood, in every ghetto, there's always going to be that brother that gets in trouble. Willie was that guy."

The night after the Mount SAC Relays, the Rams played their charity basketball game against the Brea Fire Department and a handful of varsity players from nearby Olinda High School. Willie walked in just before tipoff. Darryl introduced him to Rex, who sat with Willie in the stands during the game. Afterward, Rex drove back to Darryl's house; Darryl rode with Willie to a nearby TGI Fridays restaurant.

Darryl and Willie were shooting the breeze over appetizers, checking out Willie's new personal trainer business cards—embossed "Body By Will"—when Darryl's pager went off. He looked down and saw "23" on its display. Tracy's code.

"I was working as a waitress at Zendejas Mexican restaurant," Tracy would write later. "He is the kicker for the Rams. It was Saturday night and T. J. Rubly [sic] the 3rd string quarterback was in for dinner with his girlfriend. . . .

"[Rubley said] Darryl had played [basketball] with him that night. I didn't even know he was in town. I was so upset. I went to the pay phone."

After Tracy's second page, Darryl called her back and listened to her complaints about how she'd found out he was in town. She asked where he was. She pulled into the TGI Fridays parking lot a few minutes later.

Darryl introduced Tracy to Willie in the restaurant. They hit it off instantly. Darryl excused himself a few times, walking away with his cell phone to his ear, which gave Willie and Tracy plenty of time to talk.

When they left the restaurant that evening, Tracy and Darryl drove to his house in her 1986 Toyota Celica, while Willie got into an SUV and went his own way. Tracy would later claim that as she and Darryl drove away from TGI Fridays she asked what Willie did for a living, and Darryl replied that Willie worked in real estate and traveled "to different states transporting a lot of cash." According to Tracy, nothing was mentioned along these lines for the next month and a half, until "around the end of May," when she and Darryl "had a long talk."

"We talked about if we were to get married and how we would raise our kids," she wrote in her statement. "I also told him how unhappy I was with my job at Zendejas. This is when he suggested that maybe I could work for Willie. He explained to me that I would be paid 3 to 4 hundred dollars. I would carry a suitcase filled with a lot of cash. I told him that it was a lot of money to do something so easy. He said he would talk to Willie and see if he needed me to work. He also said that Willie paid people well so they wouldn't be tempted to run off with the money. Darryl explained that it was easier for young white people to do this because black people looked suspicious. I asked if I was in any danger and I remember him kind of laughing. He said no not at all. How could you be in any danger unless you tell people you have a lot of cash in your bag. He explained that I would fly out in the morning and back at night. It sounded easy and good to me."

Henley, who did not testify at his own trial, spoke for the first time about these events some ten years later, while sitting in a prison. He remembered Tracy's complaints about waitressing, which to him seemed aimed at convincing him to whisk her away from her problems and into the work-free life of an NFL girlfriend and perhaps wife. He acknowledged that he spoke with Tracy about "working for Willie," but in far less detail than she indicated in her statement. "'Willie might have something for you to do' is as far as it went," he said. Their conversation did not include discussion of marriage and kids, he added, and as later evidence would irrefutably prove, their talk could not have happened when Tracy said it did.

"So much of this story got twisted around while it was going on, and for all the wrong reasons," Darryl said. But all that would come later.

Right now it was April 1993, and Darryl was back in Atlanta, at Freaknik, an annual event that had begun in the early 1980s as a prim college picnic but by 1993 had become the number-one spring break destination for young African Americans nationwide. The event lured an estimated 200,000 young black people to Atlanta each spring, causing horrendous traffic snarls and other civic blights, and accidentally creating what one witness in the Henley trial called "a place where a lot of the drug dealers go, show off their cars, show how much money they got. You know, it's sort of like a showcase."

With his Freaknik excursions by night and his one-on-one workouts on the Spelman campus by day, Henley's schedule was nothing if not full. So when he allowed his trainer Eric Johnson, a part-time Spelman policeman, to drag him across campus to meet someone, Darryl kept one eye on his watch. Johnson's friend turned out to be a pretty Spelman sophomore named Shetelle Clifford, with whom Darryl became immediately smitten. Independent, educated, and opinionated, Shetelle was not the kind of woman Darryl was used to dating. She wasn't the Freaknik type, for one thing. Darryl had to have lunch with her three times before she allowed him to take her to dinner. By that time, though, the Rams' rookies had started reporting to minicamp in California. Only one thing could have pulled Henley from Shetelle and put him on that flight back to LA, and fighting for his job was it.

After practice one day, Darryl and Tracy had dinner and ended up in his room at the team hotel. "When we got there we watched T.V.," Tracy wrote, "but ended up in a huge water fight. He was drinking water and kept spitting it on me. So I got a cup of water and threw it on him. We ended up completely wet and so was the rest of the room. I always had so much fun with him. I had sex with him that night and left around 2:00 a.m."

Cinco de Mayo (May 5) was two days later. Tracy and Darryl planned to meet up after she finished a cheerleading promotion at a restaurant. "At my promo that night a man walked up to me and showed me some pictures," she wrote. "He was a fan of the Rams and wanted to see if I were in any of his pictures.

"There was a picture of Darryl holding a little boy. I would say around one years old. This man said that it was Darryl's son and that the picture was taken at Darryl's parents Fish Store. . . . I had asked [Darryl] before if he had any children. He told me that he didn't but wanted kids very badly. [The photo] really upset me because I didn't know what to believe."

Conflicted, Tracy drove across town to meet Darryl and some other friends at the Zendejas Mexican restaurant. "Darryl asked me to go outside. He could tell that something was wrong by the way I was acting. I asked him about the picture and he explained that it [the child] wasn't his. We talked for a while and decided to go back in before it looked too obvious. He was going to LA with some of the players to go dancing. As the night went on we decided that I would just follow him back to the hotel.

"When I got there I called my mom. I told her that I had too much to drink and I was spending the night at a girlfriend's. She hated Darryl so much. She didn't want me even to be friends with him. I could tell by her voice that she didn't believe me. I had a little too much to drink to worry about it at that time. Darryl and I had sex that night."

Until that point, Tracy's mother had been little more than a nuisance, but the next day, when Tracy's sister spilled the beans about where and with whom Tracy had spent the night, Tracy and her mom "got into a huge fight."

"I thought she was being prejudice [*sic*] and wouldn't give Darryl a chance," Tracy wrote. That night Tracy had dinner with her father, a retired policeman who had divorced Tracy's mom six years earlier. "I don't think that he approved," Tracy wrote of his reaction to the Darryl news. "He was just trying to support me. When I got home that night, my mom and I fought like we never have before. It was awful." Shirley Donaho told her nineteen-year-old daughter that if she wanted to date a twenty-six-year-old black man, she'd have to do it under someone else's roof.

"At the end, I was so tired of fighting that I gave in," Tracy wrote. "I told her I would never see him again, though I knew I would.

"Throughout that horrible day, Darryl and I talked several different times. It seemed to bother him a lot. I remember him saying, 'Tracy, I can't change the color of my skin.'"

When Darryl arrived back in Atlanta, he told Tracy that if things got tough between her and her mom, she could use his garage code to hang out at his house. It was a gesture of friendship, he said later, for by then he had made the decision to start distancing himself from Tracy. There always seemed to be some kind of drama with her, he explained later, and although they'd had sex several times, the spark between them wasn't powerful enough to build a relationship on, or to put up with her Mom issues or her habit of inviting herself to wherever he was or weird freakouts like the baby photo thing. Tracy was cool to hang out with, but she pressured Darryl to call her the moment he set foot in LA. Even Alisa knew that didn't fly. Plus, Jennifer and Shetelle had entered the picture by then. They didn't know about one another's existence, but Jennifer and Shetelle were individually glad that Darryl was back in Atlanta and would be there the whole summer.

Tracy visited 2105 Wildflower Circle several times while Darryl was away, often bringing a cheerleader friend or two with her — or her sister Sherry, or her friends Wendy or Stacy. The girls usually went jogging, sat in the Jacuzzi, and watched TV.

Darryl later wrote a timeline about his life in Atlanta at that time:

"05/13 Thursday: D cooled out; took rest of week off. Spent time with Shetelle (her apt) during the day and with Jennifer (Post Chastain double) at night . . . started to deal with Earl Thomas about property."[1]

Willie McGowan came to Atlanta to visit Darryl about a month after they reunited at the track meet. He stayed in the downstairs bedroom left vacant when Jennifer's daughter went to her grandma's for the summer. One night, as Darryl and Willie were enjoying one of Jennifer's home-cooked meals, Darryl tried to persuade Willie to train him for the upcoming season. David Lang was also coming to Atlanta, Darryl explained, and Willie could work out with him, too. Always moving at warp speed, Henley had it all figured out: "You could stay here until Jennifer's daughter gets back, then you can find your own spot. You know I'm going to take care of you [pay you well]."

Henley had received a series of salary advances from the Rams to help cover his home construction in Atlanta; Willie had even watched him open one of the checks, for $150,000. How quickly Darryl's new house would be completed would depend on the size of his next contract, which would depend on his performance during the upcoming season — his last before becoming a free agent. His performance depended partly on what kind of shape he was in for training camp. And what kind of shape he was in depended, in Darryl's mind, on Willie.

Willie was only in town for three days. On the third day, he put Darryl through a workout that made it clear he knew what he was doing. Eric Johnson was a good enough trainer, but Willie brought the added benefit of putting Darryl through football-specific footwork and technique drills. Plus, Will could throw. Johnson meant well, but his passes were limp and imprecise.

Off the field, Willie had developed a deep appreciation for Darryl's lifestyle. Before he flew back to LA, Willie went on a double date with Darryl, Shetelle, and Shetelle's roommate. Willie had watched Jennifer cook for him one night, and now Darryl was chilling with a girl as fine as Jennifer the next night. He knew Darryl had a handful of girls he could call as soon as he touched down in LA, including that white girl Tracy. He'd seen heads turn each time Darryl's Benz rolled up outside a strip club, and he'd seen more turn when Darryl walked in the door. Darryl got love from all the high rollers in the clubs, including that guy he introduced Willie to at Magic City. Dude from California called G.

Willie was jerked from these thoughts, and back to the blind date, when Shetelle asked him what he did for a living. Willie smiled, pulled out a thick roll of cash, and said he was a professional gambler. The conversation stopped uncomfortably. Shetelle's roommate, an old-fashioned southern girl, looked like she'd eaten a bad bite of food. Willie chuckled. "I'm just playing. You want to know what I do for a living?" he said, sliding his money roll back into his pocket. "Nothing."

Darryl and Jennifer flew to the Cancun Jazz Festival on May 23. Flight records confirmed this trip and their return flight to LA a week later—a paper trail that would later become important. Medical records and witnesses would later prove that Darryl spent most of that return flight in the lavatory, fighting a case of salmonella poisoning that would send him to Brea Community Hospital the next morning. He spent the next four days in bed at his parents' house in Upland where, unable to keep anything down, he lost sixteen pounds. With training camp just six weeks away, he knew he needed every one of those pounds and then some. He needed Willie.

Shriveled to 154 pounds, Darryl flew to Atlanta and placed the task of preparing his flaccid body for training camp in Willie's hands. Willie's plan was simple: conditioning work with Eric Johnson in the morning, then football drills and weights with Willie in the afternoon. Jennifer's cooking, plus plenty of amino acid pills, would rebuild the muscle Darryl had lost.

The plan worked early on. Darryl stuck to it through June, interrupted only by a two-day family reunion in Texas. But after that, his workouts began to suffer. As July approached, Darryl's training often amounted to a light jog around the block while Willie trolled behind in Darryl's Mercedes, bumping hip-hop on the Alpine. Most days they were still drained from the previous night's social activities. By summer, Darryl's training had become something to muddle through so they could hit the clubs again. Thanks to Jennifer's work in the kitchen, most of those sixteen missing pounds returned, but Darryl could have been in better shape. These days, though, his body wasn't the problem.

Back then, and for the rest of his life, Darryl would refuse to believe that Willie's wheels had been turning from the moment they bumped into each other at the Mount SAC Relays track meet. It would have been natural for a businessman with Willie's experience to see the possibilities at hand. A kilo of cocaine sold for a lot more in Atlanta than in LA — $25,000 versus $16,000. Considering Willie's connections in California, and the people Darryl was rubbing elbows with in Atlanta, the path to wealth seemed simple: all Willie had to do was find a supplier in LA, a distributor in Atlanta, and a courier to deliver the drugs from West Coast to East. The rewards would be at least six figures. He'd probably have to tell Darryl about it at some point — maybe even ask for some start-up money. But not yet.

Darryl and Willie had just finished working out one day and were eating at a Jamaican restaurant near Morris Brown College when Darryl found the courage to ask Willie why he had quit football at PCC — why he had abandoned his dream. The question had always fascinated Henley, no matter which former athlete he was asking. *What made you stop?*

Willie answered Darryl by pulling up his shirt and showing him a scar on his back that looked like the result of a knife fight. After his second year at Pasadena, Willie explained, his sister fell ill and needed a kidney. Giving her one of his had ended Willie's football aspirations but had prolonged her life. Darryl was willing to bet that all those people in Duarte who thought Willie was a worthless hustler didn't know what he had done for his sister. At that moment, and throughout the summer, Darryl found himself looking up to Willie again, as if he were seven years old and Willie ten.

When Willie was in the right mood, he would regale Darryl with stories of his days in the drug game. Willie recalled that he wasn't at all surprised when the Colombian cartel he'd been working with "fell" (got busted), because the Colombians had been too flashy — snorting their product, flaunting their money, engaging in needless bully crimes, partying every night. Their high profile is what landed them in the pen, Willie said, and his low profile was why he was walking free in Atlanta.

I got something big in the works, Willie announced. But I can't invest in it. I can't get it started because I can't move my money from place to place as easily as you can.

You tryin' to launder some money? Darryl asked with a chuckle.

Nah, it ain't like that. I'm talking about taking it on a plane. Moving it from one spot to another.

Darryl asked if that was legal.

Well, I ain't exactly paid taxes on it, Willie said. But if the right person is carrying it, she won't even get looked at twice.

Who you got in mind?

Willie grinned.

That's who I thought, Darryl said.

I remember you telling me she's broke, Willie said. Always complaining about how she hates waitressing.

You talk to her about it? Darryl asked.

I was hoping *you* would.

You're sure we're talking about money now? Darryl said, still smirking, knowing full well that Willie wasn't talking about money at all.

Just mention it to her, Willie said. See how she reacts.

As it happened, Tracy reacted positively. This was the conversation in which Darryl, according to Tracy, explained to her that she "would be paid 3 to 400 dollars. I would carry a suitcase filled with a lot of cash. I told him that it was a lot of money to do something so easy. He said he would talk to Willie and see if he needed me to work. . . . He explained that I would fly out in the morning and back at night. It sounded easy and good to me."

One day not long after he had this conversation with Tracy, Darryl returned home from a Spelman workout with Eric Johnson to find Willie on his couch watching TV. G was with him. It was the first time Garey West had been inside Henley's home.

Come downstairs, Eric Johnson whispered to Henley.

Outside, Johnson asked: You know who that dude is?

Yeah, man. He straight.

You ain't never heard of Garey West?

Yeah, he's from the neighborhood. Played ball at Montclair.

You better take care of that shit, Johnson said, tilting his chin upstairs. Dude in your position doesn't need to be anywhere near that shit. Johnson left.

Darryl returned to his apartment and ate dinner with Jennifer, Willie, G, and G's female companion—a young woman named Toni.

The next day, Willie approached Darryl and, according to Henley, told him: "Everything is all lined up. I just need you to look out for me."

Tracy's flight would be from LA to Memphis, Willie continued, and all Darryl had to do was guarantee her delivery. In other words, Darryl would have to come up with $100,000 in the unlikely event that something happened to Tracy's suitcase between the time it was handed to her in California and the time she handed it to Garey West in Memphis.

Darryl looked confused.

Willie broke it down. Sometimes a guy will give another guy something up front, Willie explained. He'll give it to him with the promise of being paid later. It's called "fronting." But Dude A will only front Dude B if he feels sure Dude B can turn a profit and pay him back. Willie had a friend in California named Eric Manning who knew a cocaine supplier with that kind of trust in him. Once this supplier's suitcase arrived safely in Memphis, G would sell its contents for twice what people in California were paying, Willie said, and after they paid the supplier back they'd have over $100,000 profit left over.

The only snag was Manning's supplier in California. He was a Mexican dude who kept insisting on insurance—a guarantee in case something went wrong. "That's where you come in, D," Willie said. "I need you to look out for me."

Darryl would have walked away had it been anyone other than Willie talking. He'd always taken a stand against drugs, having spoken about them in schools and participated in the annual "Just Say No" event at Chris Leggio's car dealership. He had conveyed that very message on behalf of the NFL at the Super Bowl where he met Tracy. Introducing Willie to G and letting them do their thing was fine, but Darryl had never even smoked a joint. (Willie refused to believe Darryl on this point, and every few weeks asked him *Really?* out of the blue, posing different scenarios in hopes of cracking Henley's armor: *Not even at* UCLA *with all them ghetto dudes you played with? Not even one hit?! Come on, D. You can tell me. You ain't never smoked no weed?!* Nope. Never.) Yet Darryl was seriously thinking about "looking out for" Willie on this cocaine thing. Willie made it sound so easy.

The package was going to Memphis, first of all—seven hours from Atlanta. There was no way Darryl could be connected to it. Second, no money would leave Darryl's pocket. All Darryl had to do was give his word that he'd pay the supplier if something went wrong—if Tracy had to ditch the drugs, for example, or if she got busted, both highly unlikely scenarios.

Who all knows that you came to me with this? Darryl asked.

This is between me and you and the dude [supplier] in California, Willie said.

What's his name?

Willie laughed. See? Why do you need to know that? I'm trying to keep you clean.

Darryl felt uneasy. Part of him felt downright scared. But a smaller part felt intrigued by it all, and this particular part of him seemed to grow in influence with each passing second. It was the same part of him that had always wanted to live the hip-hop lyrics he listened to instead of being just another pro athlete who blasted Dr. Dre's *The Chronic* in his Lexus . . . while driving home to his three-bedroom house in the white-ass suburbs. Darryl hated those guys. He was one of those guys. And so he listened as Willie kept on talking:

All you gotta do is back this thing 'til it goes through, and then I'ma turn around and give you—

Nah, Darryl interrupted, waving his arms like a referee. I don't want *no money* from this. I don't want nothing connected to me, no way, no how.

That's cool, Willie said. Shit, more for me.

At that point Henley, the cornerback who loved to take chances, looked into the eyes of the guy whose uniform number he had worn during his first Pop Warner games, the man whose white tape and moves he'd mimicked, and said:

"Ah-ight."

With that one word—it wasn't even a word—Darryl became part of a conspiracy to traffic Schedule II narcotics, a violator of a federal law whose punishment was exceeded only by the punishment for murder. But the words Willie had used were much smaller than those. And Will was a friend. He had flown to Atlanta as soon as Darryl asked him to so he could help Henley put his Can-cun weight back on. Helping Willie with this thing, without lift-ing a finger — without a cent leaving or entering his pocket — it was the least Darryl could do. *Willie was right*, Darryl thought. *If he hadn't given up his kidney to save his sister, he would be where I am. What would he do if our roles were reversed? Would he look out for me?*

In making this decision — the one from which the rest of his troubles would grow like a spidery, runaway cancer — Darryl gave no thought to the crippling effects cocaine was having on the world, particularly Americans of his own race. He gave no thought to the thousands of people doing unspeakable things at that very moment to get their hands on the drug, and he gave no thought to the legions of babies who were born hooked on it. He ignored all he had heard and read about people killed over cocaine, all the bullets fired, all the families ruined. Instead, he focused on the attractive darkness of the scheme before him. This was Darryl's chance to be a part of something countercultural and illicit and risky. If nothing else, it would make a good story down the line: *Man, back in the day I looked out for this dude Willie on this thing he was doing. Shit scared the hell out of me. I swore I wasn't never doing nothing like that again.*

And so Darryl Henley — the parochial school product who got ribbed by his teammates for being square, the dwarf among giants who was known for having a bit of a Napoleon Complex — decid-ed to play Scarface for a day. Years later, he would compare those pivotal days in July 1993 to driving drunk: "You know you need to call somebody or whatever because you can't drive. You even entertain the disaster possibilities, but you go against that. You're too drunk to get in that car, but you get in anyway and something tragic happens.

"From the beginning of the month when everything was fine to the 15th when Tracy got busted — that's a downward spiral that happened so fast."

Chapter 7

July 1, 1993

Willie McGowan and his friend Eric Manning arrived in Atlanta by plane at 1:25 a.m. on Thursday, July 1, 1993. They most likely hit a couple of after-hours clubs before checking into the Hampton Inn at 6:34 a.m.

Before leaving LA, they had asked Tracy Donaho to send an overnight package to an apartment in suburban Atlanta that turned out to be the home of Garey West's mistress, Toni. Henley said later that he knew nothing about this package, which was never recovered but was believed to have contained two kilos of cocaine. Henley also didn't know that Manning had flown to Atlanta under the name "Darryl Henley" or that Manning's purpose for the trip was to retrieve the overnight package and distribute its contents.

Car rental records showed that Darryl Henley rented two cars on July 1 — cars that the authorities would later allege had been rented with drug running in mind. At 1:50 p.m., he rented a maroon four-door Mitsubishi Diamante while "approximately five other unidentified black males remained outside the McFrugal [rental] office during the transaction," according to a later DEA report. These five black males, according to Darryl, were actually four: Willie McGowan, Eric Manning, Garey West, and Rex Henley.

July 2

Darryl worked out with Eric Johnson in the morning, then he drove Jennifer to the airport so she could fly to Dallas to spend the holiday with her brother. Henley's teammate David Lang flew in from LA to attend the massive pool party that NBA player Cliff Levingston threw each Fourth in Atlanta. "After Lang's arrival, [Darryl, Rex, and Lang] head to Club Nikki's, a strip joint, dinner, then to Club 112 where it is jam-packed," Henley wrote to his attorneys later that year. "A ton of women are there and plenty of attention is [paid] to the out of town folks! There are at least 9–10 women at our table. D sees many athletes in the club as well."

Willie and Manning flew back to California the next day. Before they left, Willie briefed Darryl on the specifics of Tracy's flight to Memphis, which was just a few hours away.

Darryl called Tracy at her mother's house shortly after 9:00 p.m. His purpose, he said later, was to make sure she had her flight and hotel information. They spoke for fifteen minutes, phone records show. He called Tracy again, shortly past midnight, but this time she wasn't home. Tracy wasn't home because she was at Darryl's house in Brea, retrieving the suitcase from Eric Manning that she was about to transport to Memphis.

July 3

Tracy's flight was scheduled to take off at 1:05 a.m.[1] As the flight was boarding in California, Darryl was in Atlanta calling an old flame named Terri, to whom he spoke for four minutes before nodding off on his couch.

69

His ringing phone woke him at 5:00 a.m. It was Willie, calling with bad news: Tracy had missed her flight. Rex, who was supposed to have flown with Tracy that night, called Darryl with the same news. "That dude Eric [Manning] didn't drop her off at the airport 'til one o'clock," Rex said. "How were we supposed to make a 1:05 flight?"

"Where's Tracy?" Darryl asked.

"She went home."

It was almost 2:30 a.m. in Yorba Linda when Darryl got in touch with Tracy, who repeated what Rex said: Eric Manning had been late getting her to the airport. Stranded, with no more flights and no ride, she and Rex had had no choice but to take a cab home. "Then you called."

Willie McGowan clicked into this conversation between Darryl and Tracy, spoke with Darryl briefly, then called American Airlines to try and set up another flight.

"Willie wants to know if you can try again in the morning," Darryl said to Tracy. Willie clicked in again. Tracy's new flight would leave Burbank airport at 7:00 a.m. Tracy agreed to meet Willie at Darryl's house at 5:00 a.m.

At 7:00 a.m. sharp, Willie was sitting ten rows behind Tracy on American Airlines flight 1320, Burbank to Dallas. He had reminded her to act like she didn't know him. When they landed in Dallas, he helped Tracy retrieve her rolling suitcase from the overhead compartment, then escorted her to her flight to Memphis. They parted ways at her departure gate, and Willie boarded his flight to Atlanta.

As Darryl waited to pick Willie up at the Atlanta airport, he received a page from a 901 area code — Memphis — and called it from his cell phone. Tracy answered.

Hey, I'm in Memphis but the Marriott's full. What do I do now?

Fuming at the lack of foresight shown by what would soon be his codefendants, Darryl told Tracy he'd call her back. He couldn't believe that no one had reserved a room for her in advance, especially on Fourth of July weekend. He was way too involved in this thing. It wasn't supposed to go like this.

Willie stepped off the plane in Atlanta to meet a jaw-clenched Darryl, who slapped his cell phone into Willie's hand and told him, Call Tracy at this number, goddammit. Willie did so and told Tracy that someone would be by shortly to pick her up. He seemed calmer than Darryl would have liked. Darryl was certainly angrier than Willie would have liked. For the first time, Darryl feared that all he had ever worked for was about to be taken from him because of this stupid favor he was doing—this completely unnecessary risk he'd taken—for Willie McGowan.

But it would take several more days, and a few more people, for that to happen.

Gary Dabney was a former gang member and cocaine dealer who, like his longtime friend Garey West, was originally from Montclair, California. (The locals there called him "Little G" to avoid confusion with West's "G.") Dabney was living in Memphis in the summer of 1993 when he received a call from West, who asked if he could borrow Dabney's car. Dabney knew West's line of work, so he wasn't surprised when West said he needed it to pick someone up from the airport. [2]

Shortly after G came over and picked up Dabney's 1989 Hyundai, he called Dabney to ask another favor. "Can I bring a white girl over to your place?"

Darryl was in Atlanta at that moment, explaining to Willie that this was a lot more complicated than he'd thought, when Willie's pager went off. Willie looked down at the device and grinned. *Touchdown*, he said. Tracy had just handed her suitcase to G. You don't ever have to worry again, he told Darryl.

By afternoon, Darryl had calmed down. He even brought Willie with him to Shetelle Clifford's apartment in suburban Stone Mountain, where Darryl met Shetelle's parents, who were in from out of town for the holiday. Showing no signs of having stayed up all night discussing flights and suitcases, Darryl and Willie watched a baseball game with Shetelle's dad, then Darryl led everyone on a driving tour of the posh neighborhood where his home was being built. Shetelle's parents were impressed both by Darryl and his property, which, although it had only recently been cleared of trees and brush, called forth a vision of the sprawling home that would stand there one day. Darryl had given his builder, Earl Thomas, a select few instructions, the most important of which was that he wanted it so that "everybody in my family can come here for Christmas and nobody would have to leave for anything."

Tracy Donaho looked so young that when she entered Gary Dabney's Memphis apartment, Dabney's girlfriend, Amy Thompson, thought she was still in high school. Tracy asked Garey West when she could fly back to California. West said it might be a while. First he had to round up some money to pay for her ticket. Tracy sat on the couch and watched TV with Amy while West sent Dabney to the parking lot to get the all-important suitcase from the Hyundai's trunk.

"I can't remember who paged Darryl," Tracy wrote later, "but he called. . . . When I got on the phone he got really mad. He couldn't believe that I was still there and not on a flight home. He had the guy that picked me up [West] get on the phone."

Tracy wrote that when the phone call ended, "I remember saying to [West] that if he took some money out of the bag, I would just go ahead to the airport and wait for my flight.[3] He said no, that he would get the money and I could stay there and watch TV. . . . I watched TV for awhile. . . . The two guys were in the bedroom. The door was open and I heard them talking and laughing. The bag was sitting by the front door. At one point the guy who picked me up came out and got it. Took it to the bedroom."

West and Dabney stashed the suitcase in a bedroom closet, told the girls they would be back with the money for Tracy's flight home, and left. Tracy, who hadn't slept all night, dozed on the sofa. Amy also fell asleep. When the guys returned, West told the girls to arrange for a cab to pick Tracy up at 7:30 p.m. Then they left again.

"The cab showed up around 7:25 pm," Tracy wrote, "and the guys were not back yet. Finally around 7:35 they showed up. [West] gave me the money. I think around $840. My flight was seven something, a little for the cab fair and to get something to eat he said."

July 4

The next day, while Darryl and his friends were enjoying Cliff Levingston's celebrity-laden pool party in Atlanta, G was returning to Dabney's apartment in Memphis, where he retrieved the suitcase from the bedroom closet and took it to his place.

July 5

Darryl had heard that Tracy was back in California, but she hadn't called him yet. When she finally paged him at 1:51 p.m., he called her back, made sure she was okay, then scolded her for not calling sooner. Tracy giggled in response, he recalled, and told him: "Oh, you're being paranoid." Now that she was back in California, her Memphis trip seemed fun for her—a daring walk on the wild side. "What's the worst that could've happened?" she asked.

"Don't call me anymore about whatever you and those dudes got going on," Darryl said he replied. "Leave me out of it."

That night Henley hit the clubs with David Lang. They did not return home. Phone records indicate that Willie McGowan spent that evening at Henley's Atlanta apartment, making two incriminating phone calls—one to Gary Dabney's home, the other to Eric Manning's pager.

July 6–12

Darryl drove to the Atlanta airport on July 6, where he dropped off David Lang and picked up Jennifer Wilson in one fell swoop.

Tracy called him the next day to complain that Willie had yet to pay her for her Memphis delivery. Tracy "really needed the money," she said later, so she could attend a girlfriend's bachelorette party in Vegas that weekend. Western Union records confirmed that Darryl wired $1,000 to Tracy on July 9, 1993.[4]

"I got back from Vegas late Sunday night [July 11]," Tracy wrote, "and early Monday morning Willie called. He said that he really needed me sometime that week and could I please do it one more time. I said no. Later that day I took the stuff I had bought in Vegas to show my sister in her room. We talked for a little while and she asked me where I had gotten the money. I explained that Darryl had a friend that I flew to Memphis for. I carried a suitcase full of cash for a real estate deal. She thought it sounded a little weird and suggested that maybe the cash was for something else, like drugs. I explained to her that Darryl would never do anything to hurt me."

Tracy's written statement did not mention the calls she had made to Darryl's pager that day or the following night. Henley's phone records showed that he did not return either call. He explained years later that he'd been trying to distance himself from Tracy while preparing for his cruise to the Bahamas with Shetelle, set to depart in two days. Looming after that was the most important training camp of his career. He had recently closed escrow on a townhome in Marietta, just outside Atlanta — a place for Jennifer Wilson and her daughter to live during the season. Darryl agreed to let Willie move into the vacant apartment they were leaving behind under the condition that he help Jennifer move out. Darryl informed the management at the Post Chastain apartments that his "cousin" Will would be staying there for the remainder of July.

July 13

Willie called the phone company and transferred Darryl's landline at the Post Chastain apartment to his own name. By evening, Jennifer was settled into her new home in Marietta and Willie was settled in his. The events of the next forty-eight hours, however, would bring any sense of stability they felt to an end.

July 14

Willie called Tracy in the morning. [5]

"He said that he really needed me that night and I would fly to Atlanta," Tracy wrote. "I said no. Around 2:30 pm or 3:00 p.m. I received a page to a 404 area [code (Atlanta)].

"When I called, Willie answered and said hold on, because Darryl wanted to talk to me. Darryl started in about how he needed me to do this and how I would get to see him. He said how he missed me, and wouldn't care if I didn't want to do this anymore, but just this one last time. I still said no. We talked longer and he talked me into it."

Sitting in prison, Darryl remembered that conversation much differently. Willie didn't answer the phone, Henley said. "I answered it. Then she asked for Willie. So I gave him the phone." Willie entered the kitchen so he could speak with Tracy in private.

Alone in the living room, Darryl scanned the apartment's walls, spending a moment in the place where he'd gotten his start in Atlanta. It hadn't been a smooth start, but he was moving forward now, and the stupidest, most dangerous thing he'd ever done had passed without incident. Ninety-three was going to be his breakout season. He could feel it. It was his contract year, and his agent was already tossing around numbers like "five years, $8 million," which made the game of Russian roulette he'd just played with Willie seem even more foolish.

But all that was over now.

Willie returned from the kitchen and handed Darryl the phone.

Hello? Darryl said.

Hey, was that you who answered? Tracy asked.

Yeah.

Why didn't you say anything?

I didn't know it was you, Darryl lied.

Well, what are you doing tomorrow?

I'm in *Atlanta*, Tracy.

I know. That's where I'm gonna be tomorrow.

Oh, really.

Yeah, I'm flying there for Willie.

Darryl paused, his eyes darting to Willie, his mind ripping through the consequences.

So, what are you doing tomorrow? Tracy repeated.

Working out.

Are you gonna take a break, or—

Nah, I'm not taking any breaks.

Their conversation trickled to an awkward end. As soon as Henley hung up, he tracked Willie down in the kitchen. I thought you were done with her, Darryl said.

It was a last-minute thing, Willie replied, hoping his calmness would once again put Darryl at ease. This is the last time right here. I'm shutting it down after this.

I *already* shut this shit down, Darryl said, storming out of the apartment. He drove to the new townhome in Marietta and called Tracy to advise her to skip the flight she was about to take and all future flights. But no one answered. (Phone records showed that this call lasted less than a minute, indicating either a very brief conversation or that no conversation took place.)

Willie, meanwhile, was on the Post Chastain landline calling his partner Eric Manning in California, then Darryl's travel agent so he could book Tracy on a red-eye from LA to Atlanta. Phone records show each of these calls, just as they showed Willie's call to Tracy's pager earlier that day. Tracy's subsequent seven-minute call to Willie's new number was the one she later pinpointed as the call in which Darryl "talked her into" flying to Atlanta.

Thirty-seven minutes after making that call, she dialed Willie again, but "Darryl was gone," she said later. "I told Willie that I would do it, and he said that my flight was around 9:00 p.m. and to meet Rex at Darryl's house around 7:30 p.m."

Chapter 8

DEA REPORT OF INVESTIGATION

BASIS OF INVESTIGATION — On July 15, 1993, TFA Hogan received information from Det. Mike Ortiz, Ontario, CA Airport detail, that a Tracy DONAHO was traveling on a one-way, cash ticket on American Airlines to Atlanta.[1] DONAHO had purchased the ticket just prior to departure. . . . TFA's Lisa Roey and Al Hogan conducted a consensual interview of DONAHO at [Atlanta] Hartsfield International Airport at approximately 10:10 a.m. . . . A search warrant was obtained for DONAHO's suitcase which contained approximately 12 kilos of cocaine.

Darryl was peeking through the front window of his townhome in Marietta, Willie's words still ringing in his ears: The feds got her. . . . I'm in the wind. . . . See you in the next life. He looked around outside, trying to ignore

Jennifer's questions: You waiting for someone? What's going on? Who was that that just called?

When the maroon Mitsubishi pulled up—the car Darryl had rented two weeks earlier, a two-ton reminder of his mistakes—he still felt as if he could get out of the whole mess unscathed. All he had to do was tell the cops the truth. Or at least most of it. He told Jennifer he'd call her later and walked out into the Georgia humidity toward the car, the sound of cicadas screaming from the nearby woods.

The floorboard in the back of the Mitsubishi was littered with marijuana roaches, a pair of ladies shoes, and a tube of red lipstick. [2] As he sat, Darryl received a page from a local number, followed by Tracy's code: 23.

That's the third time Tracy's paged me, Darryl said as the Mitsubishi pulled away from Jennifer, who was standing on the doorstep, hands on hips, watching him go.

Don't call her back, Willie said. Willie was in the passenger seat, staring out the window, biting his thumbnail, his caramel skin gone gray. Garey West was driving calmly. A few minutes later, when G turned right onto Peachtree Road, bringing the Lenox Mall into view, Willie told Darryl that now was the time to call Tracy back. He put his ear next to the phone, listening while feeding Darryl his lines:

"Where are you?" Darryl asked Tracy.

"I'm at a mall near the Marriott."

Willie mouthed the words *Is anybody with you?* Darryl repeated them out loud.

"No," Tracy said.

"The police aren't with you?"

"No."

Willie frowned. He felt sure she was lying, that she'd been flipped and was working for the cops. He fed Darryl his next line: "Anyone follow you?"

"*No*, Darryl!" Now Tracy was angry. "Don't you wanna know how I'm doing? I'm scared to death and all you wanna know is if—"

"Where's the suitcase?"

"They took it. The DEA people at the airport took it."

(The suitcase hadn't been opened. The DEA investigators needed a search warrant, which they wouldn't receive until that afternoon.)

"I'll call you back in five minutes."

"Please call me back, Darryl. Willie won't return my calls."

Willie mouthed the words *Hang up*, and Darryl did, the cell phone beeping like the end of a video game.

Darryl insisted that they go pick her up, but Willie wanted to prove to Darryl that the feds had already convinced her to cooperate, so Willie told G to drop Darryl off outside the mall. Willie told Darryl to call Tracy from his cell phone in five minutes and tell her to take a cab across the street, where G would be waiting. Willie said he was headed inside the mall to watch her and make sure she followed these instructions. If she didn't, he'd know she was working with the DEA. "If you see her walk out of the mall before I do," Willie told Darryl, "call Jennifer and have her come pick you up somewhere. You don't have to worry about being mad at me anymore because you ain't ever gonna see me again."

Darryl got out of the car. G drove away. Darryl called Tracy.

"Darryl told me to take a cab around the mall to Bennigans and wait out front," Tracy wrote in her statement. "The man on the phone next to me said that if I just walked through the mall and out Saks Fifth Avenue's doors I would see Bennigans. That way I could save money. So that is what I did."

Darryl was waiting outside the mall entrance. It was a Thursday morning, so the parking lot was empty when Tracy emerged from the mall on foot. Darryl sprang up and started walking. *Willie was right*, he thought, breaking into a jog. *The cops must be right behind her.*

"Darryl!" Tracy yelled. "Where are you going?"

Henley was almost in a sprint when Willie leapt in front of him, his palms raised. "She cool, she cool," Willie said, panting. "She just can't follow fucking directions."

Everyone calmed down.

G drove over and picked everyone up.

"I got in the back seat with Darryl," Tracy wrote. "Willie was in the front passenger seat and the guy who picked me up in Memphis was driving. We drove around for awhile. The driver didn't say much. Willie asked a lot of questions and so did Darryl. Just what I said to the people at the airport and what they said to me."

When Tracy told Willie and Darryl that she'd given the DEA officers her fake ID, Willie and Darryl sighed with relief, thinking that the feds had no way of knowing her real name. G didn't sigh. He still hadn't made a sound since they'd picked Darryl up. Only when Tracy said, "I also gave them my real ID" — an utterance that made Darryl and Willie literally slump in their seats — did G finally speak:

"We should take her to Alabama."

It wasn't an awful idea. Getting Tracy out of Atlanta, preferably out of the South altogether, was now their top priority, but trying to put her on a plane at Hartsfield would have been as foolish as the scheme that landed her there. If they could get her to Birmingham, though — and the sooner the better — she might be able to board another flight undetected.[3]

Birmingham was three hours away by car, though, and the guys figured that by then the cops would have discovered the suitcase's contents and issued an APB for Tracy at every airport in the United States. So the Alabama idea was scrapped. During all this, Darryl's pager kept shrieking its high-pitched beeps, thanks to Jennifer. The scene in the rented Mitsubishi was tense, but as Tracy recalled: "They never showed any anger towards me. They kept saying everything would be alright."

Darryl surveyed the situation: he was one of three black men in a car with a young white woman "in white-ass Buckhead" (as he described it later). "We were begging to get pulled over." Thinking quickly, he suggested that G drop him and Tracy off somewhere. G pulled over at a Greek restaurant on Roswell Road called Café Dimitri.

"Hi, I'm Darryl Henley. I play pro football for the Los Angeles Rams," Darryl said to the waiter inside. "Do you have a pay phone?"[4] The first person Henley called was Chuck Knox, the Rams' head coach. He left a message on his voicemail: *Call me at this number as soon as you get this.* Darryl's next two calls were to assistant coaches Rod Perry and Joe Vitt, to whom he repeated the message: *Have Knox call me at this number, ASAP.*

Willie had said he'd be back to pick them up later, so Darryl sat with Tracy at a booth near the window so he could keep an eye on Roswell Road. They ordered food. Neither ate. "At this time, Darryl said that the valuables were gone and we couldn't get them back," Tracy wrote later. "'Our biggest concern is you.' When he referred to the contents of the bag as valuables, I knew for sure there must not have been cash in the suitcase. . . . I still didn't ask because I didn't want to hear it."

Darryl asked her again what had happened at the airport. Tracy told him that the DEA people approached her at baggage claim and asked to search her bags. She allowed them to search her carry-on, but not the suitcase, claiming that it belonged to a girlfriend of hers named Allison Coats whose father was sick in an Atlanta hospital. He'd just had a heart attack, Tracy had lied, so Allison had asked Tracy to bring some clothes to her from California because she'd be in Atlanta longer than expected.[5] Tracy told the DEA officers that she'd been given the suitcase by a white guy at a Red Lion Inn in Ontario, California.

Darryl's stomach churned. He looked out the window at Roswell Road.

It was well after lunch now, and Café Dimitri had closed its doors to give its staff time to eat and have a smoke before the dinner rush. Darryl and Tracy were allowed to stay at their table in the otherwise empty dining room as the afternoon temperature peaked outside. Darryl asked Tracy if she wanted to stick with the Allison Coats story or tell the truth. Tracy said she wanted to stick with the story.

The restaurant's pay phone rang. It was Chuck Knox. Darryl

told his coach that a girl he knew had just had her luggage confiscated at the Atlanta airport and that the situation involved some friends of his—friends he didn't know that well.

They were using her as a mule, Knox said in his John Wayne drawl. "What's a mule?"

The image of sixty-one-year-old Chuck Knox describing drug trafficking lingo to thug-in-waiting Darryl Henley, while the latter stood at a pay phone in an empty Greek restaurant in Dixie, was one of the more surreal images in an altogether surreal day. Nearly as unexpected was Knox's advice that Darryl take the girl back to the airport. Maybe they made a mistake, Knox said. His starting cornerback certainly didn't seem like the type to be mixed up with seized suitcases and mules.

Before he hung up, Knox gave Darryl the phone number for Joe Molloy, who was not only Anaheim's chief of police, and not only the Rams' head of security, but the father of a young man who had graduated with Darryl from Damien High in 1984. Darryl called Molloy from Café Dimitri and filled him in. Molloy asked to speak to the girl. Darryl handed Tracy the phone. Henley was only privy to Tracy's half of the conversation, which he recalled went like this:

"No. [pause] No, he didn't. [pause] No sir, not at all. [pause] No. [pause] Yes, I'm sure."

Tracy handed the phone back to Darryl.

"You're in the clear," Molloy told Henley. "She said you had nothing to do with this. I'm gonna call [Rams president John] Shaw and tell him the same thing. Be careful." *Click.*

Shortly afterward, G and Willie pulled up outside Café Dimitri accompanied by a white van. At the wheel of the van was a local defense lawyer named Joe Maccione, who had been having a run-of-the-mill Thursday until he received a call asking him to drive to the Amoco gas station off I-285. Maccione had been greeted there by two young black men who handed him $200 cash and asked him to follow them to a Greek restaurant.

Darryl introduced himself to Maccione, then he and Tracy

climbed into the back of Maccione's van. Maccione drove them around—just the three of them, talking things over in Maccione's office on wheels. As they did so, Maccione became certain that this football player was no cocaine trafficker. He'd handled similar cases for years, and his intuition was telling him that Henley, who was doing most of the talking, was clean. Darryl's main concern, Maccione later testified, was Tracy's well-being.

Darryl and Tracy took turns telling the Allison Coats story as convincingly as they could, after which Maccione looked in his rearview mirror and said, "This may sound crazy, but I can get you off." Tracy nearly fainted with relief. "You *do* need to go back to the airport, though," Maccione added, looking at Tracy. "And they *are* going to arrest you."

Tracy began crying again.

"After that the attorney dropped us off at another restaurant called Stage Deli," she wrote. "We sat there for along time. Darryl was on the phone for so long that I fell asleep at the table. I was exhausted. When he came back I remember him saying that Willie didn't think that it was a good idea that he [Darryl] went to the airport with me. We talked about it for awhile, and [Darryl] was going with me."

Tracy used a pay phone to call the number the DEA guy had given her that morning.

DEA task force officer J. J. Stubbs picked up the phone in the agency's cramped office at the airport. When Tracy told him who she was, Stubbs's eyes widened and he nudged his colleague, Al Hogan, and mouthed the words *It's her.*

Stubbs asked Tracy if she was in any danger.

No, Tracy said.

You sure?

Yes.

Stubbs asked if she was alone.

No.

"Why don't you let me know where you are so we can come pick you up," Stubbs said. "I think you might be in danger."

Tracy got scared and hung up.

Had the feds traced the call? Were they on their way right now? Darryl wasn't going to wait around and find out. Willie and G had just arrived at Stage Deli with a second rental car, which Darryl used to drive Tracy to his Post Chastain apartment. The plan was to rehearse the Allison Coats story with her, then take her back to the airport.

It was ninety-six degrees in the middle of the afternoon in the middle-most day in the middle-most month of the year, in a town nicknamed Hot-lanta. Darryl and Tracy were sitting in the air-conditioning of the empty apartment he'd just moved out of, sweat cooling on their backs, clothes clinging to their skin. Darryl made sure once again that she wanted to stick with the Allison Coats story. Neither he nor Tracy were convinced that the DEA officers had bought it that morning (they hadn't), but it was what she'd already told them, so they stuck with it, practiced it, and agreed to try and make it seem as if Tracy had been fooled by her drug trafficking girlfriend named Allison.

They drove to the airport at 8 p.m. On the way, Tracy used Darryl's cell phone to call Hogan's pager number.

Hogan had already left for the day, so he returned Tracy's call from his home. He told her he hadn't been able to get a search warrant for her suitcase (a lie), and arranged to meet her at baggage claim in fifteen minutes so he could give the suitcase back to her. As soon as he hung up, he called his partner, DEA task force officer Lisa Roey, who left for the airport as quickly as he did.

Darryl parked the rental car along the same curb where he'd stepped into a Kodak-sponsored limousine four and a half years earlier as a freshly minted college All-American. Only now, he and an NFL cheerleader were pulling up in a dusty rental car, its air conditioner blowing futile and full-blast, as the DEA's two newest targets. Darryl told Tracy to stay in the car while he went inside and bought her a plane ticket home. He returned, ticket in hand, and walked her inside the terminal, where Tracy spotted Hogan wearing the same thing he had had on that morning: blue jeans, short-sleeve shirt, no handcuffs, no gun.

Hogan gently steered Tracy away from the guy she was with and asked her if he had anything to do with her suitcase. Tracy said no, describing Darryl as a friend who lived in Atlanta and had nothing to do with this. Hogan introduced himself to Henley, who did likewise: "I'm Darryl Henley. I play football for the LA Rams." According to Hogan's trial testimony, he liked Darryl right off the bat, seeing him as an uninvolved friend who was there merely to support Tracy. Tracy, on the other hand, was a suspect and his only lead on what was becoming a very interesting cocaine bust. "Let's go over here to the office, and I'll get your suitcase for you," Hogan said to her.

Lisa Roey was not as quick to befriend Henley. During her routine patdown of Tracy in the DEA office, Roey kept a close eye on Hogan's patdown of Darryl, who joked about how unnecessary the frisking was. Darryl and Tracy took a seat. Hogan drew the blinds. Darryl and Tracy sat close and held hands.

"I wasn't exactly honest with you earlier," Hogan said to Tracy. "I got a search warrant for your suitcase." He then plopped a handful of Polaroid pictures in front of her, which depicted the suitcase wide open, filled with the twelve bricks of cocaine nestled in a pile of random clothing. "The color completely left her," Hogan testified later, "just like I yanked a carpet out from under her feet. And she looked at Mr. Henley and then she looked at her hands and she just buried her hands in her face and she started to cry. [It] just completely took the wind out of her."

Darryl placed his hand on Tracy's back and rubbed softly as Hogan read her her rights. She waived her right to remain silent, opening the door for Hogan to ask once again what had brought her to Atlanta. Wiping tears, Tracy repeated the Allison Coats story while Darryl tried to polish the lie with interjected details. Hogan asked Tracy where she had gone after leaving the airport that morning.

"The Hampton Inn," Tracy said.

"We know that's not the truth, Tracy."

Tracy glanced at Darryl, then turned back to Hogan. He was sitting on the edge of a desk staring down at her, his arms folded. "Well, okay, okay," she admitted, "I'm lying there. I know I'm lying. I just didn't want to tell you anything different than I told you before. I did go to the Marriott. But that's the only thing I'm lying about. Everything else is true." At that point Hogan produced a pair of handcuffs. Darryl asked if that was really necessary. Hogan said that it was.

Darryl said he couldn't believe someone could take advantage of her like that and mentioned his involvement with antidrug programs in California. But it was no use. Two local police officers arrived, took Tracy into custody, and led her out of the airport.

Holding Tracy's small overnight bag as he followed along, Darryl told Hogan: "We're going to get this thing straight. . . . I know you can do it, and I wish you could get this thing taken care of because she's just been—she's been duped."

The final sentence of Tracy's handwritten statement, which she completed five months after her arrest, was: "At that point I knew I would tell the truth, just not with Darryl sitting next to me."

But after she told it, that truth would change.

Chapter 9

Ontario Police detective Mike Ortiz was the man who had raised the red flag at the Ontario airport when he learned that a young woman had just paid cash, at 12:30 a.m., for a last-minute ticket to Atlanta. Ortiz had responded by calling the DEA office in Atlanta, and now, some twenty hours later, unaware that Tracy had just been arrested, it was Ortiz who drove to the Donaho home in Yorba Linda to follow up.

Shirley Donaho, Tracy's mother, answered the door to find a tall plainclothes detective who told her that her daughter Tracy probably wouldn't be coming home that night. Sherry, Tracy's twenty-one-year-old sister, came downstairs at that point ("visibly upset," Ortiz reported) and spilled an explosive, unprovoked bit of information: "Tracy delivered a suitcase for Darryl."

"I knew he'd get her in trouble," Mrs. Donaho added.

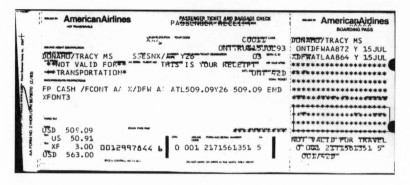

Plaintiff's exhibit 5-A, *United States v. Rafael Bustamante, et al.*

"Darryl who?" asked Ortiz. He'd never heard of the football player.

Mrs. Donaho declined to give Darryl's last name. Sherry panicked and called her father, who said he was on his way. Then, to Ortiz's surprise, Sherry continued talking. This wasn't the first time Tracy had made such a trip, she said. Tracy had also delivered a suitcase to Memphis that "contained money, and Tracy knew the money was involved with the purchase of narcotics." Ortiz's pen strained to keep up.

Terry Donaho, a former drug cop with the Downey Police, arrived at his ex-wife's home and told Detective Ortiz that Tracy had already called him from jail in Georgia and lied to him — something about delivering a suitcase for a girlfriend. Mr. Donaho said he had cut her off at that point and told her: "That's BS. I've already spoken with Darryl." (Phone records confirmed that Tracy's father was the first person Henley called after Tracy was arrested.) Tracy probably knew what she was doing all along, Mr. Donaho said.

When the phone rang, no one expected it to be Darryl Henley, but that's who it was, calling to offer Terry a ticket to Atlanta so he could help his daughter. Terry asked Darryl if he could bail Tracy out and get her a lawyer. Darryl said he would work on both. He gave Mr. Donaho his home number and asked him to call if he needed anything else. But their alliance, it seemed, dissolved the moment Terry hung up the phone. As Ortiz wrote in his report, "Terry Donaho assured me that he would fly to Atlanta and have Tracy fully cooperate with authorities and if it meant arresting Darrell Hensley [sic], that's what would have to be done. Terry furnished me with Hensley's phone number."

When Darryl hung up, he began packing for what he'd told Jennifer would be a three-day youth football camp in Miami, but was actually a cruise to the Bahamas with his other Atlanta girlfriend, Shetelle Clifford. This deceit, plus the timing of the cruise—the morning after Tracy's twelve-kilo delivery—would become two clues pointing to Henley as the cocaine conspiracy's mastermind. He would look more like a womanizing drug lord fleeing the country than a pro football player taking his usual pre-camp vacation.

Across town, meanwhile, at the Clayton County jail, efforts were already under way to turn Tracy Donaho into a government witness. A scared nineteen-year-old raised in the suburban bubble of Orange County, Tracy could not have been more suited for the role had she been genetically engineered for it. She had no criminal record, nothing to fuel an attack from the defense on her credibility. She'd smoked marijuana a few times in her life, had swindled a TV dating show out of a couple hundred bucks once, and she wasn't the most diligent student in the world. But a jury wouldn't care about those trivialities once they saw her and heard her story about Darryl and the suitcases. Plus, her father's law enforcement background would give her a trusted advisor to help navigate the intricate legal plumbing ahead.

At some point during his daughters' upbringings, Terry Donaho had told Tracy and Sherry that if they ever got in trouble, to talk to him before talking to anyone else. When DEA investigators Hogan and Roey began pressing her for information, Tracy remembered this advice and told them she wanted to talk to her dad again. Terry Donaho and his ex-wife were already in the air, headed to Atlanta.

In finding Tracy a lawyer, Darryl knew he would need someone willing to drop everything and fly to Atlanta as well—someone adventurous yet trustworthy, someone who would bend the rules if need be, a confidante who would protect Tracy's interests while also looking out for Henley's. He needed someone who could connect with Tracy. An attractive woman, maybe.

He had known Angela Wallace for years, having dated her sister Cara at one point, and he knew of Angela's reputation as a criminal defense attorney on the rise. Henley had no way of knowing, however, that in the months and years ahead, Wallace's methods and personal liaisons would be called increasingly into question, or that she would eventually be sentenced to six years in jail for insurance fraud.[1] Wallace was, as Garey West put it, a "Mob lawyer"—a too-specific term that meant she was willing to proclaim the innocence of known criminals as vigorously as she kept their secrets. After Henley briefed Wallace over the phone on the Tracy situation, Angie (as he called her) booked a flight to Atlanta.

Darryl also hopped on a plane, but his was bound for Miami. His Caribbean cruise with Shetelle would turn out nothing like the relaxing getaway he'd envisioned when he scheduled it. He spent the entire first day in their cabin on the MS *Fantasy*, a 70,000-ton city on the sea, handwriting his account of the preceding six months, just as Angie had asked him to. As the ship steamed east toward Bimini, Shetelle sat bored on the balcony, staring at the sun-flecked sea. "Be patient, girl. I'm almost finished," Darryl said. An hour later Shetelle looked back to find him asleep on the bed. While he slept she read what he'd written to that point and, English major that she was, grabbed a pen and began correcting his grammar.

"Hey, that's between me and my attorney," Darryl said, jerking awake. He called Wallace on the boat's ship-to-shore line and asked what he should do now that Shetelle had breached their attorney-client privilege. Wallace said not to worry about it, so Shetelle finished her corrections and faxed the final draft to Wallace's office in LA, completing a process that would later do irreparable harm to Henley's legal defense.

The document that rolled off Angie Wallace's fax machine in Los Angeles represented Darryl's best effort to protect everyone involved and reflected the delusional overconfidence that was his best on-field attribute and the key to his personal downfall. The fax contained numerous lies. For one, Darryl made it seem as if G had been behind the whole "money delivery" thing, not Willie or Eric Manning, who were hardly mentioned in the fax. Lies aside, Darryl wrote candidly that he'd given Tracy access to his house so she could escape "racial problems [she was] having with her bitch-ass mom." Shetelle didn't edit that line, one that would hardly paint Darryl in a favorable light when he'd need exactly that. But at the time the fax was between him and his attorney (and now Shetelle), and he thought it would go no further.

In it he wrote incriminating details linking him to all the players and all their suitcases and flights, but he maintained that he was only on the fringe of things; he knew these people, but he didn't know what they were doing. He did not tell Angie that he'd guaranteed the Memphis delivery for Willie; in fact, he would never divulge this fact to *any* attorney at any point. At the end of the fax he added another telling passage:

"Angie — As long as this chick and I are the same on who was contacting her then I don't care who else's name she tells. We need to make sure she always says that Willie always let her know what was going on and that she always took a cab to the airport and met the guy getting her the luggage at the Brea Mall. She does not want to incriminate me, so these two details will be extremely important. That is, if she hasn't said them already. After I gave [Willie] her pager [number], from that point on, we only conversed about regular issues. The other things you have to deal with are 1. Her trip to Tennessee and her calls to me. 2. Her Vegas money wire from me. 3. Whether or not she told them that we all picked her up [in Atlanta on July 15] or just me."

The sight of her daughter in an orange shift and prison-issue sandals brought Shirley Donaho to tears, which brought Tracy to tears, which moved Terry Donaho to wrap his arms around both of them and squeeze. The Donahos had reportedly been flown to Atlanta by the government—an unusual gesture for a suspect caught smuggling twenty-five pounds of cocaine, as was the ten-minute private talk they were granted in an adjacent room. (Other inmates at the Clayton County jail were required to meet their visitors in the guard-monitored visiting room.) Those on Darryl Henley's side of the legal fence would later point out that Tracy was an experienced drug courier by that point, a transporter of multiple kilos of cocaine through five major airports, a criminal whose parents—the very people with whom she was given a private visit—had already indicated that she knew what she was doing all along. So why allow them to huddle with Tracy alone?

Even Steve Israel, who had more derogatory things to say about Darryl than any of his other Rams teammates, could not abide the government's methods. "The picture they painted about how Darryl lured her into this elaborate scheme is false," said the retired cornerback, who had also socialized with Tracy on occasion. "This girl knew what she was getting into. . . . I didn't follow every single detail of the case, but I heard D-Hen wined and dined her, took her to Vegas, all this. She just got caught up in it. He didn't catch her up in anything. There's a difference. She allowed herself to get caught up in the fast life he was leading, and I'm not talking about drugs at all. I'm talking about money, fame, all that. She had to know she was taking a chance on some level. And they obviously wanted him more than they wanted her."

Tracy Ann Donaho was born August 17, 1973—six weeks after another Yorba Linda native, President Richard Nixon, created the DEA. Terry Donaho had been with the Downey police for six years when his wife, Shirley, a homemaker and part-time dance teacher, gave birth to their second daughter, whose path to the NFL was much like Darryl Henley's in that it began in Texas and with Pop

Warner football. Tracy began cheerleading during the family's brief move to Texas in the early 1980s, and like Darryl she showed exceptional ability, nimble feet, and a charming personality. After her family moved back to California, Tracy cheered every year until high school, when she fell in love with her mother's passion: dance. Esperanza High School boasted one of the top dance programs in the country, with a full trophy case to prove it. They won a national championship during Tracy's first year as cocaptain, but the team's most talented dancer was no spoiled diva. Tracy's family was not as wealthy as most of her friends' families, so she worked at a frozen yogurt shop during her junior year, then as a waitress at the Original Pancake House—a position she still held at the time of her arrest.

She learned about the tryouts for the 1992 Rams' cheerleaders just two days before they were scheduled to begin, when she overheard a college teammate complaining about how a hundred girls were competing for just a dozen openings. The tryouts would last several weeks, Tracy learned, and would include impromptu dance, personal interviews, and singing—three things Tracy had never done before. Most of the candidates had been preparing for months. Tracy simply walked in and made the team. She met Darryl Henley at the Super Bowl nine months later.

And now she was meeting with her parents inside the Clayton County jail, with federal drug trafficking charges hanging over her head. One of the DEA investigators later reported overhearing Tracy's father tell her: "Everything is going to be okay. You know, you'll get out of this. Everything is going to be okay, Tracy. . . . All you have to do is tell the truth." When the Donahos emerged from their private meeting, Terry Donaho announced that his daughter was ready to cooperate.

It was at this point that the government began referring to Tracy Donaho as "SG3-93-X045" or "the CI" (Confidential Informant or Cooperating Individual) as often as they referred to her as Tracy Donaho. Angela Wallace got there too late, as it turned out. During her brief, anticlimactic meeting with Tracy, Wallace advised her against speaking to anyone, especially the government. Tracy replied that she hadn't spoken to a soul, when in fact she had met with DEA investigators for almost five hours by that point, helping them produce a five-page report that implicated Darryl Henley as the man behind the twelve kilos of cocaine she was caught carrying.

Tracy was released from jail three days after her arrest on $25,000 bail. This was a surprisingly low amount for such a large quantity of cocaine, but the rules were different now that Tracy had become a government informant. A line had been drawn between her and Darryl, thick and permanent.

Darryl snuck out of his dorm room on the first night of training camp for a covert meeting with his agent, Marvin Demoff, and Rams executive John Shaw.[2] A small, fortyish man who was considered one of the toughest men in the Rams organization, players included, Shaw was intensely private and was known among players as a cutthroat contract negotiator. The more mature members of the team knew that deep down Shaw was their friend. That's how Jackie Slater described him when Slater was inducted into the Pro Football Hall of Fame in 2001. John Shaw was certainly a friend to Darryl Henley, and to the surprise of many, he would remain by Henley's side long after Henley's other friends quit.

That night on the Cal State Fullerton campus, Shaw and Demoff advised Darryl that "Tracy would say I was behind all of this to save herself," Darryl wrote later. "And she did just that." Shaw told Henley that if his troubles went public, the Rams would release a statement announcing that he had taken a leave of absence. It would be a *paid* leave, Shaw added, which meant that Darryl would not have to apply to the NFL for reinstatement when it ended—whenever that might be. The theme of that night's three-man meeting was *This is an awful situation, but it can blow over if we handle it right.*

Hiring an attorney was Henley's next step—a crucial one that could mean the difference between swift exoneration and a ten-year prison term. Choosing a lawyer was like grinding a key that had to fit perfectly into the legal system's locks, and because Henley and his advisors did not have much time, they went with Demoff's first choice, Gerald Chaleff, a thin, bearded Harvard Law product who had cut his teeth years earlier in the LA County District Attorney's Office. Chaleff, possessor of an outrageously keen intellect, had since gained fame by defending the Hillside Strangler during the disco days. He was one of Los Angeles's most gifted and renowned trial lawyers. Money had obviously been no object.

After the Rams' scrimmage against the Chargers under the blazing Fullerton sun, John Shaw showed up at Darryl's dorm room. "I know what you're going through," he said, sitting on the spare bunk. "This might not be what you want to hear, but you're probably going to be indicted for this. Between now and then you're going to have good days and bad days. You're going to want to talk about this thing, but you can't. With anyone." Darryl appreciated the advice, but he knew he would have to tell his family — if not the whole story, then at least a warning that he might be arrested for something that would quickly be cleared up. He knew he had to tell them before it hit the papers, which could be tomorrow morning for all he knew.

He told his little brother, Eric, first and asked for his input on how to break it to their parents. A week passed before Darryl could bring himself to do it. "We were at the fish market one day," Dot Henley remembered, "and he came in and told us what was going on. He said that somebody, maybe it was Chaleff, had told him, 'Don't tell your parents.' And Darryl had said, 'I've *got* to tell my parents.'"

Darryl's older brother, Thomas, was working as an intern on Wall Street when he found out. His mother called him shortly after the fish market meeting and said, "Darryl is in some trouble. It has something to do with drugs, so obviously he's innocent."

"I knew that something had happened, and it was not

insignificant," Thomas said years later. "And it wasn't until I got back [to California] that I began to understand the magnitude of what we were talking about."

That same magnitude began to sink in on the Rams' defensive players when, after they all shaved their heads as a sign of solidarity, Henley said no thanks to the clippers. Ordinarily he would have been first in line, but these days he knew he had to look like a clean-cut citizen, not some chrome-dome convict, in case he was called into court on short notice. "Darryl started getting quiet at work," Steve Israel recalled. "I could tell something was wrong with this dude." Todd Lyght sensed it, too, so he asked Henley about it one day after practice. Henley replied that he was caught up in something that had to do with a friend who had been arrested. He didn't tell Lyght that the situation involved drug trafficking, or that the friend was a Rams cheerleader, and he certainly didn't tell Lyght that this cheerleader had partied at Lyght's house recently. Henley had been told by his attorneys that mentioning any of this would place his teammates at risk of being called as witnesses. Giving Lyght the bare bones, however, meant that he had to do the same with all the cornerbacks.

"It was me and Darryl and Todd and Robert Bailey," Israel remembered. "He sat us down in the lunch room and was like, 'We're a family, we have to stick close, on the field and off. I want you to know about this first, before it gets out, because this is probably going to hit the papers soon. They're going to try to make it seem like I did this and this and this, but I didn't do it.'

"I remember just sitting there at the table with my mouth open," Israel added. "I was waiting for the old Darryl to pop up at any moment and say, 'Sike!' But something about him—I knew he wasn't joking this time. Robert [Bailey] just started laughing. And he *kept* laughing. During practice Robert was running around with his hands behind his back like he was wearing handcuffs. Darryl must have been mad, but he couldn't do anything because then he would have had to explain it to everybody."

"Yeah, I remember messing with him that day," Bailey recalled. "You've got to remember, though, Darryl was the biggest prankster on the team at that time. We always messed with each other. He didn't tell us it had to do with cocaine. He just said it was no big deal, so I was trying to make light of it. . . . We all thought he would be playing forever."

Chapter 10

"We are on tape right now with Tracy Donaho. Detective Roy Kaiser of the Los Angeles
Police Department and Detective Mike Ortiz of the Ontario Police Department. It is
Sunday afternoon at 2:35 p.m., and we are at
Tracy's mother's residence. This is the twen-
ty-fifth of July, 1993. . . . Okay, Tracy, we are
going to kind of go through this whole scenario here again. Basically how long have
you known Darryl Henley?"

"I met him on Super Bowl Sunday. About
six months, I guess."

Asked what Willie McGowan had said to
her the day before she flew to Atlanta, Tracy
replied: "He said, you know, 'Are you willing to — What is your schedule like today?'
I said that I had practice. He said, 'What is
your schedule like tomorrow?' And I had a
promo. 'Is there any way you can get out of it?
You know, I really need you to do this.' And I
said, 'I really don't think I could.' And then

about an hour later Darryl called me back and he was saying, 'Well, you know you are going to get to see me though. Come on, Tracy, you can get out of this stuff.'"

Later in the interview, Tracy clarified who had been behind the delivery of the Atlanta suitcase: "I was told it wasn't for Darryl, it was for Willie. Willie. I was doing this for Willie, Darryl's friend."

These and many other statements from Tracy Donaho would change dramatically in the coming months.

When the interview was over, Detective Kaiser kept his tape recorder running and asked Tracy to call Darryl's pager. Kaiser wanted her to sound frightened and overwhelmed, to lure Henley into contacting her. When Darryl's voicemail picked up, Tracy turned thespian: "Darryl, um, this is Tracy. Listen, um, I'm really scared right now and I don't know what to do. Can you please call me back? I know that you've been trying to get a hold of me. Can you please just call my voicemail and leave a number where I can reach you because, um, my dad doesn't want me to get a hold of you, and so I want to call you whenever I can get a chance. So I'll just keep checking my voicemail, okay? Bye."

Her appeals to his sympathy worked. Darryl called back and left his own message. His voice was quiet, almost a whisper: "Hi Tracy, uh, listen, uh . . . [exhale, long pause] This machine's going to cut me off. Listen to me, um, I have been nothing but honest with you and your friend [Willie McGowan], okay? Period. And you need to call me at that same number and just be honest with me. . . . I haven't lied to you. I've never tried to hurt you. So, uh, I think if you call me and tell me what's going on, if you're not bullshitting me, I'll know. And if you are, I'll know. Just call me back and take as much time as you need to take on there, and just talk."

Tracy called the next day. The police were with her, listening:

"Darryl, it's Tracy. . . . I'm scared to death, and I don't know what to do. . . . I'll see if I can get away from my father, because I don't know what to do anymore. Please get back to me because I'm so scared."

Her acting seemed less convincing this time than during her first message. Darryl did not call her back. He and Tracy never spoke again.

A few nights later, Darryl met his alleged cocaine supplier for the first time. Coincidentally, it was the same week that Boston Celtics star Reggie Lewis died of a cocaine overdose, a tragedy that saddened and surprised the sports world in light of Lewis's reputation as a community spokesman with a spotless past and a happily married father of two. Darryl Henley still considered Reggie Lewis a straight arrow, still a devoted family man. He probably just got mixed up with the wrong people. Might have known them a week. Maybe less. As Darryl knew all too well, it didn't take long.

The news of Lewis's death brought Henley back to the summer of 1986, just prior to his sophomore year at UCLA, when within eight days of each other Len Bias, who would probably have been Reggie Lewis's teammate with the Celtics one day, and Don Rogers, Darryl's favorite UCLA player growing up (and the "big brother" to Darryl's "big brother," James Washington), died the same way Lewis would. Bias's cocaine-addled heart stopped beating less than forty-eight hours after he was picked by the Celtics in the NBA draft. Rogers's fatal overdose came on the eve of his wedding.

These were the thoughts on Darryl's mind as the defensive backs' meeting broke up and he walked toward his car in the dark. When Darryl noticed the lowered blue pickup rolling toward him in the parking lot, he wasn't scared. The driver's door opened, and a pudgy, young black man stepped out. The truck's interior light revealed him to be Eric Manning, Willlie's friend, the guy who over the summer had turned Darryl's house into a cocaine distribution center.

"Get in," Manning said.

Darryl chuckled — *Yeah right* — until he saw the Glock dangling from Manning's hand. Darryl looked in the truck and saw a thick Mexican guy around his age sitting in the passenger seat, staring him down. "You know who I am?" the Mexican asked.

Darryl looked him over. He was short, well dressed, and in thick bodybuilder shape. He had a thin moustache and pockmarked cheeks, as if he'd had acne as a kid.

"Nah," Darryl said.

"You don't know why I'm here?"

"No."

"Get in," Manning said again, and at the insistence of Manning's gun, Darryl did, climbing into the extended cab behind the front seats.

I'm here about my fucking money, the Mexican said.

I don't know nothing about your money.

Yeah, you do, said the Mexican. You're in this, Darryl. You may not want to be, but you're in it, and you owe me the respect of a fucking meeting when I page you.

Page me? Man, I don't know noth—

Just don't go anywhere, the Mexican said through clenched teeth.

"If you ever wonder where I am," Darryl replied, "just turn on your TV on Sundays."

Moments later, Darryl was standing on the blacktop watching Manning drive away. He went straight to Chuck Knox's room. "Goddammit," Knox snarled, "now they're coming after you where you work." The old coach was sitting on his bed, Henley remembered, his gray hair tousled, reading glasses on the tip of his nose. Take tomorrow off, Knox said. Get with your people and sort this thing out.

From Knox's room Darryl walked to the nearest pay phone, where he called his Atlanta friend Ant, the guy who had introduced him to G back in April. It was late in Atlanta, but Ant was awake.

G told me not to talk to you, Ant told Darryl. He says you're working for the feds, trying to set dudes up.

Man, what?

I know it ain't true. I'm just telling you.

Man, this shit's getting crazy, Darryl said.

This shit's been crazy. You know G keeps a couple cars here at my spot, right? A Benz and a silver Range [Rover]. In my garage. Some dude came by yesterday, said he was picking up the Benz and driving it out to California. If G knew I was talking to you, he'd send somebody over here to scoop up the Range, too. He don't trust nobody, man.

I'ma let you go, Darryl said with a sigh. He hung up, returned to his dorm room, and tried in vain to get some sleep before the next morning's practice.

Garey West was not an easy man to find—perhaps because most everyone who knew him knew him only as "G," or perhaps because the authorities thought his name was Charles Williams or Deandra Woodall. West had forged documents to back up both aliases; one was the doctored birth certificate of a toddler born to one of his mistresses.

Born eleven months before Henley, Garey West was known in his hometown of Montclair, California, as a basketball player more than a hustler. But by the time he met Darryl in the spring of 1993, G was no longer the svelte high school guard he had once been. Forty pounds heavier than during his school days, West had amassed an equally cumbersome criminal record, having been caught by two policemen in June 1986 (the same month that Len Bias and Don Rogers died) selling crack outside an apartment building in Montclair. He pled guilty and was sentenced to three years in state prison. He'd been busted because an informant told the cops his MO: West sold crack out of one apartment while living in another one a few doors down.

Seven years later, West was using the same ruse in Georgia. The DEA had investigated the package Tracy overnighted on June 30 to Smyrna, a suburb of Atlanta. When they interviewed the mail carrier who delivered it, she told investigators that when she approached apartment C—the apartment the package was addressed to—"a black male ran up from apartment A and said, 'That's mine.'"

The man was so big, she said, and had come up on her so quickly that she forgot to have him sign for the package, which was addressed to "A. Woods." The residents of that apartment were two black women in their twenties named Antonnia Champion and Ursula Woods. Their mailbox contained letters addressed to Garey West's aliases. Toni Champion, it was later learned, was another of West's mistresses. She was also the woman who had had dinner with G and Darryl and friends at Darryl's apartment back in June — the day Eric Johnson warned Darryl about West.

West was part of a fuzzy picture that was slowly coming into focus for DEA special agent Kevin McLaughlin. McLaughlin knew that West had a wife and son in Memphis, and that he was the guy who had picked Tracy up at the Memphis airport on July 3 and accepted delivery of her suitcase. But West was elusive. As soon as his scheme at the Smyrna apartment was uncovered, the two women moved out and their final rent payment was made by a large black man in a silver Range Rover. This was two weeks after Darryl learned about the silver Range being removed from Ant's garage.

Darryl, meanwhile, took Chuck Knox's advice and told his advisors about the Mexican who had visited him in the parking lot. Shaw told Darryl to pay the Mexican half of what he was asking, but Darryl stood his ground. Parting with six figures might have been easy for Shaw, but Darryl wasn't about to give in that quickly, especially when he didn't think he owed anyone a dime.

Shaw countered: Sure, it's a lot of money, but you can make this whole thing go away.

Again Henley declined.

Ted Woolsey believed Darryl when he said he didn't owe Bustamante a thing. A burly fifty-three-year-old PI who had joined the defense team as part of the Gerry Chaleff package (and could have been cast as "LA Gumshoe" in a movie based on looks alone), Woolsey had what Darryl's father, who would come to know Woolsey better than he ever intended, described as a "cops and robbers mentality." Over his career Woolsey worked numerous death penalty cases, most of them with Chaleff as lead defense counsel, so he was no stranger to high stakes. After the incident in the Fullerton parking lot, Woolsey gave Darryl a 9mm Glock for protection. "I didn't know shit about guns," Henley said later, "but I wasn't about to get scooped up again, I knew that much."

"Okay, today's date is 7/28/93," Detective Kaiser said into his tape recorder. "The time is 7:20 p.m., and we're going to be placing another page into Darryl's pager." This time Tracy's voice was a monotone, her faked fear not nearly as convincing as it had been two days earlier:

"Darryl, it's Tracy, and it's Wednesday, and I really don't know what to do anymore. You're not returning my phone calls. I'm—I'm scared. I need to meet with you as soon as possible, or at least give me a phone number where I can reach you. I don't know what to do. I'm scared. I don't think you understand how scared I am. The least you could do is give me my things back, you know. My money and my credit cards.[1] So please call me as soon as you can." Considering her poor attempt to sound helpless, the investigators probably weren't surprised when Henley didn't call back.

Henley was preparing for the Rams' next scrimmage—his next chance to vent his frustrations. He didn't count on being beaten for a deep touchdown by an obscure Chargers receiver named Johnnie Barnes, but the bench-clearing brawl that followed Barnes's TD was no surprise. There had already been one fight, after the Chargers' first score, when the violence had spilled from the field onto the track and had swept an official into it like a tumbleweed. After the second fight, Henley redeemed himself by intercepting two passes, returning one for a touchdown.

His house in Brea, meanwhile, had been turned into a crime scene, so he was living at the Quality Inn near Rams Park. Other than that, his life was basically the same. He was still driving his Lexus to work; he was still an NFL starter; he was still seeing several women at once. The differences in his life were less obvious. He had never known such stress, for one thing, nor such discomfort at having to hide it. Hardly a second passed without his mind drifting to what Tracy was doing at that moment, who she was talking to, where her allegiances stood, what he should be doing to help himself. He had given up the nightclub scene. That was the most noticeable difference. Darryl stayed in his hotel room most nights, protecting a secret that would have been revealed by even the slightest, most unrelated off-the-field trouble.

Twenty of his twenty-six autumns on Earth had been spent playing football. He had never been cut from a team—had never come close—but now he could sense such doom approaching. His livelihood, his passion, his very identity, football was also his escape from the dreadfulness of all this, and it stood to be ripped from him at any moment. That it was happening so methodically and privately made him feel as if he had a terminal illness. He found himself looking through the chain-link fence during practice, waiting for the inevitable convoy of television vans to pour into Rams Park.

An injured shoulder kept him out of the next preseason game, which was played the day after the DEA swept his Atlanta apartment for drugs. They found nothing in the carpet, nothing in the air-conditioning filter, nothing anywhere.

Chapter 11

As Henley's legal troubles were crushing him, four years of playing as the league's lightest defender began to take its toll. If it wasn't his knee, it was his hip, and when his hip felt fine, his shoulder didn't—or his other knee hurt. Cracked fingers and strained hamstrings were nearly as common as neck pain, which he had lived with every day of his adult life. And now all these aches were joined by one that throbbed daily between his temples and had nothing to do with football.

The day the Rams' plane departed for a preseason game in Cleveland, the DEA conducted a search of Henley's home in Brea. Ten agents scoured the house for two hours at the end of the quiet cul-de-sac, and what they found would intensify Henley's headache. Inside two kitchen drawers were several rolls of Saran Wrap like the kind that encased each of the twelve kilos in Tracy's suitcase. The exact number of rolls was never determined because the DEA agent who led the search, Kevin McLaughlin, failed to seize them as evidence, but clearly there was a lot more Saran Wrap in the house than a young bachelor needed.

There wasn't much else in the kitchen. Darryl had been in Atlanta the whole summer, and it looked as if Rex and whoever else had been staying there had preferred to either dine out or order in. More likely, someone had cleaned the place after Tracy's arrest. If it was the latter, they'd forgotten the stockpile of Saran Wrap, which not only screamed *cocaine trafficking* but also corroborated Tracy's story about hearing "strapping noises" — like tape being pulled from a roll — coming from upstairs on the evenings of July 2 and July 14 as she waited for the suitcases to be brought to her.

The preseason game in Cleveland gave Darryl a chance to catch up with Eric Metcalf, a player he had befriended four years earlier at the Hula Bowl college all-star game in Hawaii. The Browns' most dangerous offensive weapon and one of the league's best return men, Metcalf could sense the same ennui in his friend that Darryl's teammates had sensed, and he could tell that it was unrelated to the shoulder harness Henley was wearing. Over dinner, Metcalf kept asking Darryl if there was something bothering him.

I just got a headache, Darryl said.

They made it all the way back to the hotel before Henley cracked. When Metcalf said once again that Henley seemed "off," Henley recalled: "I just vented. E-Met must have thought I was crazy. I mean I told him everything. *Everything.* Just rambling. Tracy, Willie, all the drama in Atlanta."

Metcalf didn't say much in return. As they sat in Metcalf's car outside the Cleveland Sheraton, he put his hand on Darryl's head and told him he was there for him. And that, Henley said later, was all he had needed.

Moments later, when Darryl entered the Sheraton, the Rams beat reporter for the *LA Times*, T. J. Simers, approached him from across the lobby. "Darryl, you got a minute?"

"Nah, not right now," Darryl replied, continuing toward the elevator.

His relationship with Simers had started shakily during Henley's rookie year and had since become one of icy tolerance. Simers's persistence and fearlessness, however, were his meal tickets. He pressed:

"Just a couple questions, Darryl."

"Try to grab me tomorrow, man."

Bing. The elevator arrived.

"I know about Atlanta," Simers said.

Darryl's body went cold. He slipped into the elevator, hit the "Close Door" button, and called Chuck Knox as soon as he got to his room. Knox reacted the same way he reacted to any startling news: with complete calm. "Forget about him," Knox said in his gunslinger's drawl. "He's just fishing." Then, as he had done with *mule*, Knox explained what *fishing* meant: "It's when a reporter repeats a rumor to a guy hoping he'll panic and spill the whole thing." When Darryl and Knox hung up, Darryl noticed that his phone was blinking. He called the message service and listened to an unfamiliar voice say: Mr. Henley, this is Special Agent Kevin McLaughlin of the DEA. We're downstairs here, and we were hoping we could have a word with you. We don't have a lot on you, to be honest. You look pretty clean on this thing. We were just hoping you could help us connect some of the dots.

McLaughlin left his phone number. Darryl called Gerry Chaleff instead.

Do not call him back, Henley's attorney barked, his voice more stern than McLaughlin's.

But this guy sounds like he's all right, Darryl said. He didn't threaten me or anything. He said they didn't have anything on me.

Chaleff let out an exasperated breath. You really don't understand how this works, do you? These guys are flesh-eaters, Darryl. They'd give up their own grandmothers for the chance to talk to you without a lawyer. Do *not* call him back.

When Darryl hung up, the red light blinked again.

Darryl. Special Agent McLaughlin again. We know you're up

there because we saw you get in the elevator. Look, we've been patient on this thing. We haven't gone to the media, even though we could have. Trust me, the best thing you can do for yourself is call me back.

Darryl called Chaleff again. If you call this guy back, Chaleff said, you're gonna have to find yourself another lawyer.

As soon as Darryl hung up, the phone rang. He let it ring until the red light blinked.

I've tried to be nice. But you've left me no choice but to arrest you tomorrow. At practice. Would you like that? No, you know what? We're going to arrest you at the *game*, Darryl. On television. With all your teammates and coaches watching. Is that the way you want it? Then call me back.

Chaleff was furious. Darryl had never heard his lawyer swear before, but Chaleff made up for lost time when he was told about McLaughlin's third message. He asked for McLaughlin's number, and most likely he called it, because Henley said he did not hear from the DEA again. At least not while he was in Cleveland.

Kevin McLaughlin was on a roll. The Atlanta-based DEA agent was coming off a conviction in the Southern Lights marijuana case, which McLaughlin had initiated by walking into a small hydroponic gardening store in Georgia and asking its owners to let him secretly videotape their customers. According to the owners, Gary and Steve Tucker, two brothers in their forties, McLaughlin gave them an ultimatum: cooperate or have your store shut down. "We figured a percentage of our customers were growing pot," Steve Tucker told a reporter years later. "But we had store rules that if anyone asked us about marijuana, we'd ask them to leave. . . . Most of the stuff we were selling, you could buy at Home Depot. We had a legitimate business."

The Tuckers told McLaughlin no. McLaughlin promised to "get them somehow" and left.

Two years later, after McLaughlin had helped fill a courtroom with scared, reluctant informants testifying to reduce their own sentences, Steve and Gary Tucker, along with Gary's wife, Joanne, were convicted of an incongruously named charge known as "conspiracy to manufacture marijuana" and sentenced to a combined thirty-six years in federal prison. They were never accused of growing a single plant or possessing a single joint. "I got ten years for selling lightbulbs," Steve Tucker said. [1]

Tracy Donaho had been arrested less than a month after the Tuckers were, so for a while McLaughlin worked both cases simultaneously. One DEA agent recalled that early on during the Henley investigation, "McLaughlin got into Darryl's dad's face and told him, 'I'm going to put your son in prison,'" before cooler heads pushed him away. A Los Angeles County sheriff's detective who worked with McLaughlin on the Henley case offered a dissenting opinion, calling McLaughlin "fantastic. He was a gentleman. He never tried to overpower us or bamboozle us in any way."

The Rams lost in Cleveland, dropping their preseason record to 0-3. The good news for Darryl was that he had not been arrested, and his drug story still hadn't hit the papers. Simers had never followed up on his fishing trip, and things got back to normal — or as close to normal as they could for a man with a drug trafficking indictment looming over him. Ironically, on the day the Rams lost to the Browns, an *LA Times* article mentioned Henley as one of several NFL athletes who had spoken to area youths about the dangers of drugs.

Chris Hale was on the freeway when he first heard. He was talking on his car phone with a relative who was going through a legal ordeal of his own, when his relative announced, "Darryl Henley's doing dirty."

"I said, 'No way,'" Hale recalled. "'That's impossible. . . . This guy's making way too much money. He's got too many positive things in his life. He has no reason to do anything like this.' [My relative] said, 'I'm *telling* you. I heard it from the inside.' I never believed it up until the day it hit the papers. Until that day, I refused to believe it."

The Rams' final preseason game was a night game against their crosstown rivals, the Raiders. Darryl blocked out his throbbing shoulder long enough to play for the first time in weeks. After the game, as he was signing autographs, he was handed a program and told, "Put your number on there." Darryl looked up and saw Eric Manning. "Be cool," Manning said. "Just put a number down where I can call you." Darryl did as he was told, in permanent silver ink. This scrawling would later be entered into evidence at his trial. Manning took the program and walked away.

Kevin McLaughlin also wanted to speak to Henley. When McLaughlin called Chaleff's cocounsel, Roger Cossack, to request a handwriting sample, Cossack promptly drove Henley to meet McLaughlin at a local police station so he could provide it. The date was September 1, 1993.

As always, McLaughlin was neatly dressed in a tie and pressed white shirt that matched the feature Darryl remembered most about him years later: his blinding white teeth. McLaughlin told Cossack that he wanted to speak with Henley alone. Cossack's chuckled and said, "I don't care what you want." Eventually it was agreed that Henley would accompany McLaughlin and his mild-mannered colleague, Special Agent Brian Sullivan, into a private room where he could complete his handwriting sample while Cossack watched through a window. Don't say a word to these assholes, Cossack told Henley as he walked away.

Henley sat at a table in the center of the room and got started. The sample required him to copy six pages of typed material in his own handwriting—one page in cursive, another in print, some uppercase, some lowercase. It was as tedious as the time he'd had to sign five hundred footballs at the Kodak All-American celebration in Atlanta—only this time he was writing names like Stancil O. Torque and Ulysses T. Velez. He signed and dated the bottom of each page as McLaughlin paced behind him. McLaughlin wasn't about to pass up this opportunity to question his high-profile suspect. He turned his back to the window and whispered: You know you really should talk to us.

Darryl kept writing.

Your lawyer's a clown, Darryl. Look, the sooner you cooperate, the sooner you're out of this mess.

Darryl spoke without moving his lips, so Cossack couldn't see: Are you talking to me?

RAP-RAP-RAP!

It was Cossack, pounding the window with his knuckle. He straightened his finger and shook it. Not a fucking word! he yelled.

A half hour later, Darryl was still writing, McLaughlin's arms were still folded, and Cossack was still watching their every move. When Henley finished, he rose and handed the papers to McLaughlin. Never one to turn the other cheek, he told the DEA agent, "Roger's right, you are a fucking asshole," and walked out. Another line had been drawn in the sand, and both sides would do more than cross it in the months ahead.

Four days later, the Rams opened the 1993 regular season with an embarrassing loss, 36–6, in Green Bay. It was the most lopsided opening game in NFL history. Henley tore his pectoral muscle on the first play from scrimmage and played in excruciating pain until halftime, when he told Knox he couldn't go anymore. The three players the Rams had signed in the off-season to bolster their defense also suffered injuries that day—a strained groin for Shane Conlan, broken thumb for Henry Rolling, and shoulder stinger for Fred Stokes. Whatever optimism that had survived their winless preseason crashed like the Hindenburg into Lambeau Field.

Anthony "Q" Newman, the starting free safety, wept tears of anger during the defensive backs' meeting the next day. It was typical of Newman, a player whose wildly shifting emotions could display a winsome smile and volcanic temper within seconds of one another. Once, while being criticized by an assistant coach, Newman marched off the practice field and proceeded to bludgeon a tree with his fists. And not just a couple of jabs, either. Newman mixed combinations with haymakers, battering whatever demons he'd imbedded in the poor oak, hammering it like a heavy bag for five minutes straight. During games, his deep-seated hatred for the enemy often led him to chase plays blindly, which placed him embarrassingly out of position as often as it produced bone-crunching hits. He played with Henley on the Rams' charity basketball team, and one night he body-slammed a firefighter so he could make a steal and the game-winning dunk. The fans were as appalled as the fireman. "I was like, 'This is for *charity*, Anthony!'" Todd Hewitt recalled.

The Rams' coaches wished Newman's competitive fire would spread to his teammates, who were often the subject of opponents' jokes. No one doubted the team's talent, especially on defense, but the Rams of the early 1990s were plagued by an inability to make crucial plays when they needed them. The rest of the league considered them soft. Hammer them long enough, the argument went, and the Rams will either choke or fold. It was a strategy that worked too often for the Rams to argue against it. Many of Darryl's teammates believed it themselves.

Since his standout seasons in 1991 and 1992 — when he'd played in all thirty-two games and recorded seven interceptions — Henley had developed into one of the Rams' locker room leaders. Several veterans had been traded or had signed elsewhere, so Henley and Conlan, the linebacker the Rams had just signed away from the Buffalo Bills, were often called upon to keep teammates from phoning it in. During one film session, as secondary coach Rod Perry stood before his troops and wondered aloud if they even *cared* about winning anymore, Anthony Newman clenched his fists and began swearing under his breath. Darryl sensed what was coming next. Newman vaulted out of his chair, lifted it over his head, and let out a roar that shook the drywall. Darryl hugged him around the waist and persuaded him to put the chair down, and after a few angry breaths between gritted teeth, Newman stormed out of the room in tears, leaving his teammates to say what they usually said after such tantrums: "Go get him, D."

Years later, Newman was an avowed family man who bore few traces of the hell-bent menace he'd been with the Rams. The co-owner of a successful construction firm, Newman also conducted youth sports camps in the summer and filled his autumns as a football commentator for the University of Oregon, his alma mater. "I remember me, [Michael] Stewart, Darryl, we were all at Darryl's house, sitting in his living room," Newman said, reflecting on the carefree days of 1992. "We knew D was about to get paid. He was the one we always mentioned. 'Out of all of us, you're the one who's about to get paid, D.' Then, before training camp in '93, I'm washing my Dooley outside my house,[2] and Darryl pulls up [and says,] 'I think I messed up, Q.' I asked him what was wrong. 'I can't talk about it now. I think I messed up. I can't tell you.' Then he went away. Physically, emotionally. He just went off to himself. I remember trying to reach out—"

Like most of Henley's friends, Newman's memories were interrupted by tears and long, telling pauses. "Anyway, that's when it all started. I thought he had gotten a girl pregnant or maybe lost some money in a car deal or gambling in Vegas or something. I wasn't thinking about drugs. That was the last thing on my mind with Darryl."

"In camp, he was put in a [dorm] wing by himself," Newman continued. "We were told by management, 'There are some things going on.' That season, he would call me and ask me to come over. So I'd walk over to his house and find all the curtains closed. I could tell there were people inside, but no one would answer the door. There was nothing I could do but walk home."

Chapter 12

Until Rafael Bustamante showed up at Rams Park on the afternoon of September 8, 1993, it was like any other Wednesday at Rams headquarters. It was three days after the Rams' blowout loss to the Packers, and a few of the prouder players had stayed late to watch film of the Steelers, their next opponent. Darryl was one of the last players to leave.

The story of what happened next, told in numerous personal accounts, law enforcement reports, and pages of sworn testimony, began when Darryl steered his Lexus toward the exit and saw Eric Manning standing at the edge of the parking lot, coolly lifting his shirt to reveal a pistol in his waistband. Darryl stayed calm and eased the Lexus to a stop. As Manning approached, Henley noticed that the portly twenty-two-year-old had a black eye and a busted lip. Henley was an accelerator-punch from freedom, but he didn't want a scene, and he sure as hell didn't want bullets to fly, so he lowered his window to hear Manning out.

Don't fuck with these dudes, Manning said, flicking his chin toward a blue Camaro parked in the distance. They'll straight up kill you. Darryl could see two Latino men in the Camaro, one of whom he recognized as the pockmarked Mexican from the training camp incident. Let me in the car, Manning said. Darryl was wondering how quickly he could get his hand on the Glock stashed under his seat. Manning looked like a little kid, and he had always struck Darryl as soft. But after glancing again at the Mexican, Darryl fingered the automatic door-lock instead. Manning climbed into his Lexus.

Drive around for a minute, he said. Take me around the block or some shit.

Darryl nudged the gas, and the Lexus whirred smoothly around the perimeter of Rams Park, leaving the Camaro behind.

You need to talk to these dudes, Manning said to Henley. They feel like you're disrespecting them.

I'm about to go eat.

We'll go with you.

The feds are watching me. I can't be seen with those dudes.

You got to pay these motherfuckers, man.

I don't owe them shit.

You think they're trying to hear that? All they know is, one, you got money, two, you're tied up in this thing, and three, if this shit hits the papers, you got more to lose than anybody.

Darryl's heart caved in. All three points were true.

What happened to you on Monday? Manning asked.

What're you talking about—Monday?

We had a meeting set up.

Set up with who?

You, man. You were gonna hand over a hundred [thousand].

Shit, I don't know what kind of bullshit messages you left on my pager. Put a hundred g's in *your* hand? Please.

These dudes ain't gonna leave you alone 'til you at least talk to 'em.

Henley had circled Rams Park and was approaching the main entrance again. He parked the Lexus in the parking lot and in his rearview mirror saw the Camaro easing up behind him, now just a few feet from his bumper.

I'll talk to 'em, Darryl said to Manning. But there ain't no way I'm getting in that car. He got a cell phone?

The two Mexicans in the Camaro watched Darryl step out of his Lexus and walk alone toward the Rams' offices. When Manning climbed out of the Lexus's passenger door, the pockmarked Mexican leapt out of the Camaro and socked him in the gut, then the face. The other Mexican pulled him away, yelling, "*Cállate!*" (Calm down!)

Where the fuck is he going? the pockmarked Mexican yelled at Manning. I said I wanted to meet with him, and you're gonna watch him walk away?!

Darryl was inside by then, running toward the pay phone in the players' lounge. The first person he called was Ted Woolsey, who said he was on his way. Then he called the number Manning had just handed him. Manning answered. Talk to these guys, he panted. I'm tired of being on the line for you. Henley heard an angry Latino voice yell, *Fuck these niggers!* followed by a commotion, during which the phone changed hands.

Do you love your mother? said a panting voice.

Huh?

You heard me. You love your fucking family? You want to see them again? You think we don't know about the fish store, motherfucker? You think this is a game? You think we don't have people over there right now?

What do you want? Darryl asked, his voice quaking.

You know what the fuck I want, motherfucker.

I told you I don't owe you no —

You at least owe me the respect of a meeting.

Darryl agreed to meet the Mexican in a distant corner of the parking lot, where they would be separated by a chain-link fence. Henley drove his Lexus there, and the Camaro pulled up on the other side. Henley left his engine running, his door open, and his Glock under the seat. He and the Mexican squatted on either side of the fence.

You got to kick back, Darryl told him. I can't pay you until I sign this next contr —

You never answered me. Do you love your mother?

Darryl looked into the muscle-bound Mexican's eyes, searching for any trace of a bluff, finding none. Darryl lowered his head and cursed himself for the millionth time for getting anywhere near Willie McGowan. He looked up at the Mexican. I'll take care of this, Henley said. You just got to —

When? the Mexican chuckled. I've got motherfuckers threatening *my* life because *your* stupid ass girlfriend lost my package, and you want me wait on a motherfucking *football contract*, motherfucker? When you gonna give me my money?

I don't know.

And that's what did it. "It was the one answer I didn't want to hear," the Mexican said years later. "You don't say that to somebody when you're in his situation. 'I don't know.' It was like an insult. Come up with a plan. Ask for a week or two. Give me a date. Don't tell me I don't fucking know. When he said that shit, I lost it."

The Mexican leapt over the fence, but Darryl was already in a full sprint by the time the Mexican's feet hit the pavement. The Mexican ran after him, but Henley was, of course, way too fast. So instead of breaking Darryl's ribs — his reason for hopping the fence, he said later — the Mexican hopped in Henley's Lexus and tore off. The Camaro followed him, its v-8 rumbling through the parking lot. Witnesses later recalled Henley yelling, "Security! Security!" as he ran toward Rams Park, but the only thing Henley remembered coming out of his mouth was directed at teammates Shane Conlan and Michael Stewart, who had witnessed the last few seconds of the conflict and sprinted into the Lexus's path to prevent the carjackers from leaving. "Get out the way! Get out the way!" Darryl yelled. "He's got a gun!"

"I was in the press room at Rams Park," remembered sportswriter Dave Strege. "I remember Darryl whizzing by the door, running at top speed. Jim McCurdy [of the *Press Telegram*] got out of his chair and walked to the door [saying], 'What the hell was that all about?' We should have gotten up and followed Darryl. Talk about missing a story."

Henley ran directly to the coaches' offices, where Knox and a handful of assistants were watching film. "I just got jacked in the parking lot," Darryl said breathlessly. He called his brother Eric at the fish market and told him to close up shop and get out of there immediately. Then he called the Anaheim police. When they arrived, he helped them fill out a stolen vehicle report, sticking with the "carjacking" explanation but confessing to the cops that he had left an unregistered gun under his seat. He also admitted, according to the police report, "that he is being investigated by the DEA in reference to an earlier arrest made by them of a girl he had dated for a short period of time . . . [and] that since he had dated this girl, he met up with an old friend of his named 'Willie.' [Henley] said Willie and this girl he met somehow got together without his knowledge, and apparently these two people became involved in some unknown amount of drug trafficking [*sic*]. The details of this activity are sketchy."

Anthony Newman was also one of the last players to leave that day. He had heard Darryl yelling, "Get down!" but like everyone else he thought Henley's car had been stolen, an all-too-common crime in 1990s LA. Everyone on the team knew that fullback Tim Lester had been carjacked at a gas station down the street the week before.

The day after what all the lawyers would call "the Rams Park incident," Todd Lyght told his fellow cornerbacks, "Yo, I'm keeping my gat with me from now on." It was a common utterance that week. Several Rams who weren't already armed became so.

As for the Mexican, his name was Rafael Bustamante, and

between his birth in Chihuahua in 1965 and his run-in with Darryl Henley at Rams Park in 1993, he had lived a life that—had it not included drugs and crime (or perhaps *because* it had, depending on one's view of America)—might have made for an inspiring story about the American dream.

Bustamante's parents split when he was two. When he was seven, his fractured family moved across the border to Hobbs, New Mexico. "When I started school in Hobbs, I didn't speak any English," he explained later. "There was no one to show me what to do. I felt completely lost, and I was never able to catch up. Work was a different matter for me. I discovered that if you worked real hard, you could compensate for almost anything." Bustamante got his first job at age ten as a grocery bagger, then worked as a porter at a car dealership, then as a paper carrier for the *Hobbs Daily News*. In middle school, he worked full-time at a supermarket. Hobbs had been a booming oil town in the early 1970s, but when Bustamante's stepfather lost his job in the oil fields, fifteen-year-old Rafael moved to California in search of work.

He lived in a group home and worked as a waiter in West Covina, a suburban town near Duarte. He was working at a car wash when an opportunity arose to assume ownership of its detailing department. Bustamante's younger brother Rigo drove out from New Mexico, and together they poured all they had into making Grand Car Wash the success it would eventually become. Along the way Bustamante became an avid weightlifter and a devotee of the bodybuilding lifestyle that swept California in the 1980s. A passionate sports fan, he found himself living in the same metropolis as some of the most talented athletes in the world. On the rare occasion when a Dodger, Laker, or Ram had his car detailed at Grand Car Wash, he would invariably be asked for an autograph, and most times he would have his picture taken with the proprietor, who by that time sometimes called himself Ralph. On the wall of his business, Bustamante kept framed photos of himself posing with Fernando Valenzuela, Magic Johnson, and a litany of boxing champions that included Muhammad Ali, Thomas "Hit Man" Hearns, and Bustamante's hero, Julio Cesar Chavez.

In 1991 Bustamante was pulled over by a California Highway Patrol officer who discovered that the decals on his 1984 Porsche were fake and that its VIN number had been defaced. The officer also discovered a baggie in the glove box containing cocaine, another baggie in the trunk containing marijuana, "a plastic baggie with a white substance resembling 'crack' cocaine under the carpet," a paper bindle containing traces of cocaine, and a tightly rolled dollar bill. Bustamante had been convicted in 1986 for carrying a concealed, loaded firearm, and in 1987 he had been arrested for drug possession. These priors moved him to plead guilty in the 1991 Porsche incident, for which he was sentenced to three years' probation. That probation was still in effect in June 1993, when Eric Manning approached him about fronting kilos of cocaine to a friend of his named Willie McGowan.

Bustamante didn't know Willie McGowan, so he was lukewarm about the idea until Manning told him that a Rams player would guarantee the deal. As Bustamante's attorney would later state at trial, Henley was "the bait" Manning used to hook Bustamante.

Now, with the whole deal gone to hell, and with the confrontation at Rams Park less than two minutes old, Bustamante was speeding north on the 57 Freeway in Henley's stolen Lexus, trailed by the Camaro driven by the larger Mexican, whose name was Alejandro Cuevas.

Cuevas followed Bustamante to the town of Rancho Cucamonga, where they pulled into a barren strip mall. Bustamante hid the Lexus and returned to the Camaro on foot. He climbed into the backseat and immediately tore into Eric Manning for making their trip to Rams Park a waste. "I'm gonna beat your ass!" Bustamante screamed at Manning. "I told you not to let him out of your sight until he meets with me! I gotta squat down next to a fucking *fence* and talk to the guy?"

Cuevas, a sculpted linebacker-type who had sparred with ranked heavyweights before, had been brought along as part enforcer, part mediator. Because of his gentle demeanor and his day job as a mortgage assistant, Cuevas was thought by Bustamante to be a skilled negotiator—an assumption that would soon prove fatally false. They knew each other from the gym. Cuevas was 6'3" and 240 pounds, every ounce of it muscle. He had seen the wrong side of the law before, and he also had seen Bustamante's temper before, so it was his job to calm such storms before they arrived. In this respect, Cuevas had failed at Rams Park as plainly as Manning had, but for now Bustamante's wrath was aimed solely at Manning.

Cuevas had heard enough. "You're looking at grand theft auto here, man!" Cuevas yelled at Bustamante. "You beat Eric up, you curse me out, tell me to shut up, then you *steal a car*?! This isn't what we talked about!"

"Relax," Bustamante said. "Everything will be fine."

They drove in the Camaro to the seafood restaurant where they had met up earlier that day. Bustamante was still calling Manning racial epithets and blaming him for the whole mess. "I ought to put a cap in your head," Bustamante said.

Cuevas told him again: "*Callate.*" Cool off.

They ate. Bustamante ordered Manning to attend the upcoming Rams-Steelers game so he could try again to get Henley to meet with Bustamante face to face. Manning said he couldn't make it; his wife was in Colorado for a wedding, and he was supposed to be there the next day. "You're not going to the wedding," Bustamante declared. "You're going to help me get my money back."

And that was that.

By the time they parted ways outside the restaurant, everyone had calmed down. Manning even joked with Bustamante about getting him a good seat for the Steelers game. The three men seemed to be on decent terms again, but the most important fact still lingered in each of their minds: Rafael Bustamante did not have his money.

122

Ted Woolsey picked Darryl up at Rams Park just as Henley was wrapping up his conversation with the Anaheim police. As he drove Henley to his parents' house in Upland, Woolsey remarked out of the blue: "There are plumbers in the world, Darryl, who are bad at what they do for a living—can't fix pipes, don't take care of their customers—just like there are bad doctors and bad lawyers and bad car salesmen and whatever else. These so-called drug dealers who are mixed up in this thing—I've never seen a dumber group of hothead idiots in my life." Darryl looked at Woolsey, intrigued. "They use a teenage girl who's dumb as a box of rocks to do their legwork. Then after they lose twelve kilos, do they hide? Hell, no! This Mexican guy—the pineapple-faced guy—the government has never *seen* him! *You* couldn't ID him, *Tracy* can't ID him. But what's he do? He calls you 'til your pager explodes, then he shows up and starts waving guns around outside a pro football practice. *In broad daylight!* You're trying to run away from this thing, and he's walking right into it!"

The "Rams Park incident" would have lasting, irreversible effects. The most immediate was that it made Darryl Henley look like a drug trafficker. Team executive Jack Faulkner would soon report seeing "'a short, chunky black male' brandishing a gun in the Ram parking lot." The team's starting right cornerback had granted this chunky black male entrance into his gold-trimmed Lexus. Other witnesses saw Henley squatting by a fence talking to an angry interloper. As Garey West said years later: "That thing at Rams Park—that's when the DEA really started thinking Darryl had something to do with this." It was the explosion that convinced the DEA that Darryl had lit the fuse.

Willie called Darryl the next day. Darryl hadn't heard from him in weeks. More surprising than Willie's call, however, was the reason for it.

Chapter 13

COVINA POLICE DEPARTMENT

REPORTING OFFICER: TREVOR GAUMER #1301

DATE/TIME REPORT TAKEN: 09-09-93 / 0107

AT THE ABOVE DATE AND TIME I RESPONDED TO 1155 N BARSTON REGARDING A RADIO CALL OF SHOTS FIRED AND A MAN DOWN IN THE AREA. . . . THE DEAD MAN WAS A BLACK MALE LYING ON BARSTON AVE IN FRONT OF 1155 N BARSTON, FACE DOWN WITH HIS HEAD TURNED TO THE RIGHT. . . . THERE WAS A PROJECTILE WOUND TO THE FRONT OF THE VICTIM'S HEAD AND AN APPARENT EXIT WOUND NEAR THE REAR BASE OF THE SKULL. . . . NEAR THE VICTIM'S BODY I SAW THREE 9MM SHELL CASINGS. . . . AT APPROXIMATELY 0450 HOURS DEPUTY CORONER CROW ARRIVED AND . . . REMOVED IDENTIFICATION FROM THE VICTIM'S WALLET IDENTIFYING HIM AS ERIC EARL MANNING.

Willie thought that Bustamante had done it. So did most everyone else. Bustamante had been leaning hard on Eric for nearly two months about the money he'd lost in the Atlanta bust—he'd slapped him around a few hours before he was killed for failing to get his money back—so it made sense that Bustamante was the guy who pulled the trigger. But LA County homicide detective Frank Durazo and his partner, Sue Coleman, had never heard the name Rafael Bustamante. Unaware of the DEA's related drug investigation, Durazo and Coleman had no leads and no suspects during the first hours after the killing. All they had was Manning's body, the shell casings, and testimony from some of the "ear-witnesses" who lived near Manning's home on Barston Avenue.

One witness said he looked out his window after the gunfire and saw a white or silver vehicle driving away with its lights off. It was a newer model, he said, and small—possibly foreign. Other witnesses corroborated this description, but no one reported seeing the car's license plate or occupants. Within days, when the links between Manning's murder and the Henley-Bustamante DEA investigation were tied, the early inference was that this "white or silver vehicle" had been Darryl Henley's Lexus, which Bustamante had stolen a few hours before Manning was gunned down.

Three witnesses were of particular interest to Detectives Durazo and Coleman. The first was Christopher Dodds, a thirty-three-year-old white friend of Manning's who had been with him until moments before the murder. According to Dodds, he arrived at Manning's apartment that night to find Manning "holding ice on his mouth" because he "got in a fight with a guy because he owes the guy some money. [Dodds] said he kept asking [Manning] why the guy hit him, and at first [Manning] was reluctant to answer. [Manning] finally told Dodds that it was because he was in debt for about $350,000." Later that night Dodds drove Manning to an apartment in West Covina, where Manning went inside, alone, for about five minutes. Then Dodds drove Manning to a service station, where Manning bought gas for Dodds's car, then to KFC, where Manning bought two chicken dinners to go. They returned to Manning's apartment at around 10 p.m. and "just sat inside eating, watching TV, and drinking beer."[1] That's when Manning's killer rang the doorbell.

"[Manning] went to the door and looked out the peephole [and] kept looking out the peephole as the doorbell rang two more times. [Manning] then motioned for Dodds to be quiet . . . [and] told him that he would be right back and he went outside and closed the door behind him. Approximately twenty seconds later Dodds heard a 'pop' and thought something was wrong so he locked the door. Dodds then heard two or three more 'pops' and called the police."

"Dodds said he didn't see who was at the door when [Manning] had answered it. He did say that [Manning] was acting like he was a little nervous. Dodds also thought it was a little strange for [Manning] to ask him for a ride in his vehicle when [Manning] owns a nice Chevy truck."

The truck came up often when people spoke of Manning after his death. It was a blue Chevy Silverado outfitted with custom paint, chrome rims, and a personalized license plate that read NO-THANG, as in It ain't no thang. His prized vehicle, lowered so close to the asphalt that it scraped speed bumps, was one of the first things his high school classmate Chris Hale remembered about Manning more than a decade after his death, and it would surface a number of times during the investigation into his murder, particularly during an interview with a witness named Edward Cloud.

Cloud told investigators that Manning (who he said had been "very depressed and had lost a considerable amount of weight") recently agreed to move $40,000 worth of drugs for a notorious pair of cocaine dealers called the Pickett Brothers. But Manning was robbed at the rendezvous point, and the Pickett Brothers had had to eat the $40,000 loss. They took their anger out on Manning by stealing his truck at gunpoint. Although the truck was returned to Manning before his murder, this incident helped explain why Manning had asked Dodds for a ride: Manning didn't want to be seen in his own vehicle, which, in a sad bit of irony, he had customized specifically to draw attention to himself.

Cloud also told investigators about the visit he had received from Manning a few hours before the murder. (The apartment that Dodds drove Manning to that night was Cloud's apartment.) Manning had mentioned to Cloud that the twelve kilos in the Atlanta deal had been "fronted" to him—to *Manning*, not Darryl Henley. This made it seem as if Manning, not Henley, had been the point man and that Manning had used the NFL player's name to convince Bustamante to participate—just as he had used Henley's home, his phones, even his identity. Cloud also told police that he had seen Manning driving a white Lexus with gold trim a few months earlier.

The third important witness, Tim Duffy, confirmed that this white Lexus was indeed Darryl Henley's. Duffy had attended the Rams-Raiders game with Manning, when Manning had ordered Henley to write his phone number on his game program; Duffy gave Detective Durazo his ticket stub to prove it. Duffy also told Durazo that after Manning approached "football player #20 of the Rams team . . . to have him sign his football program," Manning asked Duffy, "How would you like to have an NFL player's home telephone number?"

Five hours after Manning was killed, Detectives Durazo and Coleman searched his home, where they found a .22-caliber revolver under the couch and a .25-caliber Derringer hidden in the nursery. Manning's baby, a little girl who was staying with her grandmother while her mom was out of town, turned one month old the day her father died.

Willie McGowan showed up at the murder scene at 11:00 a.m., ten hours after his friend was killed. During an impromptu interview with Durazo, "McGowan stated he went to the apartment only to determine if Eric Manning, in fact, had been shot and killed . . ." the police report stated. "Willie McGowan asked Investigators if the suspect was Mexican or Black. Willie McGowan shook his head in response to being told the suspect was Black and stated that he knew nothing of why this happened. . . . He stated that a friend, Darryl, might know more about Eric and that he would advise Darryl to call Investigators."

In McAllen, Texas, that same afternoon, Garey West was pulled over for speeding. The Texas Highway Patrolman who approached West's car didn't realize that the man he had just stopped had an outstanding warrant for his arrest (for a counterfeiting charge in Tennessee) or that he was about to become one of the more sought-after drug criminals in the country. As far as the patrolman knew, the speeder's name was DeAndra Woodall. That's what his driver's license said. As West drove away, he slid his bogus ID back into his wallet—right behind the one that said his name was Charles Williams—and tossed the ticket out the window.

Darryl was at practice in Anaheim that afternoon, but his mind was elsewhere. He knew that Manning's murder would change everything, that it would act as a bolt of lightning illuminating everything beneath it, including his own involvement in the drug conspiracy. For now, though, Henley had to put himself first. At his agent's request, the Rams restructured Henley's contract after the murder so Henley could pay for increased security from Ted Woolsey and his team. For the remainder of the 1993 season, Woolsey would drive Henley to work each morning, circle Rams Park once, then drop him off at a hidden nook between the offices and the field. Henley arrived at his job most days by hopping a fence near Chuck Knox's office. When equipment manager Todd Hewitt spotted him doing this one morning—knowing that the sight of a black guy hopping a fence in Orange County could result in as much trouble as whatever it was Darryl was trying to avoid—he asked Darryl to at least call ahead so the guards could open the gate and let Woolsey drive in.

Woolsey assigned a bodyguard named Mike Lara to float between guarding Darryl and his parents, while an employee of Lara's, a 6'5", 260-pound man the Henleys knew only as Big John, was assigned to protect the fish market and the Henley home in Upland. "Big John would drive us home every night," Darryl's father recalled, "and he was the first one in the house. He'd draw his gun and look all over, looking behind doors. He wouldn't let us in until he came out." Woolsey helped Darryl move in the middle of the night from the Quality Inn to the Marriott, where Henley checked in under the name of his publicist, Kim Etheridge. Not even his parents knew where he was.

The following Sunday he was in Anaheim Stadium, where the Rams shut out the Steelers, 27–0, in a game that Eric Manning would have attended had he been alive. Darryl certainly had more pressing issues in his life than football, and so did Rams fans, apparently, as the home opener drew the smallest crowd since the team's move to Anaheim in 1980. That same day Darryl's brother Thomas returned home from New York City, where he had spent the summer as a Wall Street intern. Thomas's wife found an apartment for them near UCLA, where he had enrolled in the MBA program.

That Wednesday Thomas was at his parents' house in Upland when, hearing a knock at the door, he looked out the window to find two Latino men in their late twenties standing on the doorstep wearing shirts and ties. Through the window they introduced themselves to Thomas as Julio and Frank, but their real names, respectively, were Rafael Bustamante and Alejandro Cuevas. Thomas asked warily what he could do for them.

Are your parents home? Bustamante asked.

"Nah, they're actually out of town," Thomas said.

"They asked me who else was there," Thomas recalled later. "My aunt was there . . . but I told them I was there by myself. They said, 'Well, who's the lady that we saw?' So clearly they had been casing the place. I said, 'Listen, they're out of town. I'm here by myself. I'd be happy to leave them a message.' And the more they talked the more I could see that they had some serious other motives. . . . At that time there was a bodyguard who was down at the restaurant. I called down there and they rushed up to try to get there, but the guys had already left." The two visitors were "dressed like salesmen," Thomas said, "but I could tell they weren't selling anything."

Ted Woolsey wrote that just as Bustamante and Cuevas were "knocking at the Upland front door, Darryl was leaving [Rams Park] to go home. I met him in the parking lot across the street. . . . Darryl was being followed by two male Latinos. They appeared to be moving in for a takedown; we departed. . . . I know we were close to having a problem." On the drive, Darryl continued to claim innocence in the drug deal, Woolsey said, and he still refused to pay Bustamante.

"I got a call from Darryl later that day," recalled Rams equipment manager Todd Hewitt. "Darryl had left his car in the parking lot. . . . He called and asked if I could take his car back to his place. So we called a tow truck. I went across the street with the towing guy and just as the guy was about to hook up the car, I took a stroll behind the tire store next door. When I came back, the guy was like, 'Where'd you go?' And I said, 'I want to make sure that if that car blows up, I'm not gonna be there.' That's how it was at the time. No one knew what was going on."

Darryl's teammates were scared to come to work. "Todd [Lyght] and I were talking about it one time," Robert Bailey said, "and we were saying, 'Man, we went to parties at D's house when these people were looking for him. We could have been killed.'"

"The feeling around Rams Park," Anthony Newman recalled, "was, 'Don't stand next to Darryl, you might get shot.'"

I mean narcotics isn't full of niggers and Mexicans. They're full of white guys that wear cowboy boots.

—LAPD DETECTIVE MARK FUHRMAN, April 7, 1987[1]

Chapter 14

DEA special agent Steven Kinney was in Las Vegas when he first heard the name Darryl Henley, a name he would hear more often over the next three years than the names of his own children. Kinney was attending a narcotics enforcement seminar that had become like most other seminars in Vegas — "an excuse to gamble, drink, and blow off steam," he said — when his boss pulled him aside and told him he was needed in California. Cocaine case. Something about a football player.

Kinney didn't want to leave. He had gambled away all his per diem money and wanted to win it back. Plus he was anything but a sports fan, having been laughed at by his peers once for turning down rink-side seats to see Wayne Gretzky and the LA Kings play. "Who's Wayne Gretzky?" Kinney had asked. His response to Henley's name was identical.

"That's why they want you," his supervisor replied. By placing the unknowing Kinney in charge of the case, the DEA could preemptively dismiss any claims about the Henley investigation being an NFL player witch hunt.

Kinney's ponytail, Fu Manchu moustache, and the thirty extra pounds he carried around his middle betrayed his standing as an elite, Washington-trained criminal investigator who had followed his education at the DEA Academy with a gig as an FBI instructor at Quantico. After that had come a ten-year assignment with the Department of Defense's Special Investigations division, followed by his move to DEA, where Kinney became an expert in, as he phrased it anytime he took the witness stand, "the methods used by traffickers to manufacture and distribute narcotics and evade apprehension by law enforcement." The tropical shirts Kinney preferred were often matched with boots, even in court, when they were accompanied by what appeared to be his only suit. On such occasions, Kinney hid his two stud earrings in his pocket.

Once he learned who Darryl Henley was, Kinney viewed the high-profile case as a way to get promoted to the DEA's coveted GS-13 income level, skipping the usual waiting period of three years. But he immediately butted heads with his supervisors about how to proceed. Kinney wanted to make an example of Henley by aggressively gathering evidence, drawing links, and passing these results along to the prosecutors, who would pass it along to the media. As Kinney saw it, "in the war on drugs, a sports star and sexy case with lots of high-profile players makes the press." He wanted the Henley conviction to speak loudly to those who considered themselves above the law, a group he wasn't merely disdainful of, or just committed to stopping, but one he sometimes wished to punish with violence from his own hand without interference from the bureaucracies around him. Kinney's bosses considered the Henley thing just a measly twelve-kilo bust in a region up to its ears in five hundred–kilo hauls coming up from Mexico. The bosses wanted to get Henley, sure, but Kinney had other drug cases to work, too.

So Kinney did his best with what little resources he had. One of his first moves was to have Henley's Atlanta apartment searched thoroughly for drugs, instructing investigators to look in every crevice for hard-to-find cocaine residue. Although Darryl's home in California was where Tracy had heard the suspicious strapping noises prior to her deliveries, this same search was not repeated there. In fact, Kinney would never set foot in the Brea house during his fourteen-month investigation. He knew Henley had been in Atlanta the whole summer, and Henley was the man he wanted to get, so Atlanta was where he searched. His sweep found nothing.

DEA special agent Kevin McLaughlin, whose efforts to that point had been unproductive, would now work beneath Kinney as a grumbling second in command. McLaughlin was miffed not only because Kinney had been handed the reins of the case but also because it had been decided that its trial would be held in California, not Atlanta, where McLaughlin was based. McLaughlin's in-your-face style contrasted sharply with the MO of Kinney, who liked to say that his pen and pad were his favorite weapons. One of the few things the two men had in common was a belief that physical aggressiveness was often necessary. Statistics showed that DEA agents were more than four times as likely to experience a violent episode than other law enforcement officers, including their rivals at the FBI. So Kinney and McLaughlin presented a brusque, don't-fuck-with-me attitude to each suspect, each interviewee, each defense lawyer they encountered in the Henley case. Anything else showed weakness, and weakness didn't win cases. Despite this similarity, from the very beginning neither Kinney nor McLaughlin was eager to share the limelight that the Henley case promised to bring.[2]

Predictably, their partnership began deteriorating as soon as it started. McLaughlin felt squeezed out, and Kinney would later accuse him of withholding information, then waiting until after-hours before investigating his own leads, alone. Probably the most important issue they disagreed on was Tracy Donaho. McLaughlin considered Tracy an innocent damsel who had been hoodwinked by older black guys intent on using her. He was adamant that Tracy be spared indictment. Kinney thought that was ridiculous; Tracy had been caught in an airport carrying twenty-six pounds of blow after taking plane trips with guys who had told her to pretend she didn't know them. She was dirty as hell. Kinney saw Tracy as his most prosecutable suspect.

Kinney's strength was unearthing the details, the human side of a drug conspiracy. He wanted to look into the threatening visit he heard the Henleys had received from two Latino men, but his superiors saw it as a distraction; Kinney was also advised to ignore the extortionate phone calls the Henleys had been getting. Because the DEA did not investigate these matters, Ted Woolsey did.

The defense team's top investigator, Woolsey tapped the phones at the Henley house so that when Alejandro Cuevas called Darryl's father on the night of September 16 — the day after knocking on their door with Bustamante — Woolsey's tape recorder was rolling. Again, Cuevas used the alias "Frank."

CUEVAS: The only reason you're involved, your house, your phone number, is because [Darryl] is refusing to contact us. If you can give me a number for us to reach him at, that's fine, but we don't know what he's doing. . . .

MR. HENLEY: I'll tell you what he's doing. You know what he's doing. Darryl is playing football. He's playing with the Rams. . . .

CUEVAS: According to him, he doesn't have access to money because the feds are watching him. Has he told you this?

MR. HENLEY: No, he ain't told me nothing like that.

CUEVAS: Okay. You can tell him that we told you that. This is his excuse for putting us off. . . . We don't want to threaten his life.

MR. HENLEY: I understand that three guys jumped in his car Wednesday and took his car, okay? And had guns on him. Now if that's not threatening his life. . . . And then they threatened to shoot my wife. That's the thing that really upset me.

CUEVAS: Oh, absolutely, if somebody told me that, I'd be upset myself. But did he tell you why they did that?

MR. HENLEY: No. He did not tell me why.

CUEVAS: He's not being honest with you, sir. He's not. Because if he was honest with you, he would tell you, "Hey, look, Dad, I made a mistake and now I, you know, I need help to take care of it, or I need to work it out." But he's not telling you the truth.

MR. HENLEY: Okay, I'll get back in contact with Darryl.

CUEVAS: We want him to go back to playing. That's the way it should be. He shouldn't be all stressed out. We have to take care of this. This is very serious.

MR. HENLEY: Okay.

CUEVAS: . . . Ask him to please be honest with you. All we want is for him to take care of his debt.

MR. HENLEY: Okay.

CUEVAS: . . . Mr. Henley, can I trust you that you're not going to call the police?

MR. HENLEY: No. Now I'll tell you what. Now remember now the police department's already involved now, because of his car.

CUEVAS: Okay. . . . Everything will come back to normal, and it will be taken care of. If the police does get involved — and we have to get involved with the police — it's going to involve him just as well. And I can guarantee you after this all blows up, he will not be playing ball.

The next morning, Woolsey gave the tape of this phone call to Steven Kinney, who responded by routing the Henleys' phones to DEA headquarters and asking Darryl's father to come in and receive more calls from the extortionists.

Darryl, meanwhile, had no idea any of this was happening. Woolsey had seen Darryl's emotional side and had decided to leave him out of the loop. Besides, Darryl was preparing for the New York Giants.

On September 16, Bustamante and Cuevas placed another call to Darryl's father, who received it sitting in Kinney's office.

For the next few minutes, Mr. Henley continued to doubt Darryl's involvement. Listening to the call later, it's clear he wasn't helping the DEA so Darryl could get a sentencing break; he was helping because he was convinced his son was innocent and he wanted to prove that.

CUEVAS: Just from speaking to you I get the impression that you doubt that your son would ever do anything wrong.

MR. HENLEY: No, no, that's not it. But, see, I know my son. I know my son. Now he might do something that's off key, but Darryl will never — I'm telling you now, listen to me, and I don't care what goes down later on — *Darryl will never get involved in dope.* Darryl will never — now read my l — listen to me now, now you might think otherwise and your boss might say otherwise, but Darryl Henley — my *son,* okay? — will *never* get involved in dope. . . . Now don't get me wrong here. I'm not trying to just take up for my son and think my son is perfect, because I know he's not, Frank. Okay?

CUEVAS: . . . We had done business with the people he's involved with before. One of the people that he's involved with got hurt. And it had nothing to do with us.

MR. HENLEY: What do you mean got hurt?

CUEVAS: Uh. Um. Dead.

MR. HENLEY: . . . Frank, we're going to work on trying to get this to you. . . . Try to give me a week or so.

CUEVAS: That's too long. I need to talk to you before then. . . . I'm going to get you a number where you can get a hold of me.

MR. HENLEY: . . . It had to be somebody else that framed him, Frank. If you investigate, if you really get down and investigate and find out what happened you're going to find out that Darryl wasn't even involved.

The next morning, Eric Manning was eulogized in the same

church where he had been baptized seventeen years earlier and by the same pastor who had dipped his head in the water. The flyer given to mourners that day noted: "Eric's many interests were complimented [sic] by his magnetic and humorous personality. . . . God blessed him with many talents. A smile that was like a greeting card to others, a warm personality that would brighten a cloudy day, and a strong love for the Lord displayed by his ushering, singing, and playing the drums for his church." Eric Manning was twenty-two.

The next day Alex Cuevas called Darryl's father again.

CUEVAS: I'm going to give you until next week to talk some sense into your son. . . . We want our money. . . . If you go to the cops, he will not play ball any more, Mr. Henley. I can guarantee you that. We're not playing games. If he wants to live in denial, that's his choice. . . . If he doesn't pay our money, I don't care if he stops playing ball and he moves. We will find him. We want this taken care of. . . . Did he get a hold of G?

MR. HENLEY: . . . How can he get a hold of G?

CUEVAS: Okay, he has Monday and Tuesday off.

MR. HENLEY: Darryl does?

CUEVAS: Yes.

MR. HENLEY: How do you know that?

CUEVAS: We know everything, sir. He has Monday and Tuesday off. He better get on it. . . . We know where he lives.

MR. HENLEY: And how much money did you say was involved in that?

CUEVAS: Now, with the interest, it's three-sixty. . . . We gave him a chance to make payments and he never came through.

MR. HENLEY: . . . You know this is a great sum of money.

CUEVAS: I understand that. If he wants to make a commitment to pay, it better be a serious one. . . . He better not come up with five thousand dollars. No no no no. If he wants to make a payment, tell him to come with a hundred grand. . . . If he doesn't, he won't play ball, sir.

MR. HENLEY: Okay. Well, he'll play ball. You don't determine that unless you—unless you just kill him. . . .

CUEVAS: We don't want that to happen to him.

If Bustamante didn't receive at least $100,000 by September 25—the day before the Rams' game in Houston—Darryl would be kidnapped and possibly killed. But first there was the Giants game. Darryl rode in the back of Mike Lara's Bronco to catch the team flight to New York. Huddled behind the passenger seat wearing a Kevlar vest, Henley asked Lara to stop at the bank on their way to LAX. "There won't be any stops today, partner," Lara replied.

As he lined up against Darryl Henley that Sunday, Giants receiver Mike Sherrard still thought of him as the upbeat little freshman he had gone up against in practice at UCLA. Sherrard had no reason to think that his former teammate's life was anything but California sunshine. His only issue with Darryl was a minor one: Henley was always ducking his dinner invitations. Sherrard and fellow Bruins Flipper Anderson and Duval Love often dined together when Sherrard played for San Francisco, and they always invited Darryl, but he never made it. Too much going on, Darryl would say. Too busy.

The Giants' receivers had been running hitch routes and outs all day, to combat the Rams' defensive strength: their pass rush. Still, by the end of the second quarter, quarterback Phil Simms had been sacked four times; his feet were impatient and his arm was eager to get rid of the ball. For a defensive back, this is the soil from which interceptions grow. When Sherrard hit the brakes to turn back toward Simms on another hitch, Henley predicted the route, leapt in front of Sherrard, got both hands on the ball—and dropped it. As he jumped around like a pouting child, furious for blowing what would have been a certain touchdown, CBS commentator Randy Cross said, "That's the kind of defensive back he is. Phil

Simms said, 'This guy likes to take chances. He can hurt you, but by the same token you can hurt him.'" On cue, Darryl blitzed on the next play, and Simms found Henley's man for a twenty-eight-yard gain that set up a Giants field goal before the half.

The Rams still had a chance to win when Henley recovered a fumble in Giants territory in the fourth quarter, but their offense moved backward five yards on the next three plays. Despite the unveiling of rookie running back Jerome Bettis, who made his first NFL start that day, the Rams gained only 171 total yards and lost, 20–10.

Ted Woolsey picked Henley up at LAX that night and drove him to Santa Monica where, battered and sore, Henley burned the midnight oil with Gerry Chaleff in his posh law office on Ocean Avenue. Manning's murder had removed the only buffer between Henley and Bustamante, which along with the extortion calls had heated the case for everyone and required a long conference between lawyer and client. The behind-the-scenes effort to keep Henley not only out of prison but alive began in earnest that night.

The next day, DEA agent Kevin McLaughlin received the first photos he'd ever seen of Eric Manning. McLaughlin promptly drove to Orange County and showed them to Tracy Donaho, who identified the man in them as the Eric she had been telling McLaughlin about for weeks — the Eric who had driven her to the airport in Darryl's Lexus.

This same day, a small battalion of law enforcement personnel, led by Kinney, tracked down Willie McGowan at his sister's house in San Dimas. The first few questions they asked Willie were about Henley. "Yeah, I know Darryl," McGowan said tentatively. "His dad coached me since I was nine. Darryl and I grew up in the same community." Willie refused, however, to answer questions about whether he had seen Darryl recently or where Henley was living. Tellingly, and quite out of the blue, Willie announced to the investigators that he was a better football player than Henley. According to Kinney, Willie made this point several times and also mentioned that "he'd played minor league baseball and would have got to the majors but chose to donate a kidney [to his sister]."

These disclosures "touched me," Kinney said later, and were "a turning point in outlining in my mind how this case involved Darryl and others, sort of put the human nature and why [into] the equation."

As he questioned Willie in that house in San Dimas in the fall of 1993, Kinney would have liked to have asked more questions about the Manning murder, but he had been advised by the U.S. Attorney's Office to focus only on the drug case. The U.S. government, after all, wasn't waging a war on murder.

In 1993 America's war on drugs was at its zenith. Bill Clinton had replaced George H. W. Bush as president the week before Darryl Henley met Tracy Donaho, in part because Clinton had convinced voters that he would be as "Tough on Crime" as his predecessor. The drug war was a politician's dream. Only after it began turning sour did high-level officials like U.S. district court judge Nancy Gertner point out the difficult truth that had helped initiate the war in the first place: "The war against drugs provides politicians with something to say that offends nobody, requires them to do nothing difficult, allows them to postpone, perhaps indefinitely, the more urgent questions about the state of the nation's schools, housing, employment opportunities for young black men, the condition to which drug addiction speaks as a system not a cause. They remain safe in the knowledge that they might as well be denouncing Satan."

The early 1990s were a complex time with regard to federal drug policy. Law enforcement was ordered to secure as many drug convictions as possible, with legal ethics often cast aside, and lengthy, "mandatory minimum" prison sentences were enacted for those caught using and selling drugs. The death penalty was sought for drug kingpins. Meanwhile, millions of Americans clamored for legalization, making America in 1993 a bit like Sherlock Holmes: both crime fighter and drug addict.

By the time Clinton took office, even the judicial branch was expressing displeasure with the drug war, with senior U.S. district judge Whitman Knapp writing that "after twenty years on the bench, I have concluded that federal drug laws are a disaster." The ill-conceived battle plans of politicians had created a vicious cycle, Knapp said, citing Nobel laureate economist Milton Friedman: "Law enforcement temporarily reduces the drug supply and thus causes prices to rise. Higher prices draw new sources of supply . . . resulting in more drugs on the street. The increased availability of drugs creates more addicts. The government reacts with more vigorous enforcement, and the cycle starts anew."

One of the more controversial aspects of the drug war was its mandatory minimum sentencing laws, which required judges to hand down predetermined sentences to those convicted of certain drug crimes, including loosely defined conspiracy charges. Mandatory minimum sentencing, or MMS, had been enacted in response to basketball star Len Bias's cocaine overdose in 1986, when House Speaker Tip O'Neill, a Boston native with more than a passing interest in the death of a Celtics draft pick, began turning political wheels that would remove judges from the sentencing process in most of their now-backlogged drug cases. Among its many effects, O'Neill's policy would help fracture hundreds of thousands of American families. Far less damage was being inflicted, many argued, on the nation's drug problem.

Before drug offenders could be sentenced, of course, they had to be convicted. For this purpose the government began allowing its law enforcement agencies to employ dubious tactics in their use of informants. These tactics proved especially effective when prosecuting conspiracy cases, particularly the ones in which multiple defendants were facing prison time. This was Tracy Donaho's situation. She was an informant under indictment who had been offered a chance by federal prosecutors at a drastic reduction in her mandatory sentence. All she had to do was provide information about Darryl Henley and his friends. Information that increased the prosecutors' chances of winning was preferred.

There existed no evidence that Tracy Donaho was paid by the government, but the fact that federal law would have allowed for such compensation was the kind of thing that exasperated opponents of the drug war. A defense attorney caught paying a witness, they argued, would be disbarred and possibly prosecuted. U.S. attorneys around the country, meanwhile, could put informants on the dole without repercussion.

Prison overcrowding became another unforeseen problem for the politicians who had declared war on drugs. Even those in support of the drug war conceded that it was crippling the corrections system, creating what General Barry McCaffrey, the former drug czar himself, referred to as a "drug gulag." In 1986, 38 percent of federal inmates were drug offenders; by 1998 it was 60 percent. In 1985 the average federal drug sentence was twenty-three months; by 1997 the average for a *first-time* offender had swelled to seventy-eight months (six and a half years). [3]

These were the bleak circumstances, the howling black hole of a future that Darryl Henley stared into every day. There could not have been a more challenging opponent for him to prepare for under these circumstances — and with his life in jeopardy — than the Houston Oilers, whose "run-and-shoot" offense deployed as many as five receivers at a time to catch the laser spirals of quarterback Warren Moon. Henley had been told by then about the threats against his family, but he didn't know about Bustamante's ultimatum — *Give me $100,000 by Saturday, or we'll get Darryl*. Henley spent his nights in his room at the Anaheim Marriott, lying low and studying the Oilers' pass routes. Three days before Bustamante's deadline, Darryl drove to a café in Westwood to meet with his lawyer, Roger Cossack, and Detective Frank Durazo, the man in charge of the Manning murder case. Henley arrived four hours late. The only reason Durazo waited was because Cossack, one of the world's premier conversationalists, had waited, too, and because Darryl's brother Thomas had arrived on time and identified a photo of Rafael Bustamante as one of the men who appeared at his parents' home on September 15. When Darryl finally arrived, he identified Bustamante as the man who had stolen his Lexus at Rams Park on September 8.

That same afternoon, Ted Woolsey found Darryl's stolen Lexus in a rundown parking garage in Tijuana. The two attendants on hand told Woolsey that they had been working there the day the Lexus arrived. They identified Bustamante and his brother as having driven it into the garage.

During the first six days of Bustamante's seven-day ultimatum, neither he nor Cuevas called Henley's parents, but those six nights were far from quiet. Things went bump at the Henley house. A window screen disappeared. Departing tires chirped. One evening, when Mrs. Henley let the family's two Rottweilers into the backyard, the dogs darted to the fence and began barking at a group of shadowy figures just beyond it. Mrs. Henley heard frantic male voices in the darkness shouting, "Shoot 'em! Shoot 'em!" The intruders turned out to be the cops — federal or local, they weren't sure, but there were "at least four unmarked cars," Eric Henley recalled. "When I went out there they had their guns drawn on the dogs, but everybody was in regular clothes. I was like, 'Where did they come from?'" The officers left without telling the Henleys their purpose.

So T.H. Henley was more than a bit displeased with Kinney and his law enforcement brethren as he sat in Kinney's office making another recorded call to Cuevas. He didn't have much choice, though. He had twenty-four hours to give Bustamante $100,000, or Darryl would be at risk of physical harm. There wasn't much acting going on anymore. Darryl's dad was a scared, angry father playing a scared, angry father.

CUEVAS ("FRANK"): What kind of progress have you made?

MR. HENLEY: Hey, we've been working on it and, uh, we've come up with some monies.

CUEVAS: How much?

MR. HENLEY: Uh, around the figure that you asked me for.

CUEVAS: Very well.

MR. HENLEY: Okay, but my problem is I need to meet with you, Frank, because . . . I just can't give the money to you without proof that my son is involved. . . . Can I meet with you?

CUEVAS: We can work something out.

MR. HENLEY: Frank, now look, I am afraid, man. I'm afraid [for] my family. Have you guys been watching my house?

CUEVAS: We have left you completely alone like I promised.

MR. HENLEY: I don't think that's true, Frank, because I've had people come around my house.

CUEVAS: I gave you my word that you wouldn't be bothered.

MR. HENLEY: Okay.

CUEVAS: . . . You know what I want to know?

MR. HENLEY: What?

CUEVAS: If you went to the police.

MR. HENLEY: That's another thing I wanted to ask you. . . . *You* might be the police yourself, and I got this money out here and—

CUEVAS: Well, I'm going to tell you what's going to happen, okay?

MR. HENLEY: What's up?

CUEVAS: If you involve anybody but yourself in this—

MR. HENLEY: Uh huh.

CUEVAS: There's going to be consequences.

Cuevas eventually agreed to meet with Mr. Henley in person.

CUEVAS: But I'm going to tell you something. If something goes wrong—we're gonna be clean, we're not going to be packing or anything—if something goes wrong, there's going to be a contract on Darryl. . . . I can get bailed out of jail. . . . That's not a problem.

MR. HENLEY: All I want to do is take care of my family, Frank. That's all I want, Frank.

CUEVAS: . . . I'm a man of my word. I know that we met with your son, and I know that your son told us to our face, "I guarantee it." We've been doing business for four years with NBA players. We never had a problem. Two years ago we got involved with NFL players—never had a problem.[4] . . . I want you to listen to me very well. If anything goes wrong, and any member of my organization goes to jail, you're putting your son's life on the line. Are you ready to live with that?

MR. HENLEY: Frank, I don't want no one to get hurt, Frank. I don't want no one to get hurt.

CUEVAS: Okay, okay. I just want you to know who you're dealing with.

MR. HENLEY: Okay.

CUEVAS: We've got family in Mexico, Colombia, and the United States. We're a big organization. We have people doing time. If your son goes to jail, we can get a hold of him in jail a lot easier than out here. It's not a problem. All he has to do is pay his responsibility. I just want you to know something. If you talk to the cops and the cops are promising you security, the cops will not bring Darryl back to life. Just keep that in mind.

Cuevas called back that evening. An exasperated Mr. Henley spoke with him for a while, then put his "cousin" Reggie (DEA investigator Reggie Bennett) on the phone.

CUEVAS: If we hang up the phone right now, you can tell Mr. Henley that he'll be getting a call from his son when we pick him up. They've guaranteed me we'll get him. But this time there ain't going to be no talking. . . . We're going to hurt him first. . . . The point is, we do not know if you guys have contacted the police.

REGGIE: Man, it ain't no contacting the motherfucking police. . . .

CUEVAS: You want to meet with me alone?

REGGIE: I'll meet with you alone.

CUEVAS: Okay. You and me. . . . But I'm going to tell you something. . . . If I go to jail . . . Darryl is gone. There's not going to be no more talking. You tell that to his dad. . . . If I don't go back within five minutes with a hundred thousand dollars, then Darryl's life is over.

Chapter 15

Darryl's leg was gushing blood. He'd been returning a punt return during practice when the buckle on a teammate's helmet raked against him, opening a six-inch gash. He hadn't returned punts in over a year, but that morning the Rams had released their usual return man, which meant that Darryl would have to fill in against the Oilers in addition to covering their army of receivers. And he'd have to do it with a heavily wrapped wound on his leg.

Before he boarded the team flight to Houston, he called his mom from a pay phone in the airport, having phoned her on the eve of every game he'd played since college. On this occasion Darryl could tell that his off-field troubles were weighing on her. He'd look back later and realize how frightened she must have been — someone had come to her house to kidnap her — and he'd realize how desperate she must have been to tell him about the threats, the calls, and his dad's cooperation with the DEA. But she couldn't. She knew Darryl would have flipped out. He couldn't have done anything about it, anyway. It was Saturday. Bustamante's one-week deadline was up.

CUEVAS [to undercover DEA investigator "Reggie Henley" Bennett]: At 3:30 you're going to receive a phone call. . . . You'll be given a destination on where to drop off the money. It's going to be one male Caucasian, a white man. . . . If he does receive the money, you will receive a phone call at 4:30 confirming that we have the money and everything is up and up. . . . If you break any of these rules, we're going to pick [Darryl] up. If we cannot pick him up, we're going to fly somebody in and have him killed. . . . If you guys do not pay the money, we're not coming after the family. . . . We're coming after *him*.

"REGGIE HENLEY": Well, then you're still coming after the family.

CUEVAS: We're coming after him only. And I can guarantee you that if he's under protection, we're going to get to him sooner or later because he's going to play ball, and as soon as he plays ball, we're going to make a hit. So you guys make a decision. . . . If his life is worth a hundred thousand dollars, you guys have the money there. . . . If he's not there, Darryl is dead.

Cuevas called back and set the handoff for 5 p.m. in the parking lot behind the Marie Callender's restaurant in Covina. Mr. Henley watched an agent check out $100,000 cash from the evidence room, place it in a satchel, and hand it to a local sheriff's deputy named Eric Manker, who for the next hour or so would play the role of "Eric Henley," one of Darryl's cousins. The plan was to have Manker show the money to Bustamante's bagman, then demand a face-to-face meeting with Cuevas. "It was hoped that this ploy would lure Frank [Cuevas] out so he could be apprehended and identified," the investigative documents said.

As the families inside Marie Callender's were finishing their Saturday lunches, Steven Kinney and ten other law enforcement officers were setting up surveillance in Room 524 of the adjacent Hampton Inn, which overlooked the restaurant. Bustamante's interests were represented less thoroughly by his brother Rigo, sipping iced tea on the restaurant's back patio. Deputy Manker pulled into the parking lot driving a gray Chevy pickup and dressed how he thought the cousin of a pro football player would dress. Bustamante's bagman, an unemployed white handyman he knew from the gym named James Saenz, pulled up next to Manker on a Japanese street bike that Bustamante had borrowed for the occasion. When Manker, who was wearing a wire, showed Saenz his bag full of cash, the agents in Room 524 noticed a brown Camaro pulling up on the other side of a chain-link fence. Cuevas got out, watched the meeting through the fence, then got back in the Camaro and drove away.

Manker told Saenz to bring his boss to the parking lot at 6 p.m. and he would give him the money then. Said Saenz: "There will not be a second time around, bro. . . . Like I said, I'm just the middle man, you know. I got no power of nothing. I'm a nobody, man. I'm a fucking nobody."

Cuevas's Camaro reappeared at the fence. He watched Saenz mount his motorcycle and leave the parking lot empty-handed. Cuevas caught up with Saenz at a nearby red light, where Saenz looked at him and shook his head: *No money.* Just before the light turned green, two unmarked cars squealed in front of them and Cuevas and Saenz were arrested. In Cuevas's Camaro investigators found a gym bag containing a loaded .380 Taurus handgun, plus eleven spare rounds.

Darryl Henley was in Houston at that moment, arriving at the Rams' team hotel from a visit to the Houston home of his old UCLA friend (and Olympic track medalist) Mike Marsh. Henley was greeted at the hotel by a group of FBI agents and U.S. marshals who informed him of the arrests at the restaurant in California and the most recent threats against his life. Henley remembered the marshals telling him they'd be by his side for the remainder of his stay in Houston.

Even during the game? Darryl asked.

Especially during the game, the head marshal replied.

Henley remembered the marshal's next words vividly: "They might get you, but they're not going to get you in Texas."

Alejandro Cuevas was also surrounded by federal agents, but they weren't there to protect him. Steven Kinney had been working for forty hours straight by the time he sat down in a bleak police interrogation room to interview Cuevas. As Kevin McLaughlin stood close by, Kinney informed Cuevas that, as one of the last men to see Eric Manning alive, he was responsible for Manning's death. A panicked Cuevas proceeded to give Kinney exactly what Kinney's accusation had been intended to get from him: a blow-by-blow description of the Rams Park incident. Audibly nervous on the tape of the interview, Cuevas also ran down the two-week extortion effort that had followed the murder. "And everything went by, everybody got deeper and deeper and got worse and worse and by the time I tried bailing out, you know, I was hooked," Cuevas said. "I knew too much and that was like a threat towards me. [Bustamante said,] 'You can't get out, not until you take care of it.'"

"Did you take that as a threat?"

"Somebody dies, I mean, what would you take it as?"

"What do you feel is the threat level for the Henley family?"

"His [Bustamante's] words to me, and he kept telling me to tell Mr. Henley over the phone, is that he would not come after the family, that he would come after Darryl himself, and he looked like he meant it. . . . He goes, 'You don't rat nobody out, because if you rat somebody out, it's all over.'"

"What was he referring to when he said it was over?"

"I don't know," Cuevas said. "You got to figure it out. I mean, I take that as one of two things: he's not going to bail me out, or two, he's going to put a cap in my ass."

Kinney's next move was to get a search warrant for Bustamante's home in Rancho Cucamonga. It was a modest brick house on a hill, just down the street from a school, with an immaculate lawn shaded by a squat palmetto. Inside, investigators found a cache of firearm ammunition including hollow-point bullets, plus five types of anabolic steroids, assorted drug paraphernalia, a loaded .38-caliber Smith & Wesson, and four grams of cocaine.

Detective Mike Ortiz, meanwhile, was grilling Bustamante's bagman, James Saenz, in an interrogation room not unlike Cuevas's. "This is a major deal," Ortiz told Saenz. "People are going to go to jail and serve twenty- and thirty-year terms for this, and just the mere fact that you were there to pick up the cash, you're going to sink down right with them."

"Jesus Christ," said the overwhelmed handyman. All he'd wanted from Bustamante was a little extra cash to help him move his family out of crime-infested La Puente. Now he was facing a federal drug rap.

"That's what conspiracy is all about," Ortiz continued. "Everyone who takes part in completing the transaction is involved, and you're part of it now. . . . You're not going to have to worry about a place to move or stay because you're going to have a place for the next ten years."

Saenz cooperated as best he could, but he didn't have much to offer.

"I can't believe that you're going to let these guys step all over you, and all you can tell me is that you're pissed about it," Ortiz said.

"I can only tell you what I've seen," Saenz said. "I can probably make up some good drama for you."

"I don't want drama."

"I haven't seen anything!" Saenz pleaded. "I haven't physically seen anything!"

Bustamante's threat to "fly someone in" to Houston and have Henley killed at the Astrodome was very real. The relaxed airline security in 1993 would have allowed virtually anyone to fly anywhere, undetected. Even if there were snags via air, Bustamante's home-town of Ojinaga was less than ten miles from one of the most po-rous sections of the Texas border. He could hire a hit man to drive to Houston, do the deed, and be back in Mexico by the time the Rams' flight departed, one player lighter.

Adding to Darryl's worries headed into the game were all the rel-atives who had driven down from Waco to watch the most famous Henley play in their home state. Darryl was in his dark Houston ho-tel room on the morning of the game, curtains drawn, cramming for his test against Warren Moon, thumbing through his notes on the Oilers' run-and-shoot offense. The other Rams were staying in a five-star hotel across town, but Darryl was in this out-of-the-way Best Western for his own protection, registered under an alias. The media still had no idea that the Rams' starting right corner-back was the target of both a DEA investigation and a murder plot.

As the heat of midday began to oppress Houston, a black Crown Vic rolled into the hotel parking lot, blinking its lights as a signal to the guard stationed outside Darryl's door. Darryl emerged into sunlight that stung his eyes and began his long ride to the Astro-dome, touching the tinted window to feel the ninety degree heat outside. When the car arrived outside the dome, he got out and walked with two escorts to the Rams' locker room. "He had these two huge Texas Rangers escorting him," remembered Todd Hewitt. "They were as big as some of our defensive linemen. I remember them hanging around in the locker room trying to be undercov-er, but everybody was like, 'Who are these guys?'"

During the game, Henley did not listen for clicking rifles in the stands or scan the fans for hit men, but the idea that his as-sassin might be in the echoing Astrodome "was definitely on my mind." On one third-and-long, Henley went after Moon on a cor-ner blitz. Running back Lorenzo White dove at Henley's bandaged shin, sending him into an airborne somersault that allowed Moon to sprint ahead—right into the arms of Rams defensive end Fred Stokes. That sack forced a punt, and as he jogged downfield to receive it, Darryl knew that he was about to be more exposed, as both a football player and a murder target, than at any other time in the game. He waited at his own 10-yard line, surrounded by a sea of blank green turf, until he heard the *boom* of the punt in the distance. He almost felt grateful to see ten opponents running at him full speed. He probably should have called for a fair catch, but instead he made the first man miss, then darted upfield for seven tough yards, allowing the Rams to get started beyond the 20-yard line. He jogged to the sideline, where armed bodyguards sidled up to him as inconspicuously as they could.

With four and a half minutes left in the game, the Rams led 28–13, but the Oilers were deep in Rams territory. Henley and his teammates had blown plenty of games like this before, and to lesser teams. Moon completed a pass to the flat, hoping his receiver, Willie Drewrey, could make his man miss and slip into the end zone. But Henley hit Drewrey firmly and slung him to the turf, venting a frustration that only he could understand. Two plays later, Henley assisted on a fourth down tackle that sealed the Rams' win.

He recalled later that he was the first player to reach the locker room. Chuck Knox—one of the few people who knew why the burly guys in sunglasses had been connected to Darryl's hip every second Darryl hadn't been connected to an Oiler receiver's—awarded Henley the game ball. Knox had become like a grandfather to the young cornerback, and he winked knowingly at him as he handed Henley the turf-burnt pigskin. Then the marshals escorted Henley to the team bus, where, alone and unshowered, he changed from his sweaty uniform into the jeans and T-shirt he'd worn to the stadium that morning.

Five days later, Rafael Bustamante turned himself in at the federal courthouse in Santa Ana and pled not guilty to extortion charges. To his surprise, he was then jailed without bond. He'd thought he would just pay a private bondsman and leave—his attorneys had all but promised him so — but now he was behind bars indefinitely, and there was nothing he could do about it. With Bustamante's arrest, the membrane between Darryl's problems and the media was now thin to the point of bursting. It was only a matter of time until the most famous name in Bustamante's case file became known to the press.

Henley was a shell of himself during practice that week. The Rams, in turn, played like a shell of the team that had just defeated the Oilers. The final score was Saints 37, Rams 6, and it wasn't that close. Henley made four tackles and broke up a pass. It was the last game he played that season.

The next day, Alejandro Cuevas pled guilty and was *also* sent to jail pending trial. In Cuevas's detention papers, the judge twice referred to Henley, Cuevas's extortion target, as a "drug dealer" — something that had been neither charged nor proven. To Darryl, learning of Cuevas's decision to testify for the government was like watching a weather report on TV that showed a swirling tempest approaching. The storm will hit by morning, Henley thought.

He was in a defensive backs meeting when it struck. Secondary coach Rod Perry answered the phone on the wall, then turned to Darryl and said: "For you, 20. It's the boss." Darryl thought it was Knox, but when he put the phone to his ear, the voice he heard was John Shaw's:

"The media's on their way."

"I don't even know if I hung up the phone," Henley recalled.

His teammates remembered Henley running out in a blur, jumping in his Pathfinder, and squealing out of Rams Park. He drove a half hour north, straight to his parents' home in Upland, where he found a small media gathering and a phone that wouldn't stop ringing. Realizing he was in the third-worst place imaginable if he wanted to avoid the press — the first two being Rams Park and his home in Brea — he drove to Kym Taylor's place. He'd only known her for four days, but he was about to pull Kym into a dark three-year odyssey that would change her life.

Upon meeting Darryl at a happy hour mixer earlier that week, Kym, a pretty thirty-three-year-old medical receptionist, had invited him to a pool party she was hosting on Saturday. At the party, Darryl asked if he could see her on Sunday. An hour after the Saints game ended, she arrived at his home in Orange County.

Her impression of Darryl from the beginning was that he seemed desperate for someone to talk to. "He said he had rented his house out to some other guys that summer," Kym recalled, "and that he had dated a cheerleader even though he wasn't supposed to. She was looking for work and asked if Darryl could get her a job. . . . One of the guys renting his house said he could help her out. Darryl said he knew what kind of work it was, but he left it up to Tracy. She did a few runs for the guy, then she contacted Darryl in Atlanta that day—the day she got arrested—because she didn't know anyone else. . . . [Darryl] said he was the only one trying to protect her that day. He was like, 'I'm probably going to get indicted, but getting indicted doesn't mean I'm guilty. It doesn't take a lot of evidence to get indicted. I hardly drink at all. I've never done drugs in my life. I talk to kids about the dangers of drugs. I didn't know what those guys in my house were up to.'"

"I don't know if I'm gullible or what," Kym added. "But I believed him."

In these pregnant hours after the bursting of the media membrane, Henley quarantined himself inside Kym Taylor's condominium in Culver City, leaving only to meet with his lawyers or his family. Only his mother knew his whereabouts.

The next morning, beneath a story about the American soldiers who had been overrun in the streets of Mogadishu, the *Orange County Register* ran a front-page story titled: "Rams' Cornerback under Drug Probe." Dave Strege and the *Register*'s other sportswriters shook their heads in wonderment at those words. "Darryl Henley?" they asked each other. "Darryl *Henley* did this?"

"Darryl Henley has not and will not ever be involved with narcotics," Gerry Chaleff told *Register* reporter Tracy Weber, who wrote
her "Drug Probe" piece based on what an unnamed "source close
to the investigation" had told her. This source said that "Henley
would purchase the drugs in southern California and ship them
to Atlanta, using the former cheerleader as the courier," and that
he "was apparently purchasing kilos of cocaine from Mexican
dealers through a go-between named Eric Manning." These allegations, which read like facts, were devoured by the public, posed
as they were next to the cleverly chosen photo of Darryl dropping
his would-be interception against the Giants, an image that reeked
of metaphor.

Karl Dorrell, who at the time was an assistant coach at the University of Colorado, laughed years later at the portrayals of Henley as a cocaine-slinging thug. "The people who have made that
classification, that stereotype, don't know him. Absolutely don't
know him. If they were introduced to Darryl Henley on the street
they'd think, 'Wow, that guy seems like a great guy.' And those
are the impressions of Darryl I want to keep. Because I know what
kind of person he is."

John Carroll, Darryl's high school teammate, remembered being ridiculed by his grad school classmates when the news broke.
"I wouldn't say I was in denial," Carroll said later. "It was just a
plain fact: *He would not do that.* A lot of it has to do not only with
Darryl but with his whole family. It just wasn't acceptable. I could
see myself doing this kind of thing before Darryl, and I've never done drugs in my life. . . . If we graduated with three hundred
guys, I'd suspect 285 of them before I'd say Darryl would be involved in this."

"Everything is false," Henley's father told the *Register*. "You say
that this girl was taking coke for Darryl Henley, and that is not
true. The courts will prove that he is not guilty."

Willie Abston heard about it on ESPN. He was surprised to find
himself crying, right there on his couch, in front of his new bride.

A recent law school graduate, Abston knew instantly that his high school buddy was about to be convicted in the court of public opinion long before he could be heard in a court of law. These reporters and talking heads didn't know Darryl, Abston said. These prosecutors wouldn't bother to look into what kind of person he had been over the years. How he had visited grade schools and breathed life into Abston's dreams by paying for his law school tuition and books. The media wouldn't investigate how strange the drug charges seemed to those who knew Darryl best. "He's a drug dealer now," Abston said to his wife, stating what would soon be accepted as fact by those who ingested the media's truncated version of the story. "That's it. He's a drug dealer."

He actually wanted to open the door, to actually show himself and speak. . . . [H]e was eager to find out what the others, who so desired to see him now, would say at the sight of him.

—FRANZ KAFKA, *The Metamorphosis*

Chapter 16

Aside from Knicks or Pistons fans, Darryl Henley might have been the only person in America who reacted happily to the news that Michael Jordan was retiring from basketball.[1] Jordan's retirement moved the blurbs about the NFL's renegade drug trafficker to the back of the sports pages and sometimes out of the paper altogether. But the DEA was not distracted. The day Jordan retired, Steven Kinney, Reggie Bennett, and two federal prosecutors were at Rams Park interviewing players and other team personnel about Henley. Jackie Slater, the future Hall of Fame tackle, added a rare moment of levity to his interview by admitting that he'd "joked with Henley about his vehicle being taken, telling him if he was a larger man he wouldn't have been a victim of this type of crime." Slater also said that he'd observed "a change in Henley's personality recently and described Henley as being reserved. Slater advised that he felt this was due to some recent injuries that Henley had suffered." Todd Lyght said he'd noticed Henley's down mood, too, but he didn't know the cause.

Kinney asked equipment manager Todd Hewitt, "Have you ever seen Darryl Henley trafficking anything?"

"No."

"Has Darryl ever asked you to carry anything for him on the road?"

"No, other than his player bag, and I check each of those personally. To be honest with you, there are guys in the locker room I would think could do this ahead of Darryl Henley. I've never known Darryl to do drugs or anything like that."

"We're not talking about *using* drugs," Kinney replied testily. "We're talking about moving drugs, pushing drugs, pushing them toward little kids."

As Hewitt remembered it years later, "I was like, 'Whoa, you just asked me a question and I was trying to give you a thorough answer. To be honest with you, I'd trust Darryl Henley with my children.' That's the way I felt about him. I would never have thought anything about it. This is one of the last guys in the locker room you would think would be involved in something like that."

Slater confessed to similar bewilderment. "We know Darryl is a very competent, talented person with a lot on the ball," Slater told the *LA Times*, "and if a guy like that, with so much going for him, ends up in a situation like this, then we're all vulnerable."

Flipper Anderson, who had honed his skills in practice against Darryl every day for most of his career, back to their UCLA days, chose to distance himself from Henley. "Life goes on," Anderson told the *Times*, "and Darryl is going to have to deal with what happens to Darryl. We got a game next Thursday that we have to deal with." When asked if he had been in touch with Henley, Anderson replied, "No, don't even know his phone number. I don't hang out with him. Just football friends."

The Rams draped an opaque curtain over the fence surrounding the practice field. Security guards were added, along with closed-circuit cameras and alarms. The prosecution, meanwhile, was tightening its operations as well. The lead prosecutor, assistant U.S. attorney Deirdre Eliot, had a stroke of luck when an LAPD detective named Richard Kellogg called her after executing an unrelated search warrant on the law office of Angela Wallace. One of the disks Kellogg recovered contained what looked like a letter from Darryl Henley to Wallace, faxed to her from a cruise ship in the Bahamas.

Kellogg gave the disk to Eliot and, with it, the unique privilege of reading Darryl's firsthand account of his relations with Tracy, Willie, and "Gee" leading up to Tracy's arrest in Atlanta.[2]

Deirdre Eliot's frail, blonde exterior belied an intensity that by turns impressed and annoyed her colleagues. She had been assigned the Henley case after winning convictions against members of the Colombian Cali cartel who had been caught exporting dog kennels to the United States made of cocaine-infused fiberglass. The lengths to which those traffickers had gone had both fascinated and troubled Eliot. She had the same reaction to Henley's fax to Wallace. She found a safe place for it in her growing Henley case file.

That Friday, the Rams convened for the first time in four years without Henley on their roster. He was still on paid leave, holed up in Kym Taylor's condo, his skin ashy from all the time spent indoors watching TV. Everything on reminded him of the mess his life had become. His mom's favorite show, *Perry Mason*, made him think about the spectacle of standing trial, the horror of being cross-examined; *Cops* made him feel as hopeless as one of the belligerent drunks splayed across its sidewalks; watching ESPN was out of the question. The local news told him he was unavailable for comment.

I went to Damien High School, he kept saying to himself, lying on Kym's couch. And even that defense held its own irony. He'd never felt truly at home at Damien, but now the proper upbringing it represented was his best defense — his only life preserver amid miles of ocean. As dawn snuck through Kym's horizontal blinds, Henley whispered to himself, *I helped charities, man. I didn't do this.* Yet he knew he'd done something. At the very least, he'd mingled with people whose paths had been diametrically opposed to his own. *That don't make me no damn drug dealer, though.* And so it went, as he whiled away the hours in Kym's apartment, defending himself in his own head as the television before him flashed with human conflict.

He received a letter that brought him hope. It was written by the same hand that had scrawled that fateful fax to Angela Wallace.

10/8/93

Dear Darryl,

I swear with everyday, I love you even more!! The longer I am away from you, the more I desire you & need you. These incidents & our distance has really put our relationship to the test. Plenty of times, I have thought about giving up, or wondered if in fact I'm cut out for this distance. On the same token, there is absolutely no one who makes me feel the way you do. I notice that when you are around I am full of life & overflowing with joy. As opposed to when you're not around, I am downhearted, unpleasant & unsociable. I recently just noticed this. Naturally, I knew that I very much need you & I very much want to be a part of your life. My parents love you & of course, that makes me love you even more. Sweetheart, I know this year, by far, has been the worse year of your life; but, look on the bright side, you are still here, God obviously has plans for you. There are better days ahead. Baby, no matter what happens, I am behind you 100% + 100%! . . . I wouldn't care if you never touched another football again—as long as your happy, I'm happy. . . . [J]ust remember—I love you for better or for worse!!

When the Rams flew to Atlanta the following week to play the Falcons, Darryl flew with them. He stayed with the young woman who had written the letter, Shetelle Clifford.

He hadn't set foot in Atlanta since the day after Tracy's arrest, nearly three months earlier. When he arrived this time, he was as glad to see Shetelle as he was to hear that Bustamante, Cuevas, and Saenz had been indicted for extortion back in California. The bad news was that Steven Kinney had begun testifying about the drug case before a federal grand jury, describing the late Eric Manning as Henley's "friend," someone Henley "trusted."

Manning's twenty-one-year-old widow testified before the grand jury as well. "Darryl Henley was the man where all the cocaine was going to," Denise Manning testified. "He was the person that asked for all the cocaine." It was a startling departure from what she had told Kevin McLaughlin two weeks earlier during a one-on-one interview:

"I don't—I could assume that whenever—at times it would go to Darryl," Denise had said then.

"Assume as in Eric told you?" McLaughlin had asked.

"Right."

But now, sitting before a grand jury, Denise Manning was saying that Darryl "was the man where all the cocaine was going to."

Federal grand juries consisted of twenty-three citizens, twelve of whom had to side with the prosecution in order for attorneys like Deirdre Eliot to win an indictment. Such victories were made easier by the fact that defense attorneys weren't allowed. There was no one present, for example, to take issue with some of the more dubious evidence Eliot placed before the grand jury in the fall of 1993, particularly the hearsay of witnesses like Denise Manning—who could have been charged in the drug case but had instead been promised immunity in exchange for their testimony.

The fairness of the grand jury setting had been a hotly contested item at the U.S. Supreme Court the previous year, when it was decided by a 5–4 decision that prosecutors didn't have to disclose evidence that might exonerate the accused—a staple rule in actual trials. So Darryl had no recourse when Denise Manning testified that "they all met together, all of them, Willie, Eric, Ralph, and

Darryl, met together and they agreed on this [cocaine conspiracy]."
As three of the men named in that swatch of testimony said years
later, this meeting between "all of them" never happened. More un-
fortunate, Mrs. Manning's statement that it *had* happened was never allowed to be contradicted before those twenty-three grand jurors.

Magic City and Club Nikki's were not on Darryl's agenda during
the weekend the Rams visited Atlanta. Instead, he hung out with
Shetelle and watched on TV as Deion Sanders, his roommate at
the 1988 Kodak All-American festivities in Atlanta, played baseball for the Braves in the National League playoffs one night, then
football against the Rams the next day. The Falcons trailed the
Rams 17–3 before Robert Bailey, Henley's replacement at cornerback, was beaten for two touchdowns. The second score gave Atlanta the lead for good. After the game, a skirmish erupted in the
Rams' locker room. Bailey picked up a chair and threatened one
of his teammates, yelling, "Don't tell me I cost us the game!" before being dragged out.

It was supposed to have been Darryl's contract year. He was supposed to have been showcasing himself for the Rams and anyone
else interested in his services, adding to the zeroes on his next
contract, which his agent had assured him would be worth over a
million dollars per season. But he wasn't even playing. Years later,
Henley recalled being invited to the hotel suite of an NFL executive who wanted to sign him, despite his off-the-field issues. After
wading through a litter of lingerie and empty champagne glasses—it was the day after a win—Henley found the exec lounging
on a sofa in a bathrobe. Speaking over two female voices mingling
in the next room, the exec said to Henley: "Ten years, huh?" He
paused a moment, then added, "It's just so damn *long*. Have you
ever thought about, y'know, disappearing?"

"Not once," Darryl said. "Not one time since this whole thing
went down. I'm gonna fight this."

Henley was shocked to find his locker empty when he dropped by Rams Park. "Where's my stuff, Todd?" he asked sadly. "It ain't like I'm dead." As soon as Henley left for the practice field, equipment manager Hewitt returned his helmet to his cubicle, along with his pads, cleats, and number 20 practice jersey. After practice, his trust in Hewitt restored, Henley confided in him "about how the investigators had snaked all the pipes in his house looking for stuff, digging into his walls," Hewitt recalled. "Darryl was trying to play it off like it didn't bother him, but I could tell it did. He was like, 'They're questioning all my neighbors, man.'"

Henley also confided in the Rams' head trainer, Jim Anderson, a trusted soul and renowned prankster who had once gained the distinction of saving Darryl's life while simultaneously trying to kill him. It happened during Darryl's second training camp, when Henley was in the locker room preparing to go to dinner with safety Vince Newsome. Henley's hypoglycemia struck, and Anderson, whose specialty was sports injuries, not fluctuating blood sugar, responded by feeding Darryl as many oranges, candy bars, and Cokes as he could get his hands on. When Henley began regressing into a seizure-like state, Anderson panicked and yelled for Jackie Slater and three other linemen to sit on Darryl's flailing limbs so he could hold a paper bag to Darryl's mouth. When that failed, Anderson tried an IV. He couldn't insert the needle with an offensive guard sitting on Darryl's elbow, so he grabbed the oar he used to stir Gatorade and strapped it to Darryl's arm with athletic tape, to hold it straight.

It was quite a scene—five NFL athletes playing Twister in their jock straps with a four-eyed white guy, surrounded by empty Coke cans, orange peels, Snickers wrappers, and sticky noodles of white tape. Henley's spell soon passed, but not because of Anderson. After that, Henley would cut a wide swath around the trainer and joke about how he had survived Anderson's homicide attempt. Anderson mounted the oar on the locker room wall to commemorate "the day he saved Darryl Henley's life."

Unlike his football equipment, the oar was still there when Henley dropped by Rams Park. When Anderson spotted him, he lowered his eyes, unsure of how to approach the beleaguered player. Darryl walked around him, as if in fear for his health, and the resulting laughter inside the locker room eased the tension and assured everyone that the old Darryl was indeed back, if only for a day.

According to league rules, Henley could not practice with the team, so he lifted weights and stayed after practice to do footwork drills with Joe Vitt. That too brought back memories. During the 1992 training camp, shortly after Vitt and Rod Perry were hired, Henley had been sidelined by a bad knee. Because they had never seen him practice and knew nothing of his work ethic, Vitt and Perry made a point of it to compliment the corners who *were* practicing, especially second-year man Todd Lyght, of whom much was expected. Henley, sitting on the sideline with an ice pack on his knee, was already miffed that the team had selected cornerback Steve Israel in the most recent draft. Now, as he watched Perry praise Lyght ("Man, look at those feet!") just loud enough for Darryl to hear, knowing that quick feet were what *Henley* was known for — Henley seethed. When Vitt walked up, clapped Perry on the back, and nodded approvingly at Lyght's blurry cleats, Henley made himself a promise.

The next morning, Flipper Anderson arrived at work to find the hobbled Henley alone, pulling on his pads. "Awwww shit, y'all done it now," Anderson said. "Go get 'em, D!" One of Henley's best practices as a pro followed. He stayed in Anderson's and Ellard's hip pockets all morning, batting down or picking off nearly every pass that came his way. When the final whistle blew, Henley limped off the field and told a grinning Knox that he would be unavailable for the afternoon session. Then he glanced across the field at Joe Vitt.

"All right, he can play," Vitt whispered to defensive backs Mike Stewart and Clifford Hicks, who were standing next to Vitt, helmets on their hips.

"That's what we've been fucking telling you!" Hicks said.

A year after that day, as Darryl went through drills with Vitt for the first time since the world began considering him a drug dealer ("emerging from two weeks of seclusion," the papers said), he thought back to the day he earned Vitt's trust, his respect. Over time, a special relationship had formed between Henley, Vitt, and Perry—a bond that had made Vitt and Perry the first people Henley contacted when things broke bad in Atlanta on July 15. Henley also thought about Flipper Anderson. Flip had seemed like more than just a football friend that day.

"People who know me, believe me," Darryl told the media before he left Rams Park. "And people who don't, [they] believe what they read. I'm not afraid of this. . . . Everything you guys printed . . . I'm not going to say anything. I take that [stuff] on the chin, and when it's time for me to do something, it'll be when it counts, not now."

The following day, the Rams informed Henley that league rules prohibited him from working out at Rams Park, even by himself. He was politely asked to stay away. Henley obeyed. Then he read in the paper that Anthony Newman's wife had told the press that Tracy couldn't have done this alone, that Darryl must have put her up to it. Henley called Newman several times seeking an explanation, but Newman didn't answer. So Henley drove to Rams Park, found Newman in the locker room, and invited him into the hallway. He asked Newman—who was five inches taller and fifty pounds heavier than he was—if he remembered the time Newman's father, a policeman, fatally shot someone, an incident that had left Newman severely shaken. "Whose house did you come over to that day?" Henley asked. "You sat there on my couch and literally cried on my shoulder. And now your wife is going around hollering about I'm a drug dealer?"

Newman apologized on his wife's behalf. Darryl accepted. It was all he wanted.

Newman's trademark temper must have flared in the Rams' parking lot, though, because when he returned to the locker room moments later, Darryl could tell that it wasn't because he had forgotten something. "Ain't nobody going to disrespect my wife!" Newman yelled into Henley's face. "I don't give a fuck *what* she said."

"I'm not gonna fight you," Darryl replied, calmly reaching into the back of his pants for the new 9mm Woolsey had given him. "I'll just put a bullet in your ass."

The conflict was quickly defused by cooler-headed teammates, but the memory was seared as permanently into Newman's mind as Henley's. "I was sticking up for my wife," Newman recalled years later. "*I was so mad.* I told him, 'She didn't say that!' I asked my wife about it later and she said, 'I just can't see Tracy doing that.'"[3]

That Henley and Newman immediately put their confrontation behind them was a reflection of the way professional defensive backs are trained. *Forget the last play, focus on the next one, and most important, stick together.* If anything, Henley and Newman would grow closer over the next year, a time when Darryl would need every friend he had. ·

Chapter 17

Some friends Henley did not need. Not in
the long run. He did not need the friendship that former Ram receiver Ron Brown
rekindled in late October when he told Darryl, "You should holler at Suge. He's been
trying to find you."

Darryl had remained friends with Marion "Suge" Knight since the defensive tackle's
release from the Rams in 1989, after which
Knight had returned to his job as a celebrity
bodyguard — a role that he had either willed
or strong-armed into the one he filled in 1993:
head of Death Row Records, the most lucrative rap label in music history.

When Darryl followed up on Brown's invi-
tation and walked into the Death Row offices
on Wilshire Boulevard, he chuckled knowingly at the red décor. The carpet, the walls,
the furniture, even the clocks, everything
was the color of blood, or rather, the Bloods
street gang that Suge held dear. Upon seeing

Henley, Knight embraced him with all of his three hundred pounds. Over the next hour or two, the record mogul offered his moral and financial support and encouraged Henley to fight the system at whatever cost. Knight also offered to introduce Henley to his personal attorney, David Kenner, who had helped Knight out of numerous legal scrapes over the years (and was at the time defending Snoop Dogg on the homicide charge that would inspire his hit "Murder Was the Case").

A short, tanned man with jet black hair, Kenner preferred silk suits over the worsted wool worn by lawyers like Gerry Chaleff. When Darryl met him, rumors were swirling that Kenner had helped finance Death Row's beginnings by forging a deal between Suge Knight and Michael "Harry O" Harris—the so-called Gang Godfather of South Central—in the visiting room of a downtown prison where Harry O had been locked up at the time. That story made Darryl harken back to his first training camp, when Suge had pitched him his idea for a record company. Had Henley invested in Death Row Records back then, he might have been able to afford David Kenner four years later. "I took one look at him," Henley said, "and I thought, 'This dude's going to jail right behind me.'"

Although he declined his lawyer's services, Henley's relationship with Suge Knight deepened in the fall of 1993, a time when his drug case was undergoing a bit of a lull. Both sides were gathering information, the courtrooms were dark, the newspapers quiet. It's debatable how wise it was for Henley to associate with a man of Knight's reputation while his own future hung in the balance. Henley's explanation years later was that he had a lot of time on his hands and a chance to step into the highest level of an arena he had always been interested in: the music business. The man behind one of the most successful labels in the world literally gave him the keys to the place.

Henley and Knight hatched a plan to improve Death Row's negative public image by creating community-minded relationships between Death Row and corporations. Again, the practicality of the idea in light of Darryl's legal trouble was up for debate, but Henley planned on staying behind the scenes, and Knight was the first to remind him that his criminal record had exactly zero arrests and zero convictions on it. They formed what they called Death Row Inner City Out Reach, or DRICOR. (Knight had wanted to call it DRICOP [Death Row Inner City Outreach Program] to make it more law enforcement–friendly, but Darryl considered that a bit much, seeing as how Dr. Dre — one of Knight's artists — had once made a record called "Fuck Tha Police.")

Darryl's main reason for hanging around Suge Knight, however, was much simpler and less philanthropic: security. Physical protection was how Suge had started out in the business, and his belief in the importance of bodyguards was made obvious by the team of thick-bodied silent types he kept around him in public. Henley's life was still at risk, even with Bustamante in custody. He knew that Bustamante probably had soldiers on the street intent on collecting Darryl's debt, one way or another. Being associated with the notoriously unpredictable Knight, ironically enough, made Darryl feel safe.

Suge Knight was a man of contradictions. The week before Henley's case hit the press, Knight was charged with pistol-whipping two aspiring rappers in a recording studio. He honored his mother each year by hosting an annual Mother's Day celebration that filled a Beverly Hills hotel with struggling single moms. (Knight's mother gave him his nickname as a baby because he was "sweet as sugar.") Knight loved the Bloods, yet he donated $500,000 to an antigang program in South Central. Well aware of Darryl's distaste for drugs, Knight asked those around the Death Row offices to reduce their marijuana intake when Henley was on the premises. Even Darryl was surprised by that one. "The Suge that I met was good," remembered Eric Henley. "There was nothing wrong with Darryl befriending Suge. Suge was cool. But when Suge started doing the things that he went on to do, Darryl should have backed off."

One day Suge asked Darryl to go for a ride. Twenty minutes into it, Henley still didn't know where they were going, even after they stopped at a Foot Locker to buy Henley a pair of cleats. Aiming his BMW west on Sunset, Knight drove until land gave way to sea and until Darryl spotted Ron Brown standing alone on a grass field at Palisades Park, tossing a football around.

"Yo, D, I want you to meet somebody," Suge said.

Darryl rose from tying his cleats and found himself shaking hands with John F. Kennedy Jr., right there in the parking lot. "Marion told me what's going on, and I just want to wish you luck," Kennedy said. Next thing Darryl knew, he was watching Suge play tackle football with the son of the thirty-fifth president and a handful of other guys, including a fifty-year-old white guy who he would later learn was Jimmy Iovine, head of Interscope Records. Someone's wife had brought a picnic basket. Darryl and Ron ran a few routes by themselves, near a gaggle of kids playing tag in the corner.

Afterward, the men gathered in the parking lot, where Darryl overheard Iovine telling Suge: "You gotta hurry up. This record is costing us millions!" Knight told Iovine, Death Row's distributor, to calm down and handed him a tape, which Iovine slid into the dash of his Grand Cherokee. A beat thundered from its speakers, followed by a calm voice:

With so much drama in the L-B-C
it's kinda hard bein' Snoop D-O double-G.
But I, somehow some way,
keep comin' up with funky ass shit like every single day.

According to Darryl Henley, the first time he heard Snoop Dogg's ghetto anthem "Gin and Juice" — the first time *anyone* heard it — he was standing in the parking lot at Palisades Park, watching Kennedy bob his head like he was from Compton. "Yeah, this is it right here, Suge," Kennedy said. "This is it."

Before Kennedy left, he told Darryl: "Marion knows how to get in touch with me. If you need anything, let me know."

"Thanks," Darryl said. ("Inside, I was screaming, '*Hell yeah, I need you! Right now!*'" Henley said later.)

"Man, that's the closest I'll ever get to a Kennedy," he told Knight. "Dude said he could help me out. You gotta hook that up." But either Knight dropped the ball or Kennedy got cold feet, because Darryl soon stopped asking Knight about it. And yes, the thought did cross Henley's mind that Death Row's start-up money had come from sources even more surprising than the Gang Godfather of South Central.

On October 28, 1993, two days before Darryl's twenty-seventh birthday, his parents and two brothers testified before the grand jury in Orange County. The questions asked by assistant U.S. attorney Deirdre Eliot that day followed a similar pattern for each witness. Eliot asked what they knew about the Rams Park incident, about the visit "Frank" and "Julio" had paid to their home on September 15, about the ensuing extortion calls, and about Darryl's associations with Willie McGowan, Eric Manning, and "G." Henley's family told the grand jury that they didn't know much because they had been kept in the dark by Darryl's attorneys. His present location was a well-guarded secret, they testified. Eliot openly suspected them of lying. This was their way of hiding both the truth and Henley's whereabouts, she thought. She didn't buy Mr. Henley's contention that he had no way to reach his son — not even a phone number. "If I knew [how to reach him]," T.H. explained, "then someone else would know, and his life is still in danger."

"I see," Eliot said. "Why is his life still in danger?"

"Because how [do] I know that these people that you supposedly got locked up [Bustamante and Cuevas] don't have people on the outside?"

"I see."

"We don't know that . . . and the number one concern as far as my son is concerned is safety. And I agree with him 100 percent [about concealing his location]. I mean, you guys never lifted a hand to do it, as far as his health is concerned."

"Pardon me?"

"I mean, I'm talking security-wise. You asked me why, and I'm telling you the reason why. My life is still not safe. You know, they could come up—they know where I live. You know, they've been there. My life is still in danger."

"And throughout all of this," Eliot countered, "even though you still feel that your family is in danger, you've never asked your son why this is happening?"

"No. I'm telling you, the communication between me and my son is very, very limited."

"Okay."

"*Very* limited."

Darryl's brother Thomas told the grand jury that he had never asked Darryl what all this was about.

"The family has decided that [it's in their] best interest to remain ignorant about anything that's going on so that if you are questioned before the grand jury you don't have anything to say, is that right?" Eliot said.

"I wouldn't say that," Thomas said.

Years later, Thomas said, "She made it sound like, 'It's crazy that you wouldn't ask your brother about this.' And I didn't say this to her, because I wasn't thinking, but I should have said, 'If you came home and found that your daughter was raped, knowing your daughter, would you ask her, "What did you do to entice the guy?"' I know what kind of character Darryl has, so for me to go and ask him, 'Why did you do this?' in my mind, it wasn't relevant. . . . I knew who he was, and no one in the newspaper and no one outside of our family can dictate to me who my brothers are and what kind of characters they have. So I never felt compelled to ask any questions like that. It was something that we obviously talked about, but never in a 'How could anything like this happen?' kind of way.

"She was so baffled that I just didn't know [the answers to her questions]. I'm sure she thought I was just not being forthcoming. I mean, she asked a few questions that I just *did not know.*"

The tone of Eliot's questioning became, at best, unprofessional and, at worst, antagonistic. But there were no defense attorneys present to object.

"Do you know any of the girls Darryl dates or has dated in the past?" she asked Thomas.

"I know several of the girls he's dated in the past, but that's a long past."

"I'm sure it is," Eliot replied.

"I knew she was trying to get confrontational," Thomas recalled. "I wouldn't go down that path with her. I had never been exposed to any of this stuff before, but just the whole way it was set up, it forces the person being questioned to be on the defensive. And I can see how if you allow something to get to you, you can get flustered, you can get offensive, and potentially belligerent. And I was not going to let that happen."

When Eliot asked for Darryl's phone number, Thomas asked to speak with an attorney. Eliot informed him that although he was allowed to leave the room to consult with a lawyer, the only way he could withhold information was if he felt that it might incriminate him. So Thomas asked to plead the Fifth. Eliot replied, You can only plead the Fifth to protect yourself, not your brother.

It was a crisp illustration of the unique challenges within the grand jury setting. Thomas wanted to protect his brother, whose life was indeed still in danger, and he wanted to talk to a lawyer about it. "Plus there were a lot of other issues taking place at that time," he said later. "You had two guys who showed up at the house when I was there. And the information I got was that these were pretty serious guys. And then I come to find out that one of them [Cuevas] was actually working with the government. . . . We had asked for some level of protection, and the government was completely averse to [protecting] anything. So yeah, it doesn't surprise me at all that I didn't want to answer those questions. She said, 'Well, you *have* to answer.' My position was—and I don't know the legal process at all—but I was thinking, 'I don't *have* to do anything.'"

The Rams would have struggled even if Henley were playing, but losing their best cover corner certainly didn't help. On Halloween, Darryl watched his teammates get crushed by the 49ers, 40–17. It was their fourth straight loss, dropping their record to 2-6. The team was no longer spinning out of control; by midseason they had careened off the road and wrapped themselves around a telephone pole. Within months they would leave California, hobbled and humbled—the first team in NFL history to relocate from west to east. Three days after the loss to the 49ers, the DEA reported that they had recovered a vacuum bag from the Brea home of the Rams' beleaguered cornerback and tested it for traces of cocaine. It came up negative.

The second time Suge Knight asked Darryl to go for a ride, they ended up in Las Vegas to watch Evander Holyfield and Riddick Bowe fight for the heavyweight title. Darryl didn't ride in Suge's BMW this time, but in a tricked out Dooley-style pickup that was part of the Death Row caravan. Traveling with him were Suge's resident deejay and distribution supervisor—a man named Black—and a young, athletic-looking guy whose name Darryl didn't catch. The athletic guy drove while Darryl and Black talked. When Black dropped Ron Brown's name into the conversation, Darryl chuckled and told him how he preferred to call Ron "Con" because of the defective Mercedes he had bought from Brown when Darryl was just a rookie. That story made the guy at the wheel chuckle, and the instant he did, Darryl recognized him.

He had to rewind a year or so, to the dispute between Henley and Brown over the bad Mercedes. That day Darryl found himself paying more attention to the two men Brown brought with him than to Brown himself. Both were over six feet tall and wore scowls and gun-shaped lumps under their armpits.

"That was me," the driver of the Dooley said as Darryl recounted the story. "Me and my brother Donald."

And that's how Darryl met Suge's cousin Ronald Knight, who would become one of the most influential people in his life, for better or for worse, depending yet again on who was telling the story.

Ronald and Donald Knight were fraternal twins whose only physical resemblance to one another was their deep brown skin.[1] The unbreakable bond that was about to form between Ronald and Darryl Henley was best described by Kym Taylor, who was still sheltering Darryl, both literally and figuratively. "I waited on Darryl hand and foot," Kym recalled. "Then Ron came by and I didn't see Darryl at all. He was always at the Death Row office or with Ron. I had more competition from Ron than I did from other women."

When Kym asked Darryl what Ron did for a living, Darryl told her he was a probation officer. Kym didn't buy it, but it was the truth. (At least for a few more months it was, until Steven Kinney alerted Ron's bosses to the marijuana arrest on his record, which got Ron fired and sparked a hatred between Knight and Kinney that would one day result in courthouse fisticuffs.) As he drove Darryl to Las Vegas for the title fight, Ron Knight was indeed a law enforcement officer, legally armed with a pistol holstered to his ribs. As it turned out, he had also played football against Darryl in college.

Where'd you play? Henley asked, stunned.

Long Beach State, Ron said. We played y'all in '86.

Ron had been a starting linebacker that year, and although Darryl didn't remember him, he remembered the game like it was yesterday. It was a lopsided UCLA win that might have been worse had Long Beach not rushed its punt team onto the field at each fourth down to prevent the Bruins' All-American punt returner from setting up. "I had to make seven fair catches that night," Darryl told Ron. "I hate fair catches."

By the time the opening bell sounded, Suge Knight had bet $30,000 on the fight's outcome and had dropped at least that much in the casinos. Darryl and Ron had ridden a run of luck at the roulette tables that netted Henley $10,000. The fight itself turned out to be epic. Not even the helmeted parachutist who tumbled into the ring in the seventh round (sparking a melee that delayed the bout twenty minutes) could dampen the electricity. Seated near ringside, Henley watched Holyfield win a grueling decision over Bowe to regain the belt that Bowe had taken from him a year earlier.

It was fitting that the highlight of Darryl's relationship with Death Row Records was a bloody, twelve-round prizefight. Although physical violence was not as common at Death Row as the media would make it seem, the intensity of it when it occurred is what remained with Darryl a decade later. As often as Death Row's walls shook with sounds destined for the Billboard charts, they trembled too often for Henley's liking because an assault was taking place in the next room. Henley left Death Row not because of the violence but because of the constant threat of it. He noticed that the staff at Interscope Records — Jimmy Iovine's company, usually stayed locked inside their part of the building from nine to five, then rushed to their cars at quitting time. Henley began steering clear of Death Row himself. When he *was* there, he leapt at opportunities to leave, like the time he offered to deliver a box of promotional material to a bad neighborhood and invited Heron — Suge's top bodyguard — to come along.

It was a crisp autumn day, so Henley dropped the top on his convertible Mercedes. Heron seemed to like the open air at first, but as they neared their destination, Darryl noticed him sinking deeper into his seat. Henley realized why when he began noticing youths on the sidewalks wearing navy bandanas, Dodger jerseys, and Rams caps. This was a Crip neighborhood, where blue meant you could roam undisturbed, and red meant you stood to get "run up on." Heron was wearing black, but the people on the sidewalks didn't need a color to recognize him. They knew Suge Knight's 250-pound bodyguard by face.

Henley parked outside a storefront. He asked Heron to come inside with him, but Heron shook his cinderblock-size head and said in his deep voice, "I'm gon' stay in the ride, nigga." When Darryl walked inside to make the delivery, he was greeted by three frowning young black men.

"What you doing bringing that Slob around here, nigga?" they asked (Slob being a derogatory term for Blood). Darryl put the box down and left. By the time he arrived back at Death Row, Suge had heard about it.

"You can't just run off and drive over there," he said. "You're playing with your life."

The last straw came on a Friday at the close of business, when Darryl, Suge, and Heron stood waiting for the elevator. When the doors opened, two black men whose size indicated potential as NFL linemen, walked out. It was the only time Darryl ever saw Suge Knight worried.

"We need to see you," one of the men told Knight.

"You caught me at a bad time, homey. I'm just about to—"

"We need to see you *now*."

They brushed past Knight and entered his office. Knight and Heron followed reluctantly. Darryl waited by the elevators. He heard a loud argument in Knight's office that got louder. He heard the sound of furniture moving and large men efforting against each other. Suddenly the noise stopped, and the two visitors walked out, their clothes unruffled, and pushed the elevator button. Only after the elevator came and went did Knight and Heron emerge from the office, looking just as calm but slightly more rumpled than their guests. They got in the elevator with Henley. No one spoke. In fact, Henley didn't mention the incident to anyone for more than three years. (When he finally did mention it, he was in prison, and the man he mentioned it to was the man who had sent those two enforcers to Knight's office that day.)

After that, Darryl knew that his days at Death Row Records were numbered. For all the comparisons between Suge Knight's record company and organized crime, it was true that in the mid-1990s, leaving Death Row was like leaving the Mob. The place held a lot of secrets. Suge trusted Darryl, however, and he understood his need to leave. They were both disappointed that the "DRICOR" idea had never gotten off the ground, but they parted as friends or, rather, with as much of a friendship as Knight and Henley allowed themselves to have at that turbulent time. As a going-away gift, Knight introduced Henley to another attorney he knew, a guy named Johnnie Cochran.

The soon-to-be-world-famous Cochran had a lot in common with the young athlete about to retain him. Cochran's roots were in the South (his father had fled the Louisiana sharecropping life in favor of Los Angeles); he and Henley were UCLA alumni and members of one of the "Original Eight" black fraternities; neither man was a fan of the local authorities, Cochran having built a reputation over the years for blowing the whistle on LAPD misconduct, including the suspicious murder of Ron Settles (who, like O.J. Simpson, had been a local college running back) and the conviction of former Black Panther Geronimo Pratt for murder.

Like most people who met Henley, Cochran liked him immediately. More important, Henley's case intrigued him. Cochran found the disparity between Henley's open, polite manner and the sordid details of his cocaine case irreconcilable. Henley, in turn, liked Cochran and gave him a $100,000 retainer. Unfortunately for Henley, another case involving a local football hero was about to send Cochran, his services, and the attention of the civilized world elsewhere.

Chapter 18

For all his street bravado, and despite his ponytail, DEA special agent Steven Kinney made an excellent grand jury witness. He knew when to use phrases like *It was my understanding that* and *I have received information that*—wordplay that implied fact but swerved just clear of it. Kinney was confident on the stand. His answers were short yet thorough, his vocabulary was plain, and his testimony moved along swiftly.

Dorothy Henley, on the other hand, was a difficult grand jury witness. She made it obvious that she trusted neither the prosecutors nor the court. She was evasive in the face of questioning and was so openly protective of her son that her flattering testimony about him carried little weight. Her growing disbelief over the blindness of the jurors and the corruption of this whole thing alienated the grand jury even more. She admitted years later that she'd been trying to take care of Darryl the best way she knew how, but objective readers of the transcript agreed that her testimony probably harmed Darryl more than it helped. When asked if she was familiar with the name Tracy Donaho, Mrs. Henley testified: "No, I'm not. . . . My sons don't date white girls. They don't have white girlfriends if that's what you're consider[ing]."

The man asking the questions that day was assistant U.S. attorney John Rayburn, a handsome, aggressive thirty-three-year-old who had joined forces with Deirdre Eliot. When Rayburn asked Mrs. Henley if she had ever questioned Darryl about "why these people wanted $360,000 from him," Mrs. Henley said no. "And the reason is because I don't believe it," she added. "Because my son doesn't deal with drugs. He doesn't smoke, he doesn't drink, he doesn't deal drugs. And for—and to say that this is involving drugs, I don't believe that. . . . You have destroyed his credibility. You have destroyed his values, his beliefs, and his biblical principles, and there is no way I believe, you know, all of this—the charges that you are bringing against him. I say he goes out and speaks to junior high, elementary kids . . . high school kids, talking to them about saying no to drugs. And all of a sudden his values and his belief[s have] been destroyed by the charges that you are trying—the DEA is trying to bring against him."

Rayburn asked if she had ever spoken with Darryl about those charges.

"No. I didn't have to, because I don't believe it."

A grand juror stepped in: "It seems that—you seem to be based more on your belief than [on] find[ing] out more about the facts. . . . Are you willing to find the truth?"

"I'm willing to find the truth, and I know what the truth is."

Darryl Henley was indicted that afternoon on federal cocaine charges, along with Tracy Donaho, Willie McGowan, Rafael Bustamante, and Garey West. Each faced a mandatory minimum ten years in prison. Darryl turned himself in at the federal courthouse the following morning and was arraigned and released on $200,000 bond. DEA agents Steven Kinney and Kevin McLaughlin attended his first court appearance, where McLaughlin, still furious that Tracy had been indicted along with Henley and the others, sat in the front row so he could lean forward and whisper to the athlete: You know we're going to get you, right?

Darryl turned and replied (accurately, as it turned out): "I know you're gonna watch me walk out of here in about a half hour."

When the hearing ended, McLaughlin's partner, Special Agent Brian Sullivan, asked Darryl for a moment alone. Henley's counsel relented based on Sullivan's experience and professionalism. (His DEA tenure was longer than Kinney's and McLaughlin's combined, not counting his years as a cop in Washington DC.) Sullivan spoke openly with Henley:

Y'know we still don't have a lot on you, he said. You might win at trial, but you might not. This *is* Orange County.

Just in case Henley hadn't understood him, Sullivan drew closer and spoke softer: If you lose at trial, Darryl, you're gonna lose ten years off your life. Maybe twenty. You can make this thing go away if you work with us. I know how bad that sounds, but believe me, this is just going to get messier and messier.

No, thanks, Darryl said.

At that moment, something in Sullivan turned. "He was grinning, thinking this was gonna be a cakewalk," Sullivan said years later. "I told him, 'I'm gonna wipe that smile off your face.'"

Kinney recalled that in the days following Henley's indictment he "begged Darryl" to cooperate. "I told him I didn't think he was the leader," Kinney wrote in a 2005 letter. "I actually thought he'd been used by Willie McGowan. But he wouldn't budge. . . . He laughed at me."

Suge Knight insisted on paying Henley's $200,000 bond. Henley fought him on it, but Knight didn't lose many battles of will. Save your money, Knight told him. You're gonna need it, believe me.

As if on cue, that morning's *Register* featured a quarter-page graphic titled "Tangled Web of Drugs and Death," which included a map of the Henley case's important sites, a timeline of events, and photos of the eight alleged participants. Henley's photo was on top, positioned ominously next to that of Eric Manning, "found shot to death Sept. 9." The court of public opinion was in session.

Two important developments occurred around Thanksgiving. The first was the assignment of Rayburn to the prosecution team. The second, likely related to the first, was that Tracy Donaho hired herself a defense attorney.

Stephan DeSales had been friends with Tracy's father for years, and his hiring was no small event. After all, Tracy had cooperated with the authorities over the previous four months, walking them through every detail of the conspiracy as she knew it—identifying faces, houses, restaurants, and hotels, placing staged phone calls on their behalf—so the hiring of a defense attorney was an abrupt about-face. Her cooperation with the DEA had been her father's way of asking the government for mercy when it came time for her sentencing. By Halloween, though, the rules had changed, and Tracy and her family wanted out. This whole "CI" thing was more complicated than they'd thought.

It didn't sink in for Terry Donaho until just before he hired DeSales that Tracy could really be sentenced to prison. Sure, she might have her "mandatory" ten-year sentence knocked down a bit by a sympathetic judge, but by how much? Could he trust Eliot and Rayburn's promises of leniency? All they could do was *recommend* a lesser sentence to the judge, but the judge—whoever that might be—would have the final say.

So Tracy's dad got cold feet. In October and November, Tracy had had no contact with the DEA whatsoever, and as the holidays approached she seriously considered standing trial with her four codefendants. Her new attorney, and the weighty questions he asked her, prevented that.

*Will a jury believe that you flew to Atlanta with Willie and Eric
in the middle of the night so you could deliver "real estate money"?
What will these suburban jurors think about you delivering a suitcase
to the apartment of a former gangbanger and drug dealer? Can the
jury get past the fact that you're the only defendant who was caught
holding twenty-five pounds of cocaine?* In the end, Tracy and her father decided not to risk it. On December 1, she signed an agreement to plead guilty and testify for the government at trial. (The
plea agreement also acknowledged that she had been "a member
of the conspiracy knowing that its object was to distribute a controlled substance"—an admission she would later contradict on
the witness stand.) Five days after she submitted this guilty plea,
Tracy switched back to *not* guilty—in essence tearing up the plea
agreement. A bondsman forked over her $25,000 bail, then Terry
escorted Tracy out of the courthouse, where she fainted into his
arms moments after DeSales described her role in the conspiracy
to the media as that of "a young, impressionable, star-struck girl
who got caught up in the excitement of the situation."

Two weeks later she changed her mind again, changing her
plea back to guilty. She was on the government's team for good
now, seated before U.S. district court judge Gary L. Taylor—the
man who would preside over the trial—wearing the beaten look
of a woman who had been promised a decade behind bars if she
took this to trial. The prosecutors had been primed and ready to
attack Tracy's "I thought I was carrying money" alibi. But with
Tracy back on their side again, their task would be to stand behind it and make a jury believe it.

A fit, good-looking, white-haired man who had just turned fifty-
five, Gary L. Taylor was precisely the kind of judge that Henley's
defense team did not want on the bench. His slim, kind face, dom-
inated by large, square-rim glasses, had frowned many times over
the years at top-dollar Angeleno hotshots like Roger Cossack and

Gerry Chaleff. Taylor was unapologetically both conservative and Republican—a third-generation Orange Countian who had been raised in the heart of that right-wing stronghold. He'd been appointed to the state bench by a Republican governor in 1986 and elevated to federal status by a personal phone call from President George H. W. Bush himself. Years later he would be instrumental in helping build the Ronald Reagan United States Courthouse, "on almost the exact site," the *Times* reported, as the movie theater Taylor had frequented as a boy.

Taylor was inexperienced with drug cases. He had practiced business law in Newport Beach for twenty years before becoming a state judge, and prior to that his only experience with criminal law had come during his stint as an army lawyer in the 1960s. He was well liked among his fellow jurists, however, and respected by prosecutors, although pockets of defense lawyers (being pockets of defense lawyers) grumbled about what they saw as his pro-prosecution slant. Try as they might, though, no one could muster dislike for a man who enjoyed his job so much that he came to work whistling each day, a judge the *LA Times* once called "the voice of calm humanity," a pillar of the community who hosted an annual mock trial competition among area high schools, a self-proclaimed "cheerleader for the legal profession" who told anyone who asked that he had the greatest job in the world. Judge Taylor was by all accounts a good man, which made what was about to happen in his courtroom even more confounding.

One explanation might have been that John Rayburn had once been Taylor's clerk. Now Rayburn was standing behind the prosecutors' table in Taylor's courtroom, trying to send a high-profile defendant to prison.

Rayburn didn't look much different in 1993 than he looked in the 1978 Damien High School yearbook.[1] He and Henley played football within five years of each other at that suburban parochial school, which graduated fewer than two hundred students each year—a coincidence that moved the Henley family to suspect that

Rayburn had been assigned to the case because of Deirdre Eliot's inability to "dig up dirt" on Darryl. Surely a Damien boy would know where to look. This conspiracy theory sounded far-fetched until the Henleys learned that Rayburn had also spent nearly a year clerking for Judge Taylor. After that, they felt they had reason to watch things very closely indeed. [2]

With Henley finally under indictment, Rayburn and Eliot's new task was to pressure him into pleading guilty. They privately offered him five years in prison in exchange for his guilty plea. It wasn't an unexpected offer; about 80 percent of federal criminal cases were settled this way. And Darryl might have taken the deal if he had been given the option of pleading *only* to the Memphis suitcase. But the prosecutors felt sure they could prove his involvement with the twelve kilos in Atlanta as well. So faced with the choice of pleading guilty to both deliveries or neither, Darryl chose neither and continued preparing for trial.

He could not have known how strongly the government would react to his decision to stand trial, how deeply they would dig their trenches, how fully they would load their weapons, and how unflinchingly they would fire them. DEA agent Brian Sullivan had warned Henley that federal drug cases could be ugly things, especially with a wealthy defendant involved. There had already been challenges and taunts issued, but they were merely the first jabs in what would become a bloody four-year war whose final death blow no one could have foreseen back then, during those last days of 1993. From this point on, the prosecution would pull no punches, and they expected the same from the defense.

"He was being portrayed as Pablo Escobar," said attorney Jerome Stanley, a sports agent and intermittent advisor to Henley. "Darryl got bad advice from his lawyers, it's that simple. . . . Someone should have sat him down and said, 'Darryl, we've got a problem. We need to stop the bleeding, because you can bleed to death.'

And that's exactly what happened. It just bled, and bled, and metastasized, and grew."

As a condition of his bond, Henley was required to live at his parents' home in Upland. Defense investigator Ted Woolsey didn't like that at all, noting in a memo to Chaleff that the news had been "printed in the newspaper; the world knows where Darryl is sleeping. If anybody wants to get to Darryl, all they have to do is go to the Upland house, during the night, and Darryl will be there." Woolsey theorized that Bustamante, "the suspected killer of Eric Manning . . . [could] have his operatives put the pressure on Darryl again now that he knows where Darryl is sleeping." Bustamante's brothers lived near the Henleys, Woolsey noted, "very convenient to do a drive-by. . . . The government has set Darryl up for his execution."

Darryl never spent another night at his parents' home. Over the next year, he would hopscotch between hotels and friends' residences, usually relocating at night.

He was at Ron Knight's house the day the Rams were beaten by the 1-12 Bengals. It was one of the ugliest games of that NFL season. The Bengals' soon-to-be-cut quarterback, David Klingler, passed for a career-high 223 yards, in forty-degree weather, against a Rams secondary that included a recently unemployed man named Dexter Davis at the position Henley usually played. Todd Lyght had wrecked his knee during pregame warm-ups Thanksgiving weekend, and Robert Bailey had a knee injury of his own, so the Rams were literally hiring cornerbacks off the street. They would end up starting six players at Henley's position who *hadn't even been on the roster* back in September. Knox called it the worst spate of injuries he'd seen in his thirty-one years in the league.

There had been merrier Christmases at the Henley house. As everyone was opening gifts, and as Darryl's mother came up behind him and whispered that she loved him, something she'd told him practically every time they shared the same space, he noticed that she wasn't looking him in the eye as often as she used to. It was as if she couldn't bear to see the pain he was in. It was a long-standing family joke that an invisible nerve ran between Dot and Darryl. When Darryl was happy, she was ecstatic. When he was in pain, she was inconsolable. The day after Christmas, Darryl and Ron drove to Anaheim and watched the Rams get pummeled by the lowly Browns, 42–14, in front of the smallest crowd to see a Rams home game in thirty years. Afterward, Eric Metcalf told Darryl that the Browns needn't have bothered with the loudspeakers they'd used during practice to simulate crowd noise. "It was so quiet I could hear what was going on in your huddle," Metcalf said. Browns quarterback Vinny Testaverde set an NFL record by completing 91 percent of his passes that day, against a defense that Shane Conlan called "pathetic." One Cleveland coach called the Rams the worst team he had seen in two years.

Two years. If only Darryl could travel back that far. He would have been happy to play for the team that was worse than the 1993 Rams. He would have been happy, and his mother would have been ecstatic, and he would have run from the Willie McGowans and Eric Mannings and Garey Wests of the world as soon as he sensed them nearby.

Football had been his refuge from this mess, but now he had no escape except his confidence that he would be acquitted, an idea that would become more delusional with each passing day. The trial would be held in Orange County—a Klan hotspot since the 1920s, a place that Judge Taylor, the whitest white man he had ever seen, once called "the garden spot of Nixonia." A Barbie doll from nearby Yorba Linda (Nixon's hometown) would be the star witness against Henley, whose lead counsel, Gerry Chaleff, had never tried a federal case before. Chaleff would be going against a charismatic "Damien boy" prosecutor who had once clerked for the judge. Henley would have many more reasons to doubt the justice system by the time his trial was over, but the sense of foreboding he felt that Christmas made for an early start.

Chapter 19

The sun was out, but the freeway was empty. Not a car in sight, like the end of the world. Darryl Henley and Ron Knight were standing at the edge of the 91 Freeway with hundreds of other Angelenos, waiting to see in person what they had seen on television moments earlier: a white Ford Bronco cruising north out of Orange County, trailed by cop cars. Of all the emotions swirling around them, though, Henley was likely the only person there who was feeling relief. Relief that the life of some other hometown football hero was unraveling, for the Bronco chase meant that O.J. had done it. The NFL-legend-turned-actor had cut his ex-wife's throat and stabbed her friend to death in her front yard in Brentwood five days earlier, and now he was on the run. Henley wasn't proud to admit it, but the load on his shoulders somehow felt lighter.

He and Ron had planned on working out

at the Compton College weight room that day, but when they saw game five of the NBA Finals preempted on TV in favor of the Bronco chase, they hurried down the street to the 91, which cut through Compton like a belt lying on a pile of laundry, and watched the traffic go from thick, to sparse, to nothing. And here it came, headed due west now, toward the ocean. The white Bronco was so close Darryl could reach out and touch it. The spectators around him began shouting, "Run O.J., run!" and "Free the Juice!" as the Bronco continued on the path that would one day lead to Simpson's acquittal.

The man who would engineer that acquittal, Johnnie Cochran, had called Darryl a few days before the Brentwood murders to remove himself from Henley's defense team. "Gerry and I are two quarterbacks," Cochran had said politely, referring to Chaleff. "We would both want the ball in our hands at the crucial moments. It just wouldn't work." It would be fortuitous timing for Cochran, whose departure from the Henley team probably had more to do with his simultaneous defense of Michael Jackson (in a child-sex case) and Snoop Dogg (on his murder case) than his unwillingness to share limelight with Chaleff. However, Jackson and Snoop's cases were about to be swatted off the public radar by the alpha and omega of celebrity legal proceedings.

Gerry Chaleff had been in the running for a spot on Simpson's "Dream Team" of defense attorneys, but Simpson, who had been advised that his LA jury would probably be predominantly black, was motivated to hire a lawyer who shared his skin tone. Henley did not know yet the perils of standing trial in Orange County—the county that Simpson had fled in his Bronco that day. Its jury rules and racial topography had already guaranteed that Henley's jury would be a white one.

Nineteen ninety-four was a tumultuous year, and not just because of the Northridge earthquake that rocked Los Angeles. It was the year of Tonya Harding and Nancy Kerrigan, the year of the major league baseball strike. It was not a banner year for fairness, for 1994 was also the year that a congenial Colombian soccer player named Andrés Escobar was murdered shortly after he returned home from the World Cup in Los Angeles, where he had contributed to the Colombian team's elimination by mistakenly kicking the ball into his own goal.

Willie McGowan considered Darryl a fool for believing in such fictions as law and order. Willie was a fan of that old Richard Pryor skit in which Pryor said that justice meant "just us." He liked to point out what a joke the DEA was, and on this at least the facts bore him out. The agency that employed Steven Kinney and Kevin McLaughlin had revealed itself as a company rife with racial animus, bitter competition, and cancerous inner politics. Thomas Constantine had taken over as DEA chief in 1994, but according to a *U.S. News & World Report* story the following year, Constantine was loathed by his own agents, who had become distrustful of him and each other to the extent that they often tapped each other's phones. The DEA's head agents in Miami, Chicago, Atlanta, Los Angeles, Phoenix, and Houston all departed their posts in the mid-1990s, along with at least five others among the administration's brass. As *U.S. News* reported, "One agent in the Midwest said, '[M]orale here isn't just low, it's underground.'" This was the agency that had a photo of Darryl Henley tacked on the wall of its Southern California offices.

Because of his bond agreement, Henley had to ask permission to travel outside the five-county area that encircled Los Angeles. Although his request to attend the Super Bowl in Atlanta got no further than a chuckle at the prosecutors' desk, Henley *was* allowed to travel to Las Vegas — a surprising allowance that he would be granted even during his trial. He was returning home from Vegas in that spring of 1994, cruising west through the Mojave Desert, when his pager went off, displaying Angela Wallace's number. His cell phone was out of range, so he had to endure Wallace's repeated pages while driving across miles of cracked earth in search of a pay phone. Standing outside a McDonald's in Barstow, with eighteen-wheelers whooshing past, he learned that Willie had been arrested. The DEA had traced Willie's beeper and found him hiding out in San Diego.[1]

Not only had Steven Kinney traced Willie's beeper but he had made a duplicate of it, which enabled him to collect the phone numbers of McGowan's most trusted associates and prove that McGowan's relatives had been lying when they told Kinney they didn't know where he was. Kinney also learned that McGowan had an array of girlfriends aside from his main lady, Vicki, and that his male friends used a two-digit code when paging him—45, his old football number. Interesting as all this was, however, it had nothing to do with Willie's whereabouts, so McGowan remained as elusive to Kinney as he had been to all those high school linebackers in the 1980s. Until April, that is, when an informant told the DEA about Willie's plans to help a lady friend move from one San Diego apartment to another. On April 29, Kinney and a band of U.S. marshals followed McGowan to an apartment building in the North Park section of San Diego, where they made a quick and uneventful arrest. During the drive to jail, Kinney asked Willie why he had left LA. "We would have let you go [on bond] if you'd stayed put," Kinney allegedly said. "All we want is the football player."

Rex Henley had also left LA. He had been laid off from his job at Lockheed, and with his daughter on summer break in Texas and a big family wedding coming up in Waco, Rex had returned to his home state. A few days later he was indicted by an Orange County grand jury on drug trafficking charges.

With an arrest warrant for Rex in hand, Steven Kinney set about finding him. He knew Rex was in Texas, and he had a good idea what part, so he had a DEA secretary call Rex's father and identify herself as a Lockheed representative who wanted Rex to return to work. An excited aunt replied that Rex had gone out for ice cream with his daughter, but he would be right back.

Rex Henley wasn't shocked at the sight of helicopters hovering over his car that afternoon, nor at seeing the two sheriff cruisers in his rearview mirror. Rex's arrest, which came two months after Willie's, was just as plain. He knew why they were taking him in, but he had yet to realize the speed with which the case had gained momentum. Two DEA agents met him at the county jail in Texas and told him about the drug charges he was facing in California and the ten-year sentence attached to those charges. They offered to put Rex on the phone with prosecutor John Rayburn, right then and there, to discuss a guilty plea and a possible sentence reduction. Rex told the agents that he had already spoken with the government and had nothing more to say. [2]

Rex spent the next three weeks in holding cells all over Texas and Oklahoma, undergoing what was known as "diesel therapy"—a tactic intended to wear witnesses down with changing environs, impromptu van trips, and maddening uncertainty. The informants who were rotated in and out of Rex's cells were remarkably bad at doing what they had been asked to do. Some simply came right out with it ("So what happened with this Darryl thing?") while others never said a word, their eyes flitting to and away from Rex like a shy schoolboy at a dance. One morning Rex awoke to find his new cellmate peering down at him, their noses just inches apart. "What the hell's going on?" Rex said, shoving the guy away. A more experienced prisoner told Rex later that the guy had been waiting for Rex to say something in his sleep.

When he finally arrived in LA, Rex was placed in a small lockup to await arraignment. Sitting in the cell with him were a short Latino man and a tall white guy who were discussing the Henley case. The Latino whispered the latest: "I guess Henley's uncle's talking. I heard they picked him up."

Rex couldn't hold his poker face. "Nah bruh," he said with a laugh. "Not me."

The Latino's jaw fell. His name was Ralph Bustamante, and although he was about to be portrayed as Rex's partner in crime, he had never seen his new codefendant in his life. Their chance meeting in the holding cell was also noteworthy in that, according to Rex, neither he nor Bustamante nor James Saenz—the white guy sitting next to Bustamante (his bagman at Marie Callender's)—appeared before a judge that day. Rex suspected that they had been put together so the authorities could listen in and see if they said anything revealing to each other. If that were the case, the only thing they learned was that Rex and Bustamante didn't know each other from Adam.[3]

Rex's new defense attorney, Jim Riddet, would end up putting in the longest service of any defense attorney in the Henley saga—and there would be dozens of them. Bald and bearing a facial resemblance to bespectacled Syracuse basketball coach Jim Boeheim, Riddet was known for his calm courtroom demeanor and his years of experience within Orange County legal culture. He knew Judge Gary L. Taylor well. With hotshot LA lawyers Chaleff and Cossack on board, the defense team needed a hometown face Taylor would recognize. Riddet fit the bill perfectly. His first move was an impressive one, finagling Rex's release on just $50,000 bond.

"Get up!" Ron Knight shouted.

It was the first thing Darryl heard most mornings during the wait for his trial. But he didn't want to get up. He was sleeping late again, a sure sign that he was depressed. Only when Ron reminded him that he was about to be exonerated would Darryl roll out of bed to resume his training for the upcoming season. Then he would quit ten days later when the trial was postponed again. He spent entire days in Roger Cossack's office, wondering why he was there and what all these documents were about, hoping it would all go away.

Trusted advisors urged Darryl to take a plea deal, but as he told

T. J. Simers that summer, "I have to have that trial if I want things to get back to normal — well, halfway normal again. . . . If the government said for some reason — and God knows they won't — that they were dropping charges, that would do nothing for me. I don't want to risk my life going to jail, but this has to be addressed."

One of the defense attorneys he'd hired to address it, Roger Cossack, told Judge Taylor that if the trial didn't begin soon, he might have to excuse himself because of his side-job as a commentator for CNN's O.J. Simpson coverage. Taylor set a firm date for the Henley trial: January 10, 1995. This one would stick.

On August 1, 1994, NFL commissioner Paul Tagliabue reinstated Henley to the league. Two days later, Henley signed a one-year, $350,000 contract with the Rams, declaring his loyalty to the team by declining a more lucrative offer from the Seattle Seahawks. The LA Times published a handful of letters to the editor about Henley's return. Most of them didn't want Henley back.

The Rams wanted him back. As Henley strode into the locker room to begin the sixth training camp of his career, he was greeted by two factions of teammates: veterans who knew him and were glad to see him, and a smaller group — mainly free agents and rookies — who believed at least some of what the media had told them and half-expected Henley to pull a switchblade on them, Tony Montana style, in a cocaine-addled haze. Flashing his easy smile and plopping his bag in front of locker number 20, Henley felt confident about what would be his first practice with the team in ten months. He'd been working out consistently with Chuckie Miller, his former UCLA teammate, and he felt so sure of his readiness that when a reporter asked if he was concerned for his safety, Henley joked: "I play corner. I don't know about the safety."

His teammates were willing to laugh it off as well. There had been no more wild carjackings in the parking lot, no more bomb scares, no one left puzzled by the sight of Darryl jumping the fence to get to work. Most of the Rams thought of Darryl's legal situation as "a matter of wrong place at the wrong time," said quarterback

T. J. Rubley. "The Rams seemed to know more than we did about it, and the fact that they brought him back into the fold and supported him throughout the whole process made us think it would all blow over."

Henley was barred from flying to the Rams' preseason game in Green Bay because of his travel restrictions, so on the eve of the game, with his teammates in Wisconsin, he drove across LA to appear on Joe McDonnell's popular radio show. "Darryl was very careful as to what he said," McDonnell said of that day's in-studio interview, "but he denied being part of the drug thing." With Ted Woolsey seated beside him, Henley spent an hour and a half taking calls. "And some of them were tough on him," McDonnell recalled. "They were jumping him, but he took all the calls."[4] Then, to everyone's shock, John Rayburn called in.

Live on the air, the prosecutor warned McDonnell's listeners that they were "hearing one side of the story," McDonnell recalled. "He said, 'We have evidence against Mr. Henley, and we wouldn't have brought this [to trial] if we didn't think we had a conviction.'" Rayburn spoke directly to Darryl, McDonnell said, "and challenged him on a few things, and Darryl just didn't say anything, which I thought was smart on his part."

Darryl was released by the Rams three weeks later. It had nothing to do with the McDonnell show, and as Henley said at the time, "I find it hard to believe it had anything to do with my performance on the field." It had everything to do, as it turned out, with his travel restrictions. The Rams were not going to pay him $350,000 to play in half their games. His absence from the team would last only eleven days, however, before his lawyers and the court worked things out. Judge Taylor lifted Henley's travel ban but ordered the Rams to pay an extra $2 million bond and Darryl to pay $200,000 more himself. Taylor also ordered a police officer to shadow Henley during road trips.

Except for the bucket of ice water Robert Bailey dumped on him when he entered the locker room, and aside from Anthony

Newman soaking his street clothes and stashing them in the ice machine during practice, Darryl's reception at Rams Park was warmer this time. Still, he urged his parents to stay away from the stadium on game day. "I was terrified," he told Simers. "I didn't want my mom to sit up there and be subjected to whatever. My dad said he didn't care what people said, he had gone to all my games and he wanted to be there, but I couldn't let him. . . . I was terrified about going to the stadium myself, about how people were going to react. I arrived, gave my name at the gate, and looked at the people's expression. Okay, it was positive, but how were the other 25,000 people in the stadium going to react? . . . I got out of my car, [and] there were people there for autographs. Do they believe you? Do they believe *in* you? . . . The real true Ram fans sit in the end zone, just outside the tunnel, and I want to tell you, I felt fright. What were they going to say when I came down that tunnel? I remember coming out, there was nothing bad, and I know, because I was listening for everything.

"I know it's a negative thing with a majority of people. They're saying, 'How in the hell can this person look at himself in the mirror, not even give a reason to anyone for what has happened, and then just line up and play football like everything is okay?' . . . I would love to write with a can of paint on this big window: 'I am innocent.' I want to tell my story, but I can't. I feel that would be risking my life."

The last sentence of Simers's story was a warning from Henley that "if any kid is going to get anything out of this, I'd tell them to beware, just beware."

Chapter 20

Henley was hemorrhaging money. Aside from the $200,000 he'd been ordered to pay for his travel bond, John Shaw had made Henley insure himself with a $70,000 policy with Lloyd's of London. Then Judge Taylor increased his travel bond to $600,000. More broke than he'd been since college, Henley had to request an extension before he finally paid a portion of what he owed, just two days before the Rams' first road game—in Atlanta of all places.

He entered his first regular season game in over eleven months—his first under federal indictment—in the fourth quarter, with the Rams trailing the Falcons, 24–7. Fox's play-by-play man Joe Buck, after a week of in-house discussions as to how to handle Henley's status as an accused cocaine kingpin, announced Henley's presence several minutes after he entered the game with what sounded like a warning to fans inside the Georgia

Dome: "Henley is here. He does have someone with him, the Rams do, with regard to the federal indictment on drug trafficking charges." The moment seemed to warrant such an announcement, for as Steve Bisheff wrote in that day's *Orange County Register*: "No one on the Rams would ever admit it. But there is an added element of tension on this team merely because of Henley's presence." The Rams lost, 31–13. Of Henley's return, Chuck Knox said, "Shoot, he can play. What else was I supposed to do in this case? Let him go somewhere else to play? I am not here to judge."

The NFL concurred. "The Commissioner decided to treat this the same as someone in the NFL who gets a DWI," said league spokesman Greg Aiello. "Everyone is innocent until proved guilty. We don't discipline a person charged with a DWI until he is convicted. It is the same in this case."

Henley would battle three Taylors in the coming weeks—Judge Gary Taylor of the U.S. district court, receiver John Taylor of the San Francisco 49ers, and his lady friend Kym Taylor, of Culver City. The first battle had to do with Darryl's ongoing fight to play (he had only paid $220,000 of his $600,000 travel bond), while the second took place on the infield dirt at Anaheim Stadium, which had been abandoned by the Angels due to the baseball strike. The Rams had not beaten the 49ers since Henley's first NFL start, back in 1990. John Taylor had faced him in that game as well, just as he had faced him in an exhibition game in Tokyo in 1989, as the first pro receiver Darryl ever covered. Now it was September 1994, and the wispy Taylor approached Darryl after the game's first play to tell him, "Nice to have you back to battle." It was the most human, most earnest thing anyone had said to him in a while, but that was the end of Taylor's good manners. He would elude Henley to catch six passes that day, including a three-yard touchdown, while Henley, who was still rusty, let a potential interception slip through his hands, contributing to yet another Rams loss, and moving Fox's Joe Buck to remark that Henley was "playing these days with a lot on his mind."

A decade later, when asked to sum up the 1994 season in one word, Henley's former teammates chose "sad" or "hard," as if they had kept in touch over the years and agreed on those two adjectives. For the most part, they did not keep in touch. In addition to its other calamities, 1994 was the year that *two* NFL franchises left Los Angeles, a community whose devotion to the Rams in the 1950s had convinced baseball's Dodgers to move west from Brooklyn. The *New York Times*'s Tom Friend captured the sadness of the Rams' departure, writing: "They beat the Dodgers to the West Coast, the 49ers to the Super Bowl, and the Lakers to Showtime. . . . The Los Angeles Rams were first to Hollywood and are about to be first to leave."

The 1994 season was the best Darryl Henley ever played, college or pro. Not because his absence from the game had made his heart grow fonder of it somehow, or because he feared football might be taken from him. Henley knew he would be exonerated in court—*knew* it. Everyone around him told him so. No, the true and less romantic reasons for his inspired play in 1994 were his comfort within the Rams' defensive scheme and the brother he discovered in Shane Conlan, who had assumed unofficial cocaptain duties with Henley after crowned captain Anthony Newman drifted from his teammates during a difficult contract year.

There were uplifting moments for the 1994 Rams, but they would only serve as cliffs from which the team would fall, Icarus-like, when things got good. Knox had promised his players two days off—a rare and precious incentive—if they defeated Joe Montana and his new team, the Kansas City Chiefs. The Rams responded by handing Montana the only shutout of his career. At home versus the Falcons, though, after Henley and Lyght held star receiver Andre Rison to just two catches, Rison made two clutch grabs on the final drive to propel Atlanta to the winning touchdown. The final score, 8–5, was better suited for an Angels game. The joke among the 30,000 present that day was that the Rams played like they were on strike, too.

Things got no better the following week in Green Bay, where

Henley's interception of Brett Favre set up a Rams touchdown and a 17–3 halftime lead, only to have the final score end up 24–17, Packers. In New York, Newman picked off a late pass intended for Mike Sherrard to seal a Rams win. A grinning Conlan staggered off the field, victorious and bleeding from one eye. His reward would be a visit the next day from Deirdre Eliot and Steven Kinney, who grilled Conlan about the Rams Park incident. They even made him draw them a map.

To that point, Henley had done "an exceptional job of coming to work smiling, as if nothing was happening," Robert Bailey recalled, "and the rest of us fed off that. Our record didn't show it, but he handled everything so strong." ESPN aired a brief feature about Henley's legal situation in which Henley said: "Eventually everything that is said has to be accounted for, and I don't think I've blinked in this whole thing, and I'm not blinking now."

Are you saying you're innocent? Henley was asked.

"I'm saying I'm not blinking."

His life was a solitary, silent existence. He traveled with what amounted to his own Secret Service, lived sequestered in hotel rooms, and worked with teammates who feared being near him. The only time he spent in public was during practice and games. He'd lost touch with old friends like James Washington, mainly because he would have had to explain everything to them. Darryl's main man now was Ron Knight. He didn't have to explain anything to Ron. It was hardly an exaggeration to say that Darryl and Ron spent most of their waking hours together between November 1993 and March 1995.

One of the law enforcement community's greatest misconceptions about Ron Knight was that he and his first cousin Suge were partners in crime. The government would probably have been surprised to learn that Ron and Suge didn't hang out much and, in fact, didn't get along very well. There was a latent alpha-dog competition between them. Ron was the only person Darryl ever saw tell Suge to go fuck himself, without repercussion.

Kym Taylor had her doubts about Ron. She wondered about his motivations for befriending Darryl (his money? his athletic fame?), and she certainly wondered why Darryl was always with Ron. But by this time Kym was starting to have doubts about Darryl, too. One day she was supposed to meet him at his house to help him prepare for his trial, but when she got there no one was home. Luckily, a girlfriend of hers lived nearby, so Kym crashed at her place to avoid the long drive home. When she drove by Darryl's house the next morning, she found him waking with another woman. Kym left in a huff.

But she came back. Kym always came back.

One of her subsequent dates with Henley was a Sunday service at a local church he had been attending. A regular churchgoer, Kym was particularly moved by the pastor's sermon that morning, which was about forgiveness. For the first time in her life, she felt as if she was being preached to directly. Years later, she was still attending that same church, choosing to look back on her first visit there as "proof that good things can come out of bad."

"He was a good guy trying to be something he wasn't," Kym remembered. "Maybe he was caught up in the culture of the time. It was cool to be kind of 'hip-hop hard' back then. He grew up Mr. Suburbs, with both his parents in the same house, always encouraging him. He was a straight-A student. Then something went wrong."

James Washington was determined to find out what had gone wrong. When his calls to Darryl went unreturned, he stopped by Darryl's parents' house. There he encountered a weathered T.H. Henley, who had taken on the added burden of coaching Damien High's defensive backs. The jeers and stares T.H. absorbed each Friday night, Washington learned later, were almost too much for Damien's other coaches to bear. Head coach Dick Larson and his staff, despite T.H.'s emotional armor, could see that the whispers (*That's his dad right there — the drug dealer's dad*) hurt T.H. to his core. All that pain flooded forth the night James Washington dropped by the home that T.H. and his wife would soon be forced out of. "He just looked at me and started crying," Washington recalled. "Because he thought he had failed."

"I tried to do everything I could possibly do to find out what the fuck was going on and protect him," Washington said of Darryl. "But he was in too deep. The web was weaved. And none of my power, nobody I knew, could save him."

So mainly it was just Darryl and Ron. Except when the Rams were traveling. Then it was Darryl, PI Ted Woolsey, and a bodyguard. As one team employee remembered, "Nothing was really different except we had an increased police presence and more private security around, and on our itinerary [Henley] was listed under an assumed name when we were on the road. Sometimes they would put one of the security agents in the room under Darryl's fake name, and Darryl would sleep in the security guy's room."

This had become business as usual.

"When he had those undercover bodyguards on the plane," said Bailey, "a couple of us would poke holes in our newspapers and watch Darryl through the holes. That was our joke, like Inspector Clouseau. We just tried to make light of it. It was something we had to go through until the whole thing got cleared up."

Despite these distractions, Henley posted a career-high eleven solo tackles against John Elway and the Broncos, earning a game ball. Convinced that his acquittal was just a matter of time, Henley was playing for something he called "get-back"—his vision of exoneration, a multimillion-dollar contract, and a middle finger for his accusers. It wasn't a bad mind-set to have with the 49ers next on the schedule.

At first glance, the low pass that Steve Young completed to John Taylor in the second quarter looked like any other first down. Only when Taylor got up did it become clear that Henley was hurt. His limp body slid off Taylor's back like an overcoat and lay face-down on the grass, motionless except for his right leg, which kicked the turf like a metronome. "It has been a tough year and a half for

Darryl Henley," said ESPN's Mike Patrick. A minute passed, and still the only thing moving was Henley's right leg, kicking the sod while his facemask stayed buried in the grass. Surrounded by the Rams' medical staff, he was finally picked up and helped off the field, one man under each armpit, limp as a doll, with the tip of his right shoe carving a wet trail. Two plays later, Jerry Rice carried Todd Lyght into the end zone to give San Francisco a two-touchdown lead at halftime.

Henley would watch the rest of that memorable game from inside the Stanford Medical Center, where he heard Mike Patrick tell viewers that he had a groin pull. Henley knew he didn't have a groin pull. He had never known such pain in his life. In the cold mist of Candlestick Park, meanwhile, injured Rams quarterback Chris Miller led his team on a stunning fourth-quarter comeback that lifted the Rams to a three-point lead over the eventual Super Bowl champions. Then, in rapid succession, the Rams punted, Lyght got hurt, and Rice burned Steve Israel to set up the winning touchdown. It was Rice's sixteenth catch of the game, a team record, and Henley watched it from a hospital bed, his hip throbbing as the game clock hit 0:00.

The doctors told him he'd broken a bone in his hip and torn a muscle there—a recurrence of the weird injury he had suffered during his second year in the league. They said he was done for the year, but the following Sunday he woke up in San Diego feeling good enough to play against the Chargers. The game was as sloppy and uneventful as the Niners game had been brilliant. The Rams instantly reverted to awful again and lost by two touchdowns. "We are not just losing," Henley said afterward, removing his hip harness, "we are self-destructing." Ranting about what he called "loser's delight" ("You know what that means? It means when you have been losing so long, you become surprised to find yourself winning"), he said he felt sorry for Chuck Knox. "It's not that we are unprepared. . . . It's not the coaching, it's not the scheme, it's not who ran it or who should have thrown it. It's the people in this locker room. The guys on this team just aren't doing it." Strong words from a man who had let his teammates down so profoundly with his off-the-field actions, but Henley wasn't done: "It's an attitude. Someone forgot to tell us it's not okay to lose week in and week out."

Shane Conlan was more economical with his words: "I'm just tired of this crud."

When the team returned from San Diego, coaches Rod Perry and Joe Vitt were interviewed by federal prosecutors Eliot and Rayburn at Rams Park. They didn't know it, but Perry and Vitt, both master scouts themselves, were being scouted as potential trial witnesses. Perry hid his cards that day. Vitt spoke more freely. According to the DEA report, "Vitt advised that because Henley came from a great family, he would be surprised if Henley was involved [in drug trafficking]. . . . Henley has always advised Vitt that he didn't do it." Regarding the Rams Park incident, Henley "told Vitt that he had never seen his attackers before and did not know who they were. Henley told Vitt that the suspects were asking for money, but Henley did not say why. Vitt advised that Henley absolutely did not [k]now the people who confronted him at Rams Park. . . . Henley did not act like he knew the man that was murdered."

"Henley mentioned to Vitt that he and [Willie] McGowan went to school together and that McGowan had been living with Henley," the report continued. "Henley told Vitt that he thinks McGowan set him up. . . . Vitt described Henley as a leader."

Henley and his injured hip flew to Tampa for what would be the Rams' most typical loss of the season. They contributed thirty-seven yards in penalties to one of the Bucs' touchdown drives; there were fights after almost every play; Zendejas had a kick blocked; an unknown Bucs receiver named Charles Wilson scored two touchdowns, including one in which Henley and Newman collided while trying to stop him. By the fourth quarter, the Tampa players were laughing openly at their opponents. After the game, several Rams converged with the Buccaneers at midfield—not to fight them, but to chuckle right along with them. We are a joke, aren't we? Henley was already in the locker room, his hip on fire, his patience gone. "We just lost to the Tampa Bay Buccaneers," he said. "This is terrible. Terrible."

They lost by two touchdowns in Chicago, allowing the Bears to score more points than they had scored in over a year. "We're not dead," said defensive end Fred Stokes, "but we probably wish we were dead. . . . I don't know, it's like you have this intense pain and you just wish it would go away. . . . I thought this was going to be our day, but then it just fell apart, kind of like our whole season."

That Friday the team gathered solemnly at Rams Park for what everyone could sense would be the final team photo in Los Angeles Rams history. Georgia Frontiere was the only no-show. A team representative said she had bronchitis. The next day, at the Rams' final home game, a different team official said laryngitis. The *Register* reported that she didn't attend the game. The *Times* reported seeing her in a skybox. Her whereabouts were as secret as the discussions she was having with her courtiers in St. Louis, Frontiere's hometown, where the Rams would soon move.

The final game was on Christmas Eve. Henley, the only player remaining from the Rams' 1989 draft class, walked onto the Anaheim Stadium grass beside living legend Jackie Slater. His assignment that day was to cover Henry Ellard, the veteran receiver who had shown him the ropes at his first training camp back in 1989—the player who best exemplified the Rams' collapse since that time. The Rams had allowed Ellard, their all-time leading receiver, to sign with Washington during the offseason, declaring him too expensive (which Ellard didn't mind) and too old (which he did). Ellard took the field that Christmas Eve having gained more than 1,300 yards that season, third-best in the NFL. His attitude all day was *Too old, my ass.*

Ellard got open on the Redskins' first series, but Robert Bailey darted in front of the aging receiver, who coiled himself to go up and get the tipped pass anyway. Henley leveled Ellard in midair, Newman caught it instead, and raced twenty yards for a touchdown. The first man to greet him in the end zone was Henley, who had greeted his brother Thomas in that very end zone twelve Decembers earlier, after helping him score in the high school state championship game.

The Rams still had a chance to win when their meager pep band began playing "St. Louis Woman" in the fourth quarter. The ragtag musicians were practically the only fans left in the stadium other than the die-hards who were chanting, "GEORGIA SUCKS! GEORGIA SUCKS!" with acres of empty plastic seats making their jeers both louder and more poignant. Miller and Knox, the gutty quarterback and the grizzled old coach, willed the Rams into field goal range with four minutes left. Zendejas, the only sure thing on the Rams' roster, jogged on for the thirty-three-yard kick that would send the game into overtime and send the Rams toward a triumphant end to their stay in LA. Zendejas had made nineteen straight from inside forty yards, but this time he kicked a hunk of turf before he kicked the ball, which wobbled wide right, no good. Ellard beat Henley for a first down, ending the game, the season, and an era—as well as Henley's career. That quiet hum to the north, incidentally, was the Los Angeles Coliseum, where the Rams had played before 100,000 fans back in the 1950s. On this Sunday, the Coliseum housed 64,000 fans who didn't realize they were watching the Raiders play in LA for the last time, too.

And so the Los Angeles Rams, born during the Truman administration, died during Bill Clinton's, going out with a shameful denouement of five straight losing seasons and seven straight losses, the last of which was witnessed by a bloated estimate of 25,000 fans—by far the smallest crowd to see a Rams game since the team moved to Orange County in 1980. Two *high school* games at Anaheim Stadium that month had each hosted more spectators.

Moments after the loss, as Todd Hewitt gathered equipment for the final time in the stadium where he grew up, someone handed him an envelope. "I was like, 'Cool,'" Hewitt recalled. "'A Christmas card or a Good Luck in St. Louis card.'" It was a subpoena for Darryl Henley's trial.

It had been a sad year. Sad and hard. It was fitting that the Rams' best defensive back had participated in it only because his attorney and what the papers called "a traditional bail bondsman" had sprinted into a courthouse back in September carrying $60,000 cash.

Henley granted an interview to Barbara Kingsley of the *Register* a few days before his trial began and recited a poem for her—"Invictus," by William Ernest Henley (no relation)—the second half of which he had memorized as an Alpha Phi Alpha pledge:

> Beyond this place of wrath and tears
> Looms but the horror of the shade,
> And yet the menace of the years,
> Finds, and shall find, me unafraid.
> It matters not how straight the gate,
> How charged with punishments the scroll,
> I am the master of my fate;
> I am the captain of my soul.

"You know, you think of the horrors of the shade . . . [those are] the charges," Henley explained to Kingsley. ". . . It's how people perceive you. It doesn't matter how straight the gate, or charged with punishment. . . . It doesn't matter how this looks, how that looks. I am the master of my fate. I am the captain of my soul." He called the allegations made by Rayburn and Eliot "incredible" and "impossible." "You're talking about someone who never ever smoked a joint. . . . Never ever physically even *seen* cocaine. Never! . . . There are some things maybe close to something and they require an answer, then there are other things that are so ridiculous. . . . How could I answer to a ridiculous statement?"

He likened his preparation for trial to his preparation for an NFL game. "I know what happens to you when you're not ready to play: you get beat. . . . Everything I do at that trial, I'm going to have to relate to football in order for me to be functional. When I walk into this courtroom, when I'm at home getting dressed for court, that's how I am preparing for a game. . . . [This is] my battle. This is me against the government.

"I cannot wait to get this on. I cannot wait."

Chapter 21

It rained hard that January, and the temporary courthouse where Orange County's federal caseload was heard looked even more depressing than usual. Nearly everyone who worked there considered the building an embarrassment — the equivalent of a portable classroom outside an overpopulated high school. Cynical lawyers called it "deals on wheels." Hometown boy Gary Taylor didn't brag about the place, but he stood firmly behind what it represented and his role in maintaining that representation. He kept a bucket by his bench to catch the raindrops leaking through the roof.

The trial of *United States v. Rafael Bustamante, et al.*, which was predicted to last three weeks, would instead last ten. At its outset, Gerry Chaleff and Roger Cossack knew that to win an acquittal for Henley they would have to portray a black football player as the victim and a pretty, white cheerleader as the villain. Not an easy thing to do, especially in Orange County.

Each of the five defendants had separate counsel. The crowded defense table featured lawyers of every type, from the respected Riddet and esteemed Chaleff, to the likes of Erwin Winkler, Garey West's lawyer, who would be disbarred the following year for misappropriating funds from his clients. (The youngest lawyer at the defense table, Winkler missed a pretrial hearing because of what was rumored to be a nervous breakdown. Turned out he was vacationing in Mexico.) [1] In all, the defense boasted attorneys who had represented, or would represent, the Hillside Strangler, the Menendez brothers, the Church of Scientology, Heidi Fleiss, Winona Ryder, rock singer Scott Weiland, serial killer Randy Kraft, and one of the policemen who beat Rodney King.

John Rayburn and Deirdre Eliot represented the federal government. Everyone close to the trial who reflected on it years later would mention how young the prosecutors were and how surprisingly effective their lawyering was. The thirty-four-year-old Rayburn (cocksure, diligent, and movie-star handsome) and the thirty-two-year-old Eliot (herself physically attractive and known as a pit bull in chihuahua's clothing) did not treat their tenure in the U.S. Attorney's Office like most young lawyers, that is, like a paid internship before moving on to the more lucrative field of criminal defense. One of seven children raised by an electrical engineer father and a homemaker mother, Rayburn had been following his dad's technical footsteps when he fell in love with the law. He worked his way through law school specifically to become a prosecutor, and nothing in Eliot's record suggested she had done otherwise. Rayburn drove what one of his colleagues called "the crappiest car in the parking lot." His and Eliot's was a cold, thankless job whose pats on the back came largely from within their own ranks.

And then there was Darryl Henley. Unlike his codefendants (and unlike the most famous defendant of all time, standing trial a few miles north), Henley understood what was going on at all times during his trial. He even looked like a young attorney, having ditched the bright designer look he preferred in favor of his attorneys' advice that he go conservative. The stoic expression Henley wore in court fit well with his new suits, and was only interrupted by a brief furrow of his brow or nibble at his lip when he was thinking hard or listening closely. Over the next ten weeks he would do plenty of both.

The first order of business was to assemble a jury. Jim Riddet, who represented Rex Henley but was being paid by Darryl,[2] had already filed a motion calling the jury pool unfair, citing a recent court order that reduced the counties from which Orange County jurors could be drawn from seven to just three. Los Angeles was one of the counties eliminated, which meant that over one million black candidates had been disqualified from serving on the Henley jury, which would decide the fates of four black defendants. The seats left open by those missing LA jurors would be filled instead by citizens of Orange, Riverside, and San Bernardino Counties — places that, in addition to being considered less educated and less cosmopolitan than LA, were irrefutably less black. In the end, there would be more black women on the twelve-member O.J. Simpson jury (seven) than black *people* in the entire pool of 160 candidates from which the Henley jury was chosen (five).[3]

While attorneys on both sides were selecting jurors, defense investigator Ted Woolsey was looking for witnesses. Woolsey tracked down the travel agent who had booked all those ill-fated plane trips back in the summer of 1993. Justo Rios told Woolsey that "during June and July 1993, other persons started calling Travel Associates using the name of Darryl Henley." Woolsey could envision Rios saying the same thing on the stand (supporting Chaleff's stance that Henley had been used), especially when Rios added that these bogus bookings happened numerous times and that his supervisor never questioned them because the customers paid in cash. Rios went on to describe the "lax" airport procedures that allowed impostors to fly under assumed names — "You can fly under anybody's name and nobody ever checks" — and noted that this abuse of Henley's account had led to a policy change at his agency because one of the men who had forged Henley's signature misspelled it so badly that the agency had to wait five months to receive payment.

It was a revealing interview, but it became a useless one once Woolsey learned that Rios had a criminal record that included registration as a sex offender. Knowing that the government would tear him apart on cross-examination, Woolsey essentially tore apart his interview notes. Several behind-the-scenes issues like this one crippled Henley's defense. Some were brought on by Henley himself.

The prosecution flew Shetelle Clifford to LA as a government witness, but they didn't count on Henley picking her up at the airport or sleeping with her in his home that night. Rayburn was not pleased when he heard about it, and he was even less pleased when he learned that Eric Johnson, another government witness from Atlanta, had hung out with Darryl and Shetelle that same evening. Rayburn was not surprised by the pro-defense responses given by Clifford and Johnson during their government interviews the next day. (Darryl dropped Shetelle off fashionably late for hers, in his Mercedes.) "Your case is full of holes," Eric Johnson told DEA agent Kevin McLaughlin. "You've been working on this thing for two years, and you haven't gotten anywhere." According to Johnson, McLaughlin was "not happy" with him when the interview ended.

Shetelle would later testify that McLaughlin had spent much of their interview "asking and probing about [her] sex life with Darryl," and pointing out that Darryl had not only dated Shetelle, Jennifer, and Tracy at the same time but also another woman — a "mystery girl" whose name McLaughlin said he couldn't reveal. He asked Shetelle if Darryl's womanizing might make her less eager to protect him. Shetelle answered no; she said she knew as much about Darryl's other women as she did about all this drug stuff, which was nothing. Like her friend Eric Johnson, she said later that McLaughlin was "not happy with her" when she left.

When Shetelle flew to California a second time, McLaughlin and his partner staked out her hotel to prevent Henley from contacting her. They were parked outside one night when the hotel clerk received a call from someone asking for Shetelle, with "loud gangster rap music playing in the background." Moments later McLaughlin watched Shetelle exit the building carrying an overnight bag and climb into a large Dooley pickup truck with personalized plates that read NFL. The truck, which police would soon learn was registered to Anthony Newman, was driven by Darryl Henley.

Once inside the truck, Shetelle told Darryl about the DEA agents who had been shadowing her, at which point Darryl called the hotel on his cell phone and asked the desk clerk to deliver a message to the agents. He would later take issue with McLaughlin's report, which stated that Henley's message had been: "Fuck you, Kevin McLaughlin." Darryl claimed that he'd actually told the clerk: "Tell Kevin McLaughlin he's a fucking asshole." Whatever his words, McLaughlin was furious. He notified the local police, who pulled Henley over near his home later that night. Rex Henley and Eric Johnson were also in the truck, and after a brief chat with the policeman who pulled them over, Darryl and his friends were allowed to continue on, having received another subtle reminder as to who was in charge. However, Shetelle did sleep in the defendant's bed again that night.

The next day, perhaps not by coincidence, Rayburn submitted a stern forty-page memorandum that laid out the rules as he saw them. Two stood out:

"Evidence of a defendant's possession of a mobile phone and paging equipment and his cash purchases of vehicles and weapons is probative of an overall narcotics trafficking conspiracy."

"Evidence of a defendant's possession of firearms is properly admissible to show a defendant's involvement in drug trafficking."

Unfortunately for Henley, these two items were also probative of being an NFL player. In court, Rayburn raised the issue of the other NFL star standing trial by questioning "Mr. Cossack's role as an expert on CNN." The prosecutors were concerned that jurors might recognize Cossack from his Simpson commentary and give more weight to his words than their own. In the end, Taylor ordered the prospective jurors to refrain from watching CNN. But there was no avoiding the Simpson trial, especially in Southern California and especially in January 1995. Even in its early stages, the O.J. trial was a media-driven bacchanal unlike any the world had seen, one that would create vast and lasting changes in the way news is disseminated.

The CNN issue compelled Chaleff to disclose his own work as a Simpson analyst for Court TV and the *LA Times*. Fatigued by the issue, Taylor dismissed it out of hand: "That case is not particularly related to this case in terms of subject matter."

It was, and it wasn't. *California v. O.J. Simpson* was a murder case, of course, while *United States v. Rafael Bustamante, et al.* was a drug case. At the heart of both matters, however, was a relationship between a black football star and a white Orange County girl, both set amid the unique racial topography of Southern California. In football terms, Simpson's trial was a "home" game for him (played in urban, cosmopolitan LA/Hollywood), while Henley was on the road (in white, ultraconservative Orange County). Had they somehow switched trial venues—had the O.J. trial been heard in Orange County, where Nicole Brown was born and raised, instead of LA, where Simpson had starred at USC and gone on to shoot his movies and commercials—surely the tone and content of each trial would have been different, if not their outcomes. As lawyer-turned-TV analyst Roger Cossack said in 2004, on the ten-year anniversary of the Brentwood murders, "It was impossible to convict O.J. Simpson in Los Angeles. [He was] the prince of the city."

Not so Darryl Henley in Orange County.

LA's neighbor to the south was known for its wealthy, white suburbs and nice beaches. Orange County was not as well known for being a hotspot of antiblack sentiment since its origin. As recently as the 1920s, the Ku Klux Klan held a powerful foothold in

Anaheim, the county's largest city, by controlling its daily newspaper, electing four Klansmen to the city's five-member Board of Trustees, placing nine policemen on its ten-member police force, and posting signs that greeted newcomers with the acronym "KIGY" (Klansmen I Greet You). In those days, only about 140 black people lived in Orange County — less than 1 percent of its population. Not a lot had changed in that regard by 2001, when the census confirmed that blacks had never composed more than 1.8 percent of Orange County's population in its history. That same year, one Orange County police department admitted that some officers still wrote the letter *N* on traffic citations, for Negro. In 2003 a black Vietnam veteran who'd lived in Anaheim Hills for twelve years "awoke to a 10-foot-tall burning cross on his front lawn," according to the *Register*. The racist skeleton in Orange County's closet was but one reason why its jurors were considered more inclined than those in LA County to take the side of white women like Tracy Donaho and Nicole Brown, the leading ladies of the two trials, who turned out to be quite similar themselves, despite having been born fifteen years apart.

Nicole Brown had been a high school homecoming princess in Dana Point; Tracy was cocaptain of the dance team at Esperanza High. Nicole had worked as a waitress when she was eighteen, the year O.J. Simpson entered her life. Tracy, also a waitress, said it was "exciting" to have Darryl Henley sweep her off her feet at age nineteen. Both women were raised in a family of girls — Nicole and her three sisters, Tracy and her one. There were two glaring differences between them. The first was that Nicole's family had money and the Donahos did not, and the second difference had more to do with how the women were perceived than with the women themselves, and it arose in 1995, when their names were being tossed around criminal courtrooms.

In the words of Jeffrey Toobin, author of *The Run of His Life* (the most credible among the glut of Simpson books), the heavily black, heavily female Simpson jury sided with O.J. in part because they viewed Nicole as a "blond temptress who had snared this black hero." The Henley prosecutors, meanwhile, wanted Tracy to be seen as the opposite: a blonde heroine who was fighting back against Henley, the dark Rasputin. It made for an interesting irony, particularly because Tracy was a convicted criminal and Nicole was not. Somehow, though, these two facts were about to be reversed in the minds of the two juries, such that Nicole Brown would end up a villain and Tracy Donaho closer to a martyr.

Race was never an issue in the Henley trial—at least not on the record. The Simpson trial was *all* race, of course, especially its latter half, when a jury that included seven black women, one black man, and zero white men inched toward its stunning verdict. Once the Henley trial began "and everyone took their places," said one of the Henley defense attorneys, "it took on its own personality, as every trial does, and those present who weren't kidding themselves could not deny that there were strong racial overtones." Gerry Chaleff and Roger Cossack knew better than to play the race card in Orange County. Of the 2.8 million people who lived there, only 43,000 were black—a startling 65:1 ratio. Yorba Linda, Tracy's hometown, was populated by 44,000 whites and just 600 blacks. Villa Park, where the Honorable Gary Taylor made his home, had a population of 6,300—fewer than 50 of whom were black. It was a ratio similar to John Rayburn's graduating class at Damien High School, which boasted only two black students, one of whom had written as his senior quote, "A fox should not be on the jury at a goose's trial."

Chaleff and Cossack knew that asking the outnumbered blacks on their jury to save Darryl from the clutches of corrupt white law enforcement—like Johnnie Cochran was doing with his jury in LA—would not work, even though Henley's past would have supported such an argument better than Simpson's. Henley was revered within a number of African American communities around Los Angeles. He still attended the same black church where he had been raised. The predominantly black block in Inglewood where he and Eric Ball had lived as UCLA undergrads welcomed him back each time he returned. He'd visited minority schools frequently during his career, from college through the pros, on his own time. But Henley's support from the black community during his trial would be, to quote one observer, "nonexistent." In contrast, "Blacks rallied around O.J.," wrote Harvard law professor Randall Kennedy, "even though — before the murders — he ignored, and was largely ignored by, most blacks."

Positioned against the enormity of the Simpson trial, the Henley trial was the clever independent film no one saw because it hit screens the same day *Titanic* did. Like most good indie films, it featured compelling conflicts between rich characters. One day during a break, as Darryl walked past John Rayburn, he told him, "Coach Larson says hello" — a reference to their former high school coach, Dick Larson. Rayburn quickly reported Henley's remark to Judge Taylor.

Coach Larson, of course, had never asked Darryl to relay his greetings to Rayburn. It was Darryl's way of killing Rayburn with kindness, perhaps reminding him that Larson's name was on the defense's witness list and not the government's. If so, then Rayburn's reaction had reminded Taylor in no uncertain terms: *Keep an eye on this guy.*

Tom Carroll, Damien's longtime athletic director, recalled that the Damien community was "flabbergasted" by the coincidence that one former Spartan was prosecuting another. "Some people would say, 'How could Rayburn take the case?'" Carroll said. "And my comment back to them was, 'Well, that's his job.' . . . I can't say that I know John Rayburn jumped in there and said, 'Oh hey! Yeah, I wanna do this!' I don't think so. I could be wrong, and I would be so disappointed in John Rayburn. But I don't think that ever happened." The coincidence still struck him as ripe, however. "When would that ever happen again?" Carroll asked. "That two guys from the same high school, a small school, would bump into each other like that?"

Scott Morrison, who captained the 1982 Spartans with Thomas Henley, was coaching football several counties away at the time, but was still attuned to the Damien network. "People saw it as intriguing," he recalled. "Good, bad, or otherwise . . . John had a job to do and Darryl just happened to be a part of John's job." *Register* reporter John McDonald agreed. "Rayburn told me he was not in Henley's league as a player," McDonald said. "He was proud when Darryl was starring in the NFL. When Darryl got in trouble, he had to do what he had to do."

At 6:20 a.m. on January 23, 1995, Darryl's parents were awakened by the smell of smoke. Gray haze had filled their bedroom, and neither T.H. nor Dot could see the floor as they staggered downstairs and onto their lawn. When the Upland Fire Department arrived, they discovered that a batch of computer paper had been set ablaze in the garage, sparking flames that had spread to some boxes nearby. Darryl's father didn't suspect foul play ("I didn't think nothing of it," he said), but the Upland Fire Department noted in its report that the fire's ignition was "suspicious." Eric Henley, who arrived just as the fire trucks did, recalled an investigator telling him: "Someone wanted to scare you."

Thus, on the same day that Marcia Clark and Chris Darden made their opening statements in the Simpson trial, Darryl Henley quietly asked Rafael Bustamante if he had tried to burn his parents' house down. Bustamante looked down at his shackles, as if to say: *How am I gonna burn down anything?*

What about your brother? Darryl asked.

Look, Bustamante said chillingly, if I had wanted to do it, it would have been done.

Asked years later who he thought had set the fire, Henley's face contorted as if he couldn't believe the question. Steven Kinney was now the family's answer, and it was bolstered by the former DEA agent's residence at a federal prison for unrelated but universally loathsome crimes he would commit years later. The Henleys believed that Kinney had set the fire to make it look as if Bustamante had ordered it to persuade Darryl not to testify against him or to intimidate him into paying his debt. Either reason would have made Henley and Bustamante look like former partners.

These were only theories, though, and stretches at that. In fairness to Kinney, he didn't have much time to organize an arson attempt. Most of his days began at 3:30 a.m., when he'd wake up for the long drive to Santa Ana so he could prep witnesses with John Rayburn from 5:30 until 8:45. Kinney and the prosecutors would then wheel their carts across the street for the long day in court. After adjournment, Kinney would work until 9:00 p.m. or so, then drive home and crash. Some days he left court early so he could work with Alex Cuevas on his upcoming testimony, or prepare Rayburn's telephone evidence—the government's secret weapon—which required him to thumb through and cross-reference endless stacks of phone bills. Kinney often excused himself from his meetings with Cuevas or Tracy Donaho (whose testimony he was also helping groom) to compare their stories to this developing telephone information. Sundays were his only day off, but he worked those, too.

As the skies in Orange County cleared and the rain went away, and as the jury pool shrunk toward its final eighteen members (twelve jurors, six alternates), the defense began to feel what one member referred to as "the view from the jury box." "Here were four African American defendants and one Hispanic," said Charles Hack, "with the dynamic of Orange County and the other places the jurors came from. And I'm not saying they're evil people or that they had pointy white sheets on their heads, but race is a subversive part of our culture. . . . Many of us like to pretend it's not there, but it shapes our decisions. It shapes *my* decisions. There was a feeling amongst the defense counsel that our clients were guilty before the first witness was called to the stand."

It was a common defense attorney's lament, but the abundance of white faces in Judge Taylor's jury box made Hack's complaint worth heeding, especially with regard to the trial's most famous defendant. Darryl Henley's involvement in the drug conspiracy would not be proven as easily as Bustamante's, McGowan's, or West's, but his case involved sexual relations with a nineteen-year-old girl who had grown up close by. The jurors who were about to hear those details were from predominantly white communities like Huntington Beach, Laguna Hills, and Costa Mesa. Clearly the concept of "a jury of one's peers" did not apply as directly to the Henley trial as the authors of the Magna Carta had intended.

Shawn O'Reilly was one guy the defense wanted on the jury. Not only did O'Reilly have a marijuana conviction on his record, and not only did he say on his questionnaire that he thought pot should be decriminalized, but the billy-clubbing he'd received from a cop as a teen had left him with a less than reverent view of law enforcement. There was just one problem with O'Reilly—a problem that the defense wouldn't learn until it was too late. He didn't like black people.

Twenty-five-year-old Bryan Quihuis [4] was so wired on methamphetamine during the first day of jury selection that he wore colored contacts to hide his dilated pupils. Mike Malachowski, [5] twenty-four, had a marijuana bud in his car that he planned to smoke during his long drive home to Hesperia, a town that sat simmering on the edge of the Mojave Desert—by far the farthest any juror had driven that day. An out-of-work carpenter with a wife and three kids to feed, Malachowski was desperate to make the Henley jury because the court paid extra to those who had to drive more than eighty miles to get there.

The rain returned the day the jury was finalized. O'Reilly, Quihuis, and Malachowski made the cut, along with:

Edmund "Moose" Richards, seventy-three, a white retired furniture executive from Laguna Hills. [6]

Spandan Rajpillai, thirty-five, a nuclear chemist of East Indian descent, also from Laguna Hills.

Hogan Davis, thirty-four, a white supermarket manager from Chino Hills.

Reid Johnson, fifty-nine, a black Vietnam vet and postal worker from Santa Ana.

Juan Cardenas, thirty-seven, a Latino cable installer from Montclair.

Lauren Zampese, forty-three, a white office manager from Cypress (near Anaheim).

Barbara Sussman, thirty-nine, a white municipal employee from Riverside.

Scott Turner, thirty-two, a black machinist from San Bernardino.

Roger Christian, thirty-eight, a white financial advisor from Santa Ana.

Before Taylor released the unchosen jurors back to their lives, he advised them: "Don't ever believe stories you may hear that the jury system doesn't work or something like that. It does work." Unfortunately, as Taylor's colleagues at the federal appeals court would later rule, the jury system was about to fail in the Henley trial, just as it would fail in Judge Lance Ito's courtroom thirty miles north.

Chapter 22

Darryl arrived early on the morning of opening statements, wearing a gray suit and yellow and black tie. He and Gerry Chaleff were thumbing through documents together at the defense table when their opponents entered the courtroom, pulling carts burdened with their own boxes and files. Deirdre Eliot, John Rayburn, and Steven Kinney intended those files to serve as the tools of Henley's undoing. The competitor in Darryl wanted to knock their carts across the room. The professional cornerback in him never raised his eyes from what he was reading.

"Bustamante was the cocaine supplier," Eliot told the jury during her opening remarks. "Darryl Henley was the buyer. He took delivery of the cocaine at his house in Brea, California, and guaranteed payment for the drugs. Darryl Henley's Brea house served as the stash house where the cocaine was wrapped, packaged, and concealed in suitcases. . . . Defendant Willie McGowan was a middleman. . . . He helped put the deal together for Darryl Henley. . . . Defendant Rex Henley was Darryl Henley's right-hand man in Brea. . . . Defendant Garey West was the main man in Memphis . . . [responsible for] returning profits from drug sales to Darryl Henley."

Henley sat there "impassively," the papers reported, as Eliot exaggerated his role in the conspiracy, with reporters and a stenographer recording her exaggerations so that his descendants might read them someday. He wasn't surprised that Eric Manning's pivotal role had been removed from Eliot's argument; the deceased Manning was the quintessential "empty chair" at the defense table. Incriminating him would have only dimmed the light shining on the five living defendants. As Eliot continued to preview her case, Darryl glanced back at Willie, thinking back to those long gone days on the Pop Warner field. *How did we get here?* he thought.

"The evidence will show," Eliot continued, "that in the summer of 1993, defendants Bustamante and Darryl Henley entered into a criminal partnership to distribute pounds and pounds of cocaine. Bustamante had cocaine to sell, and Darryl Henley wanted to buy it. A perfect match. Just how did Darryl Henley, who wore number 20 for the Los Angeles Rams, come in contact with Bustamante? The evidence will show that Henley turned to his boyhood friend, defendant Willie McGowan, hoping that McGowan had connections. . . .

"The evidence will show that the high level people, the people in charge of a drug organization, typically don't place themselves at risk. They get someone else to do it. . . . That someone else was Tracy Donaho, at the time a nineteen-year-old cheerleader for the Los Angeles Rams. . . .

"Donaho found herself caring for Henley, a good seven years older. They looked beyond their differences in age and race, and even discussed a future together. Henley gave Donaho the security code to his house in Brea so she could come and go as she pleased. Their relationship hit a rough spot when he didn't call her back for a while. She even told him she didn't want to see him anymore, but as Donaho will tell you, Darryl Henley had a way with words. Henley was able to charm his way back into her life. By then, Tracy Donaho was hooked. She would do just about anything for Darryl Henley, the football star."

Eliot went on to describe Willie's unsuccessful efforts to get Tracy to fly to Atlanta on July 15. "Then Darryl Henley made the call," Eliot told the jurors. "He asked Donaho to make this trip to Atlanta for him. She will tell you that Henley told her they could be together and that this was the last time he would ask. 'Just do this trip, this one last time.' Well, Donaho hadn't seen him in a while, so she agreed to take another suitcase. . . .

"This was one flight too many."

"Good morning, ladies and gentlemen. My name is Roger Cossack, and with me is cocounsel Gerry Chaleff, and this is Darryl Henley, number 20 of the Los Angeles Rams. Ladies and gentlemen of the jury, I wish to tell you Darryl Henley, the evidence will show, knows his uncle, Rex Henley. He knows Willie McGowan, although he had not seen him for fifteen years until he ran into him at a track meet in May of 1993.[1] And as far as Mr. Bustamante, the evidence will show that the way he knew Mr. Bustamante was that he turned him in to the police and identified him from a police lineup as a person who accosted him at Rams Park. . . .

"Let me take you now on a little time travel if I could for a second, and take you back to July 15, 1993. Let's go over to the Atlanta airport. Look out the window and we see the plane from Los Angeles land. It's in the afternoon.[2] It's a warm, sunny day, hot in Atlanta that time of year. Humid. People are deplaning, getting off the plane, and we notice a young, pretty woman getting off the plane. Five-six, five-eight, dressed in shorts, in a rib top and sandals." Cossack continued this narrative, telling the jury about the lies Tracy told the DEA officers at baggage claim, and how she'd continued telling the Allison Coats lie even after Darryl brought her back to the airport that night. At that point the DEA agents "arrested her, and off she goes to jail," Cossack said. "Now let's stop for a second right there, and let me tell you a little bit about Darryl Henley."

His client was the product of model parents, Cossack said, hardworking folk who had provided sterling educations for their three sons. Darryl was "a young man who, but for this, has the world by the tail. He is one of those gifted few who is good enough to be a professional athlete and, therefore, is paid a great deal of money to do it. . . .

"Now let's go back again to Tracy Donaho in the jail in Atlanta. . . . The first person she calls is her father, who is a former police officer, and she calls him and tells him the same story that she told the agents. 'You know, Dad, I don't know what happened. My goodness, I was carrying this suitcase and I met this girl at a party and she told me I should carry it, and I just carried this suitcase down to Atlanta for her because her father had a heart attack, and it had cocaine in it.'" Cossack explained that Tracy's father drove immediately to his ex-wife's house upon hearing this. Detective Mike Ortiz was waiting for him there. "It is at this time and for one of the few times, ladies and gentlemen, that I am going to agree with something the prosecution has said," Cossack continued. "There is a conspiracy in this case. There is a nasty, nasty conspiracy, and that conspiracy is the conspiracy that is formed at that moment, in the Donaho household, to frame Darryl Henley and save their daughter. . . . The drug laws in this country are very harsh. For carrying the kinds of drugs that Tracy Donaho admits that she carried, she could be facing somewhere in the area of fifteen years or more in prison with a $4 million fine." But Tracy had a way out, Cossack explained, glancing at the prosecutors. Only "the people sitting at this table" could recommend a shorter sentence. Cossack's point was clear: Tracy was here to scratch the prosecutors' backs so they could scratch hers.

Cossack delivered this opening statement on the same morning that O.J. Simpson's book, *I Want to Tell You*, was released, a book that claimed the justice system had framed him. And now Cossack was describing Tracy's framing of Darryl Henley. She did it not because he was black but because, as an NFL player, Henley "is a much bigger fish for them and for the agents to catch than this courier.

"It is also important to remember this," Cossack continued. "Until this moment, and including this moment, Tracy Donaho has never said that she knew that there was cocaine in that suitcase. . . . She claims that she thought that she was carrying cash, something that was perfectly legitimate. 'My goodness, I didn't think I was doing a thing wrong.' . . . And I believe after you have heard the complete evidence in this case and after you have had an opportunity to view the participants in this case, Miss Donaho and Mr. Henley, and hear them, you will only come to one verdict. Mr. Henley is clearly not guilty of these crimes."

It was a promising opening statement, smoothly delivered and dramatic without being overwrought, but it included several errors and several promises that would go unfulfilled, including the one about Darryl's imminent testimony. (As Darryl told T. J. Simers near the trial's end, "I wanted to testify, but my attorneys advised me not to. They said I was too animated to testify.") Darryl knew that his codefendants weren't going to take the stand. He hated that Bustamante would never be asked under oath when he first spoke with Darryl Henley; and that Willie would never be asked how many of the calls from Darryl's phones he'd made; and that Garey West would never be asked if he and Darryl were longtime friends; and that Rex would never be asked if he'd wrapped any cocaine. One of those four answers might have been the key to Henley's freedom, but the jury would never even hear the questions.

Tracy, meanwhile, would say whatever the government wanted the jury to hear in order to get her sentence reduced. She would tell them that Darryl had manipulated her into taking all those flights. Darryl was behind everything.

Rayburn's first witness was Al Hogan, the DEA investigator who had arrested Tracy in the Atlanta airport. Exhibit 1 was the suitcase. Hogan stepped down from the stand and opened it in the middle of the courtroom, revealing to a few dozen craned necks what had ultimately brought them all there. The suitcase contained the same random clothing that had been in it the first time Hogan opened it, on July 15, 1993, but its most important contents were in exhibit 3, a cardboard box filled with several separately wrapped kilos of what had once been Rafael Bustamante's cocaine.

Showing the jurors the drugs right off the bat was straight out of the federal prosecutors' handbook. Here's the dope. These guys over here are responsible. Forget the varying degrees to which they might be responsible. We're going to get all of them. It was the first time Darryl had seen a kilo of cocaine in his life.

Early on during Cossack's cross-examination of Hogan, he asked what Hogan's first impression of Henley had been that night at the airport. "I liked Darryl," Hogan testified. "Darryl came across as a charming fellow and he seemed genuinely concerned about Tracy and the welfare of Tracy and wanted Tracy to do the right thing is what it came across to me as."

But a lot had changed by the time Tracy sat down with her parents inside the Clayton County jail the following day, the point at which the exchange between Cossack and Hogan became testy. When asked about the unique visit he had arranged between Tracy and her parents, Hogan said, "I know some of the people that work down there, and I asked for a special meeting."

"So you pulled some strings for them?"

"Yeah, sure."

Cossack's "nasty, nasty conspiracy," it seemed, was starting to take shape.

Deirdre Eliot called Rams vice president Jay Zygmunt to the stand next, to testify about the salary advances he'd given Henley in the spring of 1993. Eliot felt sure that Henley had used those monies for drug trafficking, even though one of the few certainties of the case was that the kilos had been "fronted" to the traffickers, with payment suspended until later. Even if Darryl was the drug lord the prosecutors claimed he was, he wouldn't have needed any cash advances that spring. Zygmunt testified that Henley had requested the advances to help with a house he was building in Atlanta.

On cross-examination, Chaleff asked, "Is this uncommon that players would ask for advances of their salaries?"

"No," Zygmunt said.

"It happens all the time?"

"Yes."

Eliot passed on her chance to question Zygmunt again.

When Chuck Knox took the stand, he did not look like a man who'd been fired by the Rams three weeks earlier. To the contrary, the sixty-two-year-old coach seemed relieved—relaxed, even—most likely because he still had $700,000 coming to him on his contract. Knox testified that when Darryl called him from Atlanta on July 15, 1993, Henley said that a "girl had called him and said she would come to Atlanta if she could have a chance to see him." Rayburn would later theorize that "the reason Darryl Henley contacted Coach Knox [was to] make himself look innocent." It was another reach, but Henley was in a poor position to disprove it because Anaheim police chief Joe Molloy, the man Henley called after calling Knox, died twelve days later of a heart attack. Molloy, therefore, could not tell the jury that Darryl had called him for guidance, not to set up an alibi. What's worse, Henley's attorneys had no way of letting the jury know that Molloy was dead, or that Darryl had even called him in the first place, because only Darryl and Tracy had spoken to Molloy, and Tracy said she didn't know who he was. One of Darryl's most fervent prayers over the next decade would be an eternally unanswered one asking that Molloy—who'd been fit as a fiddle at the time of his death—be spared his heart attack so he could relay to the jury what Tracy had told him that day about the suitcase: "No, Darryl wasn't involved. Yes, I'm sure."

"On his way out of the courtroom," the *Register* reported, "Knox winked at Darryl Henley, who smiled back." Following Knox with his eyes, Darryl noticed that none of his teammates had come to support him. He would later point out Troy Aikman's appearance at Michael Irvin's drug trial in Dallas and the support that Rams star Leonard Little would receive during his drunk driving entanglements. As usual, Henley had brought this pain upon himself. He'd told every teammate who asked, and several who didn't, "Don't come to court." David Lang had defied these orders early in the trial—perhaps because he'd suffered his own legal issues in college—and Darryl's mother had been so happy to see him that her hug nearly knocked the wind out of him. Henley's UCLA teammate Chuck Miller went to dinner with Henley the night before opening statements, where Henley repeated his request: "Stay home." Miller honored it. "But as the trial went along," Miller said, "I kept hearing more of this 'hardened criminal' stuff. I mean, anybody who has spent ten seconds with Darryl knows that's a joke. If I thought he was going to jail, I would have gone to court no matter what he said."

It was evidence of Darryl's wavering confidence that he regretted asking his teammates to stay away. As the trial wore on, he'd worry about the effect their absence was having on the jury. *Are they wondering if my teammates even like me?* he thought. Darryl would not ask his teammates to come to court now. He was too proud for that. He just hoped that they would see his "Stay home" request as an expression of the same foolish pride that caused this whole mess in the first place. After Lang, no one else showed up.

Instead, Ronald and Donald Knight sat together in the back row. They usually wore jeans and T-shirts, and their presence was silent and brooding. The Knights arrived with Darryl and Rex most mornings and left with them at the end of each day. This is probably what led the prosecutors to start calling them Darryl's "bodyguards."

Fraternal twins who looked nothing alike facially, Ronald and Donald each stood taller than six feet and weighed more than two hundred pounds. The aura of intimidation they brought with them into the courtroom was accentuated by the way their beefy forearms stayed folded across their chests, just below their scowls. Being raised in Compton had shown them how the white man preyed on the black, how the white man thought all black folks gangbang and sling rock, how the black man was told to stop complaining if he even hinted at being discriminated against. The Knights had seen what happened to Rodney King happen on their block a dozen times, the only difference being the absence of a video camera. When they saw the King beating on TV, they were not as surprised that it happened as they were by its appearance on the white man's news shows.

This judge is white, thought Ron. *Prosecutor's white. This Kinney dude, over there sitting with the prosecutors every day—that's the biggest redneck I ever seen in my life. Walking by us like he bad. With his pudgy ass. D's lawyer's white. Rex's too. Ten out of twelve jurors—white as a motherfucker. Media people white. Damn right we're gonna sit here with our arms crossed, watching this thing like hawks.*

A rotation of Darryl's aunts, uncles, cousins, and friends showed up in shifts. As a potential witness, Darryl's mom was ordered to sit in the hall outside the courtroom. She sat as close to Darryl as she could without being held in contempt, staking out a bench right outside the double doors. Darryl's dad did not come to court. He tried, but it hurt too much, he said later. Dorothy was there every day, Bible in her lap, whiling away the hours copying verses of scripture, mostly from Deuteronomy. On her way to or from the restroom, she'd steal glances through the swinging doors to try and get a fix on what was happening. The sight of Darryl sitting there, handsome in the new suit they'd picked out together, gave her hope. *They've got nothing on that boy*, she thought.

She did not hear Judge Taylor rule that the letter Darryl had faxed to Angela Wallace from the cruise ship would be admissible as evidence—a reversal of the ruling he had made several months earlier. To support it, Taylor pointed out that Darryl had fallen asleep and left the letter on the bed, thus failing to prevent Shetelle from discovering it.[3] The trial was filled with such issues. Because they had to be argued outside the jury's presence, one juror recalled his most prominent memory of the Henley trial as "all the times we had to walk in and out of the courtroom so the lawyers and the judge could talk about whatever."

The jurors, who had gotten to know each other by the second week, spent these quarantine periods playing cards and doing crossword puzzles in the jury room. The man who would become their foreman, Edmund Richards, showed them how to do the daily cryptogram puzzles in the *Register*. Well liked because of his age and kind disposition, Richards shared stories with the other jurors of a life that to that point had been a tapestry of experience—from his youth in 1930s London, to his escape from the Nazis as a European Jew, to his successful furniture business nearby, and his current work with the local Big Brothers program. Richards hit it off immediately with Reid Johnson, the fifty-nine-year-old black ex-Marine. The two oldest jurors, Richards and Johnson played a perpetual card game throughout the trial while the lawyers and the judge did their dancing next door. Mike Malachowski played cards with them sometimes. The ante was only nickels and dimes, but Malachowski cheated often enough for Richards and Johnson to tell him to get lost. At the time, no one gave a second thought to Malachowski's affinity for breaking rules.

A twenty-four-year-old father of three, Mike Malachowski seemed proud that he didn't have to work for a living, thanks to an injury he'd suffered during his most recent job and his subsequent collection of unemployment, workman's comp, and now jury service checks. Bryan Quihuis, the only other twenty-something male on the panel, was considered "just as loud" as Malachowski but not as abrasive. Quihuis was just immature. The other jurors felt uncomfortable that the defendants' lives were in the hands of a guy who proudly flashed his JUROR badge to pedestrians during lunch breaks, as if he were a celebrity.

Quihuis sliced deli meat at a supermarket in Rialto, a town that Malachowski would have passed had he driven to court alone, so they agreed to carpool together. Their families knew one another. Quihuis had once worked at a construction company owned by Malachowski's cousin, who was a close friend of Quihuis's uncle. In light of later events, it was wondered if Malachowski and Quihuis hadn't crossed paths personally before the Henley trial. But early on, Mike and Bryan seemed harmless. Young and impulsive, but "too dumb to be dangerous," as one juror put it.

Shawn O'Reilly was an unlikely recruit into their carpool group. The forty-one-year-old truck driver was fifteen years older than Mike and Bryan, but he seemed cool enough to keep quiet if, say, one of them defied the judge's orders by talking about the case. Sometime during the trial's first few weeks, as this threesome was driving home on the 91 Freeway, Malachowski asked the other two jurors if Rayburn had seemed particularly angry that day.

"Yeah," O'Reilly said, "but I don't know why."

"Maybe because that Shetelle chick is supposed to be *his* witness," Mike said.

"Man, I wouldn't want to have Rayburn mad at me like that," O'Reilly added.

A silence passed. The tires hummed.

"She's hot," Mike noted.

"Who?"

"That girl, Shetelle. Darryl's girlfriend."

"It's a shame she fell for that guy," said O'Reilly. "I've got three girls at home, and if I found out one of my daughters was dating a guy who was hiding a couple other girlfriends, I'd wring his neck."

"Sheesh."

"The guy's a snake," O'Reilly added.

"Who?"

"Who do you think?" O'Reilly said.

233

Chapter 23

Tracy Donaho entered the courtroom wearing a flowered dress hemmed tastefully below the knee. "There was a feeling in the air when she took the stand," remembered *LA Times* reporter Susan Marquez-Owen. "A sense of high emotion." As Darryl watched her fold her dress behind her knees and take her seat at the witness stand, he was reminded once again of all the mistakes he had made. He had certainly played a part in bringing Tracy into this courtroom, and now he had the sense that he was about to pay for it. Within moments of John Rayburn's first question, once it became clear that Tracy would try and play the role of the dim-bulbed damsel who had been lured into all this, Henley remembered that no one had held a gun to her head and *made* her carry those suitcases. He could still hear her laughter, now two summers old, when she'd called him "paranoid" for telling her to think twice about flying for Willie.

Tracy Donaho leaving court with her mother and attorney. (*Orange County Register*)

"When you met Mr. Henley," Rayburn asked his star witness, "how old were you?"

"I was nineteen."

The defense attorneys scribbled furiously. The transcripts wouldn't be available for another day or two, so all they had were their short-term memories and notes to prepare their cross-examinations. Roger Cossack wasn't scribbling. He could look at Chaleff's notes if he had to. For now, Cossack was watching Tracy, studying her eyes and hands, looking for signs of weakness the way his client did with opposing receivers. Cossack and several others, jurors included, noticed that after each of Rayburn's questions Tracy would turn to the jury and answer with rehearsed clarity before turning to Rayburn again for the next question. Her replies were robotic and coached, falling right in line with what Cossack and Chaleff had expected from the prosecution: that they would use Tracy's blonde, youthful looks to seduce the jurors into thinking she was blameless, just as she had convinced security personnel in five airports.

Henley didn't see Tracy as malicious as he watched her on the stand. There was nothing vindictive about her. He could tell she was scared. At recess he told Rex that he felt sorry for her. Her skin had lost the tanned glow it had radiated back in the summer of 1993. It was winter 1995 now, and the freckles the sun had once sprinkled on her nose—the freckles he used to tease her about—were gone, replaced now by pallor. Tracy "spoke in a well-amplified voice and kept her eyes on the jury when she talked," the *Register* reported. "She avoided looking at Henley, the man with whom she once discussed marriage and children."

"At this time, would you please take a look around the courtroom and see if you recognize Mr. Henley?" Rayburn asked.

". . . He's right there. . . . He has a gray suit on, a white shirt. I can't really see his tie."

The value of her testimony hinged on whether she could stick to the sixty-seven-page statement she had written for the prosecutors, as well as the various interviews she had given the DEA. Any variations from those scripts would give the defense a chance to plant their petri dishes of reasonable doubt. Rayburn began with the blossoming of her relationship with Darryl. "He was very funny," Tracy testified. "He seemed to think highly about his position with the Rams. . . . He was very outgoing. . . . A lot of the time [we spent together] was joking around, play fighting or wrestling. . . . It made it a lot easier [to relate to Darryl], I felt a lot more comfortable with him because of that. . . . I found Darryl to be very easy to talk to."

Next, Rayburn pointed out his star witness's more unfavorable attributes, to lessen the damage of having them revealed by the defense. Tracy admitted to smoking marijuana three times in her life: once at her house, in high school, when she and a girlfriend had been hanging out with "two guys out front by their car smoking marijuana"; a second time at a party during her community college days, when she and some friends "kind of passed it around and I then again took another—I inhaled it one time"; and a third instance at the home of Travis (the guy she had been dating when she met Darryl), when she "again did take another smoke or inhale the marijuana." She admitted to cheating on a TV dating show once, when she and a male friend had pretended to be strangers, then faked a love connection so they could walk away $500 richer. It wasn't high-level fraud (although the defense would later try and make it seem so), but Rayburn knew that Chaleff knew about it, so he had to get it and the marijuana thing out of the way early.

Rayburn tried to use a large calendar to assist Tracy with the timeline of her testimony, but the defense objected on the grounds that she seemed to be remembering things just fine. Taylor sustained, and the calendar was put away while the jury listened to Tracy's day-to-day account of her relationship with Henley—from the Super Bowl where they met, to the Vegas trip where they slept together for the first time, to the meeting at TGI Friday's where the conspiracy was born, all the way to her arrest in Atlanta on July 15. Darryl was unprepared for how rehearsed it seemed. Most of her answers were delivered in the same template—"Yes, I do," "Yes, it is," "No, I'm not"—and even for these quick replies she would turn toward the jury, then turn stiffly back to Rayburn to field his next question, which she seemed to know already, like a novice actress mouthing her leading man's lines.

Rayburn eventually was allowed to use his poster-size calendar to refresh Tracy's memory, which made at least one juror "wonder if they were refreshing her memory, or trying to tell her 'This is how it went down.'"

According to Tracy, the first time she had sex with Darryl (in their hotel room in Las Vegas) she felt "confused." She didn't resist, she just "didn't feel like she knew him well enough to be having sex with him." Darryl leaned toward Cossack and whispered, "I thought she enjoyed it." Jim Riddet had to look away so Taylor couldn't see him laughing. The defense felt confident enough to joke at this point, based on the less-than-solid testimony Tracy was putting forth. She testified that when she and Darryl returned from Las Vegas, he went a full day without calling her, which made her feel "very hurt." Darryl repaired this rift, she said, by surprising her with flowers and a balloon at her waitressing job, which made Tracy feel as if "things were going very well. I was very happy." She took a photograph of the flowers as a keepsake. Rayburn entered it into evidence.

Then the roller coaster began. Tracy said she stopped hearing from Darryl in the days leading up to a Rams promotion at which they were both scheduled to appear. This made her feel "very hurt" and "very upset," so she switched with another cheerleader so she could avoid Henley. He responded by leaving her a voice message — *I get the picture. You don't want to see me anymore* — which made Tracy feel "upset," "really hurt," and "as if he was leaving me in a situation where I was never going to talk with him again or be able to explain myself or get an explanation from him."

Darryl called the next day, as Tracy was preparing to go to Disneyland with Travis. "I got real upset," Tracy said. ". . . I started hysterically crying and ended up hanging up on him saying, 'I don't care if I ever see you again.'" But she *did* want to see him again, she said, a dilemma that left her "crying so hard and frantic." She called every number she had for him to try and make amends, but she couldn't get through. Then she went to Disneyland with Travis.

Darryl looked at Cossack with wide eyes. See? This girl was cray-zee.

Rayburn was allowed to use his calendar to help Tracy pinpoint the day she went to the movies with Darryl and he "opened the glove compartment and he pulled out a gun."

The courtroom drew in a collective breath, but Darryl kept his cool. He knew that this gun business appeared nowhere in her statement, in none of her interviews with law enforcement, and nowhere in the government's discovery. "Because it never happened," he said later. What did happen, he said, was that after more than a year of trying to dig up dirt on him, the prosecutors came forth with this gun thing. "I got really scared," Tracy testified. "I didn't think I was in any danger. Just guns in general scare me, and I got really upset and asked him to please put it away." *Now* Cossack was scribbling.

Rayburn quickly moved on to the Rams' charity basketball game. Tracy became "very upset" at the news that Darryl was in town and "hadn't bothered to tell me. . . . I went straight to the pay phone . . . and called [Darryl's house] and spoke with a man." She was rude to this unnamed man, she said, who told her that Darryl wasn't home. When she called again, after work, this same man told her that Darryl should be home soon. Darryl called Tracy a few minutes later and told her that he and a friend were headed to TGI Friday's for a bite to eat. He invited her to come along.

Darryl remembered that conversation differently. Tracy invited *herself* to Friday's, he said. But he agreed with her testimony about their discussion as they were leaving Friday's, when she noticed a fireman sticker on the back of Willie's vehicle and asked Darryl if he was a fireman. Darryl replied that Willie was "involved in a type of real estate construction," Tracy testified, "that he traveled around different states transporting cash."

Darryl flew back to Atlanta the next day. He did not return to California until the Rams' minicamp, two weeks later. Tracy said she only saw Darryl twice during minicamp. They got ice cream together one night, and went back to the team hotel where they had a playful water fight in Darryl's room, followed by sex, and her departure at about 1 a.m. The second time was Cinco de Mayo. A few hours before she met up with Darryl, "an older man . . . a big Rams fan" approached her at a cheerleading promotion and showed her a group of snapshots, one of which showed Darryl holding a small boy. This made Tracy "really upset," she testified, "because I had asked Darryl earlier if he had any children and he said no, he didn't." She gave Darryl the cold shoulder that evening, until Darryl asked her to step outside the restaurant so they could talk. In the parking lot, Tracy "started crying" because Darryl had lied to her about not having children. Darryl responded: "Look, if I had kids, you'd know about it. I'd take them everywhere. I wouldn't keep that from you."

When Tracy calmed down, Darryl asked her to come back to the hotel with him. "And I said yes," Tracy testified.

"Did you talk with your mom that evening?" Rayburn asked.

"Yes, I did. . . . I told my mom I was spending the night at a girlfriend's house."

"But you went with Darryl back to the hotel?"

"That's correct."

"How long did you stay at the hotel?"

"I spent the night there."

Tracy had described that night much differently in her statement, writing: "When I got [to Darryl's hotel] I called my mom. I told her that I had too much to drink and was spending the night at a girlfriend's. She hated Darryl so much. . . . I had a little too much to drink to worry about it at that time. Darryl and I had sex that night." Her trial testimony omitted not only her excessive drinking and her mother's hatred for Darryl but also the fact that Tracy slept with Henley yet again. If these three blemishes were going to be revealed to the jury, Rayburn was going to make the defense work for them during cross-examination. That work never happened, and the story of Tracy the ruined angel lived on.

Everything else Tracy said about that night was true, Henley said—as true as the decision he made around that time to start easing away from her. "She had some issues," he said. "I don't know if it was an abandonment thing that had to do with her dad leaving all the time or what." (Tracy testified about experiencing some "ups and downs" with her dad over the years "due to separation with him living far away.") "She was just real clingy." He shrugged, as if admitting his own mistake. "She was young."

Rayburn guided her testimony through the rest of May, a period when Tracy spoke with Darryl over the phone but didn't see him because he was in Atlanta. It was here that her testimony made its most dramatic departure from her written statement. Her statement contained a critical conversation with Darryl that she said occurred in "late May." Needing to present an exact date at trial, the prosecution pinpointed Sunday, May 30, as the day Tracy drove to Henley's house during a break between her waitressing jobs and spoke with him about having children. If Darryl were to choose a mother for his child, he told Tracy, it would be her. He said he would put her in an apartment and take care of her, Tracy testified, because "he didn't think I'd go and sue him for all the money he had."

This conversation on May 30, Tracy testified, was also the first time Darryl spoke to her about working for Willie. She'd been telling Darryl how tired she was of waiting tables, so he presented an opportunity for her to fly suitcases of cash to other states, making $300 to $400 per trip. "At one point I asked him if I could be in any sort of danger doing this," she testified, "and he said to me — I remember him kind of laughing — 'Well, the only kind of danger you could be in [is] if you tell somebody your bag is full of cash. That's just like saying, Knock me over the head and take my bag.'" Tracy testified that she and Darryl went to a movie that night, then to dinner. "He then asked me if I would make love to him that night," Tracy continued. "And I said that I would, and we then went to 7-Eleven to buy condoms."

On that note, Rayburn announced that he'd reached a good stopping point.

As it turned out, Tracy's testimony about May 30 was one long falsehood. It would be proven by travel records and the testimony of four other travelers that Darryl Henley returned to LA from Cancun on the night of May 30 — too late for him to have seen Tracy during the day, then gone on a date with her that evening.

(Hospital records proved that Henley was also battling a post-Mexico case of salmonella poisoning that night.) But Tracy would not be cross-examined on this point until two days later, by which time she had grown conveniently foggy about the exact date.

"Well, do you remember . . . testifying in this court when Mr. Rayburn asked you the questions that you met with Darryl on May 30?" Cossack asked.

"Yes."

"All right, and does that refresh your memory as to the day that you met with him?"

"Yes."

"And it *was* May 30?"

"Yes."

Cossack had pinned her to that date again, but surprisingly, that was the extent of his cross-examination on the subject. May 30 was no small thing. The prosecution had declared it the day that Darryl lured Tracy into his cocaine trafficking scheme. But someone in the U.S. Attorney's Office had skipped the critical step of making sure Henley had been in town that day — or even in the country. Years later, Henley would still be upset that his attorneys hadn't taken the government to task over the liberties they had taken with his whereabouts on the weekend the cocaine conspiracy began. But there was little Cossack could have done other than glue Tracy to that date again. Besides, he and Chaleff thought the evidence they would present later — evidence that Darryl had returned from Mexico on the night of May 30, sick as a dog — would be enough to prove Tracy a liar.

May 30, 1993. No cocaine was even moved that day, but it would become one of the most important dates of the trial. Soon everyone became weary of dealing with it — everyone except Darryl, who thought that it hadn't been dealt with enough.

A guy walks into a bar and asks the bartender if there are any criminal attorneys around. "That's the only kind we've got," says the bartender, "but we can't seem to prove it."

— OVERHEARD IN HALL AT HENLEY TRIAL

Chapter 24

"Miss Donaho," Rayburn said, "I believe yesterday when we left off, we were talking about Sunday, May 30, 1993. Do you recall?"

Tracy's testimony continued: they were driving to buy condoms after dinner when Darryl began playing a rap tape in his Lexus and talking about its lyrics. "This is your part if you work for Willie," Darryl allegedly said to Tracy. "Here, listen to your part. This is your part." Tracy testified that Darryl rewound the tape for her four times, but she still couldn't understand the lyrics.

The song in question was "Gotta Let Your Nuts Hang" by a rap group called the Geto Boys, which described the profits and perils of drug running and how a gambler's mentality (i.e., "letting your nuts hang") could lead to success in that field. Darryl had played the song for Tracy, the prosecution argued, as a playful joke about the mischief she was getting into. But the "rap tape," as it became known, was a legal tightrope for John Rayburn. Riddled with slang about moving drugs, selling drugs, buying drugs, and smoking drugs, the song was supposed to have supported the idea that Tracy thought she was carrying cash. But it contained no allusions whatsoever to carrying money.

When Rayburn produced a transcript of the song's lyrics, the defense objected immediately on the grounds that government paralegals might not be the most accurate transcribers of gangster rap. Indeed, in a glaring example of the differences between the defendants' world and the world in which they were being tried, the transcript contained no fewer than thirty-six errors, not counting its misspellings and its complete lack of punctuation, which resulted in a single run-on sentence that went on for more than two pages. The word *fiend* was mistyped three times as *feign*. *Slinging*—selling drugs—was typed three times as *swinging*. And according to the transcript, the Geto Boys, products of Houston's squalid housing projects, were not from "the land of the heartless" but "the land of the horseless." Taylor sustained the defense's objection without comparing the transcript to the song.

A better translator might have been found on the witness stand. Tracy was quite a fan of rap music. It was one of the reasons Darryl liked her from the start. Her attraction to his hip-hop-chic Karl Kani outfit had sparked his interest, and he knew that her affinity for rap was practically a requirement for her job as an NFL cheerleader. Since high school Tracy had choreographed many a dance routine to its bass-and-snare undercurrent, and she was more than familiar with the slang in its lyrics. (A DEA officer would testify later that Tracy's voicemail greeting was "a recorded message of rap music.") Cossack questioned in court why this "rap tape" story of hers, like the gun-in-Darryl's-glove-box story, had not been mentioned in any of her lengthy interviews with the DEA or in her handwritten statement. As for the song itself, Cossack said he was "baffled" that a transcript should be necessary. "It seems to me if you're going to play it, I think the jury should hear what she heard."

So Rayburn played the tape in court, twice. "Tracy's part" — the part that Darryl allegedly asked her to listen closely to — was:

The dope is getting short up in New York, too.
We sell it for thirty-three, they sell it for forty-two.
See what we gotta do is come together.
They trying to cut shit short, and they will if you let 'em.
Now let's go out on a boat,
Pretend to be lawmen, and come out with dope.
But first we gotta find a bitch with nuts,
A down-ass bitch who doesn't give a fuck.
Distracts the cops on duty,
Walking around, shaking nothin' but booty.

"Now, Miss Donaho, after hearing that tape several times, . . . what did you understand your role to be in working for Willie Mc-Gowan?" Rayburn asked.

"I understood that I would be taking the suitcase full of cash for him, and I understood that they used a girl because it helped things to go a little more smoothly."

"Let me back up just a moment," Rayburn said, his rehearsal with her on this point having failed. "What did you understand that particular portion of the tape to be saying?"

"Just that you had a girl carry it for you."

"When you say, 'you had a girl carry it for you,' what did you understand 'it' to be, in regards to the tape?"

"A suitcase."

"What did you understand to be *in* the suitcase?"

"Money."

Rayburn was trying to get Tracy to say that the song was about drugs, so she could save herself from being bludgeoned on this point by the defense. "Now again," he continued, "I'm talking about the tape, on the tape itself that you just listened to, what was the focus of that part?"

"They in the tape were transporting drugs."

245

"You understood the tape to be involving a woman carrying drugs, is that correct?"

"Yes. At that point, I hadn't really heard the whole song, but at a later point I did."

"Later on, as you were listening to the tape more clearly, what did you understand your role to be in terms of transporting the suitcase?"

"That I was to carry the suitcase of cash."

"You still understood your role to be a courier of cash, not narcotics?"

"Yes, I did."

Whether Tracy knew there was cocaine in her suitcase would be covered at great length later, but this was an insightful prelude to that chapter in the trial. Rayburn had just asked the jury to believe that after Tracy listened to a song that contained fifteen references to cocaine and zero references to cash, she had thought she was carrying cash — cash, by the way, that she believed had nothing to do with drugs. Rayburn did not ask Tracy about what she had written in her statement: "The song that we listened to was about drug running."

Rayburn returned to May 30. Tracy testified that she had sex with Darryl that night and the next night, too. "Things seemed to be going pretty well at that time," she testified. "I was happy." Their contact was sporadic through the first weeks of June — just phone calls and voice messages.[1] She had quit working at the Zendejas restaurant and was trying out for the Rams' cheerleaders again. She testified that Darryl called her after her audition and, pretending to be a Rams official, told her she had made the team. His laughter at her overjoyed reaction blew his cover, which got Tracy laughing, too. (Henley recalled that this gag actually happened.)

Rayburn moved on to the next time she spoke to Darryl about working for Willie. "That would have been the 28th of June," Tracy testified. Five days before her fateful flight to Memphis.

"Can you describe Mr. Henley's demeanor?"

"He seemed sort of panicked to me. And he seemed panicked, yeah."

Henley told her that Willie really needed someone to fly to Memphis, she testified. Tracy agreed to make the trip, but the plan fell through.

A couple of days later, she was lying by the pool at her mom's house when Darryl called and asked her to pick up a package at his house and overnight it to him in Georgia. She drove to Darryl's house, where, just as she said in her statement, a black man in the garage gave her a $100 bill and pointed to a package, which she took to the post office. Darryl called her the next day and told her the package didn't arrive. Tracy felt horrible, responsible, until Darryl's chuckling once again gave him away. "It got here. I was just kidding," he said. (A fabrication, according to Henley. The prosecution's clever continuation of the cheerleading gag.) Henley denied then, just as he denied a decade and a half later, that he had any knowledge of the package Tracy overnighted to Smyrna, Georgia, on June 30 — other than owning the house where Tracy picked it up and owning the phones from which the calls to her had been placed. The government would hammer both those points home: Henley's house, Henley's phones.

Rayburn moved on to July 2, the date Darryl called Tracy a second time about flying to Memphis. Henley told her that when she "got to Memphis, I was to take a cab to, if I remember correctly, to the Doubletree Hotel. I was to check into a room and then page him." She was told to keep her suitcase with her as a carry-on during the flight.

"Were those instructions from Mr. Darryl Henley?"

"Yes. . . . [Darryl] then told me I would make $1,000 for making this trip. . . . I was told that there would be people watching me or that I would be watched over very closely and make sure everything went okay and that yes, I would be protected."

". . . Willie McGowan ever give you any instructions about this trip?"

"No, I never talked with him."

She went to Darryl's house that night and "waited around for somebody to show up."

"Who arrived?"

"Eric."

"Did you know Eric?"

"Yes."

"What's Eric's last name?"

"Manning."

". . . Had you ever met Eric Manning prior to that time?"

"No, I hadn't."

Darryl glanced at Cossack. *Didn't she just say she knew him?*[2]

Tracy heard "sounds like tape being pulled or like Velcro ripping" coming from upstairs. Manning came down lugging a suitcase and drove her to the airport in Henley's Lexus. When she got out of the car at the airport, she saw Rex Henley waiting for her.

It was all true—everything she said about that night. Darryl *did* call her with details about the trip, he *did* tell her that her ticket was reserved under the name "Maggie Williams," and Rex *did* meet Tracy at the Ontario airport so he could escort her and her suitcase to Memphis. Rex's attorney would deny it throughout the trial. He would even put Rex's wife on the stand to present an alibi. But Rex would admit to it years later. He didn't know what was *in* that suitcase, he said, but he wasn't blind, he knew it wasn't above board. "I knew what was going on," Rex said. "You kind of know what was going on, but you *didn't* know." So he kept his role simple: "Fly here, pick up this, bring the money back, whatever."

But there would be no flight that night.

When Tracy and Rex missed their plane, she went home and received a call from Darryl at about 2:30 a.m. The government's phone evidence would later show this call from Darryl's Atlanta apartment to Tracy's mother's house at 2:24 that morning. This forty-seven-minute call, more than any other piece of evidence, was irrefutable proof that Darryl Henley had been involved in moving drugs. It made his claims of innocence about the overnight package to Smyrna seem flimsy.

Near the end of this call, Darryl told Tracy to meet Willie at the Brea house at 5 a.m. so they could catch a 7:30 flight, Tracy testified. Darryl called Tracy again when she arrived at the Brea house. "And before I got off the phone, he said that he loved me."

"Had Darryl ever told you before that he loved you?"

"No, he hadn't."

Her testimony about what happened when she landed in Memphis fell right in line with her previous statements, with one exception. She testified that either Garey West or Gary Dabney paged Darryl from Dabney's apartment. This conflicted with what she had told the DEA (that *she* had paged Darryl), but the defense never pointed out this discrepancy, which made Henley appear to have been in cahoots with two known drug dealers. The defense also did not protest when Tracy said she considered the Memphis trip "very scary. I thought that I definitely knew that I didn't want to do it again." From his chair at the defense table, Darryl silently disagreed. He remembered her asking him less than a week after that trip if they were going to use her again.

"At some point did you talk to [Darryl] about being paid for the [Memphis] trip?"

"Yes, I did." When Tracy drove with her friend Stacy to pick up the money from Western Union, she told Stacy it was for some work being done on Darryl's house. When asked why she didn't tell Stacy the truth, Tracy testified: "I'm not really sure why I didn't."

Tracy identified the Western Union transfer in question — for $1,000, sent on July 9, 1993. The government's handwriting expert would testify that the "Darryl Henley" signature on it had indeed been signed by the football player. Darryl knew he had signed it, and ten years later he clung to the same explanation he had been dying to blurt out in court that day. He wired the money to Tracy because she kept complaining that Willie hadn't paid her yet, that she was broke, and that she needed it for her bachelorette weekend in Las Vegas. "I sent it to her to shut her up," he said. At trial, this wire transfer looked like proof that he had been in charge of a cocaine conspiracy. Not even Henley could deny that he had paid a courier to deliver a suitcase that he knew contained cocaine.

When Tracy returned home from Vegas, she spoke with Willie over the phone. He asked her to fly for him later that day. Tracy said no. Willie said fine. When they hung up, Tracy showed her sister some of the things she had bought in Vegas. "She asked me where I got all the money to go and have this trip," Tracy testified. "And I told her that Darryl had a friend that I had worked for." When Tracy told her sister she'd made $1,000 just by flying across the country, Sherry said she "thought that that seemed to be a lot of money for doing just that, and could there possibly be something wrong and implied that maybe it was something illegal."

This was a milder account than the one Sherry Donaho gave Detective Mike Ortiz on the night of Tracy's arrest ("Tracy knew the money was involved with the purchase of narcotics"), but moments after Sherry said that to Ortiz, her father had shown up, setting off Cossack's "nasty, nasty conspiracy" to frame Henley. Sherry would retract her incriminating comment within two months of speaking it, further supporting Cossack's conspiracy theory, as did the prosecution's decision not to call Sherry or her father to the witness stand at trial. The notion that Tracy didn't know she was carrying drugs was becoming a hard sell.

Rayburn moved on. "Let's talk about Wednesday of that week, July 14." The day before her arrest. "Do you recall receiving a telephone call that day?"

"Yes I do. . . . If I remember correctly, it was Willie. . . . He said that he really needed somebody to make a trip for him and could I please do it. . . . I said no."

Later that day she received a page from an Atlanta number she'd never seen before. When she called it, Willie answered and said, "'Oh, hold on a second. Darryl wants to talk with you, let me get him.' And he put Darryl on the phone and Darryl said that Willie really needed somebody to fly out that night and could I do it. I would be flying to Atlanta and we'd get to see each other, and I said no. I had practice that night and I had a promotion the next day and I really wasn't going to be able to do it. We talked for a little while longer and I can't really remember all what was said. We were—I hadn't seen him it seemed like in a while and want-ed to—by the end of the conversation, I had decided to change my plans, and I told him that I would try to change my plans and that I would get back to him . . ."

"During that conversation, did Darryl mention anything about you and he seeing each other?"

"Yes, he did. . . . He really stressed the fact that we would get to see each other and we would get to spend a little time together."

Later in his life, Darryl would want to travel back to this mo-ment in the trial and bring with him a copy of the Western Union money transfer made on July 14 in the amount of $700 to "Tracy Donahoe" and signed, in what appeared to be a forgery, by "Darry Henley." Then he'd want to shoot ahead six weeks to the handwrit-ing expert who testified that the signature was a forgery. It would be boring when the handwriting guy said it, but if he could walk through the doors and say it now, *right now*, and if Cossack could place his own transparency showing Tracy's inconsistent state-ments next to the one showing all the phone calls between Tra-cy and Willie, it would be mind blowing. *The jury would see that I had nothing to do with her trip to Atlanta.*

But trials don't work like that. Not even Cossack's deft cross-ex-amination skills could pull it off. The evidence was going to stay spread out, its individual impacts padded by the time between them, as the government had ingeniously planned.

"Why did you make a flight arrangement [to Atlanta] for one o'clock in the morning?" Rayburn asked.

"Well, I had already lied to my mom. . . . I thought I'd make one for late that night and go ahead and go on to Atlanta so I could see Darryl as soon as I could." In her statement Tracy said it was "because I had nothing else to do." Now, at trial, her reason for flying at 1 a.m. was that she wanted to see Darryl.

"At that point, what luggage did you have with you?"

"I had the suitcase that I had brought for Darryl and Willie." ("I was told it wasn't for Darryl, it was for Willie," Tracy had told Ortiz after her arrest. "I was doing this for Willie.")

Tracy testified that after she was stopped by the DEA in Atlanta, she went to a pay phone at the Marriott and dialed the number she had used to reach Willie over the previous twenty-four hours — a number she'd called nine times, with no one but Willie having ever answered. "When you called that number, who did you expect to answer?" Rayburn asked.

"I expected to speak with Darryl," Tracy testified.

"When you called that number, what occurred?"

"Willie answered the phone." (It had been much simpler in her statement: "In the lobby of the Marriott, I called Willie from the pay phone.")

Tracy began to cry on the stand as she explained why she had wanted to see Darryl so desperately that day. "Because I was very scared and I trusted him." ("Your Honor, perhaps this is the time to take a recess?" Cossack asked. But Judge Taylor saw through Cossack's attempt to play to the jury's sympathies: "No. I don't think so, counsel. Continue, please.") Tracy tearfully recounted the remainder of July 15, up to the moment Darryl told her, "The valuables are gone, so now we need to worry about you." It was at that point, Tracy testified, that she "realized that there was something illegal in the suitcase."

She testified that Darryl had indeed been seated next to her during her interview in the DEA office, but she did not mention that they had held hands throughout it or that they'd leaned their heads on each other's shoulders, hugging, as DEA officer Lisa Roey would testify later. Tracy merely recalled that "every once in a while, [Darryl] would tap my leg or rub my leg." Rayburn did not want the jury to wonder why Tracy had been cuddling with the man who—according to her story, and according to the Polaroids Hogan showed her—had just duped her into muling drugs for him, so he did not probe further.

Rayburn asked what else Darryl did during the interview.

"Just sitting next to me and tapping my leg. That was about it."

She had almost forgotten to say that Henley told her to lie. Rayburn nudged her toward it. "Did Darryl ever say anything to you while the interview was going on?"

"Yes, he did. . . . First he asked the agents if he could speak alone with me, and then he told me just stick to the story and you'll be fine. Just stick to the story."[3]

Later in the trial, Rayburn set up a reenactment of this all-important interview, asking Roey to position two chairs at a right angle, the way Tracy and Darryl had been seated in the DEA office that night. In an odd bit of casting, Roey played the part of Darryl while Reggie Bennett, Kinney's 220-pound, black coinvestigator, played Tracy.

Nine years later, Darryl set up the same scene in the visiting room of the federal prison in Beaumont, Texas, demonstrating how foolish it would have been for him to have leaned toward Tracy—"with Hogan right there, and with Roey watching me like a hawk"—and told Tracy to "stick to the story and you'll be fine." If he'd done that, Henley said, then why did Hogan testify under oath that he found Darryl to be "a charming fellow [who] wanted Tracy to do the right thing"? If Henley was behaving suspiciously, why wasn't he even questioned after her arrest? "Because I didn't whisper to her," Henley said, calmly sliding the visiting room chairs back into place.

Inconsistencies like these abounded within Tracy's testimony. The last sentence of her handwritten statement, which described her mind-set when the DEA interview ended and she was handcuffed, read: "At that point, I knew I would tell the truth, just not with Darryl sitting next to me." This, of course, conflicted directly with the call she made to her father that night, when she told him the Allison Coats lie, hoping he would buy it. Darryl had not been near her then.

The prosecution had prepared Tracy well, though, and she and Rayburn together dodged these bullets. One juror remarked after the trial, "We all agreed there was no way Tracy Donaho could have concocted this whole story . . . but some people thought she might have been coached too much."

It is tempting to imagine that as Roger Cossack rose to begin his cross-examination of Tracy, John Rayburn reminded himself not to object. Tracy wasn't his client, the government was. And it wasn't Rayburn's job to protect someone who'd pled guilty to cocaine trafficking. Tracy was on her own.

It's just as tempting to imagine Cossack reminding himself to tread lightly. His task was to prove Tracy an outright liar while not making a villain of himself in front of the jury. Juries typically do not like older male attorneys who make pretty young witnesses cry, but Cossack knew that that's exactly what he was about to do, "bringing [Tracy] to tears," the *Register* reported, "in ten minutes."

He started with her lack of education. No, she hadn't gotten good grades in high school. No, she didn't know how many college credits she had, which courses she had taken, or whether she had passed or failed them.

"Did you drop out?" Cossack asked.

"I stopped—I can't remember."

"Did you just stop going?"

"I might have. I think so."

Cossack moved on to the motivations behind her guilty plea. Tracy had already testified that she "pled guilty because there were so many things that were suspicious. . . . I should have known," but to Cossack she admitted that she was indeed guilty of trafficking drugs. Then she said she didn't think she'd been carrying drugs. Cossack pointed out the conflict at hand and asked if she had ever considered "going to trial and telling the jury that you didn't know what was in that suitcase?"

"Yes, I did."

"But you chose against that . . . because you believe that the jury wouldn't believe you?"

"Not necessarily."

"You didn't want to take the chance, isn't that correct?"

"That's correct."

Tracy said she didn't understand "exactly what went on" at her arraignment, and didn't grasp "all the legal terms" in her plea negotiations, so she "had to have someone explain" it to her. Darryl couldn't help but notice the parallel between Tracy not knowing what was in her suitcase and not knowing what was in her plea deal.

"So you believe you're guilty of cocaine trafficking?" Cossack asked.

"It depends on how you look at it, I guess."

Cossack paused and took a step closer. "You don't believe you're guilty of cocaine trafficking, do you?"

"No."

Back during the holiday season of 1993, Judge Taylor had been so clear about the point Tracy was now stuck on. During her plea hearing Taylor had asked her, "Do you understand that the court is simply not allowed to accept a guilty plea from somebody who claims that they really are innocent. Do you understand that?" Tracy had answered yes, but Taylor had wanted to make doubly sure: "Do you follow me? Do you need me to say it over again?"

"Yeah, one more time," Tracy had said. So Taylor had repeated it, and Tracy had once again said she understood.

Tracy was crying again by the time Cossack arrived at July 14. "Is that the date that you say that Darryl Henley called you and begged you to come to Atlanta?"

"I believe so."

"Is that in your handwritten statement?"

"I don't recall."

It was the *climax* of her handwritten statement, the culmination of Darryl's plot to con her into moving drugs for him.

"And do you recall when you wrote your handwritten statement?"

"It was—it began after my public defender in Atlanta asked me to, and I continued after I got my attorney's stuff. And it was at different times that I would put it down and pick it up again."

"You only completed about a page and a half in Atlanta? . . . And the remainder was written here in Orange County?"

"Yes."

Cossack's repeated mention of Orange County—and not, say, "Yorba Linda" or "here at home"—had a purpose. It was an appeal to the seven non–Orange Countians on the jury, residents of hardscrabble towns like Riverside, San Bernardino, and Rialto, who might have had a bone to pick with the affluent, right-wing stronghold to the south—the kind of place where a conspiracy to frame a black man might take root. The defense believed—and tried to make obvious by the end of the trial—that Tracy's statement had been written not to reveal the truth but to keep her out of prison. Darryl had never felt more optimistic about his fate.

Reporter Barbara Kingsley expressed doubt about Tracy's testimony, writing in the *Register* that "while Donaho could remember a July 11, 1993, phone call from alleged coconspirator Willie McGowan, she had trouble remembering dates defense attorneys asked her about. When Cossack asked her if she had a good relationship with her father during 1993, she answered, 'I can't recall.'"

hearsay evidence n (1753): evidence based not on a witness's personal knowledge but on another's statement not made under oath.

—*MERRIAM-WEBSTER'S COLLEGIATE DICTIONARY*, 11th ed.

Chapter 25

Gary Taylor was inexperienced in presiding over federal drug cases, having broken in with the Colombian dog kennel case prosecuted by Eliot and Rayburn just two years earlier. But he had certainly done his homework since then. He knew that hearsay was a crucial part of most drug conspiracy trials, which were characterized by scant physical evidence—no dead bodies to examine, no serial numbers to trace, and in this case, no eyewitnesses to the handling of the drugs. Taylor knew that at the heart of any conspiracy were its closely guarded conversations, and he knew that the secondhand accounts of witnesses like Denise Manning, Eric Manning's widow, were the government's only way of bringing such conversations to light.

Taylor was committed to taking on an excruciatingly thorough process designed to weed out improper hearsay. This meant that the Henley jurors were often excused for hours at a time so that Taylor and the attorneys could listen to witnesses' testimony raw and discuss it before Taylor decided which parts of it the jury could hear.[1]

Among its many effects, the war on drugs had changed hearsay from a dirty, objectionable word into a valuable tool for prosecutors — one for which intricate exceptions could be made to render it usable in court. Without such exceptions, thousands of very dangerous criminals would surely have avoided jail, but the motives behind a witness's testimony, unfortunately, were not always analyzed as thoroughly as the testimony itself. Denise Manning, for example, was motivated to side with the prosecution. She'd admitted knowing of her husband's drug dealing and doing nothing to stop it, and she said she'd discussed his crimes with him. By law, this exposed her to prosecution for conspiracy. But as Riddet would point out, "She wasn't charged, and the [DEA] agents offered to keep it that way." As long as she testified at trial.

Another motivation for Denise Manning was that her husband, whom she called "the innocent one in all this," had been killed by a gunshot to the head. She was certain that Bustamante had pulled the trigger or ordered someone to, and her trial testimony was seen by many as her opportunity to punish Bustamante and the five other men she held responsible for removing Eric from her and her daughter's lives.

As Denise testified without the jury present, it became clear that she not only intended to tell the jury what she'd heard Eric say, but what she'd heard him say *about what he'd heard someone else say.* The defense made every hearsay protest they could, but Eliot had planned her long-winded rebuttals in advance. Denise's testimony was Eliot's baby — her biggest responsibility of the trial — and her fight to let the widow speak unfiltered to the jury became so impassioned that Taylor eventually asked Eliot to "slow down just a tad. We can't wear out our reporter before we even start the trial portion of the show."

While the admissibility of Denise Manning's hearsay was being considered, her brother Bernard Lee took the stand to have his own hearsay strained for the jury's consumption. He too relayed several statements made by Eric Manning, including one in which Manning confessed to Bernard that he'd been seeing someone other than Denise. This mistress lived in Atlanta, Bernard added, the city to which Manning had invited him that summer to help him pull off a drug deal. Manning had told Bernard all about the deal, using code names for his partners.

"The Mexican was the hookup," Eric told Bernard Lee, according to Lee's testimony. "The Big Man was in the NFL . . . the one who was more or less going to get rid of it [sell the drugs]."

When Manning told him about the twelve kilos that had been popped in Atlanta, Bernard was glad he had chosen to pass up Eric's Atlanta opportunity. After the Atlanta bust, Manning told Bernard that the Big Man had been complaining to him about the Mexican's demands for money. The Big Man said he didn't know how he was going to pay the Mexican, and "he just wanted it over with, more or less. 'I don't know why [the Mexican] keeps bugging me.'"

"Who is Big Man?" Bernard said he asked his brother-in-law.

"Man, I can't tell you that."

"Come on, [all] this stuff is going on. Now who is Big Man?"

"Do you know who Darryl Henley is? . . . He plays for the Los Angeles Rams."

"Geez," Bernard recalled saying.

"That's who Big Man is," Manning said.

Judge Taylor asked Bernard why he thought Manning had told him all this, and within Bernard's answer was the rub when it came to trusting Eric Manning. "To put it quite simple, pretty much to brag, I guess," Bernard said. It's part of what made admitting hearsay from Eric Manning so dangerous. It was hard to be sure if he was boasting, embellishing, or saying something worth listening to.

The day Bernard Lee testified would later be cited as the day that Ronald and Donald Knight threatened several government witnesses as those witnesses entered and exited the courtroom. Edward Cloud, one of Eric Manning's friends from the neighborhood, certainly appeared to have been threatened. As he was sworn in, Cloud gave a different name than the one he'd given investigators. "I was just Eric's friend," he testified. "I'm scared. . . . I don't want to be mixed up in this. . . . I didn't know nobody in this case. . . . I just didn't want to be in it. I just didn't want to be in it. I'm so scared. I don't want to be in it. . . . I was Eric's buddy, that's it." When asked why he was frightened, Cloud said, "I didn't want to be saying nothing about Willie."

The jury wasn't present for those comments, nor did they hear Cloud talk about the white-girl courier Manning said he'd been sending on trips to Atlanta. Cloud also testified that Manning claimed to *own* the white Lexus he'd been driving that summer; he said he'd bought it for his wife as a wedding present. Manning said he'd bought Henley's home in Brea, too, Cloud added. Manning had Cloud drive him to Orange County so he could show it off. Drinking heavily during the drive down, Manning asked Cloud to stop by the Rams' practice session so he could pick up some money from a "ballplayer." (This ballplayer never appeared.) By the time Cloud pulled up outside Henley's home in Brea, Manning had consumed a six-pack of Mickey's malt liquor. He nodded off in the back seat during the drive home.

This was the man who had started the game of "telephone" that Denise Manning was about to finish — the man her brother Bernard Lee had described as "like a comedian, more or less. . . . Every once in a while, [Manning] would kind of make a story bigger than life" until it became "a feather in the whirlwind . . . it doesn't carry much weight."

Bernard added: "You can believe 60 [percent of what Manning said] and probably not believe 40."

Aside from the purpose of filtering their hearsay, the appearance of these witnesses gave the prosecutors a chance to review their testimony and the manner in which they delivered it. It was obvious why the prosecution would never place Edward Cloud before the jury. It wasn't just his nerves; Cloud's testimony would have allowed the defense to insinuate that Tracy was the white girl Manning had going to Atlanta for him. Cloud also made Manning seem like one of the shot-callers in the deal — a role the prosecutors wanted only Henley and Bustamante to fill. Even Taylor noted: "This is not the government's strongest witness."

Denise Manning wasn't their strongest witness either, but she became invincible once Taylor said following her non-jury testimony that "the indicia of credibility and reliability are strongly present in this case." For the first time in the trial, Darryl felt genuinely uneasy.

His attorneys had once been confident that Denise Manning would be barred from testifying altogether; Riddet was particularly upset that she was about to be given an open mic. With her practice run complete, the defense knew that Rayburn and Eliot could weed out the questions whose answers might hurt their case, ensuring that the jury would never hear either. The prosecutors had also evaluated Denise's ability to handle questioning from the same terse attorneys who would be cross-examining her when it counted. Denise had held up well.

Before the jurors could hear Denise's testimony, though, Joe Maccione was called to the stand. Maccione, the Atlanta attorney who had driven around with Darryl and Tracy in his van just before Tracy was arrested, did little to incriminate Henley, but he recalled that the young woman with Henley that day had struck him as "upset and nervous. Very upset. Very nervous." When Maccione was done, Rayburn asked "that we continue with Miss Donaho's cross-examination."

It was a clever and entirely fair strategy for the government to slip Tracy back onto the stand after a five-day absence, when the Denise-obsessed defense team least expected it. Wearing a peach-colored suit and pearl earrings partially hidden by her pillowy hair, Tracy helped Rayburn correct a point that Riddet had just repeated for the third time: that she'd spent fifteen hours with the prosecution preparing for trial.

It wasn't fifteen hours, Tracy said. It was "approximately seventy-five to eighty hours."

The defense attorneys' eyes widened. *They spent eighty hours prepping her?*

I don't think I've spent eighty hours with her, total, Darryl thought.

The jury didn't seem to notice. It was late in the afternoon, almost quitting time.

"Do you think Tracy's been telling the truth?" Mike Malachowski asked his carpool partners during the ride home.

"No way," said Bryan Quihuis. "She's way too coached."

Out of the blue, Mike asked Shawn O'Reilly if he'd go out with Tracy.

"I'm married," O'Reilly said.

"Well, what if you *weren't* married?"

"I'm old enough to be her dad."

"What if you were her age?"

"If I was her age, and if she wanted to go out with me, I'd ask her out."

"Would you do her?" Mike asked.

"I wouldn't kick her out of bed," O'Reilly replied with a chuckle.

These same questions were posed regarding Deirdre Eliot. Quihuis called the prosecutor "beautiful." Everyone agreed that Shetelle Clifford was beautiful as well.

"So what do you think?" Mike said. "Guilty or not guilty?"

"All those niggers are guilty," O'Reilly said.

"Why do you think they're guilty?" Mike asked.

"Because the government wouldn't bring a case to trial like this unless they had enough evidence to convict the guy," O'Reilly said.

"Well, you haven't even heard the defense side yet," Mike said. "How could you say they're guilty?"

"I just think they are. . . . Those guys are lucky they're being tried in America and not overseas somewhere, where they hang drug dealers."

Bryan piped up with a halfhearted reminder that they weren't supposed to be discussing the case.

"What's the big deal?" Mike asked. "As long as it stays in this car."

The conversation among the three jurors stopped when a report came over the radio about the O.J. Simpson trial.

"O.J.'s gonna buy his way out," Mike predicted. "Watch, he's gonna pay some juror and walk."

"He could buy me for fifty grand," Bryan said.

Mike filed that bit of information away.

Rayburn began the next morning by asking Tracy to repeat the one rule he had given her during their eighty hours of meetings.

"Just to tell the truth," Tracy testified.

"It's Judge Taylor who will ultimately decide your sentence?" Rayburn asked moments later.

"Yes, it is."

Darryl considered that scarier than if Rayburn were to decide it. Despite the time Rayburn had spent with his star witness, Henley could tell that he was no Tracy fan. Rayburn never had, and never would, call Tracy a hero or call her testimony courageous or important to the case or any other adjective, not even after the verdict. He never supported her claim that she thought she was carrying money. Instead of believing Tracy, Rayburn endured her like a driver endures the tiny spare tire that brings the car home and then gets shoved back under the carpet in the trunk.

Taylor was different. Henley felt that the judge "accepted everything Tracy said as the gospel." It was an observation shared by several others close to the trial, and while there was no evidence to support it (other than the light sentence Taylor would eventually give her), it wasn't a stretch to imagine Taylor sympathizing with a girl raised ten minutes from his house who was testifying against five men raised several miles, several skin shades, and several income brackets away.

As Darryl sat pondering once again the dreadful error he'd made in getting involved in this mess in the first place, he didn't realize the biting coincidence taking place on this, the last day of Tracy Donaho's testimony. Suge Knight was in an LA courtroom that same day avoiding trial and receiving probation by pleading no contest to felony assault. Darryl, by contrast, had chosen to dig his heels in and fight. "I was raised to fight," he said later. "There was only one 170-pound defensive player in the league, and I didn't get there by lying down." Only after the trial was complete would he see that he had been fighting an unwinnable war. But the idea of an unwinnable war was as foreign to Henley as the idea of standing trial for drug dealing had been two years earlier.

"One question," Cossack said to Tracy after looking down at his notes. "You haven't been sentenced yet, have you?"

"No, I haven't."

"And part of what the recommendation is going to be by the United States Attorney's Office depends on how you testify in court, isn't that correct?"

"Depends on me telling the truth."

"They want to make sure that you stick to the story, isn't that correct?"

"Stick to the truth."

"Stick to the story that you've told them?"

"Objection," Rayburn said. "Asked and answered and argumentative."

Taylor sustained, but Cossack had already stepped away from the lectern, announcing that he had no further questions.

Darryl wrote a note and slid it to Chaleff: *I like my attorneys. Even if they are expensive.*

Chaleff scribbled a response and slid it back: *Not expensive enough.*

After one more round with Rayburn, Tracy stepped down and

exited the courtroom, having answered her last question of the trial. ("Your Honor, I have run out of gas," Cossack said. "He [Rayburn] is younger than I am.") The newspapers reported that she had "avoided looking at Henley" during her entire testimony; Tracy averted her eyes again as she walked a few feet in front of him and pushed open the swinging door, where Darryl's mother glanced coolly at her as she passed. Some observers thought that Tracy had avoided eye contact with Darryl out of fear or out of disgust at how he'd used her. Henley's opinion was that she avoided his eyes because meeting them would have reminded her of what only a handful of people in the room knew: that it was *she* who was using him.

Chapter 26

Only an old LA noir film would have had gruff gumshoe Kevin McLaughlin taking the stand right after troubled damsel Tracy Donaho, but there he was, in real life, undergoing Deirdre Eliot's tough questioning about his search of Darryl Henley's house in the fall of 1993.

Of all the evidence McLaughlin gathered during that search, two pieces stood out. The first was a scrap of paper taken from Henley's dresser, on which Darryl had calculated his "billings" and "payoffs" — most notably, a payoff in the amount of $360,000. It was exactly what Eliot and McLaughlin said it was: Darryl's notes about paying Bustamante. That it might also have been the scribbling of a man whose mother's life had been threatened — a man considering John Shaw's advice to make the whole thing go away by paying "the Mexican" — was left unexplored. The most compelling of the exhibits, though, was a photo showing several boxes of Saran Wrap sitting in Henley's kitchen drawer.[1] Eliot placed an enlargement of this photo on an easel. "This appears to be the Saran Wrap, or similar to the Saran Wrap, used to wrap the cocaine that was seized from the airport," McLaughlin testified.

When Riddet asked McLaughlin if he'd tested the wrap for fingerprints, the agent's touchiness on the subject was obvious:

"First of all—"

Judge Taylor intervened and made McLaughlin answer the question.

"No, I did not."

It was the single investigative measure that could have blown the case wide open—*fingerprints on the cocaine*—and McLaughlin's failure to execute it was embarrassing for everyone on the government side of the courtroom. It was almost certain, of course, that the Saran Wrap shown to the jury had in fact been used to package the cocaine that ended up in Atlanta. In Darryl's mind, though, the most important fact about the wrap was that he'd been two thousand miles away when it was used.

After Henley endured the testimony of Gary Dabney's ex-girlfriend, Amy Thompson—yet another witness against him that Henley had neither met nor seen before—he watched Taylor announce his much-anticipated ruling about Denise Manning. Virtually all of her hearsay would be allowed, Taylor ruled, because "Mrs. Manning qualifies as an active coconspirator, not just a passive one." This was the needle-eye through which Denise's testimony would enter the record—that Denise, a twenty-year-old, pregnant newlywed who'd testified that she'd never dealt drugs in her life, was, as Chaleff joked, "the consigliere of the Manning drug cartel." The jurors would *not*, however, hear her testimony about being promised immunity by Eliot "about three months ago . . . orally . . . face to face . . . in Deirdre Eliot's office." That information came out when the jurors were in the next room. Eliot quickly denied granting such immunity, which would have been gravely unethical, and she put Steven Kinney on the stand to support her denial. But Kinney's brief testimony in the empty courtroom did little to dissuade anyone that a promise had been made: *Talk, Denise, and you'll walk.*

Twisting the dagger in the defense's gut, Taylor noted that Denise's freshly admissible testimony had been "corroborated by lots of other testimony in the case, much of it by Tracy Donaho."

It made sense somehow that the person Darryl later called his "best witness of the entire trial" was called by the prosecution. Jennifer Wilson, as Rayburn pointed out to the jury, was staying with Darryl's parents during the trial; Darryl's mom had given her a ride to court that morning. Based on these links to the defendant, Rayburn tried to have Jennifer declared hostile, just as he'd tried with Shetelle Clifford. As with Shetelle, Taylor denied him.

It soon became clear that Jennifer was not there to perjure herself or protect anyone but to tell the truth. It also became clear that she was not about to be bullied by Rayburn the way Tracy had been by Cossack. During an exchange that the *Times* called "pointed" and "crusty," Rayburn asked Jennifer about discussing marriage with Darryl during their 1993 romance, and her mistaken impression that he'd been dating her exclusively at the time. It was yet another attempt to prove that because Darryl had conducted his private life woefully, he was a cocaine trafficker.

The testimony most damaging to the prosecution, however—whose case Jennifer was ostensibly there to strengthen—was about Kevin McLaughlin. Jennifer recalled that McLaughlin harassed her in the weeks leading up to trial by calling her "a lot. . . . One day, I had about seven calls. . . . I was getting tired of the calls." McLaughlin informed Jennifer "that Darryl had lots of women, that I wasn't the only one . . . that he was leading several different lives and he wasn't trying to break up a happy home, but he just thought that I should know that." McLaughlin behaved as if "this would be my opportunity to get even with Darryl," Jennifer said. [2]

The testimony she gave that incriminated Henley was given of her own volition. Jennifer testified that Willie had been "like part of the family," and that a guy named E often dropped by the Atlanta apartment, and gave her friendly hugs. Darryl obviously knew and hung out with these people. Jennifer testified that several men had access to the apartment (Willie had his own key), and that they all had permission to use the phones. The aura around their Buckhead apartment was, in Jennifer's words, "mi casa, su casa" — a phrase that Chaleff hoped the jury would remember when the government revealed its phone records, which Chaleff feared (correctly) would make Darryl's pad look like the East Coast hub of the Bustamante cocaine cartel.

These phone records loomed ahead for Chaleff like a 49ers game on the Rams' schedule. He knew that his only hope of winning that battle was to plant these seeds of doubt before kickoff. He noticed that Kinney, who usually sat next to Eliot, was absent during most of these middle days of the trial. Chaleff guessed correctly that Kinney was busy preparing the phone evidence, which Chaleff predicted (correctly again) would be presented on a large chart showing numerous calls between Henley and his codefendants. Or at least from Henley's *phones* to those used by his codefendants.

But that was still days away. For now, the Henley team could only hope that this non-LA jury, which seemed predisposed to convict, and included one member (O'Reilly) who was predisposed to napping, was paying attention to Jennifer Wilson. Henley wished he could make his own chart outlining her testimony — particularly the part about how Eric Manning always showed up *with* Willie or looking for Willie, sometimes waiting for him until late at night. "He used the phone a lot," Jennifer said of Manning. Darryl also "let Willie use his phone."

During his second round of questioning with Jennifer, Rayburn finally lost his trademark composure. "Is it your testimony today that you think Kevin McLaughlin was interested in you?" he asked, his voice rising.

"I don't know if he was interested in me," Jennifer said. "He was flirting."[3]

". . . Describe how Kevin McLaughlin was treating you, let's hear it."

WILSON: He was just, you know, complimenting me on my pictures and telling me why do I need Darryl. That I was a very nice-looking woman, I could do better than that. It was just the way he carried himself, the way he moved his eyes, the way he gestured. The way he looked.

RAYBURN: . . . You ever mention to anybody else that Kevin McLaughlin was flirting with you?

WILSON: . . . I told my mother. I told Mrs. Henley, Mr. Henley.

RAYBURN: Did you ever tell me?

WILSON: No.

RAYBURN: Did you ever tell any government agent?

WILSON: No, you never asked.

RAYBURN: I didn't think to ask you. But were any of the other agents flirting with you? Maybe I should ask.

WILSON: [Special Agent] Brian [Sullivan] wasn't. Those were the only —

RAYBURN: Miss Eliot flirt with you?

WILSON: Who? I should hope not.

COSSACK: Objection, Your Honor. This is argumentative.

RAYBURN: Withdrawn, Your Honor.

COSSACK: And foolish.

RAYBURN: *Withdrawn,* Your Honor. [To Jennifer] Now, you talked about Kevin McLaughlin telling you this is your chance to get even with Darryl Henley?

JENNIFER: Those weren't his exact words. That was what it reflected.

270

RAYBURN: Let's get the exact words. Whatever the exact words were Kevin McLaughlin told you when he asked you to commit perjury.

CHALEFF: Objection.

Rayburn probably deserved a mild admonishment at this point, like the ones Taylor had been giving Chaleff and Cossack, but all he got was: "Sustained." Taylor called a recess, during which he told everyone that Rayburn had "requested that in making an objection, defense counsel not announce extraneous material."

Chaleff and Rayburn were each given one more round with Jennifer, then she was dismissed. But the judge's day was far from over.

Chapter 27

Judge Taylor always adjourned at 1 p.m. on Fridays as opposed to 4 p.m. on other weekdays. He spent the extra time eating a late lunch in his office while preparing for the long Monday ahead, which was usually full of motions and argument from both sides. On this particular Friday, however, Taylor skipped lunch so that John Rayburn and Deirdre Eliot could meet him in his chambers for an in camera hearing.[1] They were joined by three DEA agents and two U.S. marshals. There were no court reporters available, so Taylor tape recorded the meeting.

The matter at hand was serious. Taylor's clerk had just fielded a nervous call from juror Michael Malachowski, who said he'd arrived home to discover a phone message from Garey West. West had apparently "sent the juror a letter and I guess wanted to know if Mr. Malachowski had received the letter," the clerk reported.

"This may be a hoax," Taylor told the prosecutors, "this may be a nothing. It may be something very significant." Taylor did not express concern for Malachowski's safety (despite the clerk's description of Malachowski as "very nervous about staying at his house tonight"), nor did he express concern about courtroom security. Instead, Taylor said he was "concerned because I don't want to lose jurors in the case and have them have to leave the jury because of something like this." Replacing jurors took time and was often perceived as symptomatic of a sloppy trial ripe for appeals and new trial motions. No judge likes sloppy trials, but Gary Taylor *really* did not like sloppy trials. As happened several times during the Henley trial, he sought to avoid even the appearance of one. "It'll be important for me to advise defense counsel [of the Malachowski incident]," Taylor told the prosecutors, yet he would wait eighty more hours before doing so — a time during which this little mini-chapter in the trial would be flipped on its ear.

That process began as Taylor was bringing the in camera hearing to a close, when Eliot interjected: "Your Honor . . . if the court was interested now, there is other information that's been occurring that deals with this whole type of issue. . . . It just appears that there's a series of little signals or something for intimidation purposes." These signals, Eliot said, included a Christmas card she and Rayburn had received from Bustamante's younger brother, which read: "May the Lord be with you and your family through out the Holidays & The New Year to come. I wish you and your family the very best & may all of your Dreams, Wishes, & New Years Resolutions! Come True! God bless. Sincerely yours, Rigo Bustamante." Eliot said she considered it a threat.

Next, Eliot alleged that Darryl and Rex Henley had tried to intimidate government witnesses through the actions of "the two males who are typically in the back of the court." (She was referring to Ronald and Donald Knight, whom she did not name, but instead called Henley's "bodyguards.") She accused the Knights of "follow[ing] out each witness after that witness testified." This behavior, she said, had been reported to her by "different witnesses, or people, observers in the court." No witnesses were ever brought forth, though, other than Steven Kinney, whose word would years later be viewed as equal to that of the defendants'.

Eliot alleged that one of the Knights had stood in witness Edward Cloud's path as Cloud was returning to the courtroom one day. In a separate incident, one of the Knights had said into a pay phone, loud enough for another witness to hear: "Don't worry, we'll take care of [witness] Bernard Lee." Third, Eliot said that Eric Manning's brother had been told by the Knight twins: "If Darryl Henley goes to jail, it's on you."[2] Finally, one of Eliot's sources told her that Darryl and Rex would nod toward the Knights when they wanted a witness followed. (This Mafia-style behavior apparently took place in plain view of the U.S. marshals, who were seated directly behind the defendants for the specific purpose of detecting and stopping such behavior. All Eliot said about the marshals was: "I believe the marshals noticed some of this going on because they did ask a blue coat [uniformed guard] to sit back outside of your courtroom." The marshals present at the in camera hearing said nothing.)

A question loomed: What did all of this Christmas card mailing, path obstructing, whispering, and nodding have to do with Garey West's call to Mike Malachowski?

"After the court ruled yesterday that the Denise Manning information would come in," Eliot explained, "I think the timing is clear that it's the next day that this phone call is placed to the juror." In other words, Denise Manning's testimony would be so damaging that the defendants were calling jurors at home, seeking to sway them. This theory of Eliot's would only become comical two days later, when the FBI discovered that the Gary (no e) West who had called Malachowski was a harmless bill collector whose call had been legitimate. But it was dead serious business that Friday in Taylor's chambers.

"All right, I think we'll conclude the hearing at this point, and we'll take it from there," Taylor said. "This concludes the in camera hearing and the sealed transcript." *Click.*

Deirdre Eliot was by several accounts an arrogant person and, as one journalist noted, "not the most liked lawyer in that [U.S. Attorney's] office." But that she might have fabricated witness intimidation charges in order to boost her chances of convicting Darryl Henley must be considered thoroughly before being stated as fact. None of the allegations she made that day were ever proven. The only thing her private speech seemed to prove was that the case had become intensely personal for her. For four weeks she and Rayburn had held their tongues at the sight of Henley striding confidently into court each day. The athlete's subtle arrogance, which had riled Kinney and McLaughlin so deeply during their investigation, brought about a similar response from the prosecutors, who knew they would have to endure it five days a week for at least another month. Endure it, that is, because no one else could see it.

Henley was unanimously regarded as well behaved during his trial, thanks in large part to the advice of his counsel. He never spoke out, never sighed with disdain, never sucked his teeth in disgust, never made unseemly facial expressions. (Except on two occasions, he admitted later, when Kinney mouthed *Fuck you* to him when no one was looking, and Henley mouthed it back.) During even the most damaging and most dishonest testimony against him, Henley sat there like he was watching PBS. The prosecutors were waiting for a crack to show, and to that point it hadn't, so in the privacy of Taylor's chambers Eliot tried to open her own cracks.

Mike Malachowski lived at the edge of the desert—so far from anything city-like that the Santa Ana FBI agent assigned to visit him that night instead asked a colleague from the sandswept Victorville office to do it. When four FBI agents from that sunbaked outpost visited Malachowski about the call he'd gotten from Gary West, they discovered something that would soon dwarf that West call in importance. "In November 1994," read their report, "Malachowski had been empaneled as a juror, in a narcotics trial. . . . He identified the prosecutor in both trials as Assistant U.S. Attorney John Rayburn."

It was stunning news. Not only had Malachowski served on a drug case just two months prior to the Henley trial, he had served on one that had been prosecuted by John Rayburn. Jury selection was supposed to have weeded out such improprieties, but instead, one of the twelve citizens deciding Darryl Henley's fate had just returned a guilty verdict in John Rayburn's most recent drug trial. The prosecution had some explaining to do.

A three-day weekend would pass before they were called upon to do so. Eliot called in sick that day, perhaps because she regretted the hasty in camera remarks she had made on Friday, perhaps because she was sick. After clearing the courtroom of spectators, Taylor informed the defense of the phone call Malachowski had received from a Gary West who had turned out to be merely a bill collector. Darryl watched his attorneys' brows wrinkle — not because of the call (they knew the phone policies at area jails and therefore knew that the call couldn't have been from Garey West) but because as officers of the court who were supposed to have been held in the same regard as prosecutors, news of the call had been withheld from them until now.

Taylor explained it as "a totally innocent coincidence [that] has a happy ending. . . . When I was advised of this, I conducted a short, in camera hearing to learn of any current security concerns." (Taylor neglected to mention his real reason for calling the secret hearing — to ask the prosecutors what they wanted to do. "How do you wish to proceed?" he had asked. "How do you usually proceed in a situation like this?" "So what's your pleasure?") When Taylor finished, Rayburn asked to approach the bench alone so he could "inform the court of one other minor issue that did come up in the same context." He was referring to his previous trial experience with Malachowski, news that Taylor had almost certainly heard by that point (Malachowski told the FBI about it on Friday, and today was Tuesday) — news that Rayburn now wanted Taylor to help him disclose as delicately as possible.

"It appears to me it's proper to hear what counsel has to say," Taylor said.

Roger Cossack wasn't having it. "I guess it's my nature that things in camera bother me, and unless there's a representation made that this has to do with jury tampering, I would like all things out on the record."

"Well, I don't know what he's going to tell me," Taylor replied.

Cossack objected again — "This is a public trial" — but Taylor overruled him and invited Rayburn into his chambers for another private meeting. Just as the door was about to close, Jim Riddet asked if their conversation could at least be transcribed so "there's some record of what the court was told."

"That's a very good point," Taylor said. "I think you're probably right." Then, in a telling move, just before he and Rayburn excused themselves, Taylor asked the defense if they wanted to "make this all moot" by dismissing Malachowski from the jury right now.

Cossack and Chaleff answered in unison: "No."

So Taylor, Rayburn, and the court reporter met behind closed doors, where Rayburn confessed to the man he'd once clerked for, in a roundabout, self-absolving speech, that Mike Malachowski had served as a juror on his most recent drug trial. Were it not for Riddet, this important admission might never have made it onto the record, where it would survive as evidence of the paternal relationship between Taylor and Rayburn, a link that was never more obvious and never more painstakingly concealed. Taylor's order to clear the court of spectators had also cleared it of the media, thereby preventing Rayburn's prior trial experience with Malachowski from appearing in the papers. It never did.

The Simpson trial, meanwhile, was splashed across every paper in the Western world, which made Darryl Henley wonder what might have happened if a Simpson juror had been found to have served on the jury that returned Marcia Clark's most recent murder conviction. It would have made every front page in America. Roger Cossack would have called for Clark's resignation on CNN. Attorneys on both sides, after all, are required to alert the court to such conflicts during jury selection, but Rayburn had not done so, even after he'd recognized Malachowski "the first time he walked in" (as Rayburn would admit later).

When Taylor and Rayburn emerged from their private meeting and returned to their places, the judge let Rayburn break the news to his opponents: "I would notify counsel that I prosecuted a case in November of '94 . . . and I am confident that juror number five was on that jury."

Mike Malachowski, who had been kept away from the other jurors all morning, was called into the courtroom, where he said he had recognized Rayburn at the beginning of Henley's jury selection. "It's my understanding up in Los Angeles," Rayburn explained, "we often see the same jurors over and over again. I apologize. I likely should have mentioned the same thing to the court. I never gave it a thought. . . . I didn't think there was any reason to disclose it. . . . I didn't think about it at that point."

Judge Taylor was forced to speak the seven words he had desperately wanted to avoid: "Juror number five is excused for cause."

To Malachowski, he said: "You are free of the obligation not to discuss this matter . . . except you must have no contact with the other jurors in this case. . . . Will there be any difficulty in doing that?"

"Not at all. . . . Thank you, judge."

To everyone's eventual anguish, however, Mike Malachowski would have great difficulty doing that.

Because of the O.J. Simpson circus, the idea of serving on a high-profile jury was never more popular than in Southern California in

1995. Participating in the Henley trial had been the coolest, most important thing Mike Malachowski had ever done. He'd been dying to be a part of it—first because of the travel stipend and the involvement of an NFL player, later because of its firecracker participants and its themes of drugs, sex, and money. Malachowski had been willing to let his previous trial with Rayburn slide for as long as Rayburn did the same, but now the party was over. Mike didn't want to leave.

How he had ended up on the jury in the first place was nearly as interesting as how he left it. During jury selection, four panels of forty candidates each had been brought before all the attorneys for their review. Malachowski, who had lied on his questionnaire to portray himself as the sort of young freeloader he knew defense attorneys liked, strode in with the fourth and last group of the day. When Rayburn recognized the lanky carpenter—the same juror who had helped him win a drug conviction two months earlier—he most likely recognized a chance to ensure that at least there wouldn't be a unanimous acquittal.

Taylor had asked each group of candidates to look around the courtroom and see "whether you know any of these folks, perhaps, whether somebody here is a neighbor of yours, or whether you've done business with one of these attorneys before." No one piped up. Taylor turned to the prosecutors: "Counsel for the government, would you stand and introduce the people there at your table?"

"Good afternoon, my name is Deirdre Eliot. I'm with the U.S. Attorney's Office, and seated with me is John Rayburn, also with the U.S. Attorney's Office."

"Good afternoon," Rayburn had said.

It was the first time all day Rayburn remained seated. He had risen to his feet and spoken to the first three groups. Based on what happened later, his choice to stay seated for Malachowski's group would seem like an effort to hide from him. This theory was supported by Taylor's direct questioning of Malachowski, which came moments later:

TAYLOR: And you were previously a juror, correct?

MALACHOWSKI: That's correct.

TAYLOR: How many times have you served as a juror?

MALACHOWSKI: Just once.

TAYLOR: And you indicated it was a criminal case?

MALACHOWSKI: Yes, sir.

TAYLOR: Did that jury reach a verdict?

MALACHOWSKI: Yes, sir.

Rayburn had sat there silently during that exchange. [3]

In a fitting addendum to Malachowski's dismissal, he was replaced on the jury by a forty-five-year-old married white woman
from Orange County—the mother of two daughters near Tracy's
age. Despite the way it happened, and considering Malachowski's
soon-to-be-revealed sympathy for the defendants, Rayburn could
not have been unhappy with the trade.

And to think, the whole chain of events started because Malachowski didn't pay his bills on time.

It was one of those hot dry Santa Anas that come
down through the mountain passes and curl your hair
and make your nerves jump and your skin itch.
—RAYMOND CHANDLER, *Red Wind*

Chapter 28

The Santa Ana winds, an annual phenome-
non that has typified Southern California's
unpredictability since the area was settled, arrived in March 1995, as they do every March,
sweeping southwest out of the mountains
and leaving confusion and calamity in their
wake. The 1995 Santa Anas brought with
them a rainstorm of biblical proportions that
left six dead and soaked "a broad swath from
Big Sur to Orange County," the *LA Times* reported. A homeless man drowned near a golf
course in Van Nuys. Thousands were without power in Santa Ana.

Inside Santa Ana's federal court building,
the lights flickered but remained on, illuminating the damning evidence the prosecution
had gathered against Rafael Bustamante, Willie McGowan, and Garey West—the men they
called "the back row defendants" because the
Henleys sat in the front row. The feeling at the
prosecution table was: three down, two to go.

Around this time, Alisa Denmon told Darryl she was pregnant. They hadn't seen each other regularly in over a year—the conception having occurred during a fleeting moment when their affection and proximity coincided—and now Alisa was carrying their child. When Darryl asked her if she wanted to have it, Alisa said yes. Then we'll have it, he said calmly. Inside he was wondering: *What am I bringing this baby into?*

The answer to that question lay in the hands of twelve strangers, but as would prove to be the norm during the trial, the Henley jurors were not present for many of the trial's most important scenes.

Just prior to the start of the trial, the government announced that they had given Gary Dabney $3,000 to "move his residence due to security concerns." A year earlier, Dabney had written a letter to Deirdre Eliot in which he begged her not to make him cooperate. "It's just not my job," he wrote. "I feel I have cooperate [*sic*] enough. . . . Please be understanding about this and think it over please I really don't need to be involved no more than I am." But Uncle Sam paid better relocation fees than did Garey West, who after all had loaned Dabney a mere $800 to help him move to that ill-fated apartment in Memphis back in 1993. The government also paid for the plane tickets that brought Dabney to the Henley trial like a Santa Ana wind—plus $40 a week in meal money, an additional check for $200, and another check whose amount Dabney said he couldn't remember. His per diem money increased thanks to his longer-than-expected stay in California. Cooperating with the prosecution, the defense joked, had become Dabney's job after all.

If Tracy Donaho was Rayburn's witness, and Denise Manning Eliot's, then Gary Dabney was Steven Kinney's witness from head to toe. Kinney was the guy who had entered Dabney's apartment back in 1993 and warned him that he would be on TV with Darryl Henley if he didn't cooperate. They had spent a lot of time together since that day, and now Kinney was watching Dabney take his seat next to Judge Taylor. The jury was not present.

Though a former gang member, cocaine dealer, and addict, Dabney was not menacing in appearance. He had a round head, chubby cheeks, and a small, soft body. He was, however, a Crip—claiming allegiance to the Trey Five Seven set in Pomona—and he owned a lengthy rap sheet that was about to be reviewed in great detail. The prosecutors began their questioning of Dabney by having him state what had already been made obvious: Garey West was a cocaine trafficker. Dabney testified about the day West told him: "Darryl has a girlfriend that's a cheerleader with the Rams and she's supposed to be bringing a package through." Most of what Dabney said on the stand about the day that package arrived—July 3, 1993—meshed with Tracy's testimony, but he added one thing.

Dabney recalled that two days after Tracy's visit, a man calling himself "D" had called his apartment and asked to speak to "G." When Dabney said that "G" (Garey West) wasn't there, "D" gave Dabney a cell number so West could call him.

What *actually* happened was a little more complex than that and a lot more revealing. Phone records showed that Dabney's apartment received *two* critical phone calls that day. The first came from Darryl Henley's Atlanta apartment at 7:58 p.m. and lasted twelve minutes. Though the prosecutors wanted the jury to believe that *this* was the call made by Henley, it was almost certainly made by Willie McGowan, as evidenced by three calls placed on the same line that night to Willie's girlfriend, two to his sister, and two to his mother.

Just before this 7:58 call, a shorter call had been made from Darryl's cell phone to Dabney's apartment. This was the call Henley made. It did not appear on the whittled-down list of calls the prosecution presented to the jury because it would have absolved Henley of making the lengthier twelve-minute call. (Dabney testified that his conversation with D that night had lasted just "two or three minutes"—the same duration as this call from Henley's cell phone.) That Darryl had been using his cell phone that night was supported by a series of calls that the prosecution did not place on its phone summary either.

Because Darryl did not testify at his trial, the intervening years would dull the impact of what he said in a prison visiting room in 2005 about that night's phone activity. His memory for the tiniest details, which, once corroborated, informed every aspect of this book, proved just as accurate with regard to the events of July 5, 1993. Henley remembered receiving a page to call a 901 number that night, 901 being Memphis's area code. When he called, he expected Garey West to answer, but instead he heard a voice he'd never heard before — Gary Dabney's. Henley asked this stranger if G was there, and Dabney, just as he said at trial, replied: "This is G."

"No, I mean Big G."

"No, he's not." Dabney asked Henley if he wanted to leave a message.

"I gave him my home number," Henley said years later, "because I knew that's where Willie was, and I knew Willie was the guy G wanted to talk to." When his brief call to Dabney was over, Darryl called his apartment (as evidenced by his cell phone bill) and told Willie to expect a call from G. This call to Willie was the most glaring omission from the government's phone summary. Displaying it would have further proven that McGowan — not Henley — made the ensuing twelve-minute call to Dabney.

The jury would know none of this. (They also would not know that West paged Eric Manning twice that night.) Gary Dabney was never asked at trial if Willie had called him. From the beginning, the government only wanted to know about the call from "D." It made Darryl harken back to the words Willie had relayed to him from Kinney, the phone evidence's custodian: *All we wanted was the football player.*

Aside from his failure to illuminate the government's sleight of hand, Chaleff's questioning of Dabney was a cross-examination clinic. There was just one problem: the jury wasn't there to see it. Showing his inexperience with federal drug trials, Chaleff had made the crucial mistake of showing his hand too early. Indeed, Rayburn piped up with only one objection during Chaleff's lengthy exchange with Dabney. He was eager to watch Chaleff point out the weaknesses in Dabney's testimony—flaws that Rayburn would clear up by the time the jury returned.

Darryl was stunned by the kabuki of it all. He didn't know trials were like this.

The major newspapers took a hiatus from reporting on the Henley trial between February 11 and February 24, a dark spell that included not only Mike Malachowski's dismissal from the jury but also the testimony of twenty-two witnesses, including Gary Dabney. The papers had apparently decided that these unfamous characters didn't warrant the coverage given the star-studded Simpson trial or Orange County's bankruptcy (at the time the largest municipal failure in American history), both of which were given higher priority by local editors. It was the same week that Americans devoured news of the bickering between Johnnie Cochran and frustrated Simpson prosecutor Chris Darden. (Cochran: "They obviously haven't tried any cases in a long time and obviously don't know how." Darden: "Who is he talking about, doesn't know how to try a case?!") Darden was held in contempt that week—the same week, coincidentally, that the cost of the Simpson trial surpassed $2.4 million, much of it spent sequestering and feeding its jurors. Former U.S. attorney general Edwin Meese joked that week that the Simpson jurors would be locked up longer than the defendant. A poll of over three hundred lawyers conducted by the *National Law Journal* saw 70 percent predict that Simpson would go free. This was nine months before the verdict.

The following day, Gary Dabney testified in front of a real live jury. As if snitching on West wasn't difficult enough, Judge Taylor had the mic moved closer to Dabney and asked him to testify "in a nice, clear voice so we can hear you." Because of Chaleff's premature assault on Dabney, the task of impeaching Dabney's testimony fell to Garey West's erratic lawyer, Erwin Winkler. Surprisingly, Winkler proved himself up for the task. "Now, Mr. Dabney, isn't it true that you were extremely reluctant to cooperate with the government in this case, isn't that true?"

"No."

"I'm sorry."

"I said *no.*"

Dabney added that he didn't recall telling Angela Wallace he had five felonies on his record, at which point Winkler presented a recorded phone call in which Dabney told Wallace not only that he was a five-time felon but that he was reluctant to cooperate with the government.

Dabney also testified that he had lied to the grand jury. When asked how many times, he said he didn't know.

Shawn O'Reilly, meanwhile, was asleep in the jury box. Taylor had already noticed the slumbering trucker and asked everyone to "stand up and invest a minute in a stretch break," but now O'Reilly's eyelids were drooping again. "During the time we're in recess," Taylor announced at the next break, "everybody be sure and do deep breathing now so we can all return refreshed and invigorated and bright-eyed and ready to complete the day's session."

When Dabney stepped down, a Montclair policeman named Stephen Lux, who had watched Garey West sell crack back in 1986 (then pursued him, tackled him, and recovered twenty-five rocks from his pocket), took the stand. Lux testified that he'd known West for four years prior to that day. "I used to see him with Darryl." Only after the government had rested its case would Henley realize that this seven-word chunk of testimony was the only evidence in support of Eliot's claim that Henley and West were longtime friends.

The only person in the courtroom more frustrated than Henley at this point might well have been Gary Taylor. The likelihood that the Henley trial would end before his next one was scheduled to begin was shrinking fast, and Taylor abhorred postponements and delays. He also didn't like that Cossack's absences were starting to add up. On this day the dapper defense lawyer asked for permission to fly to Lake Tahoe for an attorneys' seminar. The same morning that Taylor accommodated Cossack's request, he informed the jury of the reasons for Mike Malachowski's dismissal. He steered clear of the real reason—Rayburn's prior trial experience with Malachowski—and rightly so. Mentioning the Rayburn-Malachowski connection might have influenced the jury with a matter that had nothing to do with the evidence. The troubling part, however, was that Taylor used this same spin *without* the jury present, when the truth wasn't as necessary to hide. In this sense, even the judge had adopted Tracy's defense: he didn't want to know, so he never brought it up.

It didn't help Taylor's impatience that his courtroom was about to host another witness, Alejandro Cuevas, whose hearsay had to be filtered before it could be heard in open court. And so the trial's gears were shifted down again, with Taylor expressing the sentiments of everyone present by blurting seemingly the dirtiest profanities in his repertoire: "Rats. We may need several hours by the time you ask your questions and the other side asks theirs. Nuts."

Cuevas's testimony was different than that of the other government witnesses. He hadn't been involved in the flights-and-suitcases madness of July 1993. Cuevas had entered the picture later, when his friend Bustamante asked him to help settle a debt. Rayburn called Cuevas to the stand because, as he said in his closing argument, "the very best evidence in this case [is] what happened after the crime."

The year and a half Cuevas had spent in custody did not make him any less handsome. Tall and athletically built, with brown eyes and a five o'clock shadow dusting his square jaw, Cuevas came off well on the stand, speaking more like a mortgage assistant (which he had been before his arrest) than a hired fist (which he was also). Cuevas ended each of his replies to Rayburn with a respectful "sir."

The bulk of his testimony without the jury present was not hearsay; that is, Cuevas witnessed these things himself. Cuevas had watched and listened to the Rams Park incident, for example, from inside a Camaro parked close by. So when Eliot asked him how Henley had responded that day when Bustamante asked why he was avoiding him, Cuevas's answer was important:

"[Henley] said his connection got busted and the feds were watching him."

His connection got busted. It sure sounded like drug-dealer talk, and Cuevas had just placed those words in Darryl Henley's mouth. But the only person who had been "busted" at that point was Tracy Donaho, and she wasn't a connection, she was a courier. When examined closer, this tiny statement — "He said his connection got busted and the feds were watching him," which inspired the *LA Times* headline "Henley Described Arrest of 'Connection,' Witness Says" — demonstrated how testimony could be rearranged, attributed to someone else, and rehearsed in its new form until it took on a factual life of its own.

Its genesis occurred the night of Cuevas's arrest, during a four-hour interview with Kinney and McLaughlin that stretched into early morning. The agents' tape had run out as they were asking Cuevas about the Manning murder, and on the new tape one of the agents spoke first: "Okay, let's go back to the Rams' camp again. While we were off the tape you had stated that during your meeting with Henley the subject was brought up — a deal involving a Rams cheerleader."

"[Manning] said that Darryl had a connection that was G," Cuevas replied, "a guy who he supposedly grew up with, or is his good buddy, which is his main connection, and Darryl got a cheerleader from the Rams to do the deal and that she got busted. . . . Darryl said that the cops had busted his connection and that the Feds are watching him."

Without the jury present, Cuevas had said Manning's use of the word *connection* was a reference to Tracy. This clarification was never made in front of the jury, leaving the identity of Darryl's shadowy "connection" up in the air. It could have been Pablo Escobar for all the jury knew.

Henley knew why Cuevas wasn't eager to clarify this point under oath. For seventeen months he'd languished behind bars while Darryl lived free on bail. Cuevas had lost his job. His fiancée and child had left him. Cooperating with the government had been his only chance at getting a lenient sentence and restarting his life. The prosecutors had agreed not to charge him for the loaded pistol they found in his trunk after the Marie Callender's incident, and now they wanted repayment on that debt.

During the breaks in Cuevas's testimony, the defense asked Taylor repeatedly to disclose the contents of yet another in camera hearing he had held with the prosecutors that morning.[1] It was easy to tell when Taylor was uncomfortable; he used twice as many words as were necessary, and he did so now, waltzing clumsily around the issue. In his most candid moment, even Taylor might have admitted that the Henley trial was not his finest hour. His previous drug trials had featured irrefutable evidence resulting in convictions or neatly packaged plea deals. (The infamous Colombian kennel traffickers had been videotaped dissolving their cages into cocaine.) But Taylor had never experienced a trial as complex nor as dangerous as the Henley case. Witness intimidation; a murdered coconspirator whose killer might be in the room; card tricks during jury selection. As if the Henley trial weren't challenging enough, Taylor was also presiding over preliminary hearings in the Juan Benito Castro case, the first federal death penalty case in Orange County history, a labyrinth of drugs and homicide that would have left even the most calloused judge sleepless. Gary L. Taylor, local boy made good, was no longer practicing business law in Newport Beach.

For the moment, he was focused solely on Alejandro Cuevas. In contrast to Tracy, who at times appeared uncomfortable on the stand, Cuevas displayed the perfect mix of self-esteem and remorse, of comfort and unease. Cuevas seemed eager to identify Busta-mante—pointing him out as the clean-cut Hispanic male at the corner of the defense table wearing the dark suit and flower-print shirt. He identified a photo of Bustamante's prized Porsche before Eliot could even ask him to. This was Cuevas's revenge against the man who had tried to intimidate him when they were in jail to-gether, the man who had threatened to break the legs of Cuevas's infant son if Cuevas didn't accept his $20,000 bribe and change his story. But Bustamante's clout didn't matter in court, and the man demonstrating that point was, not coincidentally, the man who had been stabbed in his sleep recently by inmates aligned with Bustamante.[2] Cuevas could feel the scar near his ribs as he testified against the man who put it there.

Again, Chaleff's hands were tied on cross-examination. Perhaps Cossack could have done more with Cuevas, but he was in Tahoe, "edifying other people rather than us," Chaleff jabbed (hinting at the growing rift between Henley's attorneys). So no one was sur-prised when the first sentence in the next day's *LA Times* story made it seem as if *Henley* had been the one threatening Cuevas's child: "A government witness testified Friday that he has ignored threats to himself and his family in order to tell the truth about the role of Ram cornerback Darryl Henley and four other defen-dants in an alleged drug conspiracy ring."

The *Times* story also said that Darryl (twenty-eight) was thir-ty years old. If only they knew how far he would fall before then.

One witness is not enough to convict a man accused
of any crime or offense he may have committed. His
guilt must be established by the testimony of two or
three witnesses.
—DEUTERONOMY 19:15 (jotted by Dorothy Henley in her
notebook during trial)

Chapter 29

Alejandro Cuevas's testimony reminded everyone that the murder of Eric Manning had
to be addressed soon. Manning's name had
been mentioned nearly as often as the defendants', but his absence from the trial had
been explained only with a vague instruc-
tion that the jurors shouldn't worry about it.
It was a touchy issue. With the testimony of
Denise Manning approaching, Taylor had to
protect the defendants from prejudice that
might result from disclosing that Manning
had been murdered. What he told the jurors
(that the killing had occurred hours after the
Rams Park incident, that he had been shot
point-blank in the head) would have a lot to
say about how the jury viewed it.

Taylor drafted a speech informing the
jury that Manning had been killed and that
there was no evidence linking any of the defendants to the crime. Rayburn agreed with
this approach at first, but after speaking to

his superiors in Washington, he did an about face: "Your Honor . . . the matter is suggesting strongly the defendants were involved." (Earlier Rayburn had asked Taylor to tell the jury: "In no way were any of the defendants involved.")

The matter was put on hold while Lisa Roey took the stand.

The Atlanta DEA officer who had helped arrest Tracy at the Atlanta airport, Roey testified that Tracy was given "a pad of paper" in jail, "to write things down on" until her parents arrived. Tracy wrote six pages of scattered notes on that pad. It was her first statement after ditching the "Allison Coats" lie, and it included a powerful swatch of recollection:

Wed July 14
Willy called 7:45 am
Asked if I could work
Didn't want to until he said it was Atlanta

Tracy's own words — "Didn't want to until he said it was Atlanta" — conflicted with her testimony that *Darryl* had talked her into taking that flight. But for reasons that were never made clear, these notes were not brought up at trial.

Roey also testified that she didn't know how many pounds were in a kilo. Fully aware that the Henley trial was not an arena for skewering law enforcement (unlike the trial he was analyzing on CNN), Cossack let it slide that the DEA interdiction expert before him didn't know the basic math of her job. He also let it slide when Roey explained why Tracy's parents had been flown to Atlanta following her arrest: "I thought they should be there to support her, and again, she was surrounded by everybody she didn't know. I felt it would make her feel better if her parents were there." Cossack did not ask Roey if it was DEA policy to fly in the family of a suspect who had already lied repeatedly to investigators, or if her job was to make suspects caught carrying twenty-five pounds of cocaine "feel better."

After a long discussion about how to address the Manning murder, Taylor stuck by his first explanation. But as he was calling the jurors into the courtroom, Eliot announced out of the blue that Denise Manning had just informed her of additional meetings between her husband and Darryl Henley—meetings that Denise had apparently forgotten during her discussions with the DEA, her grand jury testimony, her meetings with Eliot, or her testimony without the jury present. This new evidence popped up less than five minutes before she walked in to testify.

Denise Manning's testimony before the jury represented the final draft of a script that had been edited and revised many times during the previous seventeen months. In September 1993, Kevin McLaughlin had asked Denise, "When [the cocaine] went to Atlanta, was it not going to Darryl and Willie? Was that not who she was taking it to? To Darryl?"

"I don't—I could assume that whenever—at times it would go to Darryl," Denise had answered.

Three weeks later she told the grand jury: "Darryl Henley was the man where all the cocaine was going to. He was the man that asked for all the cocaine."

In February 1995 she went a step further, saying that Henley had "personally guaranteed" the cocaine deal during a meeting with Manning, McGowan, and Bustamante that had occurred in early July. This despite the evidence that Henley had not been in California between June 4 and July 19.

Other discrepancies emerged. Each time Denise was asked why the password to pick up the drug money from Western Union had been "Big Mac," she answered differently: On September 22, 1993, she said, "Big Mac might be Garey's name." On October 7, 1993, she claimed, "I didn't know what any of the meanings were or anything." And on February 7, 1995, with no jury present, Denise stated, "[Eric] said that was Darryl Henley's nickname."

293

CHALEFF: . . . Did you ever tell anybody that before?

DENISE: I can't remember.

CHALEFF: Do you remember [telling McLaughlin] you thought Big Mac might be Garey West's nickname?

DENISE: I might have.

Taylor advised Chaleff to move on. When she took the stand on March 1, 1995, with the jury present, the question was not asked.

Kevin McLaughlin's interview with Denise Manning in September 1993 was a curious piece of evidence. The interview, conducted two weeks after her husband's murder, was recorded, offering stark evidence of what Riddet would later call "coaching in the worst possible way." Most of what was said during the interview was indecipherable on the tape given to the defense. What *could* be heard could only barely be heard, and there were long stretches of silence, bracketed by audible clicks. Denise testified that McLaughlin had turned his tape recorder on and off during the interview, but that was only a partial explanation. She also said that the interview had lasted at least an hour and a half, yet there were only six pages of patchy dialogue on the transcript, which was broken up repeatedly by notations like "blank space on tape," "very faint recording," "unintel," and "inaudible." The audible portions sounded like they had been recorded in a sandstorm, but Denise said that McLaughlin's tape recorder had been lying on the table, so the poor sound quality wasn't because it had been in his pocket. There remained few possible explanations for the tape's condition other than someone's willful altering of it.

At trial, when asked to explain the changes in her story over the preceding year and a half, Denise replied: "The most I can say is God said you need to know this. So I don't know. It came to me."

Sixteen years later, in 2011, the decision that allowed Denise Manning to testify at trial was still lodged in Charles Hack's mind like a thorn. It stuck with Jim Riddet as well, but Hack, who represented Willie McGowan, saw Taylor's ruling as proof that Darryl

Henley had been ticketed for prison before the trial even started and for reasons that had nothing to do with the evidence. Hack had taken vehement exception to the 160-member jury pool that contained only five black people. He and the defense had tolerated the chumminess between Judge Taylor and Rayburn, just as they had tolerated Rayburn's subterfuge in keeping Malachowski on the jury, not to mention Taylor's attempt to cover it up. They had gritted their teeth through the testimony of criminals turned government witnesses. "And then along comes this angry widow whose husband had been killed during this mess," Hack recalled, "and it was obvious she held the defendants responsible for it, even though there was absolutely no evidence to support their involvement. . . . You could *feel* her anger."

Bustamante's attorney, Anthony Brooklier, struggled to question Denise. She was a small, young Latina woman with a pleasant face who had borne her husband's child three weeks before he was gunned down in the street outside their home. "I'm trying to think of a way to cross-examine her and be effective and not make you all mad at me," Brooklier told the jury during his closing argument.

Deirdre Eliot did not struggle at all. She began her direct questioning of Denise by reviewing her late husband's career in the drug game. Eliot then tried to portray Denise as Eric's partner in crime—to establish the "coconspirator" exception under which her hearsay was being allowed. From there, the facts became interspersed with what God had helped Denise remember. She had a hard time keeping track of who was involved in each crime. She recalled her husband telling her about a trip he and Willie made to Rams Park—a trip that was actually to Fullerton and included Bustamante, not Willie. She testified that Rex had been the intended recipient of the Memphis suitcase, even though Rex had never set foot in Memphis in his life. (Eliot had to steer Denise toward naming Garey West instead.)

Through it all, one vital question had never been asked of Denise

Manning. Brooklier, with the directness of a Mafia don's son,[1] was the man who finally asked it:

"Do you have any kind of agreement with the government that you won't be prosecuted or anything like that?"

"Yes."

"And who do you have this agreement with, Mrs. Manning?"

"I know I'm not going to be prosecuted for my testimony with Deirdre Eliot."

"When were you told that?"

"About three months ago. . . . Orally. Face to face. . . . In Deirdre Eliot's office."

"And to the best of your recollection, what did Mrs. Eliot say to you?"

"That I don't need to be concerned with being prosecuted for my testimony."

Cossack could hardly believe his good fortune. When Brooklier was finished, Cossack capitalized on this secret immunity deal—which spoke poorly of both Eliot's integrity and Denise's reliability—by pointing out how ripe Denise was for IRS prosecution (seeing as how she'd never paid taxes on Eric's drug income). "Well, isn't that what you've been promised that you won't be prosecuted for?" Cossack asked.

"That's correct," Denise said. "That's correct."

"And Mrs. Eliot told you that during one of the meetings that you had with her, is that right?"

"Yes."

"And who else was present during that meeting?"

"Steven Kinney."

Anticipating correctly that Eliot would call Kinney to the stand to deny it all, Cossack bolted the doors shut: "But you felt it wasn't necessary to have this immunity agreement in writing?" he asked Denise.

"That's correct."

"Because you believe that Mrs. Eliot would not be misleading you?"

"That's correct."

Having revealed Denise as a ventriloquist doll for the government, Cossack asked Taylor to forbid the prosecutors to talk to Denise during the break, "since there are such inconsistencies in her statement." Taylor refused. Eliot assured the court that Denise "was not given a thing," but Cossack cut to the chase. Immunity deal or not, he asked, was the government going to prosecute Denise Manning?

"Your Honor, that's irrelevant," Rayburn said.

"The answer is the government declines to say," Taylor said. "Let's move right along."

Denise Manning would soon step off the stand and into the club of informally immunized witnesses that included Gary Dabney and a car thief and Bustamante associate named Earik Silver. It was not a proud group, but it was hard to judge them without trying on their shoes. Who wouldn't cut a deal with one's own freedom on the line? With the weight of prison hanging overhead?

"Me for one," said Darryl Henley.

Chapter 30

Although the calls displayed on what became known as the "phone summary" were by definition circumstantial evidence, the exhibit was about to move the jury toward conviction more surely than any other piece of evidence, more steadfastly than any witness. From hundreds of phone bills involving the defendants and those closest to them, John Rayburn had selected 1,100 of what he saw as the most incriminating calls placed between May and October 1993. It was Steven Kinney's job to testify about these calls, which meant that it was also Kinney's job to double-check Rayburn's work — a painstaking task that required him to go back and ensure that each call Rayburn had selected for the exhibit also appeared on the original phone bills. It was hard work, but in Kinney's eyes it was completely necessary. The DEA agent was admittedly a perfectionist, often to a fault. When Kinney finally took the stand, it was with bags under his bloodshot eyes, but he knew his stuff.

Each of the phone summary's eighty-six pages had been made into a transparency, which DEA investigator Reggie Bennett laid across the overhead projector as Eliot questioned Kinney about them. The phone summary captivated the jurors. Rayburn watched from the prosecution table as the jurors sat riveted to the glowing, larger-than-life presentation before them, which, before their very eyes, made their reasonable doubts unreasonable.

The calls leading up to the critical month of July 1993 showed little aside from a telling decision by the government about when to begin their summary. Rayburn had chosen to start it on June 7, a week shy of May 30 — the date Tracy had mistakenly identified as the day Henley invited her in person to be his mule. The evidence showed Tracy making several calls from her mother's Orange County home to Darryl's apartment in Atlanta that weekend — the weekend she was supposed to have been in California talking with him about moving suitcases for Willie.

The phone summary was not without errors. The defense pointed out two calls made from Darryl's Brea house on June 27 — to Willie, and to a Memphis money launderer — that could not have been made by Darryl or Rex because airline records and witness testimony placed them at a family reunion in Texas. The calls in July weren't rock-solid. Every defendant but Bustamante had been occupying Darryl's homes during that time, and with both homes having two phone lines each, and with the carte blanche Henley had given his guests to use his landlines *and* his cell phone, it was anyone's guess as to who was calling whom. Chaleff tried to demonstrate that it would have been impossible for Henley to have placed some of the most incriminating calls. For example, when Darryl and Tracy were lying low at the Stage Deli on July 15, someone was using Darryl's cell phone to call numbers based in Detroit (numbers that Willie had called from his hotel room a few days earlier). Henley's cell phone also kept calling his pager that day, which — while consistent with Tracy's testimony about

Darryl's pager going off like crazy—made it seem as if Henley had been paging himself.

"Now, you can't testify to who was using what phone at any given time, can you?" Chaleff asked Kinney.

"No."

"All you can do is tell us there are phone records listed in somebody's name and that phone was used?"

"Yes."

"You don't know who made the call?"

"No."

"You don't know what was said?"

"No."

"You don't know why the call was made?"

"No."

Chaleff asked Kinney if he'd ever conducted research "to figure out who was using the phone."

"That would be impossible. . . . That would only be based on my assumption."

It was exactly what Chaleff had wanted Kinney to say: that the phone summary was not evidence, just an eighty-six-page assumption.

The summary's imperfections were at times glaring. The transparencies contained wrong numbers, wrong names, wrong times—showing just how quickly the summary had been prepared, how pressed Rayburn and Kinney had been for time. The revelation of these flaws forced Kinney to eat crow each time he had to correct them during cross-examination.

Many of the accurate calls were meaningless. Most lasted less than a minute, which could have meant a hang-up. The summary also did not include calls made from Eric Manning's fraudulent "chip phone," which aside from the savings he accrued was the exact reason he'd gotten it.

But the information on the overhead projector was large and bright, and it contained Darryl Henley's name on practically every page. It was as digestible for the jurors as it was frustrating for the defense, whose efforts to avoid pointing fingers at one another fell by the wayside at this juncture in the trial. The tension on the defense side must have been thick when Darryl's counsel questioned Kinney about the calls Tracy made to Willie the day before she flew to Atlanta.[1]

As much as he would have liked to hide behind Willie, though, Darryl could not escape the damning calls he'd made and received on the night of July 2 — the night Tracy flew to Memphis. Other evidence clearly suggested that Darryl was the only defendant in Atlanta that night, which meant that all the calls from his Post Chastain apartment had indeed been made by him. Here was the most disheartening evidence of Henley's inability to say no, of his persistent, childish attraction to the fast lane. Here was evidence that he had at least *helped* traffic cocaine, and the prosecutors' word for help was *conspiracy*.

As Darryl watched the pages being shuffled across the projector, he thought back to those last hours of July 2, 1993, and those first hours of July 3. "I was mixed up in this thing beyond the point of no return," he said later, "and when I saw that I couldn't get out of it, I had to make damn well sure it went off without a hitch." He wanted Tracy to do her job without error and for the whole thing to be over, he said, so he could move on to the matter of his imminent million-dollar football contract and forget that this Willie thing had ever happened. That big contract never came about, of course, and the worst-case scenario was now upon him, crushing him under its weight inside Judge Gary Taylor's sterile courtroom. The phone summary's impact helped explain why Henley did what he did three weeks after it was presented.

His trial to that point had not been the march toward exoneration he had expected. His attorneys had not exposed the warts on the government's investigation. Right now the only things on display were his criminal conversations in the middle of the night with known drug traffickers. Instead of vindication, Henley's trial had become a trip to a thorough tailor fitting him for his federal inmate's uniform.

As Darryl thought back to the night of July 2, 1993, his memories matched almost exactly with Rayburn's description of that night during his closing argument:

"[Tracy] told you around midnight Eric shows up [at Henley's Brea house]. When Eric shows up, there's a lot of discussion as to whether they're going to be able to make this trip. They're not sure whether Rex is going to be ready. . . .

"And around 12:30, Tracy told you she and Eric drive out in the Lexus to the Ontario airport. They arrive around 1:00 for a 1:05 flight which they eventually miss. . . . After they miss the flight, Rex and Tracy . . . drive back to Brea. . . . Tracy heads home . . . and she gets a call [at 2:24 a.m.]. . . . It's Darryl. . . . It was one long call with a lot of interruptions. . . . Willie calls and cuts in on the line and speaks with Darryl for a few minutes. . . . What does Willie do when he gets off the phone? Of course, he calls American Airlines to make new flight arrangements. . . . Darryl hung up the phone after his forty-seven-minute call with Tracy at 3:11. The very next minute, what does he do? He picks up the phone and he calls Willie McGowan."

Four hours later, Tracy and Willie were sitting ten rows apart on a plane lifting off from Burbank Airport.

As he sat there harkening back to it all, Henley knew how hollow his rationalizations were about no one ever proving what was in that Memphis suitcase. He felt the nausea again, infecting his conscience as it had when Willie called him on July 15 to tell him, She got popped.

The next day was a rainy Saturday in Santa Ana. Darryl and Rex were allowed to attend a family wedding near Los Angeles. It was still wet on Sunday, when Ted Woolsey tracked down Damien football coach Dick Larson. Larson described the Henley brothers' personalities—"Thomas was quiet, Darryl was more social, and Eric was somewhere in between"—and recalled former wide receiver John Rayburn having "the little guy attitude . . . he was tenacious." Coach Larson said he was puzzled by the charges Darryl was facing ("There has to be more to it") and that Henley was being prosecuted by another former Spartan ("Something is screwy about this"). When asked if Rayburn knew the Henleys back in the early 1980s, Larson replied, "Everybody knew the Henleys."

Larson would repeat none of this on the witness stand, however, because Judge Taylor had warned him not to mention that he had coached both prosecutor and defendant, "unless specifically asked about it." He never was.

Roger Cossack didn't make it to court on the day it was revealed that the cup of ice cream Nicole Brown left melting on her banister on the night of her murder was Ben and Jerry's Chocolate Chip Cookie Dough. While the western world stood entranced by that information, the Henley jurors were left to draw two conclusions from Cossack's empty chair, neither of which was good for the defense: either Cossack felt overconfident enough to start skipping trial days, or he was discouraged enough to give up and focus on his Simpson analysis.

Brian Sullivan, the DEA agent who had practically begged Darryl to take a plea deal back in 1993, took the stand after Kinney near the end of the brutal trial he had tried to prevent. It was Sullivan's job to explain to the jury how cocaine trafficking worked. Cocaine isn't manufactured in the United States, Sullivan testified. Its most common entry points are New York, Miami, and Los Angeles—massive port cities from which the drugs are moved to smaller burgs like Atlanta and Memphis. According to Sullivan, the average price of a kilo in Los Angeles was between $14,000 and $18,000 at the time of the Bustamante deal. After being moved to Atlanta, its worth increased to between $23,000 and $27,000.

After being mixed with fillers and sold in small user amounts, a single kilo could have netted as much as a $500,000 profit. These big numbers made for a powerful finish to the government's case, but the defendants were probably the only ones in the courtroom doing the more accurate and more depressing math:

The half million dollars Sullivan had tossed out as the revenue on a single kilo was more likely what Willie McGowan would have grossed on the entire deal. If the package Tracy mailed to Smyrna on June 30 had been full of sham cocaine (a test to see if she was "down") and if the agreement between Bustamante and McGowan had been twenty kilos for $250,000, as indicated by the evidence, and if Garey West had sold them for $27,000 per kilo (Sullivan's high end), then Willie's gross would have come to $540,000. Paying Bustamante would have put Willie at $290,000. West's cut would have been at least 20 percent — $108,000 — and Rex would have been thrown, say, $5,000. Willie would have netted around $180,000.

As for Darryl's cut, if Henley was the "financier" — the shrewd investor who had surely insisted on a share of the profits — then why was he clearing less than $100,000? *Less than Garey West?* It was one of the most convincing arguments in support of Darryl's insistence that he had never wanted a dime — a stance he still clung to fifteen years later. From the beginning he had only wanted to help Willie and keep his hands clean. That was it.

Now look at us, he thought. The government rested its case.

Chapter 31

The most powerful witnesses in Darryl's defense were not called by his own attorneys. Willie's lawyers, Anthony Alexander and Charles Hack, found Donna and Josh Henson, the mother and son who lived two houses away from Darryl in Brea—and they found them at the last minute.

A white, fortyish woman who had lived on Wildflower Circle since 1979, Donna Henson testified that Darryl had given her the code to his garage shortly after he moved to the quiet cul-de-sac in 1990. Since then he had asked her to keep an eye on the place when the Rams were on the road, and he paid Josh to take care of his dog. Unlike Willie and Tracy, the Hensons kept Darryl's garage code a secret.

In early 1993 Donna began seeing people she didn't recognize around 2105 Wildflower. "I had never seen these white girls at the house," she testified, "and it was kind of weird. . . . She had long blonde hair, and I knew she saw me because we kind of ended up looking at each other, like, 'What are you doing over there?' and, you know, 'What are you looking at?' kind of thing." Donna was shown a photo of Tracy Donaho, which she identified as the girl in question, having seen her clearly on at least two occasions — once when the blonde had been casually dressed, and the other when she had been wrapped in a towel, presumably after using Henley's Jacuzzi.

Josh, Donna's sixteen-year-old son, saw Tracy on still another occasion, Donna said, but "he saw something different from what I saw."

Josh Henson was a real-life Jeff Spicoli. *Dude, bro,* and *sweet* were the parlance of choice for Donna's son, who testified that he first laid eyes on Tracy in "probably April or May" of 1993, when she and another young blonde woman had come jogging down Wildflower Circle together. The image had seared itself into Josh's memory, for the young women had been wearing "midriff, tight, tight tops . . . you could see their stomach, and real short shorts." They entered Darryl's house using the keypad on the garage.

Later, in early June, Josh was riding his bike along Wildflower when he saw two black men in Darryl's driveway. He thought he recognized one of them.[1] So he stopped to ask when Darryl would be back. That's when Josh was introduced to "E," a young black man who drove a lowered blue pickup. Presented a photo of Eric Manning, Josh identified him as "E," the guy with the blue truck.

Josh's separate recollections of Tracy Donaho and Eric Manning converged when he testified about watching Tracy walk from her car to Darryl's house one afternoon. (He knew the car was hers because it had been there the day she was jogging.) Eric Manning's truck was also parked outside.

Rayburn and Eliot had done a good job of concealing their surprise to this point, but that became considerably more difficult when Josh testified that while riding his bike on a different day, he spotted Tracy and Manning hugging in Darryl's driveway — leaning on Manning's tricked-out pickup, arms around one another. "She was leaning against him and it looked like they were intimate." Hack's final question was about the time of day. "It was in the evening," Josh said, ". . . right before it was getting dark."

Deirdre Eliot, likely a shade paler than her usual porcelain, requested a sidebar. She and Rayburn had been given no notice that the Hensons would be called, and now they had a kid testifying that he saw Tracy and Manning hugging outside Darryl's house around the time the conspiracy was getting started. It was quite a blow. Tracy was supposed to be Darryl's victim, not Manning's mistress. If the jury believed that Tracy and Manning had been more than acquaintances, as this teenager was telling them, then the mask of airheaded innocence Tracy had worn on the stand would fall away. Josh Henson had just placed her in the arms of a known cocaine hustler she had admitted receiving a suitcase from — a suitcase that, if she knew Manning as well as Josh made it seem, she *must* have known had nothing to do with real estate. Taylor granted Eliot a ten-minute recess — "I hope."

When court reconvened, Eliot asked for an early adjournment so that she and Rayburn could prepare for their teenage foil. For one thing, Rayburn said he wanted to "check if this witness has a rap sheet." The defense chuckled at the thought of Josh Henson sharing a cell with Alejandro Cuevas, Gary Dabney, or any of the other criminals the government had called. "Despite the snickers from counsel," Rayburn said, "I know a lot of sixteen-year-olds that have raps." Taylor granted the early recess. When Josh was told that he would have to return the next morning, a smile lit his tanned face. "Sweet," he said. "I get to miss another day of school." But before he could leave, he was asked to stop by the U.S. Attorney's Office.

"They tried to get me to say someone had told me these things," he recalled years later. "They weren't aggressive or anything. They were just trying to get me to say that what I said on the stand wasn't true. They were probably frustrated with me more than anything."

Rayburn and Eliot asked all the questions Josh had been asked by the defense, to see if his story changed. "But it didn't," Josh said. "I knew what I saw."

Even with a night of preparation under her belt, Eliot's cross-examination of Josh Henson proved inconsequential. As it turned out, he didn't have a rap sheet.

While Darryl's neighbors were defending him in court by day, he was creating new turmoil for himself by night. His house on Wildflower Circle was still a home away from home for several women, and no one knew this better than Kym Taylor. One evening Darryl made the mistake of asking Kym to retrieve something from his study, having forgotten that he had tacked Alisa's ultrasound above his desk. Kym, who worked in pediatrics, knew exactly what it was as soon as she saw it. She picked it up like a smelly sock and asked him, What's this? Darryl told her it was a friend's ultrasound. Kym believed him.

This same game was replayed a few nights later when a young woman stopped by to see Darryl, only to be met at the door by Kym.

Who are you? Kym asked.

Who the hell are *you*? said the visitor.

And so on, until the visitor announced: I'm pregnant, and I'm having Darryl's baby.

Luckily for Darryl, he wasn't home. When he returned, he told Kym that the girl had been lying. Kym believed him again. This time he was telling the truth, but as with his trial, it was getting harder to tell the difference.

Darryl could not have hand-crafted a better character witness for himself than Bill Hanley, who took the stand just a month after his Irvine-based law firm had been hailed by the *LA Times* as one of the nation's finest. Hanley was arguably the most honorable lawyer in the room, and he was also a longtime friend of Gary Taylor's. His sense of humor is what caught Henley's attention at the 1990

March of Dimes fund-raiser where they first met, and it was what sustained their friendship over the next five years, when they went to breakfast before many a Rams home game, joking with everyone around them that they were related, despite their disparate skin tones. Hanley, whose home was five minutes from Henley's, had accepted his neighbor's version of the case as the truth: Darryl was a gregarious guy with women all around him and a few dubious friends he'd allowed to get too close. But a drug trafficker? No way.

"Would it affect your opinion as to Mr. Henley's law-abidingness," Rayburn asked, "if you were to know that he drove around town with a loaded firearm?"

"No."

Rayburn informed Hanley in various ways of Henley's womanizing. Would that affect his opinion of Henley?

"No."

Rayburn finished questioning Hanley the same way he finished with UCLA head coach Terry Donahue, [2] with Donahue's secretary Jolie Oliver, and with Henley's high school coach, Dick Larson — by asking if he had been in Darryl's presence on July 2 or July 15, 1993. It was a poignant and pertinent question, and the answer Hanley gave was the same one the others gave: "No."

And that was it. The defense closed its case, which had consisted of a few strangers who traveled with Darryl and Jennifer to Cancun, the Hensons, Coach Donahue, Coach Larson, Bill Hanley, and Donahue's secretary. The Hensons had provided a brief surprise, but the media had reported not a word of their testimony, nor that of the Cancun travelers, whose testimony made it clear that Darryl had returned to LA too late to have gone on the date with Tracy that she said marked the beginning of her involvement in the conspiracy. Before Darryl knew it, the discussion had turned to closing arguments. That the end of the trial was so near made his armpits go damp. The government's case had gone on for nearly two months. This was just the second day of his own defense, and already they were wrapping things up.

But fate again said, Not so fast. On Friday morning, Judge Taylor called Henley and his attorneys into his chambers to discuss a suspicious withdrawal Henley had made from his bank account—an account controlled by the court and supervised by a Pretrial Services officer named Jesse Flores, who was also called to the hearing.

It was not uncommon for Henley to withdraw large sums from this account, mostly for attorney fees. Flores was required to approve each transaction, and he approved the one in question, a $19,500 withdrawal that was earmarked to pay Chaleff, Ted Woolsey, and a bail bondsman. But Henley had instead given the money to a friend named Andrew Boston.

Henley claimed it was a loan to Boston to prevent his home from falling into default and that it was also a way for Henley to provide his own parents with a place to stay. He explained to his attorneys that since the fire at the Henley house on January 23, his parents had been living with relatives, and they had yet to move back into their own smoke-damaged home. Boston, who owned a cellular phone shop that catered to several Rams players, asked Darryl for a loan so he could catch up on his mortgage payments. Boston's money problems seemed like a good way to put a roof over his parents' heads and put Boston back on his feet at the same time. The plan was for Darryl's parents to move into Boston's home while Boston and his wife saved money by spending a few months in an apartment. It was a story backed up by the Henleys, by Andrew Boston, by notarized loan and mortgage documents, and most notably by court official Jesse Flores, who had had the withdrawal explained to him by Darryl's mother before she took out the money.

In the silence of Taylor's chambers, Chaleff explained the matter as "an inadvertent diversion related to an arson that occurred at the Henley house." There was certainly no need for Taylor to alert the prosecutors, Chaleff added, but the judge wasn't so sure.

"In my view, the government should know these facts," Taylor said. "Does that appear accurate to you?"

"Well," Chaleff said, "I guess my initial reaction is — and I don't mean any disrespect by this — Why?"

"Because it bears on the question of whether [Henley] should be confined or not."

Sensing that the matter was careening out of control, Cossack interjected, calling Henley's error "an unintentional mistake" with no "intent to deceive [or] flaunt the court's order — "

"Let me interrupt you a second," Taylor said. "In my view, the government may think to the contrary and may think that in combination of two factors they know and which I don't know, perhaps you don't know, that that forms an important picture of some sort." Taylor was referring to Eliot's in camera speech a month earlier about her witnesses being intimidated by the Knights.

After Taylor summoned Rayburn and Eliot to join the meeting and briefed them on the money withdrawal issue, Rayburn suggested "making a motion for detention immediately" and stepped out to confer with his superiors at the U.S. Attorney's Office. They had plenty of time to consider the matter, because Terry Donahue arrived at that moment for his appearance as a character witness. Delayed by freeway traffic, UCLA's head football coach loped down the hall, smirking apologetically, unaware that the young man he had once trusted to lock up the opponents' best receiver might very well be locked up himself by the end of the day. When Donahue saw Darryl sitting in the hall with his mother, he walked over to speak with him, but he was cut off by Chaleff, who reminded Donahue that witnesses couldn't speak with defendants. The clerk called everyone into the courtroom.

An hour later, after the merciful end to what for Donahue had been an embarrassing round of cross-examination — during which he learned for the first time how profoundly Henley's life had changed since he coached him — Rayburn asked Judge Taylor to start the detention hearing "at the present time."

"Detention of who?" asked Riddet, who hadn't been privy to the in camera meeting earlier.

"Mr. Darryl Henley."

It was almost quitting time. Taylor told the other defendants that they "certainly would not be required to be present at the hearing. . . . Is there any counsel that would want to be excused at this point?" No one budged. They wouldn't have missed this for the world.

"Apparently not," Taylor said.

For the next two hours, Rayburn stood before Taylor and described Darryl's penchant for ignoring court orders, stashing guns in his car, and threatening witnesses. He dusted off Eliot's month-old harangue about the Knights (or as he called them, the "two gentlemen . . . who we understand to be bodyguards of Mr. Henley"), accusing them of confronting "Miss Eliot and Special Agent Kinney [as they] were returning from a break during this trial," and "nod[ding] to the two bodyguards as they followed the witnesses."

"All I can say," said Chaleff, "is with regard to this incident of intimidating witnesses, I have not seen that. I have not heard that." The clerk hadn't seen it, either. Neither had the reporters. The handicapped clerk (Eliot's sole witness from a month before) was never heard from again. Neither were the witnesses who had allegedly been intimidated.[3] Taylor, who had a better view of the courtroom than anyone — having taken exception to Ron Knight's T-shirt at one point — did not witness the intimidation. Neither did Rex Henley, one of the men who was supposed to have been behind it.

What seemed most odd was the way Eliot had first raised the issue back in February. She hadn't said anything the day her witnesses were allegedly threatened. She had waited three days, until Mike Malachowski received what would turn out to be a harmless phone call from a bill collector, before bringing it up. And now Rayburn was exhuming her words after another unrelated event: Henley's diversion of funds toward . . . a friend's mortgage.

Emotion, it appeared, had once again gotten the better of fair play. It wasn't the call from the bill collector, after all, that led to

Mike Malachowski's dismissal from the jury. It was his prior trial experience with Rayburn, which still remained hidden from the media. And now Henley was being threatened with immediate imprisonment not because of a money withdrawal but because it had been alleged a month earlier that he had nodded to Ron Knight, an unproven allegation that would *not* be hidden from the media.

Eliot called Steven Kinney to testify about the four incidents of intimidation he claimed to have witnessed. The first incident happened about three weeks earlier, Kinney said, when he and Eliot were returning from lunch. One of "Darryl's bodyguards" had stepped in front of Kinney and looked at him "in a challenging manner. . . . And I said, 'Excuse me,' and he stepped out of my way, and we proceeded into the courtroom."[4] The second incident happened a week later, when Eric Manning's brother, Dwayne Manning, witnessed a black man (Ron Knight) saying into a pay phone: "If Rex and D go down on this, we'll get Bernard Lee."[5] After court that same day, as Dwayne Manning was leaving, both Knights allegedly told him, "If D goes down, you'll pay." Kinney said he spoke with Dwayne Manning later that evening, but Manning said he couldn't remember anything.

The third incident involved trembling government witness Edward Cloud, who Kinney said had complained to him about a threatening look one of the black men gave him in the hallway. Rayburn noted that, in all fairness, Cloud had been petrified to appear in court long before that. Which brought Kinney to the fourth and final incident of witness intimidation. It took place, he said, as he was escorting a witness out of the courtroom that same day. Darryl and Rex had stared at Kinney "in a challenging manner" as he exited with the witness, then Darryl had nodded, and one of his "bodyguards" followed Kinney and the witness into the hall. Rayburn asked if anything happened outside the courtroom.

"No, it didn't."

At the beginning of my case I wanted it to finish, and
at the end of it [I] wanted it to begin again.
—FRANZ KAFKA, *The Trial*

Chapter 32

If there was one thing Roger Cossack was
good at, it was thinking on his feet. It was a
nice tool to have when a hearing about a client's finances snowballs into one about his in-
citing courthouse violence. Cossack began his
questioning of Steven Kinney by asking him
his height and weight, which Kinney stated
as 6'1", 205 pounds. Then Cossack had Kinney confirm that he carried a firearm. His
point was clear: Kinney may have been the
most unintimidatable guy in Orange County.
"Would you do a challenging stare for us?"
Cossack asked.

"No, I'm not going to ask him to do that,"
Judge Taylor said.

It was fitting somehow that the best defense lawyering of the trial had nothing to
do with drug trafficking. By the time Kinney
stepped down, Cossack had made it clear that
Darryl's "bodyguards" had not approached,
confronted, or spoken to a single witness.

Cossack next called Jesse Flores to the stand. Flores, the court official who had brought Henley's $19,500 withdrawal to the court's attention in the first place, testified that Darryl's cooperation over the previous year had been "very good," and that during the trial "he stops by my office each morning, fills out his report, and comes to court." Darryl had done nothing to indicate that he might be a flight risk, Flores added.

Rayburn had no questions for Flores, but Taylor did. The judge wanted to know how Flores had first come across the money withdrawal issue. Flores explained that after notifying Darryl's mother of an unpaid bill, she had responded that "because of circumstances that had happened in their lives, they purchased a separate residence" and that the money set aside for the outstanding bill had instead been used for this residence. "I did not feel at any point that they were or anyone was attempting to hide anything," Flores said. When he had asked Mrs. Henley for documents to support what she was saying, she had handed them over, then and there.

The hearing was getting long in the tooth, and Taylor needed to make a decision. He theorized out loud that Darryl could have been trying to launder the money by diverting it to a friend, but Taylor's money laundering theory was disproven by the promissory note Mrs. Henley had had drafted on the date of the transaction, which was signed by Andrew Boston and required him to make monthly payments to the Henleys. After taking a twenty-minute break to decide on a ruling, Taylor announced that he had forgotten to ask Mr. Flores what *he* thought.

"I would recommend that [Henley] continue to be under the same terms and conditions as previously imposed," Flores said.

"I'm not satisfied with the present situation," said Taylor.

Darryl would walk out of court that day wearing the electronic ankle bracelet that Rayburn had argued was too lenient. Neither the Henleys nor the Knights would ever be charged with anything related to contacting witnesses. There would be no investigation. Not only did the government lay off the Knights, they apparently didn't even know their names. The prosecutors, perhaps eager to keep anything Suge-related off the record, still referred to the Knights only with physical descriptions. Ron was "the heavyset black gentleman which Judge Taylor asked to take his World's Gym shirt off," and Donald was "the tall gentleman with a diamond earring in his ear."

Taylor probably should have moved on after assigning Henley his ankle bracelet, but instead he made the boldest statements in a day overflowing with them. Conceding that Darryl's good behavior at trial had been "to his credit," Taylor noted that it was "also a good point for the government's argument . . . that the defendant, Mr. Henley, is making use of his position of high reputation and well-represented position of notoriety to be able to do the things that the government has alleged that he is doing. The government, you'll remember, is contending that Mr. Henley makes use of his position, makes use of his name, travels under his own name, returns to the airport with Tracy, openly and as if there's nothing wrong. . . . According to the government's case, the scam is that he is Darryl Henley, a well-known football player who wouldn't do anything wrong under any circumstances.

"The defense case so far hasn't consisted of any showing that I have seen or even attempted to show conspiracy on the part of Tracy Donaho," Taylor continued. "It's consisted mainly of character witnesses and a couple of facts concerning airline travel and travel down to Cancun."

The defense team looked ashen. Taylor had just slid all his chips toward John Rayburn. It helped explain why Taylor had seemed so hurried during these final days of the trial, and it supported Darryl's suspicion that Taylor had accepted every word of Tracy's testimony as "the gospel." Recognizing the depth of the bias he'd just expressed, Taylor backpedaled faster than Henley ever had on a football field: "It's important for everyone to keep in mind that in reaching the order today, the court does not attempt to try to evaluate the case." ("So in evaluating the case . . ." he'd said a minute earlier.) "It attempts to look at the position that each side is taking. In the evaluation of the case" — *oops* — "or in the position each side is taking, the government has completed its presentation of the evidence. And the court's evaluation for purposes of this hearing today is not intended to be, of course, for the court to state an opinion on what the final outcome of the case is going to be. That we're going to wait and hear from the jury."

The jury. They would go through more than anyone before the verdict arrived.

Barbara Kingsley, who received praise from both sides for her even-handed reporting in the *Orange County Register*, had been sitting in the back row, taking notes through the whole thing. Taylor saw her there; she was the only writer still present, and she was likely the reason for his hasty retreat. When the hearing was over, Kingsley watched several lawyers convene at the bench, where Taylor tried again to soften his still lingering comments. Everyone wondered what Kingsley's pen would produce in the next day's paper. It had been yet another interesting Friday.

That night, Darryl began what would become a ritual for him during the final days of his trial. Working amid a stack of transcripts that would have been as tall as he was had they not been as scattered as he was, Henley paced back and forth across the marble floor of his study, bookmarking testimony, underlining inconsistencies, taping Post-it notes to the phone evidence, coming back to a bookmark—in essence, putting his trial on trial. "In the beginning he was very confident about his case," recalled T. J. Simers of the *Times*. "'This is nothing, you'll see, everyone will find out.' But you get in a courtroom and you see all the people there and you realize it's the prosecutors' job to put you away. By the end of the trial he was dissecting testimony, looking for his way out." Taylor's pro-prosecution speech that day had shaken Henley, but after reviewing things that night in the house to which he was now electronically confined, Henley couldn't see how it would end up any other way than with him walking into John Rayburn's office freshly acquitted and plunking his ankle bracelet on Rayburn's desk.

Barbara Kingsley's story was resting on the defense table when Darryl walked into court Tuesday morning. "Henley Must Wear Monitoring Device," blared its headline. "L.A. Ram's Violation of Court Orders in Drug Trial Leads Judge to Consider Him a Flight Risk." Darryl pushed the paper away. He'd read the story twice already. When Chaleff asked Taylor to poll the jurors to determine if they had seen Kingsley's story, Taylor editorialized: "I thought the reporter used great restraint in that article. . . . There have been other times during the case in which something happened which I thought to myself, 'If a reporter wanted to make something really notorious and splashy and sensational out of this, they could.' And then I saw the article, and it appeared to exercise great restraint." Kingsley had indeed played it cool. Her space limitations, she said later, prevented her from fully describing the partiality Taylor had shown on Friday, when the judge had been, in her words, "pissed off" and "very cross."[1]

Two jurors admitted to having seen Kingsley's story. Chaleff wanted them both removed from the jury. Taylor said that their contact with the news seemed harmless. Rayburn agreed with Taylor. The jurors stayed.

"The financier was Darryl Henley," Rayburn said in his closing argument—a subtle retreat from Eliot's opening claim that Henley had been "the buyer." "He was the one with the stellar reputation, the good name. . . . He could guarantee payment because he was famous. He had lots of money." Rayburn explained to the jurors the concept of circumstantial evidence—the pillar upon which his case stood—by asking them to imagine climbing a dry Mount Baldy, the popular hiking spot whose peak towered over Damien High School, then waking the next morning to find snow on the ground. They could safely assume that it had snowed, even if they hadn't actually *seen* the flakes fall, right? It was yet another jury-friendly visual, one that had its own effect on Darryl Henley, who thought back to the party held in his honor at a Mount Baldy lodge back in 1989, the night he was drafted by the Rams. If the jurors had seen Darryl's UCLA friends smoking marijuana that night, they might have assumed circumstantially that Darryl had smoked, too. A urine test might have even come up positive. But as his former UCLA teammate Brian Brown and several others could attest, Henley had excused himself, gone upstairs, and stuffed a towel under the door.

Rayburn reintroduced his weightiest piece of circumstantial evidence, the phone summary, telling the jury: "The defense has suggested maybe one or two calls would be by different players," Rayburn continued, "but take a look for yourselves and you notice there are six calls from Ralph to Darryl Henley." That would be from Ralph to *phones registered* to Darryl Henley, Darryl thought. It was a distortion of the facts that even Taylor had taken issue with at one point. [2] But this was a closing argument, not a presentation of evidence, so Rayburn was allowed to continue uninterrupted.

Eric Manning "never, never calls Tracy Donaho," Rayburn told the jury. ("Of course there were no calls," Jim Riddet retorted in his closing. "Eric Manning used his chip phone.") And Rayburn did not mention that Tracy's phone number had been found in Manning's wallet after he was killed.

Rayburn continued, "You wouldn't expect Gary Dabney from Memphis to be hanging out with Darryl Henley, the star football player." *That's because he didn't*, Henley thought. *Dude said on the stand that he never met me.*

"Throughout this trial, I think you probably have gotten the idea that Darryl Henley is trying to insulate himself from criminal liability by pointing the finger at Willie McGowan." Henley might have smirked at this comment if the stakes weren't so high. *Nah, Rayburn*, he thought. *Pointing a finger at Willie wasn't an option, so I had to hire a couple more lawyers to make sure Willie didn't throw me under the bus. Damn, why didn't I just tell that fool no from the jump?*

It was the question for which Henley had no comeback. As he would tell the *Times* five years later, "Did I know what was going on [in July 1993]? Yes, I knew what was going on. I did nothing, absolutely nothing, and I could have. There was a window of opportunity. I could have literally said this ain't cool or this isn't going to happen. There was a chance to say, 'yea' or 'nay.' I didn't say either, so if you decide to do nothing, aren't you really saying okay?"

Rayburn knew he had some explaining to do about May 30. He got it out of the way quickly: "[Tracy] thought the date she had seen Darryl the next time was May 30, but that would have been when he was in Cancun. The point is, Tracy likely had her dates off."

She had her dates off? That's it? The weekend I was supposed to have asked Tracy to work for Willie — the weekend the conspiracy started — and "Tracy likely had her dates off"?!

"If you look at July 2," Rayburn said, moving right along, "the only call to Travel Associates at any point during that day is from Darryl Henley."

From Darryl Henley's phone, John. From my phone.

"Let's talk about Darryl for a moment," Rayburn said, pausing for effect. "Darryl is very articulate. He's smart. He's college educated. He's sharp. And he used those skills effectively throughout this case. One way he used those was to entice Tracy Donaho." To Darryl's horror, one of the white ladies on the jury nodded. "He's an accomplished liar," Rayburn continued. "He's good at it, he's sharp, he's smart, that's how he pulls it off. He lies to people he loves."

More nodding from the jury box. Another juror murmured, "Mm hm," forcing Judge Taylor to tell the jury "to not nod or shake your head in response to any of the points that counsel are making, and also very important, don't make comments to yourselves."

Rayburn continued: "Mr. Cossack promised you in his opening statement that you would see evidence of a, quote, 'nasty, nasty conspiracy' operated by Tracy and her family. What evidence have you seen? You've seen virtually none. . . . Ladies and gentlemen, she is not capable of putting together this master conspiracy . . . and we ask you to return the only possible verdict in this case, which is guilty on all counts. Thank you."

There would be five separate closing arguments from the defense, one for each defendant. Jim Riddet went first, arguing that his client, Rex Henley, had been an innocent bystander who may have agreed to fly with Tracy, but never actually boarded a plane with her—and certainly never wrapped any cocaine. At least one juror believed Riddet's argument that Rex had been duped "just as Tracy Donaho claims she was." Unfortunately for Rex, this juror was dismissed at lunch. He was one of two jurors who had seen Kingsley's story in the *Register*. Offering more proof that nothing in the Henley trial was what it seemed, this juror was a self-described conservative Republican who had been leaning heavily toward the prosecution before he was dismissed—except where Rex was concerned. One of the many hidden tragedies within the trial was the very real possibility that Rex might have been acquitted had this juror's eyes not flitted recklessly across his newspaper.[3]

Anthony Brooklier, second only to Cossack in his ability to make light of any situation, ended his closing argument by telling the jury: "I'd just like to say it's been very interesting and the longest three-week trial that I've ever been involved in. . . . Thank you very much and have a nice weekend."

The jury was dismissed, with only Chaleff's closing unheard. The stage was set for the bearded legal genius to end up a hero—to deliver the *something big* that everyone had been expecting from Henley's top-dollar defense team. The circumstances under which Chaleff would make his client's final plea for justice, however, would change drastically by the time he stood to deliver it.

The jury, passing on the prisoner's life,
May in the sworn twelve have a thief or two
Guiltier than him they try.

—WILLIAM SHAKESPEARE, *Measure for Measure*

Chapter 33

The whole thing started with a car horn. It was Monday night, the night before Chaleff's much-anticipated closing argument, and Darryl, confined to his house by his ankle monitor, was optimistically studying the contracts of other NFL cornerbacks. The honk startled him.

"Hey Darryl!" came a yell from outside, followed by another honk.

Darryl dismissed it. *Some yahoo fan*, he thought.

More yelling. More honking. Henley reluctantly walked to the garage and pressed the automatic door opener. The aluminum mouth creaked agape, revealing a white van idling in the dark cul-de-sac, a big white guy at the wheel waving out the window in broad strokes. "Hey, it's me, man!" he yelled. "Mike!"

Rex appeared behind Darryl, grimacing, rubbing his forehead.

2105 Wildflower Circle, Brea, California. (Courtesy of Darryl Henley)

"It's Mike Malachowski, man! I was juror number 5!"

"Government sent this dude," Rex whispered, smelling a set-up.

"Ray-burn." (Rex always pronounced the prosecutor's last name like it was two names: *Ray Burn*.)

Darryl saw a slender young white woman in the van's passenger seat. She looked as bewildered as Rex. No one was sure what to do next, until Darryl recognized the vacant smile on the white guy's face. *Now* he remembered him. No one had ever advised against contacting *former* jurors, so Henley invited Mike inside.

The dim smile was Mike Malachowski's usual expression. He was not dumb, but he was not the sharpest tool in the shed either, and one of the more endearing things about him was that he never claimed to be. Darryl welcomed Mike and his sister Debbie into his home and offered them something to drink. Mike accepted a beer, Debbie ice water. Malachowski told Henley how cool it was to meet him, how cool it was to be in his house, and how much it had "fucking sucked" to get kicked off the jury. They shot the breeze about the likelihood that the Rams would land in St. Louis ("Count on it," Darryl told him), and about what it was like to play against Jerry Rice. Like thousands of other American conversations taking place at that moment, they talked about the O.J. trial.

They also talked about the Henley trial. When Mike asked Darryl what he had done with the $300,000 the Rams advanced him back in 1993, Darryl was stunned that this relatively forgettable piece of evidence had stuck in the juror's mind—until he remembered that Mike hadn't been in the courtroom in more than a month. Defending himself on these salary advances set Darryl off on explaining his side of the entire story, right there in his den. He focused on the "why" of it all—just as Chaleff would the following day. Henley's explanation was as long-winded as it was passionate, and it ended with this: "Why would I mess around with this drug thing for a few thousand dollars when I was about to sign a contract for $8.3 million?" Henley said. "It doesn't make any sense."

Mike agreed.

Silent as a stone, and noticeably suspicious of this white guy's motives, Rex leaned his thick shoulder on the wall, arms crossed, listening.

Darryl asked the ex-juror how he thought the other jurors were leaning. Mike said he hadn't been near them in five weeks, but back in February there seemed to have been a few people—white women, believe it or not, plus his buddy Bryan—who were unconvinced by the opening stages of the government's case. Mike said Darryl had a good chance.

This tiny glimmer of hope, uninformed as it was, sent a wave of relief rolling over Darryl like a waterfall. *I have a chance*, he thought. *I have a chance.*

Darryl and Mike discussed individual jurors that Darryl only knew by physical description. Mike knew them by name. "We talked about the case practically every day," Mike said.

"Who?"

"Me and the two guys I carpooled with."

Darryl leaned back and smirked. "You know what? I'm not even surprised," he said. "No way they can expect you to deal with that crazy stuff all day and then not talk about it." A pregnant pause. "So what did y'all talk about?"

"Oh jeez, about Tracy, about Rayburn, about who was lying and who wasn't. Mainly about Tracy, though."

"You think she was lying?"

"Of course she was lying!" Mike exclaimed.

Darryl laughed. *Of course she was lying. I've got a chance.*

Mike, meanwhile, noticed that Darryl seemed to like what he was saying. Darryl seemed to like *him*. Mike kind of wished Debbie wasn't there, so he could really let his guard down with Darryl and Uncle Rex and hang out. Maybe pound a couple more beers.

The events of this night were the first of many pieces of evidence which proved that since he'd been excused from the trial, Mike Malachowski's interest in it had moved beyond the gas money it afforded him each week and inched dangerously close to obsession. His sister Debbie was an innocent bystander that night. An assistant track coach at Utah State University, Debbie was in town for a few days for a track meet in Long Beach. She'd come with Mike on his drive to Henley's house as a lark, a joyride. She didn't think Mike was going to honk his horn and start yelling. Debbie remained as quiet as Rex during Darryl and Mike's conversation, sitting on the couch, her unsipped glass of water gathering dew between her knees. During the drive down to Brea that afternoon she'd listened to Mike talk excitedly about the Henley trial. About the cheerleader's testimony, about how Mike should have never been on the jury in the first place because he knew the prosecutor, about the Saran Wrap they'd found in Henley's kitchen—the same kitchen Darryl was entering right now, as a matter of fact, to get Mike another beer. Mike had told Debbie that the Saran Wrap was pretty strong evidence of Darryl's guilt. He said he thought Darryl was done for. Now he was saying Darryl should walk. Debbie felt uncomfortable. Only Mike and Darryl seemed at ease.

John Rayburn had not sent Mike Malachowski. Mike, Debbie, and their mother had made the two-hour drive down to Brea to visit relatives that afternoon, and once Mike realized how close his aunt's house was to Henley's (he remembered the address and photos from the trial), he "got a wild hair up [his] ass" (as he explained it later), drove to Wildflower Circle, and started honking. Tall, bulky, and friendly, with large laborers' hands and a receding hairline, Mike Malachowski came off that night as a yahoo from the desert who'd had one too many. But the only thing Mike had one too many of when he pulled up outside Darryl Henley's house was wild hairs.

"You should get in touch with me if you get convicted," Mike told Darryl. "I've got some information that could help you get a new trial."

"Oh, really. What do you got?"

"Wait and see. I'm not sure you're gonna need it."

"We should keep in touch," Darryl said. He asked Mike to step into his office so they could exchange phone numbers. Mike asked if his sister could come along. Darryl said sure. The three of them moved in a pack into Darryl's study, the next room over from the den, where Darryl and Mike swapped numbers, and Darryl gave Mike a few football cards. Rex appeared in the doorway, watching, listening, his arms still folded.

Darryl recalled later that as Mike and his sister were leaving that night, Mike hung back, stole a second with Darryl alone in the garage, and asked him to call him in the morning.

The moment the van's brake lights disappeared around the corner, Darryl loped upstairs in an excited fog. During the entirety of Malachowski's visit, one of Henley's many girlfriends, a young woman named Janis, had been in an upstairs bedroom watching TV. Darryl told Janis what just happened downstairs. Her nose wrinkled with confusion. "A juror?"

"*Ex*-juror," Darryl explained. He laughed at her bewilderment. "I know, I know," he said. "I'm as surprised as you are."

"Be careful, baby," Janis said.

The first person Darryl called was Bill Hanley. You'll never believe what just happened, Darryl told him. Sure enough, Hanley couldn't believe it. Then he corrected himself: With this trial, yeah, I can believe it. Hanley advised Darryl to tell his attorneys about Malachowski's visit first thing in the morning.

Oh, I will, Darryl said.

It was after midnight when Ron Knight dropped by. He broke up laughing when he heard about the former juror's visit. This shit keeps getting crazier and crazier, Ron said.

Malachowski's visit that night had been preceded by one from T. J. Simers. Darryl had promised the *Times* writer an interview, and Simers had surmised correctly that the best way to cash in was to show up unannounced and hope Henley was in a loquacious mood. As it happened, his timing was perfect. According to Simers, "the other side" of Darryl Henley emerged that night. Simers entered what Deirdre Eliot had called "the stash house" and there encountered Henley's friends, and friends of friends, hanging out as if they were paying rent. As Simers said later, "The place was like Grand Central Station. Darryl was talking about people using different phones and different cars. I could see how it all could have happened." Henley led Simers into the same office where, a few hours later, he would give his phone number to Mike Malachowski. The office was littered with transcripts, legal pads, and DEA reports, "pages and pages he can almost recite by memory," Simers wrote, "searching for one more reason to assure himself of freedom."

"I think I will be exonerated," Henley told Simers. "I think my life can be reconstructed. But I just can't drop it. Does being not guilty make it all over? . . .

"You want to see what I do with my time?" Henley asked, pulling out a notepad. "I fantasize. I write down what I think my next contract will be. Nice, huh? . . .

327

"I was not guilty of putting Tracy Donaho up to carrying drugs, a suitcase full of drugs, to any state. Where did I make my mistake? It was in meeting Tracy Donaho. . . .

"I think the government has done everything it can to break my spirit. I think it became personal. It was high profile, a cheerleader, a professional football player. . . . Every day my picture is up there, and they've been throwing darts at it. I'm angry a lot. I don't have much patience. They say my name, and I don't like to hear it. It's always attached to something sinister."

Henley punched holes in the May 30 conflict in Tracy's testimony. "Henley has an explanation for everything," Simers wrote, "and says he is tired of having to defend himself. He ticks off the names of witnesses and says they used his name because he is famous."

"People are going to believe what they want," Henley said, "unless they go page by page through the testimony, and then it would become painfully obvious what has happened."

Phone records would later confirm that Henley called Mike Malachowski at 8:30 the next morning. Their conversation lasted less than two minutes. Henley had taken precautions before placing the call. The gut-punch effect of the phone evidence had compelled him to use Janis's cell phone to call Malachowski. The government would never know about the call. Or so Henley thought.

An hour later Darryl and Rex were walking through rainy downtown Santa Ana, approaching the courthouse. Once inside, Darryl found Roger Cossack in the hall by himself. The charismatic Cossack had become Henley's favorite ear—a confidant whose support transcended their legal relationship. (At mid-trial, Darryl had given Cossack one of his Rams game balls as a gift.) Cossack's face lit up when Darryl told him about Malachowski's visit.[1] Cossack was particularly interested in Malachowski's opinion of Tracy.

"His exact words were: She's a money grubbing bitch," Darryl said.

At this, Cossack grinned in silent celebration, praying that the other jurors saw her as Malachowski did.

"You want to tell Gerry about this, or should I?" Darryl asked.

"Gerry's an animal right now," Cossack said (according to Henley). "He's locked in on his closing right now. I'll tell him later." Cossack asked Henley who else he'd told. Henley replied: Bill Hanley, a girl named Janis, Ron Knight, his agent, and his mom. Cossack said, Keep it that way. Then he gave Darryl the same advice Janis had given him the night before: "Be careful."

The previous week, Darryl's mother had asked if she could sit in the courtroom now that both sides had rested. Chaleff had taken the idea to Rayburn, who relented, which made March 21 the first day in two and a half months that Mrs. Henley sat in on her son's trial. With baleful eyes, she watched Gerry Chaleff step to the lectern for his closing argument. Darryl scanned the jury box as he repeated to himself what Malachowski had told him about the people seated there: "Bryan's a young guy, just a regular Joe like me trying to make ends meet. . . . Shawn O'Reilly is the fat white dude. I hate to tell you this, but he thinks you're guilty as sin."

Attorneys do not get to choose the days they give closing arguments. They don't get to say, I'm just not feeling it today. Let's do it tomorrow. Had he been able to request such a postponement, Gerry Chaleff would almost certainly have done so on March 21, 1995. His hair and beard still flecked by the morning drizzle, Chaleff was coughing to save his soul. For all Darryl's criticism of him following the verdict, Chaleff had worked relentlessly during the trial. Sleep had been an afterthought. He had literally worked himself sick. His closing argument, upon which the rest of Darryl's life hinged, was delivered by a man who barely had a voice.

"While I talk to you during my argument," Chaleff rasped to the jurors, "I'd like you to keep one word in mind. And that word is *why*. Why would Darryl Henley do this?" It was the very question Rayburn had said the jurors didn't need to worry about. Subsequent interviews with those same jurors revealed that it was what they worried about more than anything else.

"Mr. Rayburn kindly got up and told you during his part of closing argument what our theory was," Chaleff continued. [2] "Unfortunately, he got it wrong. . . . What our theory is is that Darryl Henley
didn't owe anybody anything. Zero. Zip. Nothing. Ralph Bustamante thought he did. Because Ralph Bustamante was conned. . . .
Bustamante didn't know Darryl Henley from Adam." Chaleff connected the dots along this path of deceit—from Bustamante to
Manning to McGowan to Henley—with the first and last man
having never met during the conspiracy. He described how, when
Manning informed Bustamante that "the deal is guaranteed. I got
a football player, number 20 for the Rams" to do it, Bustamante
jumped on board because "Bustamante liked athletes, he liked to
hang around with athletes, he liked to have his picture taken with
athletes, and [Manning] found the perfect con. 'We got a football
player to guarantee it.'"

Chaleff called the claims made by Denise Manning and Alex
Cuevas—that Henley had dealt with Bustamante in person—"impossible. That's absolutely impossible. Darryl Henley wasn't here,
first of all, at the end of June. . . . Ralph Bustamante and Darryl
Henley never met. They were never together."[3] If Bustamante had
received a personal guarantee from Henley, Chaleff asked, then
why was the government's summary filled with calls from Bustamante to *Eric Manning*? If Henley owed Bustamante money, the
summary "would have shown phone calls between Ralph Bustamante and Darryl Henley, but there weren't any because Darryl
Henley did not owe this money." And if Darryl had been partners
with Manning, Chaleff continued, why did Manning have to sneak
up on him after a Rams game and ask for his phone number?

Chaleff wondered aloud why Cuevas, "like other witnesses in
this case," had embellished so shamelessly on the stand. "Because
they know what they're going to get if they make either the prosecutors or the DEA happy."

This last was a well-worn defense argument, as old as the system itself, but in the Henley case it rang true. Cuevas, a man who

had threatened murder over the phone, the carrier of a loaded .38 at the time of his arrest, a suspect in the case of a suspiciously dead three-year-old girl, would walk free by the end of the year, off the hook in all three cases. [4]

Chaleff rattled off a series of circumstances that distanced his client from Bustamante. There were no documents in Henley's home that mentioned Bustamante; there were none in Bustamante's home that mentioned Henley; and what did Henley do after having his car stolen at Rams Park? He filled out a police report and identified Bustamante as the thief. Hardly the acts of a coconspirator.

These were the high points of Chaleff's final argument, but unlike Rayburn, he seemed to forget at times that he was not working with an abundantly educated jury. (Rayburn had tailored his closing argument to what he'd learned from the jurors' questionnaires: only three sitting jurors had college degrees, and two had completed "less than high school.") Most of Chaleff's closing argument lingered between complex and boring and was marred by stops, starts, and detailed analyses from which he would suddenly jerk away and change topic. He beat the airline records and Western Union documents—the most sleep-inducing evidence of the trial—to death. He tried to diminish the note the DEA had discovered in Darryl's home (the calculation of his "600K" football salary minus the glaring "360K") instead of simply calling it what it was—Henley's plan to pay Bustamante so his mother could continue living.

At times, Darryl was glad he'd hired Chaleff. "If you're involved in a drug deal with somebody," Chaleff argued, "what's the last thing you want to do? Bring attention to your name. What does he do? He marches up to the DEA [in the Atlanta airport] and says, 'Here I am. I'm Darryl Henley.'" At other times: "Now what else did the prosecution bring up? And I've talked about this, the advances. Darryl Henley did get advances for large sums of money. . . . And, in fact, if you recall, I had to ask, I forgot, I think it was

Mr. Brewer looked at the backs of those checks, exhibits, I think it was 50 — I don't know what the numbers are. I can tell you, but look at the back of those checks."

That riff returned the sweat to Henley's armpits.

"Now let's turn to Tracy Donaho," Chaleff continued. "Like I said, we'd all like to believe that witnesses actually tell the truth when they get up there and swear to tell the truth. . . . We'd like to believe them, but we can't. And you certainly can't believe Tracy Donaho."

Regarding May 30: "You listen to this story, you think, 'Gee, this must have happened.' But it didn't. They made it all up. She didn't tell this to the DEA agents when they interviewed her. This got sprung from her fertile imagination later."

If there was a subject that deserved to be rehashed, it was May 30. Chaleff bludgeoned it during his closing argument, which became more erratic as it crept toward the three-hour mark. ("But we know what she said about what Terry Donaho said and what he said is he was going to tell his daughter what to do.") Judge Taylor asked Chaleff to be "mindful of the estimate" he'd given about duration.

"I hate not getting the last word, which I know I'm not going to get," Chaleff told the jury, wrapping things up. "I think what the case will show you when it's all said and done is that Darryl Henley was taken advantage of. People used his name for their own purposes to put him in the middle of all this. . . . And when you look at that in the light of all the evidence in this case and say to yourselves, 'Why would Darryl Henley do this?' I think you'll come back with only one conclusion, and that is he didn't. The evidence hasn't shown you that. His life hasn't shown you that. And then you will see that the only true verdict in this case would be to return a verdict of not guilty for Darryl Henley. I thank you for your attention."

Even the loyal Woolsey confessed that his boss had given better closing arguments. Darryl reflected upon the "Not expensive enough" note Chaleff had written him a few days earlier and sighed.

Then his pager vibrated. He knew who it was before he even looked down, but he had to listen to Deirdre Eliot's final argument before he could call Mike Malachowski back.

Eliot's closing was focused almost exclusively on the defendant with the best chance of walking, the most important defendant for her to convict. Several of her points about Henley had merit. She and Rayburn weren't required to prove Darryl's motive, she said, but "even so, if you do ask yourself why would Darryl Henley get involved in this, maybe it's because he didn't think he would get caught. Darryl Henley wants you to believe that he's a great guy and that great guys don't get involved in anything like this. . . . You've already seen that there are two sides to Darryl Henley. There's Darryl Henley the public person, a great ballplayer, a good student, close to his family. Everyone likes the public Darryl Henley. Old football coaches, neighbors, I guess everybody on the plane to Cancun. Tracy Donaho liked that Darryl Henley, too. Then there's another side. The Darryl Henley underneath the public image. . . . It's the Darryl Henley who will string along three women at that time and never come clean with any of them. You have to be pretty devious to be able to pull that off."

Then most guys in the NFL *are hardened criminals*, Darryl thought.

"And so Tracy Donaho is off a few days when she talked about May 30 and the day she heard the rap song," Eliot said, ". . . and because she's off a few days here or there, they conclude that she's lying. So acquit all the defendants in this case because Tracy Donaho is off a few days in May."

Nah, not all the defendants. Just me and Rex.

"And the defense would have you believe that Tracy Donaho and Alex Cuevas are in the clear, all they had to do was testify and that's it. But those plea agreements aren't get-out-of-jail-free cards. . . . Tracy Donaho has a drug conviction today, and she's facing sentencing with a possibility of a ten-year penalty. That's not getting off the hook. . . . [Judge Taylor] will sentence them fairly, you can be sure of that."

As it happened, the jury could not be sure of that. Tracy never spent another moment behind bars.

Concluding her argument—and the trial—Eliot told the jurors that Henley "wants you to ignore all the evidence in this case that points directly at him because he's a great guy and all those football coaches like him. And he hopes that, like Tracy Donaho, you'll be dazzled by his status and impressed with him. Darryl Henley thinks that he can walk away from this like he sailed away to the Bahamas. . . . Don't let them pull this over on you. We ask you to return the only verdict based on your reason and your common sense, and that's a verdict of guilty on all counts. Thank you."

Judge Taylor adjourned at 4:30 p.m. The attorneys and defendants hung around to make sure each of the five hundred exhibits had been properly entered into evidence. At 5:18 p.m. Darryl walked out of the courthouse. The first thing he did was call Mike Malachowski.

Mike had been busy. Since talking to Darryl that morning, he had spent the day looking for Bryan Quihuis—as evidenced by the three calls he made to directory assistance, followed immediately by two calls to the home of Quihuis's cousin. By the time Mike paged Henley, he had obtained Quihuis's home phone number. When Darryl called him at 5:18 p.m., Mike said this: "You remember that guy on the jury I told you about—Bryan, the young guy I carpooled with? . . . I think he'd be willing to work with you."

Bribing a juror. Darryl was immediately interested, even before Mike explained his ace in the hole. Bryan had used methamphetamine repeatedly during the trial, Mike said, a secret that would allow Mike to approach Bryan with the bribe offer without fear that Bryan would report him. (If Bryan squealed about the bribe, then Mike would squeal about Bryan's meth use.) This leverage, coupled with the thud of Chaleff's unimpressive closing argument, made Darryl's reluctance fade. "I jumped on it with both feet," he said later. "The trial didn't go quite the way I thought it would. And now I had jurors coming to *me* with a chance to get off? I was like, 'Where do I sign up?'"

By his own admission, Darryl Henley was a different person at that point than the happy-go-lucky ballplayer he'd been prior to 1993. Maybe hanging out with the cynical Ron Knight had brought on the change. Maybe all the punches he'd absorbed during his unwinnable fistfight with the government—a brawl he was finally starting to realize he'd lost—had taken their toll. Maybe it was all the dirty pool the government had played during his trial. Maybe it was time for Darryl to play some dirty pool himself.

I think this jury has a pretty good idea of what's going on in this case. . . . I think they are pretty bright, attentive people who have been working hard throughout the case to really pay attention. And I think they have a good handle on what's going on.

—GARY L. TAYLOR, March 15, 1995

Chapter 34

For the rest of his life, Darryl Henley's blood would heat each time he heard that he'd "tried to bribe a juror." It would be mentioned often. This was a case of two jurors looking to get paid, Henley would respond—Bryan Quihuis by selling his vote, Mike Malachowski by acting as the middleman. "This was something that was brought to *me*," Henley said years later. He pointed out that Malachowski had been out of work at the time, with a wife and three kids to feed. Henley cited bank records subpoenaed by the court that showed just $91 in Malachowski's checking account at the time. "Dude needed money," Henley said. Did Henley agree to pay Malachowski for approaching Quihuis? "Absolutely. But I didn't come up with the idea. This was brought to me."

It was a defense he had used to explain his choice to "look out for" Willie's suitcase back in 1993 and one he'd use to explain future misbehaviors as well. It was not a particularly strong defense. Years later, Henley would admit to a lifelong weakness for listening to the proverbial devil on his shoulder. He even had a name for it: "Spontaneous negligence. One of those things where if you think about it too long, you might not do it. So you just do it." It wasn't a bad trait for an NFL cornerback to have, this spontaneous negligence, but for someone whose felony conviction and prison sentence were all but guaranteed, someone whose life and family honor were hanging in the balance, it spelled a deeper doom. Soon it wouldn't matter *who* had come up with the bribe. The depths to which Henley would eventually sink would place him retroactively at the helm of this scheme to bribe a juror, and every other scheme for that matter, and would confirm to the world that he'd been a heartless, manipulative criminal from day one.

On the last day of the trial, once all the evidence had been squared away and all the jurors had gone home, Erwin Winkler invited his fellow defense attorneys to join him for a drink. Shortly afterward, a brief convoy of Mercedes-Benzes pulled up outside a local strip joint. Winkler's colleagues warily followed him inside, their tailored suits drenched in strobe lights and dry ice. The club's employees gravitated to Winkler, calling him Erwin and asking how the trial was going. One of the lawyers (Chaleff and Cossack were not in attendance) joked that Winkler seemed quite at home. "I should," Winkler replied, forking over a twenty for the first of many lap dances he would buy that evening. "I've been coming here for lunch every day."

Darryl was standing in his driveway on Wildflower Circle at that moment, watching Donna Henson and her boyfriend, Robert, strolling by on the sidewalk. "It's finally over, huh?" Donna said, wearing a relieved smile.

"The *closing arguments* are over," Darryl corrected her.

"Well, this calls for a celebration then."

Over the next half hour, neighbors emerged from their homes and gathered in Henley's garage, the site of several such soirees over the years. The defendant was clapped on the back and congratulated for making it to the end of the gauntlet. He shot dice in the driveway with Rex and Robert. Ice, beer, and soft drinks materialized. Darryl showed his neighbors the new ankle monitor they had read about in the paper. The crowd was decidedly middle-aged and white.

Donna was especially kind that night. Over the years she'd taught Darryl how to do things like jumpstart his car and use his dishwasher, and now she was playing hostess at the party marking the end of his legal problems. Darryl would be more mindful of his friends now, Donna told herself as she handed out Domino's pizza on paper plates. Soon he'd be back playing basketball with Robert and Josh in the driveway, back to being the jokester who'd thrown her in the pool, fully dressed, then offered her a hundred bucks if she could stay in the winter-chilled water for a full minute. (Donna did it, and Darryl paid up by taking her and her kids to a local theme park.) Darryl could give Donna's daughter rides to school again, on days when she missed the bus. Darryl had already told Donna of his plan to convert his home into a halfway house for wayward kids following his acquittal. "He gave me the code to get into his garage," she said years later, repeating her favorite piece of evidence. "And he let me know when the code changed. Isn't that weird behavior for a drug trafficker?"

Darryl's neighbor Fred Pollard brought his famous pineapple cake, the one he brought to all the block gatherings, and Dick, the widower who lived next door, stopped by to shake Henley's hand. Darryl had visited Dick when he was ill, and now Dick was proud to reciprocate in his neighbor's hour of triumph. Darryl's neighbor Doris stopped by. So did Lida, the eighty-year-old white lady up the street who kept a scrapbook filled with Henley's press clippings. Stan and Nancy, Henley's next-door neighbors opposite Dick, were the ones who ordered the pizza. "If we thought he was a drug dealer," one neighbor said years later, "do you think we would have brought food over to his house and helped him celebrate?"

As the garage swelled with optimism, Darryl thought for a moment about calling Mike Malachowski and canceling the plan they had set into motion. Then he remembered that these good people hadn't been in court over the previous three months.

His pager went off. Someone made a joke about the beep coming from his ankle bracelet. Darryl looked down at his pager; it was a phone number he'd never seen before, in the 909 area code. Mike had told him that Quihuis lived "in the 909"—in the city of Rialto. Darryl retreated into a corner of his garage and called the number from Janis's cell phone. A recording told him the number was disconnected. He tried again. Same result. His mind convulsed: *Is Rayburn trying to set me up by linking me to some crack house in Pomona?*

Darryl received another page. Same 909 number. He called it again. Same result: disconnected. He returned to the dice game, his forehead now filmed with perspiration. His cell phone rang.

"Hello?"

"Hey, is this Darryl?"

"Yeah, who's this?"

"This is Mike. I've been paging you."

"Where are you at?"

"I'm at a pay phone."

"It must not be able to take incoming calls."

"Oh."

Several seconds passed.

"Hey, I got somebody here who wants to talk to you," Mike said.

Like Darryl Henley and Erwin Winkler, Bryan Quihuis had been celebrating the end of the trial that evening. He was pretty drunk when a friend dropped him off outside his grandparents' house around 8 p.m. From the front porch his grandma called out: "Bryan!

Somebody's here to see you!" And here came Mike Malachowski, bumbling across the lawn toward his carpool buddy.

"You'll never believe what happened," Mike panted.

"What?"

"Let's go get a couple beers and I'll tell you."

They hopped into Bryan's Honda Accord and made their way to a nearby convenience store. Along the way, Mike told Bryan about his visit to the Henley house: the beers, the hospitality, the talk about the trial, what a cool guy Darryl is, all of it.

"You're full of shit," Bryan said.

"I'll prove it to you," Mike said. "Turn in here."

The AM/PM convenience store on Rialto Avenue had a few gas pumps out front and a bank of pay phones by the street. Just as Bryan emerged from the store with a bottle of Mickey's malt liquor for Mike and a Bud for himself, Mike dropped a couple quarters into a pay phone and dialed Darryl's pager number. They swigged beer and waited for Darryl to call them back, but the phone remained silent. Mike asked Bryan to go inside and get some more quarters. Bryan told Mike to get his own damn quarters.

I gotta wait by the phone, Mike said. Do you wanna get paid or not?

What do you mean, get paid? Bryan asked.

Mike used the new quarters Bryan brought him to call a new number. Bryan heard Mike say into the phone: "Hey, I got somebody here who wants to talk to you."

Mike handed the phone to Bryan, who would later describe his ensuing conversation with Darryl Henley this way:

BRYAN: Hello? Who is this?

DARRYL: This is D.

BRYAN: Who is D?

DARRYL: Is this Quihuis?

BRYAN: Yeah, this is Quihuis.

DARRYL: Get the fuck outta here. Is this Quihuis?

BRYAN: Yeah, who is this?

DARRYL: D. What do you want?

BRYAN: Uh, this isn't the time or place to be talking to you. [Bryan handed the phone back to Mike.]

Years later, Henley recalled this exchange exactly the same way, adding only that he'd scolded Malachowski as soon as Quihuis returned the phone to him: "What the fuck are you doing, man? Putting me on the phone with a damn juror!"

Despite Henley's anger, the call brought a hint of hope to everyone. Mike and Bryan would get paid; Darryl would get a hung jury. Mike drove Bryan back to his grandparents' house where they went to Bryan's room and closed the door. "How much do you want?" Mike asked. "Whatever you ask for, I'm pretty sure he'll give it to you."

"How much are *you* getting?" Bryan asked.

"He said he would take care of me."

"What does that mean?"

"He just said he'd appreciate it if I could touch base with you and see which way you were leaning," Mike said. "Maybe two, three grand, some season tickets . . ."

"What're you gonna do, commute to St. Louis?" Bryan laughed. Bryan didn't say so, but three grand seemed awfully cheap to help hang a federal drug trial. The whole thing sounded so sketchy that Bryan made Mike strip down to his underwear so he could make sure he wasn't wearing a wire. As Mike was pulling his jeans back up, Bryan said, "If I was going to do it, I'd want a lot."

"Like what, ten thousand?"

"More than that."

"Fifteen?"

"We're talking about something that could get me thrown in prison, man."

Bryan eventually agreed that $25,000 would do the trick.

Malachowski drove home. The plan was for him to call Darryl

that night, find out how Bryan would be paid, then call Bryan with an update.

An hour passed with no call from Mike, so Bryan called him at 11:10 p.m. Bryan told Mike he was having second thoughts about selling his verdict. He'd already violated Judge Taylor's orders about discussing the case, and he'd blown to bits the warning Taylor issued about communicating with Malachowski. Now bribery. Bryan said he was out.

Just then, Darryl clicked in on Mike's call waiting, and for the next eighteen minutes, Mike clicked back and forth between briber and bribee, with Darryl communicating several details of the deal. Each time Mike clicked over to Bryan, Bryan repeated that he was done with the whole thing. Twenty-five grand was not worth risking his freedom, he said finally, and hung up.

Mike never relayed Bryan's reluctance to Darryl. Doing so would have made Henley think he'd "screwed up," Mike told the FBI later. So he told Darryl that Bryan was good to go. Done deal. As far as Darryl knew, Bryan Quihuis, juror number 9, would return a verdict of not guilty for him and Rex in exchange for $12,500 before the verdict and $12,500 after it.

Three minutes after this three-way conversation ended, Darryl called Alisa, sounding more confident than he'd sounded in weeks. They spoke excitedly about her pregnancy. The parents-to-be hung up at midnight.

The jurors elected Edmund Richards as their foreman, without debate or disagreement. At seventy-three, Richards was the oldest juror, and with two previous trials under his belt he was also the most experienced. Aside from his habit of sharing out loud the copious notes he'd taken during the trial, Richards, a retired furniture store owner, proved to be an entirely capable foreman. The others recalled that he gave everyone a chance to speak, then made sure all opinions had been fully expressed, with time of no concern, before moving on. Richards often outlined their discussions on the dry erase board.

Two sticking points lingered in the jurors' minds. The first was that Henley's defense had been weaker than they'd anticipated. Should they factor that in? The second was motive, or as many of them referred to it years later, still mystified: "the why of it all." Most of the jurors agreed that sitting alongside three known criminals during the trial had not hurt Henley's chances; if anything, it had helped. Henley had seemed so out of place. As Richards said later, "Darryl left the middle class and entered into a class he should never have come close to."

There were vast differences between Richards, the oldest juror, an elderly immigrant of Western Europe, and the youngest, Bryan Quihuis, a Gen-X Californian of Asian and Hispanic descent. Bryan was "like a college kid," one juror recalled. The moment deliberations began, Quihuis was on his feet arguing for the Henleys' freedom. When the other jurors cited flaws in his logic, Bryan announced: "I have reasonable doubt and that's enough. That's all I have to have. I don't have to say why." When pressed, Quihuis said that his deepest doubts had to do with Tracy.

Even before the bribe offer, Quihuis believed that Tracy had lied on the stand and that she knew the contents of those suitcases the moment she was asked to carry them. About half the jurors agreed with Quihuis — "How could she *not* know?" asked one. Another juror credited Quihuis for putting forth a strong argument for the Henleys' acquittal: "He was good. He was convincing. I would almost believe him."

Only Shawn O'Reilly had Henley pegged as 100 percent guilty from the moment deliberations began. "He had his mind decided about how it all happened," recalled a juror who was not a member of O'Reilly's ill-fated three-man carpool. "And I was thinking, 'This guy was half-asleep the whole time. How could he remember? He wasn't even paying attention, much less taking notes.'" Several jurors recalled that O'Reilly's notepad was filled not with trial information but with scores from his jury-room card games. Another juror described O'Reilly as having been "off in la la land" during the trial's entirety.

The ten presumably fair-minded jurors struggled mightily with the discrepancy between Darryl's reputation and the crimes with which he was charged. No one among these ten, Richards observed later, "said, 'Of course the son of a bitch is guilty.'"

Mike Malachowski would have been deliberating right there with them had he not received an unrelated call from a bill collector a few weeks earlier. Instead, Mike was in his apartment at the edge of the Mojave Desert, fielding a call from Darryl Henley at 11:00 a.m. Darryl invited Mike and his wife to come by his house that night for dinner. He didn't say why, but his reason was so he could have Mike meet Ron Knight, whose opinion of him would be the equivalent of Quihuis's strip search; Ron could tell right away if Mike could be trusted. Ron had already advised Darryl to keep his wallet in his pocket. "None of this 'half now, half later' shit," Ron said. "Hang on to that money, D. They gotta make sure that verdict's straight first."

Mike and his wife, Shaunti, showed up at Henley's house shortly after nightfall. Donna Henson and Robert were already there, oblivious to the fact that this new guest had served on the jury. As Robert shot craps with Darryl, Mike, Rex, and Ron, he noticed that the rules of dice had changed. This Mike guy was winning a lot — when he shouldn't have been winning at all. Darryl gave Robert a friendly nod: *Be cool, let this guy win a little.* Just before dinner, Darryl asked Mike if he wanted to see his stash of sports memorabilia. Darryl and Mike broke away from the group and went to another room, where Darryl asked Mike about Quihuis: He's still on the team, right? Mike told Darryl he had nothing to worry about. But Darryl wanted proof, so at 7:13 p.m. Henley handed his phone to Mike and asked him to call Bryan. Quihuis wasn't home — or at least Bryan's grandmother *said* he wasn't home. (Quihuis had told his grandparents that if Mike called, tell him he wasn't around.)

At 9:13 p.m., Mike tried Bryan again from Darryl's house. No luck. Before Mike and his wife left for the night, he dropped an unsubtle hint to Darryl that he was having money problems. Darryl handed him $300 and told him not to worry about paying it back. Mike would use the money to make his car payment.[1]

Phone records showed that Malachowski tried to call Quihuis that Thursday, Sunday, and Monday. Malachowski called phones belonging to Darryl Henley nine times during this period. Henley called Malachowski twenty times.

Thursday morning found Darryl sitting in the courthouse hallway with Rex, awaiting the trial verdict while reading T. J. Simers's story in the *Times* about his visit to Henley's home. Henley remembered Simers asking if he thought he'd be convicted, and now he was reading his own answer: "I have not thought about it, not once. No nightmares. I don't think it's going to happen. No way. If it does, I will be fooled. I just don't think that's in my future."

When he finished reading, Darryl asked the clerk if he could leave early to go work out. "Go ahead," said the clerk. "I'm going on vacation next week, and when I come back, this jury will still be deliberating."

When Judge Taylor heard about Henley's workout, he ordered Henley to be present all day on Friday. Darryl was angry at the time, but he would end up grateful.

After Mike Malachowski's dismissal from the jury, the remaining jurors were not allowed to stray from one another during lunch, to prevent contact with outsiders. So each day they moved in a herd to one of the eateries near Fourth Street, or more often to a catered spread that was wheeled into the jury room. Combined with Taylor's orders that the jurors avoid all media, these terms brought the jurors as close to sequestration as possible without actually employing the word. The trial's sedentary demands and rich menu had added what felt like ten pounds to each juror in as many weeks, and all those days spent indoors had given everyone a pasty glow.

345

Bryan Quihuis didn't sleep the night before the jury returned its verdict—perhaps because he was wired on methamphetamine, more likely because he was under immeasurable stress. Not only was the weight of the verdict upon him, but also the bribe offer he'd turned down, and all its loose ends and ramifications. *Was it a standing offer that I can jump on at any time, or is the window closed?* he thought. *Twenty-five g's could set me up pretty nice. I couldn't go spending it like crazy, though, then everyone would know*—and then Bryan would make himself quit thinking about it and snap back into whatever the other jurors were discussing.

Mostly, Bryan wanted it to be over. The trial, the bribe, his paranoia that the other jurors thought he'd been bought already, the daily phone calls from Mike, everything. Long before his family informed him that Malachowski had stopped by yet again, Bryan had decided to stay holed up in his room at his grandparents' house and ride this thing out.

Then he opened the local Rialto newspaper. After flipping past a story about the movies the sequestered Simpson jurors were watching, Bryan glimpsed—beneath an article titled "Collectors Scrambling for Tyson's Prison Memorabilia" and next to a story about Reggie Lewis's jersey being retired by the Celtics—an article that would change the situation entirely.

The next morning Judge Taylor cleared the courtroom and asked the jurors if they'd seen Simers's story in the *Times*. None of the jurors said yes, but Bryan said he'd seen something in the *Sun*. Across the courtroom, Darryl's eyes widened. This, he thought, was Quihuis's way of squeezing money out of him; Quihuis would walk the fine line of getting kicked off the jury, right before Henley's eyes, and use it to force at least a down payment out of him. Although the next few minutes would make Henley's suspicions appear accurate, it's also possible that Bryan was using the *Sun* article to try and get himself kicked off the jury so he could put an end to all the pressure.

Quihuis was sent to the jury room while the lawyers and judge discussed the *Sun* story. Cossack asked Taylor to ignore it and "tell them to go back to work." Rayburn disagreed and asked Taylor to call Quihuis back in and learn more about the article's impact on him.

"Quite a big impact, really," Bryan told Taylor after he was called back in.

"In what way?" Taylor asked.

"Just all the attention that's being drawn towards it, and we have to make this major decision. I mean, I couldn't sleep last night for one . . ."

In the end, Quihuis said he could still decide the case fairly. Taylor sent him back to the jury room and gave the lawyers ten minutes to confer amongst themselves.

Darryl and Cossack stepped into the hall and spoke privately. According to Darryl, Cossack asked: This is your guy, right?

Yeah, that's him.

Phone records show that Darryl called Malachowski during this same break. "Your boy needs to stop playing games," Darryl told Mike.

When court reconvened, everyone agreed that the Quihuis matter would be put on hold until Tuesday. Taylor adjourned for the weekend.

As he exited the court building, Darryl called Mike again. They spoke for nine minutes. Henley called him again that afternoon. They spoke for ten minutes. Malachowski would later pinpoint these two conversations as containing orders from Henley to double his bribe offer — from $25,000 to $50,000.

The headline in the next day's *LA Times* read: "Juror Says He Read Article about Henley." The story mentioned in passing that two jurors had already been excused from the case — one because he'd seen a newspaper article, the other (the unnamed Malachowski) because of "his job demands." But Mike Malachowski had no job demands. That was part of the problem — Malachowski's abundant free time, which he used on this particular day to try and get Bryan Quihuis on the phone again.

He finally reached him Monday morning. According to Mala-chowski, Bryan expressed renewed interest in the bribe. (Other ju-rors said that this could have been true because Quihuis was still holding out for the Henleys' acquittal the following day.)

Mike hung up with Bryan and called Darryl. They spoke for six-teen minutes. Mike told Henley everything was cool—only this time he meant it. Bryan was in.

Sometime over the weekend, Willie McGowan called Darryl from the Santa Ana Jail. Though they rarely spoke during the trial, and hadn't spoken at all during the months leading up to it, the defen-dants' common goal of beating the case had silently united them in a way that Darryl had not anticipated. Speaking into a jail pay phone, Willie told Darryl: You're gonna walk, D. They can't prove nothing on you. Rex either. Shit, I got to be the fall guy for this one. Just don't forget about a nigga, ah-ight? Shoot me a letter sometime.

Willie put Garey West on the line.

We hit, man, G said, admitting defeat. We hit.

Darryl awoke on the morning of March 28, 1995, not knowing whether it would be another day of waiting, or one of unimagina-ble relief and clinking champagne glasses. That these were his last hours of freedom did not cross his mind.

Judge Taylor began the day by announcing that Bryan Quihuis would remain on the jury. As soon as Quihuis returned to the jury room, he stepped back on his Free Darryl soapbox. "How could he have known what was going on at his house when he was in Atlanta the whole summer?" one juror quoted Quihuis as saying. "Why would he take Tracy back to the Atlanta airport and sit with her right in front of the DEA people?"

One of the jurors did the math, estimating that Darryl would have made about $125,000 on the deal. Bryan exclaimed: "But he was about to make millions playing football!" Richards shrugged; he couldn't explain it either. No one could. None of the twelve citizens who were about to decide Henley's fate, not the investigators, the prosecutors — not even Henley's codefendants could put a finger on his motive. At the end of this grueling, twenty-month odyssey, only one person who mattered was holding out for Darryl's acquittal: Bryan Quihuis. "I have reasonable doubt and that's all I have to have," he said again.

The phone evidence is what finally turned him. Richards pointed once more to the forty-seven-minute call from Darryl's apartment to Tracy's house on July 3 — the call that had been interrupted several times by Willie, who was also calling American Airlines. "I'm Darryl," Richards said to Quihuis. "It's two in the morning. I call Tracy. We have a forty-minute conversation. Let's say it starts: 'How you doing, Tracy?' Now take that conversation from there, Bryan, and if you can convince me that there is nothing going on, for forty-seven minutes, then I'll agree with you."

Barbara Kingsley approached Darryl in the hall. "I don't believe twelve people will convict me," he told the *Register* reporter. "The way the government put it on, they made it believable by the *story*. They didn't make it believable by the *facts*."

A clerk stuck her head out of the courtroom. "We have a verdict."

Darryl called his parents at the fish market. "You're going to be fine," his dad said. "Call us afterward. We'll be listening for it on the radio."

Dorothy Henley was not about to learn her son's fate over the damn radio. She badgered one of Woolsey's security men into driving her as fast as he could to the courthouse.

Darryl's codefendants told him later that as they were being led out of the marshals' lockup to head to the courtroom, they saw Rayburn burst out of the adjacent U.S. Attorney's Office, throw his fist in the air, and yell, "Yeah!" A few observers recalled Rayburn entering the courtroom and congratulating his government team-mates before the verdict was announced, confident that after just three days of deliberation the jury had seen things his way. Ger-ry Chaleff walked into the courtroom after making the long com-mute from West LA, visibly fearful that the jurors had seen things Rayburn's way, too. Roger Cossack didn't make it.

"All rise. This United States district court is in session."

As the jurors filed in, Darryl focused on Quihuis, who looked like he'd been to hell and back. The other jurors didn't look much better.

"Be seated, please," Taylor said.

Jim Riddet leaned toward Rex and whispered, "If there's such a thing as justice, you deserve it."

"I just remember Deirdre Eliot looked so intense," recalled Kingsley.

It was 2:15 when Edmund Richards handed his stack of juror forms to the clerk, who read aloud:

Rafael Bustamante, guilty on both counts. Willie McGowan, guilty on both counts. Garey West, guilty on both counts.

Rex Henley, guilty on both counts.

At that moment, everyone in the courtroom but Darryl—who knew as soon as Rex was declared guilty that he would be, too—felt as if things could go either way. Not a soul in the room wasn't in some way panicked, yet the place was dead quiet.

"United States versus Darryl Keith Henley. We the jury in the above-titled action find the defendant guilty as charged in Count One of the second superseding indictment, and guilty as charged in Count Two of the second superseding indictment."

There was no preparing for it. Like an astronaut returning to gravity, the blood in Darryl's body rushed toward the floor. Chaleff put a hand on his shoulder and said, "I'm sorry, Darryl. I'm so sorry." The papers reported that Darryl "bowed his head and bit his lip as the verdict was read." They did not report that when he glanced up, his eyes sought Quihuis, who was crying. More than half the jurors were crying, including all four women. Rex, his mouth agape, was looking at Darryl as if pleading for his help.

Taylor thanked the jurors for their service, noted how "attentive" they'd been, and asked everyone else to rise as the jury walked out.

"Mr. Henley," said a U.S. marshal, "if you could place your pager on the table and place your hands behind your back."

"When they said that—when they put that iron on him," recalled Charles Hack, "my heart broke. The sense was, 'There goes his life.' The whole thing had been like a parade, and once it stopped, we were all like, 'What just happened?'"

For all his faults, Mike Malachowski was equally eloquent in his view of the trial, although by the time he expressed it he had become biased by his own prosecution. "If you were there, you could see how it all happened," Malachowski said. "The young, good-looking prosecutors—I mean, who *wasn't* going to believe them? *I* believed them. They were like Barbie and Ken. And the judge," Malachowski added, moving his hands like a marionette artist, "he was like the puppet master."

A similar perspective was offered by Steven Kinney, who ten years after the verdict called Henley's involvement in the drug conspiracy a case of "poor judgment . . . a good friend trying to help those he left behind by guaranteeing a twelve-kilo cocaine front. I doubt if Darryl was ever to benefit financially."

Dorothy Henley didn't arrive until after the verdict was announced. She watched the marshals herd her son and the other four convicted drug traffickers into a van destined for the Metropolitan Detention Center in downtown LA. For the first time in her life, she felt angry at God. She had trusted Him to deliver Darryl from this, but instead He'd let her down. During the long drive home, her face ashen and drawn, she rolled down her window so she could toss her stack of handwritten scripture verses onto the freeway. Then, as suddenly as the overpasses whooshed over her head, the moment passed and she decided that the guilty verdict had been God's will, that Darryl's victory had merely been postponed, and for a higher purpose.

At that moment, Gary Taylor was welcoming the exhausted jurors into his chambers. The women were still weeping. Taylor asked if anyone had anything to say. No one said a word. "Everyone in the room was emotionally drained and very, very sad," recalled one juror. Said Richards: "We were just hoping we had done the right thing, hoping we had not made a mistake. . . . The phone [evidence] was just so damaging." Taylor asked the jurors if they wanted to leave through the front door and face the media, or leave through the back. Twelve voices answered in unison: "Back." But there was no peace there, either. Reporters drunk on Simpson coverage scurried across the blacktop in pursuit of the Henley jurors, who muttered begrudging quotes.

"It's not an easy decision," one unnamed juror said. "The decision you make, you got to live with the rest of your life."

"Why would someone so successful get involved in something like this?" said another. "That was the number one reason people had a hard time. . . . The guy was making upward of $600,000 a year."

"He was stunned," Chaleff said of his client's reaction. "We were all stunned. . . . He wasn't involved in drug dealing. Period."

"Juror Bryan Quihuis appeared to blink back tears after leaving the courthouse," the *Register* reported. "Now I can go home and sleep," he said.

Chapter 35

If not for its thin, black windows, each no
wider — by design — than a human arm, the
Metropolitan Detention Center would look
like any other tall building in downtown LA.
Constructed in the late 1980s, MDC consisted
of two nine-story towers connected by three
hammock-like terraces hanging between the
third, sixth, and eighth floors. These caged
recreation balconies were the means of escape for five inmates who, in 1989, used
bedsheets to drop themselves from the exercise area onto the shoulder of the Hollywood Freeway, whose traffic moaned at the
prison's feet. It was the first and only escape
in MDC's history. Nothing got out after that.
But as Darryl Henley would soon discover,
plenty could get in.

Henley would often compare life at MDC
to the Rams' training camp. It wasn't exactly hard time. Because it was a federal facility, most of the thousand or so inmates at

MDC were in for drugs, as opposed to violent crime. They were housed not in cells but in "rooms" with solid doors, each with a slim, vertical, wired-glass window not unlike the ones visible from the street. As the *Times* reported shortly after MDC opened in 1988, there was "not an iron bar in sight."

Rex Henley was placed among MDC's general population while his famous nephew was relegated to protective custody. Located on the eighth floor of the south tower (or "8 South"), the protective custody unit also housed suicidal or otherwise mentally unstable inmates, in addition to "high-profile" inmates like Henley, who would hear those two words, "high profile," throughout his incarceration. As with life on the street, Henley came to see too late that those words made his life harder more often than they made it easier.

The trial verdict hadn't shocked him. Darryl didn't sit in the crazy ward and stew. The phone conversations he had during his first week in MDC revealed that he was more focused on getting out of prison than on the process that had put him there. Like all calls from federal prisons, Henley's were recorded.

"They don't want me with nobody right now," he explained to his mother within hours of his arrival.

"Why?"

"Security reasons, you know. They're just watching me or something."

"Oh, really."

"Yeah."

"You want to holler at your dad?"

"Yeah."

T.H. took the phone. "How you feel?" he asked his son.

"I feel all right. I mean, you know, I'ma be all right as long as you all right. . . . We still doing some things. We still doing some things. Uh, Gerry [Chaleff] and them on their way down here so, uh, so, you know, don't worry about all of that. . . . We at the little fork in the road. I don't have all the answers to it, but, you know, you got to play out this hand."

T.H. put his wife back on the phone. "Mama, where's Ronald at?" Darryl asked.

"He's right here."

"Let me speak to him real quick."

"What's up, baby?" said Ron Knight.

"You remember what we were going to do with them people out of town?" This, Henley said later, was a coded request for Ron to get the information from Malachowski that could earn Henley a new trial. Ron said he was on it.

The phone eventually got to Alisa. "It's some other things going on with the case," Darryl told her, "and it ain't over. . . . Keep plugging away and I'm gonna be here for a while I'm sure. You sure you okay? . . . You still want to have the baby?"

"Yeah."

"You sure?"

"Yeah."

Mike Malachowski picked up his *LA Times* the next morning, rifled past the headlines about Marcia Clark and Kato Kaelin, and landed on the story he was looking for, the one in which Shawn O'Reilly said of the Henley verdict: "I feel bad. . . . I don't like to see anyone go to jail." And later: "It was real hard to do that to someone being an upstanding citizen like that, but the evidence I saw . . . did it for me." Angered by O'Reilly's disingenuous comments ("Upstanding citizen? He hated Darryl!" Mike yelled in his kitchen), Mike called Bryan Quihuis and ranted for eighteen minutes. Then he called the reporter who had written the story and ranted some more. Annoyed, the reporter told Malachowski to call Roger Cossack.

The next morning, in an unrelated event, Gerry Chaleff walked into the visiting room at MDC, plopped a thick binder on the table in front of Darryl, and opened it to reveal an eight-by-ten glossy photo of Suge Knight. The feds wanted Darryl's help nailing him, and they were promising sentencing considerations in return.

"Sentencing considerations?" Henley barked. "How about a new trial?! I haven't been locked up forty-eight hours, and you come to me talking about snitching on Suge Knight?"

Roger Cossack dropped by a few days later. "Now that it's all over, did you really do it?" Darryl remembered him asking.

"What do you mean, did I do it?" Darryl said he replied. "Did I have sex with Tracy? Did I say yes to Willie? Did I let him use my phones? Yeah. Did I sell drugs? Hell no."

Within a week, Darryl would terminate both Cossack and Chaleff as his attorneys. But first he had to get things moving with Malachowski. This thing wasn't over. Not by a long shot.

"I'm doing good," Darryl told his mother over the phone. "We got some things going on, real positive things." When his father took the phone, Darryl could tell that he was near tears. The weight of the verdict had sunk in and evoked the response Simers would describe in the *Times*: "He did not expect it, could not believe it, and would not accept it."

"I don't feel like I'm in jail, man," Darryl told his father, trying to lighten his load. "I don't know what this is. This is like a camp." Darryl heard his dad's voice crack with emotion, something he never thought he'd hear. "Come on, Dad, you my father, man."

"They take your life, they take my life," T.H. said.

"They not taking my life. They not taking nothing close to my life. Period."

"There is no way you should be in jail. You and Rex should not be in jail at all."

Within days of his arrival at MDC, Darryl was taken off the protective custody floor and reunited with Rex. From then on they would be roommates on 9 South, a loosely supervised unit where the doors stayed open from 6 a.m. until 10 p.m. As much as he hated protective custody, Henley's removal from it in favor of the shark tank on 9 South would eventually bring about his steepest fall.

Darryl called Ron Knight from one of 9 South's pay phones the afternoon he was moved there and spoke with him about "the green tablet"—another cloaked reference to Malachowski's new trial information[1]—and about selling their cars in preparation for the costly legal fight ahead. It took all of Darryl's persuasive powers to convince Ron to drive to a local IHOP and meet with Malachowski in person.

Worried about a government setup, Ron covertly pressed "Record" on the tape recorder in his pocket when he saw Mike arrive outside the restaurant. Once seated, Ron got to the point, asking Mike what he and the other two jurors had discussed during their carpool rides.

Everything, Mike said. He told Ron about O'Reilly's "Those niggers are guilty" comment, an utterance that made Ron's eyes—which didn't widen often—expand to the size of the saucers beneath their coffee cups.

Don't fuck with me, Ron said. Is that really what this dude said?

I was sitting right there.

When was this?

Like, the second week of the trial. I mean, if this stuff doesn't get Darryl a new trial, something is seriously wrong with the system.

If you only knew, Ron thought.

The rest of their conversation included details of Quihuis's methamphetamine use. He was strung out practically the entire trial, Mike said. Quihuis had told Malachowski that he wore colored contacts during jury selection to hide his dilated pupils.

Unfortunately for Henley, several other disclosures were captured on Ron's tape. Malachowski said that Darryl would have to "really take care of" him for coming forth with all this information. And when Ron warned Mike that Quihuis would tell the authorities that Mike came up with the bribe, Mike suggested that he could just say the bribe had been *Quihuis's* idea. It would be his word against Bryan's, and Mike had the reputation as a truth teller in the court's eyes for coming forth about the call from Gary West.

This recorded conversation between Mike and Ron would have been disastrous to Henley's motion for a new trial, so Darryl had no choice but to have Ron destroy it. Malachowski had promised to testify about all the other stuff on it, anyway.

Nine South was home to a main core of fourteen or fifteen inmates with a handful of transitioning inmates constantly floating in and out of the unit. One of the first things Rex had been told upon entering MDC was the importance of keeping to himself. Darryl had apparently missed that lesson during his time in protective custody. Both men knew that MDC was a transitional facility, where most inmates were awaiting either trial or sentencing, so they realized that most of their neighbors were looking to play the game Alex Cuevas had played — that is, providing information to law enforcement in hopes of getting a sentencing break. Over time, however, Darryl would either forget or undervalue this realization. His celebrity status, outgoing nature, and reputation as a drug trafficker made him 9 South's flame, and his new neighbors were the moths. Most inmates assumed that Henley's NFL career had made him permanently rich, a misconception that would spawn countless offers to harm Tracy Donaho in exchange for money. "I'll get her, D," they'd say. "I get out next month. All you gotta do is say the word." Darryl would either ignore or laugh at such offers. He didn't want Tracy dead. He wanted her back on the witness stand being cross-examined about her dishonesty at trial.

Bill Hanley, the Orange County lawyer who'd been one of Henley's character witnesses, soon became the liaison between Henley and his legal team, which was now helmed by Jim Riddet. Riddet, whose interest in the case had intensified due to the recent rumors of jury misconduct, accompanied Hanley to MDC a week after the verdict to discuss those rumors with Darryl. The three men discussed Quihuis's drug use, O'Reilly's racism, and the startling disinterest in these issues shown by Gerry Chaleff and Roger Cossack. The consensus was that Chaleff was furious at Cossack for keeping Darryl's contact with Malachowski a secret and wanted no part of a mess that could only make him look bad in the end.

While Darryl was conferring with his legal team, his football team was meeting without him at Rams Park, where training camp resumed under a similar cloud of uncertainty. Within days of Henley's conviction, the team had replaced him at cornerback by signing Anthony Parker, a starter for the Vikings the previous season. But a greater need remained unfilled—the need to know where the Rams would be playing their home games, Anaheim or St. Louis.

Henley hadn't abandoned hope that he would return to the team. During a phone conversation with Alisa that week, he said he'd been advised by his attorneys that if Malachowski was telling the truth about O'Reilly's racism and Quihuis's meth use, he might be set free. Before hanging up, Darryl asked Alisa to send him some books. He told her he'd tacked the photo she sent him—a pinup shot from the Rams cheerleaders' calendar—on the wall of his room.

That Friday evening Darryl called Ron Knight. With the sounds of the Ultimate Fighting Championship rumbling from Ron's TV, they discussed how "that guy" (Malachowski) would have to hold up under government pressure. When the subject of Darryl's lawyers came up, Ron—who was highly critical of Chaleff and Cossack's trial performance, not to mention their avoidance of the post-verdict jury issues—said, "If I see them motherfuckers, I'm gonna slap one of 'em."

"Fuck Gerry," Darryl said. "He gone."

Ron passed the phone to Alisa. "Take care of yourself tonight, love," Darryl told her.

Alisa and Ron had an errand to run.

They knew Mike Malachowski lived far away, but they didn't think it was this far. Out past San Bernardino and the winding switchbacks north of it, through two mountain ranges, so far north that it felt as if Oregon was just ahead. By the time Alisa's red Mercedes finally descended into the small town of Hesperia, with nothing around but purple sky and pitch black hills, Los Angeles's lights were but a distant fizz in her rear-view mirror.

The tone of their meeting with Mike Malachowski was cordial and friendly. It took place in the apartment Mike shared with his wife and three kids. Ron and Alisa wanted Mike to feel comfortable, and he certainly seemed so. He saw this sit-down as the beginning of an exciting three-person crusade to Free Darryl. They were all doing the right thing, Mike thought, something important, something that would provide for Mike's family in the process. When Ron and Alisa got down to the business of reviewing Mike's version of events, and warning him about the pressure he'd soon face from the government, Mike didn't seem concerned.

Four days later, Ron and Alisa returned to Hesperia, picked Mike up, and drove him to a law office in Irvine where Jim Riddet was waiting to take Malachowski's deposition on tape. Meticulous as always, Riddet had asked one of the area's top attorneys — one of Judge Taylor's closest colleagues, in fact — to sit in on the deposition as a witness.

But not even Riddet's preparation could combat the litany of lies Malachowski would tell under oath that day — lies that Riddet would not realize were lies until several weeks had passed, after the lies had begun eroding the truths in Malachowski's deposition like salt on snow. As he sat listening to Mike's responses that day, Riddet believed it all: that the bribe had been *Quihuis's* idea, that Mike had come *alone* to Darryl's house that first night (Malachowski wanted to leave his sister out of it), and that he only wound up there by accident, after getting lost. Malachowski also said that he hadn't spoken to Darryl since that first visit and hadn't spoken with Quihuis at all. [2]

Later that night Alisa reported to Darryl over the phone: "I guess everything went all good. . . . He said he got all the good things out. . . . He said that they grilled his ass up . . . but he says he feels good. He said he wasn't as nervous as he thought he would [be], because on the way out there, he was kind of like, 'Oh, here comes the butterflies,' you know. And *damn* he could talk."

Jim Riddet gave the transcript of Malachowski's deposition to the chief judge in the district. Riddet still needed proof that Quihuis had kick-started the bribe, so he sent a private investigator named Jerry Mulligan to Malachowski's home. Mulligan persuaded Malachowski to call Quihuis and lure him into incriminating himself.

The first thing Bryan wanted to talk about with Mike was how relieved he was "to get away from what was going on. . . . If I ever have to go through that shit again, man, I'll go insane. . . . You know, whether he's guilty or not guilty or whatever, it's the idea that I was part of helping sentence somebody to go to prison is not cool." Mike tiptoed toward the subject of the bribe. Bryan was the first to mention the amount — $50,000 — which he admitted would have changed his life. "But as soon as it pops in my mind I just try to get it out of my mind," Quihuis said. With Mulligan's tape recorder rolling, Mike asked Bryan what Shawn O'Reilly had said during deliberations. "He said he's guilty," Bryan said with a laugh. "He went by all the phone calls, and we started putting pieces together on who could have been where and all that, and it made sense. . . . Until that last moment when we decided he was guilty, he was innocent. And I didn't want to sentence nobody, but uh, he was the last one to do. He was the hardest one to do. . . .

"I heard through the TV that they're going to appeal it . . ." Quihuis added, "so I figured, you know, you're probably working for them or something." He chuckled.

"Yeah, mm hm, how did you know," Mike said sarcastically.

"You probably got it bugged right now," Bryan said.

"Yep, you got it, man."

"Oh, well. I tried to do my job, and I didn't take no money, so you can put that on your fucking tape."

"All right, I got that on there."

"All right, dude. I'll keep in touch."

Chapter 36

Private eye Jerry Mulligan reported back to the defense camp with only moderately good news about his visit to Malachowski's home: although Quihuis had been the first to mention the *amount* of the bribe, Malachowski had not been able to coax a confession from Quihuis about *requesting* it.

So Mulligan called Quihuis directly, introducing himself benignly as an investigator who was looking into rumors of jury misconduct. He asked Quihuis to meet him at a restaurant. Clinking glasses and waitress chatter were audible on the tape of their sitdown, which happened to take place the day after Timothy McVeigh blew up the federal building in Oklahoma City. Quihuis was still unaware that Mike Malachowski was trying to frame him for bribery, and that the man seated across from him was in on it, too. Quihuis was wary at first, but he ended up sharing quite a bit with Mulligan, like his recollection that Shawn O'Reilly had said "something like [he] thought [Henley] was guilty or whatever. . . . It didn't seem like [O'Reilly] had a open mind . . ."

"So he seemed to have a closed mind."

"It didn't seem like he was opened at all. . . . His notebook said 'Shawn O'Reilly's Scorepad for Playing Cards during Breaks.' So instead of notes in his notepad he had all the scores of all the card games . . ."

"Do you recall any statements like, um, 'All those niggers are guilty'? Anything in that general term?"

"Yes," Bryan said. ". . . I believe he said something like, uh, the government doesn't bring anything to trial unless it knows that it can win."

A waitress interrupted to ask Bryan if he wanted another beer. He drank at least two during the interview (a fact the prosecutors would later use to suggest that the defense had tried to loosen his lips with alcohol). "Okay, let's change everything a little bit here," Mulligan said. "I want you to tell me about the request that you made on the eve before deliberations for $50,000."

"The request I made for *what?*"

"For $50,000."

"I never made a request for money."

"You never made a request for money."

"I was *offered* money."

"You were offered money."

"From, uh, Michael . . . Michael Malachowski."

"Now's the time to come out and tell the truth," Mulligan said.

"Michael Malachowski had, uh — okay, this is how I believe it started." And Bryan proceeded to tell his side of the story, beginning with his family's relationship with the Malachowskis prior to trial and ending with Mike telling him that Darryl "wanted to know if anyone could get him off the trial for a sum of money. . . . I thought [Mike] was full of shit."

"I just wanna read you something here," Mulligan said moments later, pulling out a transcript of Bryan's three-day-old recorded phone call with Malachowski. As Mulligan read it, Quihuis pointed out correctly that at no point during the call had he admitted to instigating or accepting a bribe. "All I know is Darryl Henley offered me money." He'd hardly uttered this sentence before he retracted it. On second thought, Bryan said, he'd only spoken with Darryl once—from a pay phone—and the most damning thing Henley said during that conversation was, "Hey, work with me, work with me, what do you want?" (During a later interview with the FBI, Quihuis would drop the "work with me" line and change Darryl's only words to, "What do you want?")

"Darryl never discussed the money with me," Quihuis said. "Everything was always through Michael. I never discussed money with Darryl at all. I never discussed one red cent when Darryl talked to me."

So Mulligan went back to the middleman. Sitting with Mike Malachowski inside his mother's house at the edge of the desert, it finally hit Mulligan that Henley had chosen the shakiest foundation possible upon which to build his motion for a new trial. Malachowski finally admitted to Mulligan that his sister had accompanied him to Darryl's house that night, but he remained suspiciously foggy about who came up with the bribe idea. He continued to say things that would soon be easily proven false. Malachowski's house of cards was teetering, and the government hadn't even applied its pressure yet. The government didn't even *know* about the deposition Mike had given the defense, which was now two weeks old.

The prosecutors found out about the deposition four weeks after the verdict—when Quihuis's mother called Judge Taylor's office to report that "there may have been some problems involved on the Henley jury." Taylor's clerk immediately called Quihuis and put him on speaker phone. Taylor entered the room quietly, holding a tape recorder.

"Okay," Quihuis began, "when the trial was basically winding down, we were getting ready to go into deliberations. I guess Michael had talked to Darryl . . ."

And so it went, as Quihuis told his story yet again, pausing only to say, "Oh man, I'm so wound up."

Judge Taylor met with John Rayburn that same afternoon, in the first of three in camera hearings he would hold with the prosecution over the next twenty hours. The judge relayed to Rayburn what Quihuis had shared. (Which forced Taylor to explain once again, on the record, who Mike Malachowski was. Still unwilling to mention Rayburn's involvement with Malachowski's dismissal from the jury, Taylor said only that the juror had been called by a man named Gary West, "and in the course of that discussion, [Malachowski] had to be excused from the jury.") Taylor advised Rayburn that the Quihuis matter would likely "result in an invalidation of the jury's verdict. Perhaps."

Rayburn even used the word *mistrial.*

The minutes of this private meeting between Taylor and Rayburn stated that it had been called "to determine what, if any, recent information the government had about alleged jury tampering." But the real reason, which Taylor stated at the meeting's outset, was "to advise [Rayburn] of some information I just obtained within the last thirty minutes. . . . I want to notify the government and give them the opportunity to make a recommendation or to take an initiative of their own. So that's the reason for the hearing." There was no attempt to "determine what information the government had." Taylor gave them the information, then followed it with a call to action.

These minutes also stated that "the Court conducted a second in camera hearing with government counsel on the same subject." But it was not the same subject at all. During this second private meeting, whose transcripts were initially sealed as tightly as the first's, Taylor and Rayburn discussed whether the court should disclose this bribery information to the defense and whether a gag order should be placed on all the jurors.

366

Taylor's reaction to Quihuis's call—from his covert taping of it, to his private strategy meetings with Rayburn—were not out of line in and of themselves. Rather, they were the first twigs adhering to one another in what would become a tumbleweed of collusion between the bench and the prosecution—one that would not stop rolling until Darryl Henley's conviction, a conviction handed down by a jury featuring at least one racially biased man and one drug-addled man, was protected.

Mike Malachowski was surprised to find the message from Judge Taylor's clerk on his answering machine. But before he could return that call, he got one from an *LA Times* reporter who asked if he knew anything about these new jury issues (the same issues Mike had tried to tell the *Times* about the day after the verdict). No comment, Mike said.

As soon as he hung up, Taylor's office called and instructed him to speak only to the FBI or the U.S. Attorney's Office from that point on. The other jurors were called and told the same thing.

Once these jury issues were made public, a swarm of defense lawyers began dropping by Darryl's visiting table in MDC. I love your case, they'd say, as if it were some sort of compliment, or This new trial motion of yours is a slam dunk, or I've gotten people off who have done a lot worse than you. But Darryl had already decided to turn everything over to Riddet, mainly because, as he told Ron over the phone, "the judge like him." It was a choice he should arguably have made before his trial.

Mike Malachowski had made several regrettable decisions of his own since the trial began. He had always believed that everything would work out fine in the end; his favorite song was a ditty by 1980s new wave band Oingo Boingo called "Nothing Bad Ever Happens," whose flippant title said it all. But Mike's naiveté ended on April 28, 1995, the day FBI special agent Robert Cross knocked on his door and asked him to tell him what happened, one more time, and start from the beginning. Lost in the string of lies that followed was that one persistent truth: juror Shawn O'Reilly had called the defendants niggers during the trial.

The next day T. J. Simers drove to the rural hills near Riverside to interview O'Reilly himself. (The interview took place in O'Reilly's scruffy front yard, over the objections of his wife, who pleaded from their doorstep: "Don't talk to him! Don't talk to him!") O'Reilly "denied ever discussing the case with Malachowski or Quihuis," Simers reported in the *Times*, "and also denied making any racist comments." "I'm not like that," O'Reilly told Simers. "I got Mexican neighbors on this side of me and Mexican neighbors on that side. I'm not prejudiced. . . . We have black people right down on the corner and we've never had a problem with them."

That there had been racism present on the Henley jury came as no surprise to *Register* reporter John McDonald, who called antiblack sentiment in Orange County "rampant," in part, he said, because "everyone denied it." This was the county that barred citizens of neighboring Los Angeles County from its federal trials, creating a racial setting that contrasted starkly with the O.J. Simpson trial, and illustrating both Southern California's tangled ethnic history and Darryl Henley's dumb luck. If only his trial and O.J.'s could have swapped courthouses, Henley often lamented.

The U.S. Attorney's Office in Santa Ana, it became clear, was determined to defeat Henley's motion for a new trial not because they believed the verdict had been reached by a fair jury but because they knew that a successful Henley appeal would have looked horrible in the public eye — worse than an acquittal, even — and for the same reason that Henley's conviction had made them heroes. As it stood, Henley was a famous athlete who had been humbled by the rule of law. If he were awarded a new trial, the tables would turn and he'd be celebrated as a black Job — yet another African American man persecuted by the historically racist LA law enforcement club—a man who had never quit fighting until his claims of innocence were proven true at last. Specifically, the prosecutors feared that if Henley were awarded a new trial, his attorneys could take all they'd learned from the previous one and make Cossack's cross-examination of Tracy look like a tea party this time around. Rex Henley explained his view of the government's strategy as "Forget Rex, forget Willie McGowan, forget Garey West, forget Bustamante, let them win their appeal in court. We're going to ice this thing with Darryl. . . . And that's exactly how it played out. Because, you know, he was a professional football player."

Within six weeks of the verdict, each of Henley's codefendants had joined his motion for a new trial. Their sentencing was postponed. A grand jury was convened to try and sort through a mess so tangled that everyone just called it "jury misconduct." Taylor scheduled a series of evidentiary hearings. The FBI investigation intensified.

"My son is not guilty of any drugs, and that I do know," Dorothy Henley told the grand jury. "We will get a new trial because we trust in God. No one against Him is going to prosper."

Darryl hired Juliette Robinson-Slaton, a respected black attorney in her thirties, to serve on Jim Riddet's defense team. A former collegiate basketball champion at USC, Robinson-Slaton had known Darryl for years, her husband Tony having started at offensive guard for the Rams during Darryl's rookie year. Robinson-Slaton had been referred to Henley by Reverend Michael Ealey, a politically powerful pastor in Long Beach who was keeping the Reverend Jesse Jackson apprised of the Henley case.[1]

The FBI picked up its pace, too, arranging a meeting between Bryan Quihuis and two FBI agents at the U.S. Attorney's Office. There Quihuis's story began to change. According to the FBI's report of that meeting, Quihuis still maintained that O'Reilly had said, "The niggers are guilty" or "Niggers are guilty," but now "Quihuis was unsure if he was talking about the four black defendants or black people in general. . . . Quihuis felt it was more of a way for O'Reilly to blow off steam."

Quihuis admitted that he "agreed to provide Darryl and Rex Henley with a vote of not guilty for the $25,000," the report continued—a confession that left the Henley team hopeful, for even if Quihuis hadn't *accepted* the bribe, the fact that he'd agreed to it at one point proved that his ability to judge the case had been corrupted. Quihuis also confessed to using methamphetamine "every weekend during the duration of the trial." Curiously, the FBI report noted that the "methamphetamines did not effect [*sic*] his judgement during the course of the trial."

On May 25 the local CBS TV affiliate aired an in-depth interview between Henley and respected African American sportscaster Jim Hill, himself a former NFL player.[2] Hill asked Henley: "I'm wondering if sometimes, at night, when you're locked up, if you wonder, 'How the hell did this ever happen to me?'"

"I've been here about—almost two months now," Henley replied, dressed in his prisoner's jersey, his face pensive and serious. "And the first month I think I said that every night. Each day passes and, you know, it becomes a little easier. This is real. This is not a dream. And you're not going to wake up the next day and be going to the mall or going to see your family." When Hill asked Henley if he'd cried, Henley nodded. "Tears are shed for your family," he said. Excerpts from Malachowski's deposition appeared on LA TV screens as Henley, who reminded Hill that he had "never ever ever been in *any* form of trouble—never had handcuffs on prior to any of this," responded to allegations that a white juror had called him a nigger. Speaking slowly and calmly, with an air of sadness that was either genuine or impeccably faked, Henley said: "It lets me know that despite what I've ever thought about the system—fairness, judicial laws, legislature, the Declaration of Independence, all this stuff that we supposedly stand on and has created a foundation for our growing and blossoming country—it's made it very, very hard for me to cope with."

"I am considered a quote-unquote drug trafficker," Henley continued. "And when you are convicted of a charge like that, right, wrong, or indifferent, you have entered another realm. And nothing, *nothing* is going to be put past you."

Ron Knight had been scheduled to testify before the grand jury, but instead he got up and left the waiting room without permission. When he finally took the stand, he wasn't exactly forthcoming. During a morning-long exchange that was combative throughout, Knight told Rayburn that he had attended the Henley trial "until you put me out." When Rayburn tried to correct Ron by asking if his dismissal had come via the *court's* orders, Ron said: "Your orders, from what I hear." Among Ron's more dubious claims was that he'd never known Darryl to possess a cell phone. When Rayburn asked about Ron's first contact with Mike Malachowski, Ron said he called Malachowski from a pay phone at the mall. Darryl didn't ask him to do it; Ron said he made the call on his own, after finding Malachowski's number at Darryl's house.

This same day Dorothy Henley finally complied with the prosecutors' requests for her address book, which they thought contained drug- or bribe-related information but in fact contained nothing of interest except a few inspirational verses written in her perfect schoolteacher's cursive:

When the battle is over I will win. I will come forth as pure gold. — Job 23:8–10

Talent is God given, be humble. Fame is man-given, be thankful. Conceit is self-given, be careful. [3]

Give us aid against the enemy, for the help of man is worthless. With God we will gain the victory and He will trample down our enemies. — Psalm 60:9–12

After her grand jury testimony, Mrs. Henley drove to MDC to

visit her son. She hadn't missed a visiting day yet, and she would not miss one during her son's year-long stay there. "On some days she waited five to six hours," T. J. Simers reported, "and sometimes was turned away because her number was not called in time." Her efforts to rally support for Darryl were just as rigorous. Representatives from the Nation of Islam had begun showing up at the evidentiary hearings, along with Reverend Ealey, who according to Henley passed along word from Jesse Jackson that Jackson's fee for three pro-Henley press conferences, to be held on the courthouse steps, would be $30,000. Darryl was appalled by this demand, but what he didn't know was that Jackson had recently championed a widow who turned out to be involved in the murder of her husband. The Henley case was not one to take on lightly. Staying away would end up being the correct move for Jackson, politically if not morally, for as the holes in Malachowski's story widened, even Reverend Ealey began citing "other commitments" as his reason for skipping court. By midsummer, with Malachowski's credibility wilting and courtroom attendance thinning, Henley's motion for a new trial had lost what little momentum it had.

Another crushing blow came in July, when Shawn O'Reilly signed a document presented to him by prosecutors that stated, in part, "At no time did I refer to any of the defendants as 'niggers' or any other similar racial epithet." This seemed to close the book on the race issue once and for all, but the defense saw small victories within the signed statement, like O'Reilly's admission that he'd violated Judge Taylor's orders about discussing the case ("I told the others in the car that I thought Tracy Donaho was telling the truth"), and two other statements implying a presumption of guilt before deliberation ("I commented that I believed defendant Darryl Henley was a snake based on evidence of the way he treated women. I also stated that the defendants were lucky the cocaine trial was being conducted in the United States and not overseas because in other countries the penalty for a drug conviction is hanging"). But O'Reilly never called the defendants niggers, the document said—even though his two carpool partners said he did.[4] Darryl Henley's anguish that the government was using its resources to try and prove he'd instigated a bribery scheme that never came to pass, instead of revealing the truth about a racist juror, was, Henley said later, "a prison unto itself."

This is the Los Angeles into which Gia Dawn Henley was born, four months after her father was convicted of drug trafficking. Darryl and Alisa had chosen not to be informed of the child's gender before birth, figuring "there have been so many surprises around here lately, there might as well be one more." The baby, her mother, and her maternal grandmother visited Darryl in prison three days after she was born. The family would from then on talk about how Gia had lain in her father's thick arms that day, her face pressed against his government-issue jersey, her eyes locked with his, both of them unable to look away. Gia would from then on be considered a daddy's girl, despite her daddy's residence. "Each time she left the visiting room," Darryl recalled later, "she took a bigger piece of me with her."

Gia's entry into the world did not justify what her father would do later, just as the gut-punch of the phone evidence did not condone his attempt to bribe a juror, but her birth did help explain his later actions. Humiliation and desperation had become daily realities for Henley—like the distorted image of his face he saw each morning in the sheet metal on the wall that served as his mirror—and the months ahead would be clouded by new motives forged in the furnace of MDC.

During the [Simpson] trial I read a great deal of
the reporting in the black press. At first I thought
they were reporting on a different event than I was
watching; only later did I realize that I was reading a
description of American justice written by people who
had experienced it entirely differently than I had.

—ROGER COSSACK, June 2004 (on the tenth anniversary of
the Brentwood murders)

Chapter 37

"Mr. Henley has been found to be a drug dealer, handling significant quantities of drugs,"
Judge Taylor wrote in his denial of Darryl's request to attend training camp while awaiting
the outcome of his new trial motion. "The evidence has been that he manipulates people."
So instead of working out with Todd Lyght,
Darryl lifted weights with Corvette Mike, an
MDC inmate who'd been convicted of participating in a massive, Colombia-to-California
cocaine ring back in the 1980s.

The inspiration behind Michael McCarv-
er's nickname was no more complex than
the car he'd driven the last time he was a
free man. He reminded Henley of a ballplayer—fit and confident, his every move made
in slow motion—which helped Darryl establish as close a friendship with him as could
be established by two strangers who meet
in prison.

Among Darryl's other acquaintances inside

MDC was an elderly Sinaloa native who had dug a lucrative drug smuggling tunnel from Mexico to California. And Darryl spent more time than he should have with an inmate named Harry O (real name Michael Harris), Corvette Mike's former codefendant and the so-called "Gang Godfather" of South Central. A few years back, Harry O had taken a chance on a retired NFL lineman from Compton by bankrolling his fledgling record company. Rumor had it that Suge Knight and Harry O had formed Death Row Records in the MDC visiting room, with the help of Suge's trusted lawyer, David Kenner, using start-up money that included millions in cocaine sales.

Darryl and Harry O could usually be found at the pay phones, but not even the phone-addicted Henley could keep up with Harry O's pace. On the rare occasions when he wasn't talking to his "peoples" on the outside, Harry O could usually be found in his room swapping stories with Henley. During one of their first talks, Darryl mentioned the football career he was trying to return to, which prompted Harry O to ask Henley if he knew the ballplayer who used to hang out at Death Row a couple years back. I can't remember dude's name, Harry O said.

Darryl bent over laughing. When he rose, he placed the tip of his index finger on his sternum. Their combined laughter boomed throughout 9 South.

They talked at length about Suge Knight. Harry O said he respected Knight as a businessman, if not a man in general. Suge relied on too much violent "cowboy shit" to keep his throne secure, Harry O said, and he accused Knight of never giving him a proper cut of the music empire he'd helped build. When Darryl told Harry O about the confrontation he'd seen between Knight and the two Jackie Slater lookalikes at the Death Row elevators back in 1993, a broad smile conquered Harry O's face, and his finger tapped his own chest. "Those were my peoples," Harry O said. "He wasn't no cowboy that day."

375

The FBI's visits to the home of Mike Malachowski had increased from once a month, to once a week, to daily stakeouts in their unmarked sedans. Malachowski called the local police several times to report Peeping Toms, just so the feds would know he could see them. The agents apparently didn't care. The Henley mess had, among other things, widened the rift between Malachowski and his wife, who left him to go crash at her sister's place in Redondo Beach.

The FBI's stakeouts and heavy-handed interviews weren't working, so their campaign to "flip" Mike Malachowski was modified. Malachowski broke down crying during a September visit from his nemesis, Special Agent Cross, who was "very aggressive with him," Malachowski said at the time. The FBI began calling Malachowski every day after that, threatening him with an indictment for jury tampering and promising him that the next time they dropped by he'd be handcuffed and put in a cell next to Darryl Henley. They asked Mike to picture himself in court with Darryl. They called him a liar and a coward. This was the heat Ron Knight had warned Mike about—the pressure Mike had dismissed so cavalierly back in April. "You don't know how bad they want Darryl," Ron had said back then. "Just stick to the facts when you talk to Riddet [at the deposition]. Don't go off on no tangents." Mike was paying dearly for those tangents now.

Malachowski told Riddet he was "terrified" of the FBI, and reluctant to testify at any new trial hearing—news that severely wounded Darryl's fight for a new day in court. Although he hadn't flipped to the government side yet, it was clear that Mike was turning that way, slowly, like a pig on a spit. A lot of guys would have already caved in.

The government finally arrested Malachowski on a Friday—Friday, October 13, to be exact, a day and month notorious for inspiring fear. They did it on a Friday to make sure Malachowski would spend an entire weekend in jail while pondering his future.[1] He was detained in Barstow, the sandy midpoint between LA and

Las Vegas whose topography resembles rural Saudi Arabia. Deirdre Eliot gave Malachowski until the following Friday to decide if he would "truthfully testify to the court" or stand by Henley and hunker down for an extended stay behind bars.

He was released the following Monday on $25,000 bond, which his parents paid by getting a second mortgage on their home. The next day the government asked that the upcoming evidentiary hearing be postponed three weeks — its unspoken reason: to buy more time to haggle with Malachowski and his attorney. Rayburn said that Malachowski had told the FBI: "If I tell you the truth, they [referring to Darryl Henley, Ron Knight, and possibly others] will kill me."[2]

Malachowski declined to cooperate with the government, so the prosecutors turned up the heat by indicting him on Halloween. Malachowski pled not guilty to contempt of court and lying to federal agents. He stood by his story about Quihuis coming up with the bribe. More important, he still insisted that O'Reilly had called the defendants niggers.

That's when the O.J. verdict came down.

More than the pitfalls inherent in jury trials, and more than the importance of wealth and fame in mounting a criminal defense, Simpson's acquittal showed America just how racially divided a nation it still was. The battle over Shawn O'Reilly's racist remarks was overshadowed when, across the country, an astounding number of blacks reacted to the announcement of Simpson's acquittal by raising their arms in triumph, while the whites down the street, or in the next cubicle, recoiled in horror. "We have to protect our own," one of the black Simpson jurors said that day, apparently disregarding DNA evidence that placed the chances that the killer was *not* Simpson in the millions-to-one range, in favor of LAPD detective Mark Fuhrman's lie about saying the word *nigger* ten years earlier. Rendered insignificant was juror Shawn O'Reilly's use of that slur the previous month, about a man whose fate lay in his hands at the time.

One of the few American settings with no color line that day was MDC Los Angeles, a stone's throw from the courthouse Simpson had just made famous, where the O.J. verdict was met with shock, followed by fist-pumping glee. Shock for the same reason most everyone felt it; glee because the system had been beaten. Race didn't matter as much on 9 South as it did on the street, where evidence showed that Simpson had practically beheaded his wife after years of abusing her. What mattered on 9 South was that Simpson had gotten off, the system had been beaten. It was a call to rejoice.

While the men of 9 South celebrated the Simpson verdict, Henley became nervous. After the Simpson verdict, an opinion about the Henley saga that had merely been whispered previously—an opinion best summarized by James Washington, who said, "O.J. got off, so they were looking for some other brother to go down"—was heard more frequently within Henley's inner circle. It may have been laughable to assume that the prosecutions of a state murder case and a federal drug case could be linked, but the Henleys and their remaining supporters would forever believe that Darryl's demise was in some way connected to Simpson's acquittal.

The week of the Simpson verdict, CNN began airing a show called *Burden of Proof*, cohosted by Roger Cossack and devoted to sifting through the post-O.J. rubble. Cossack had become one of the founding members of what *LA Times* media critic Howard Rosenberg called "human sound bites who have been spreading on the airwaves like measles while feasting on the Simpson case as Eskimos do on a whale."[3] The actual practice of law had become an afterthought for the charismatic Cossack, who would later describe the genesis of his media career as like "hitting the lottery." That December, Darryl experienced a taste of the surreal by watching Cossack interview Johnnie Cochran on the black-and-white TV in 9 South's common area. It was the only episode of *Burden* he watched. It aired at 9:30 a.m., when he was usually lifting with Corvette Mike and a new inmate named Ced.

Henley was getting comfortable on 9 South. "Too comfortable," he said years later. His football fame, his wealth (which, unbeknownst to those inside MDC, had dwindled to almost nothing due to legal expenses), and his liaisons with notorious inmates like Harry O, Corvette Mike, and Ced McGill—a notorious Compton drug kingpin—had given Henley VIP status on the floor. Guards greeted him with smiles and questions about how his mama and baby girl were doing. They hung around him like whale-hungry Eskimos.

One night a mischievous inmate threw an orange at Darryl from across the hall. It narrowly missed Rex, who warned the assailant about his nephew's arm: "Look out, this nigga here can *throw!*" Darryl's lone chance at retaliation was slim. It wasn't that the guard was watching; the guard was as eager as anyone to see what would happen next. The problem was that the assailant had retreated into his room and was peeking through the sliver of space between the door and doorjamb. Using a right arm honed by his shortstop days on the Inland Valley Beauty Supply little league team, Darryl fired one orange and one orange only. As the aggressor wiped pulp from his eyes, incredulous as to how Darryl had just done what he'd done, the entire tier exploded into laughter, including the guard. Nine South had found its hero, its Cool Hand Luke. Darryl never considered how dangerous such status might be.

There was a guy on the floor who cooked for Darryl, Rex, and a few other guys, but his microwave improvisations smelled nothing like the aroma that came wafting down the hall one night in late October, when Darryl and a fifty-year-old OG (original gangster) named "Player Eyes" were sweeping up the common room.

Smell good, huh? Player Eyes said in his leathery voice.

Is that Italian food? Darryl asked.

Pizza Hut. One of your peoples drop money at a Western Union, you can get you some, too.

From who?

Night co.[4] That nigga Anderson.

Darryl had heard about Rodney Anderson, a guard who was similar to Rex in age and size, but he didn't trust him.[5]

Look out, though, Player Eyes warned. Dude shady. If he beats you [if he takes your money but doesn't give you any food], let me know.

Man, I ain't trying to buy no damn pizza, Darryl replied.

Player Eyes grinned knowingly. Henley had been locked up for seven months. Most guys started cracking up about MDC's food around month six. Just look out for a motherfucker, Player Eyes said. [Just give me some food when you get it.]

The smell of pizza lingered in Darryl's nostrils as he walked back to the room he shared with Rex. "Don't do it, D," Rex said. "Don't trust that fool. He a cop." But when Darryl learned that Anderson also dealt in Popeye's fried chicken, Red Lobster seafood, and soul food from the renowned M&M restaurant, the deal was sweetened considerably. Still Henley held back.

A few nights later Player Eyes told Darryl that the co wanted to see him. Darryl could already smell why before he arrived at Anderson's desk. Anderson didn't say a word. He just pushed two paper bags toward Henley, who warmed them in the microwave on his way back to his room, where Rex lay asleep. Rex's nose twitched, then his eyes opened. He'd already dug in before Darryl could finish washing his hands in the steel basin. "We shouldn't be doin' this, we shouldn't be doin' this," Rex said, his mouth full of barbecued chicken and fries.

"You gonna save some for me?" Darryl said, chuckling.

The next night, Anderson and Henley came to terms. For $1,000 per month, Darryl and his uncle would get dinner delivered to them a few nights a week. Anderson even threw in a peach cobbler every time he stopped by M&M. Rex loved their cobblers.

A few nights later, as Darryl was returning to his room following a phone call to Alisa, Anderson stopped him. I see you be using that phone a lot, he said. Within minutes, Henley's monthly payment was increased to $1,500, and a cell phone was added to his food deliveries. Henley could use the cell phone between 10:30 p.m. and 5:00 a.m.—the hours of Anderson's shift—then he had to give it back. Like Willie McGowan's "look out for me" request in June 1993, and Mike Malachowski's bribe offer, Darryl reserved the right to say no to Anderson's criminal proposition and walk away. Like those earlier opportunities, he said yes instead.

The food deliveries weren't a big deal in the grand scheme of things. It happened every night on other floors—cos paying off sports bets or scratching the backs of helpful inmates. Thanks to their influential labor union, a guard caught delivering food to an inmate could expect only a reprimand or maybe a "day off" (one-day suspension) as punishment. Drugs also flowed through 9 South, but only in user amounts and rarely from the guards' hands. Because 9 South was a transitional floor, where inmates were brought directly "from the street" before being sent to more permanent quarters, drugs would arrive on Henley's floor inside inmates who had "packed their ass" with tiny, dope-filled balloons, enough to stay high until a connection could be found inside. It was mostly marijuana and heroin. Cocaine was rare. ("No one wants to be bouncing off the walls in prison," one former 9 South resident said.) When a guard encountered an inmate who looked high, he had a choice: he could either confiscate the joint or needle, shake down the entire floor, and start the resulting paperwork, or he could keep walking and let the inmate quietly enjoy himself. More often than not, the latter choice won out. Darryl Henley, his door left open most nights because of his position as an orderly, felt his clear, unglassy eyes widen on such occasions, never fathoming that his new cell phone would be considered more dangerous than a hit of heroin. But it was. Henley's acquisition of a cell phone, in the words of one of his more experienced floormates, "was taking it to another level."

Darryl had always been a home cooking kind of guy, so Kym Taylor began preparing four-course meals for him, sealing them in Tupperware, and taking them to the gas station down the street where she handed them off to Anderson on his way to work. Pork chops, collard greens, gumbo, desserts. Rex loved Kym's desserts. She later claimed that she'd thought such arrangements were allowed for detainees like Darryl, who hadn't been sentenced. She also cited her comfort with Anderson, finding him congenial, polite, and thankful for the treats she often threw in for him. Rodney Anderson, who was working on ten years in the Marines, "didn't seem like he would be up for anything criminal," Kym said later, "but obviously I'm not very good at predicting who's a criminal and who's not."

Darryl's fear that Anderson was setting him up had long since passed, but both men knew they had to be discreet. Henley was concerned that other inmates might get jealous and turn him in, but these fears were minimized by the fact that Anderson made his deliveries after lights out, when the unit was locked down and most guys were asleep. Darryl was also comforted by the knowledge that if an inmate snitched on him, the snitch's word would be set against that of Anderson, a Gulf War veteran who was liked by his superiors and whose record with the Bureau of Prisons was clean.

MDC was still very much a shark tank. Random inmates still came up to Henley and offered to broker outside drug deals with him — some of them setups, others real. America's second biggest city was arguably its top consumer of cocaine, with a demand that did not wane because some of its most active distributors were locked up. Countless drug deals were done through girlfriends and other go-betweens in MDC's visiting room, or over the phone, via code.

Another commodity inside MDC was murder. Darryl had heard nearly as many offers to kill Tracy Donaho as offers to move drugs, most notably the chilling proposal he received from an OG who told him as they brushed past each other in the hall: "Just let me know where she at. I'll smash her." But despite all the danger swirling around him, Henley's sense of invincibility was never stronger.

Despite the warnings from MDC's more honest inmates, he had no idea how closely linked some of the other inmates were to the U.S. Attorney's Office and the DEA.

He knew there were snitches around. When he heard Garey "G" West wanted to have a word with him, Henley was wary. But the message had come from a trusted soul on 9 South. G would be at the weekly Muslim service, this trusted soul told Henley, and G said he had something important to discuss with his former co-defendant. Darryl hadn't exchanged a word with West since the verdict and had hardly seen him. He went to the mosque thinking West wanted to talk about their new trial motion, but after the minister's initial greetings of *A salaam alaikum*, West whispered news to Henley that was more pressing: Ced McGill was hot—meaning that he was working as a government informant. It was a shocking, potentially lethal bit of information, but it was coming from an unreliable source—the same guy who had run off with Bustamante's drugs, the guy who had wanted to take Tracy "to Alabama," a man with as many aliases as mistresses. Darryl didn't believe G. No way Ced was an informant.

To his eventual detriment, Darryl continued to underestimate the extent to which snitching had permeated MDC. He had achieved Big Man on Campus status inside the towering prison, the status he'd sought and thrived on since boyhood. Everyone on 9 South knew "D": the straight inmates and the hot, the white-collar white guys and the OGs trying to beat dope or weapons cases. Henley had a reputation as a big-time cocaine player, and over time he became less concerned with refuting that rep and weary of trying to explain it. He even used it to his advantage on occasion, like the time an MDC guard smuggled him to the women's wing in a food cart, where Henley had sex for the first time in eight months.

Darryl never looked more like a convict than the night he told a nationwide ESPN audience that there had been a racist on his jury.

His eyes puffy from too much sleep, his skin faded by lack of sun, Henley, wearing light-blue scrubs, sat down for a one-on-one interview with ESPN reporter Shelley Smith. Like Jim Hill's interview, the ESPN interview featured a full-screen display of Malachowski's deposition, featuring the harsh words attributed to Shawn O'Reilly: "The niggers are guilty."

"I was guilty before I stepped in the door," Henley told Smith. "According to those statements, I was guilty. I'm guilty because I'm *black*? Every day [during the trial] I heard, 'Please do not talk about the case or form opinions. Just don't even *bring it up*.' But it happened. And if I was the judge, and I said that so many times and I found out, I'd be pissed." Smith asked Henley about the conflicting versions of the bribery scheme. "I've never been affiliated with drugs," Henley responded. "And I've never been affiliated with bribing a juror. Period."

Henley's financial walls were closing in as rapidly as his legal ones. He was notified that he was in default on the Brea house, and that unless he paid $282,000 by December it would be put up for auction. In the end he chose not to save the house that had staged his ruin. Instead, his parents drove to Beverly Hills and plopped down another $10,000 for yet another defense attorney, using money from Darryl's most recent tax return. It would be the family mission in the years ahead: raising money for lawyers. It was both sad and inspiring that a family with no money to spare would somehow scrape together and borrow nearly $1 million over the next twelve years.

A unique opportunity for financial help popped up around Thanksgiving, when Darryl was told about the Colombian cocaine trafficker who'd arrived on 9 South. With Malachowski under indictment and under pressure to switch sides, and with Darryl more confident than ever that the system had failed him, the ex-athlete (and it was fair at this point to refer to him as an ex-athlete) was willing to consider any new opportunities to finance his fight for freedom. So when Corvette Mike mentioned the Colombian on the floor, Henley was interested in meeting him. How exactly does this kind of thing get done? Darryl asked with the same inquisitive mind that had mastered complex defensive coverages. Corvette Mike explained that Colombians weren't street-corner dealers; they worked in big numbers, and since taking over the U.S. market in the Wild West 1980s, they had learned to work efficiently, if sometimes lethally.

This guy's going to offer you some weight, Corvette Mike told Darryl. Don't tell him no, but don't give him no money, either. Have him front it. The irony was not lost on inmate #01915-112 that he was about to traffic drugs in order to finance his campaign to prove he wasn't a drug trafficker. But like most drug deals arranged in MDC, nothing came of this one. Rodney Anderson had left the prison to fulfill his duties as a Marine reservist, which removed the cell phone from Henley's hand. The Colombian ended up getting moved to another floor.

In an unrelated turn of events, former government witness Alejandro Cuevas was released from prison. The extortion charges against Cuevas—charges proven by the tapes still sitting in Steven Kinney's desk drawer, on which Cuevas had threatened to kill Darryl and his mother—were dismissed. Cuevas was never charged in the unrelated death of a three-year-old girl he'd allegedly struck just hours before she perished. Two weeks after Cuevas was released, Darryl's father was questioned by John Rayburn before the grand jury. T.H. was in no mood to face Darryl's accusers, particularly the fair-skinned Damien alum he held responsible for freeing the thug who had threatened to kill his wife. Their exchange that day was little more than a transcribed quarrel. "I'm trying to console my son in jail," Mr. Henley snapped. "Every time we go down there we try to keep his spirit up, not talk about the mess that you guys put up on him. You know he's not guilty. That's the thing that really bugs me. Darryl has a perfect record. Three

of my sons hadn't ever been in jail. Don't even have a menace record. I'm a hardworking father who care about his son and who
have sent—*the same school that you went to.* The same school that
you graduated from, my son graduated from. Parochial school.
Three sons there. Never been in no trouble. We never been in no
trouble. His aunt worked for the DOD [Department of Defense] in
Washington DC."

"Mr. Henley, I'm sorry—"

"I'm telling you. You ask me these questions. I'm telling you
where I am. I work hard for my son. I'm a Christian. I raise my
kids in a Christian environment. You want to break him down.
You want to break him down because he's black and he's educated.
You always talk about how articulate he is. Yes, he's *supposed* to be
articulate. I taught him that. I sent him to school to be articulate."

". . . What has your son told you about the new trial motion?"

"We know that you and Judge Taylor don't want to grant us a
new trial motion, which is obvious."

Later Rayburn asked, "How many women does Darryl have
children with?"

"Don't ask me that stupid question, John. How many women
did you have before you married?"

Darryl's mother would prove even more troublesome for Rayburn, forcing him to repeat several of his questions before giving
him un-straight answers in return. Mrs. Henley seized her chance
to sound off about the injustices her son had endured. Before she
stepped down, she handed the foreperson a copy of Mike Malachowski's deposition. "When you read it, it will blow your minds,"
she said, unaware that the deposition contained as many lies as
truths. "And besides, we don't have any blacks in here. What happened, Mr. Rayburn?"

"Thank you, Mrs. Henley," Rayburn said.

"Thank you."

Chapter 38

It seemed like just yesterday that Judge Gary Taylor had welcomed Mike Malachowski to jury selection with a buoyant "Glad to have you." On January 18, 1996 — exactly one year later — Taylor was not glad to have had Malachowski at all. An impossibly tangled web had been woven since John Rayburn chose not to remove Malachowski from the jury pool, much of it woven by Darryl Henley, who was now seated before Rayburn on the witness stand. Rayburn had craved such a situation for more than three years, and here it was, Henley sworn in and ready to testify, with the matter of whether he would stand trial again at stake.

Clad in a green windbreaker stenciled "MDC," Henley answered Rayburn's questions with obvious discomfort. He testified that organizing a football card show had been the topic of conversation the night Malachowski first visited him and during their subsequent meetings and phone calls as well—a lie he considered harm-less compared to the lies Rayburn had coaxed out of Tracy at trial. Henley believed that Tracy's lies would be exposed at his next trial, but that next trial would never happen, in part because of the nervousness with which Henley was now lying under oath. Henley would have to step aside during a recess to calm himself. He claimed it was his hypoglycemia acting up due to a lack of breakfast, but most everyone present thought it was simply anxiety.

As important as it was to prove Henley's involvement in the bribe, it was just as important for Rayburn to prove that Henley had *known* of the bribe within a week after the verdict. By law, if Henley learned of it after that time it could be considered newly discovered evidence and Henley's position would be strengthened. Rayburn won this battle easily, producing phone calls from MDC in which Darryl revealed that he'd known of the bribe during deliberations.

The courtroom was pretty empty when Henley testified, but it was near capacity on January 23, 1996, when "more than sixty supporters . . . overflowed the gallery and the jury box," according to the *LA Times*. "Family members and former classmates at Anaheim's Esperanza High School milled in the hallway." They were there to support Tracy Donaho, who was about to be sentenced. "I just want this to be over," she told a reporter in the hall. "In an hour my future will be decided, and it's scary." Tracy's attorney explained to Taylor that Tracy had "started to hyperventilate" outside the courtroom. "She has been in treatment for depression," Stephan DeSales added. "She needs to bring this to closure. . . . The prison she created for herself is not walls and bricks. It is a prison through her mind." John Rayburn stood and recommended that Tracy spend a year in the walls and bricks kind of prison. Tracy wept with gratitude as Taylor undercut Rayburn by eight months, "slash[ing] the 'mandatory' ten-year prison term she faced to four months," the *Register* reported, "possibly in a halfway house."[1] A *Times* columnist joked that the cheerleader's first words after being sentenced were: "Gimme a J! Gimme an A! Gimme an I! Gimme an L! What's that spell?"

But there would be no jail. In what many saw as the Henley trial's version of "We have to protect our own," Tracy Donaho served her four months by commuting to a halfway house in Garden Grove.

A month after Tracy was sentenced, Mike Malachowski and his court-appointed attorney met with John Rayburn, Deirdre Eliot, and FBI agent James Blanchard. "Malachowski indicated that he was now telling the truth and he finally decided to tell the truth," the FBI report stated. Malachowski finally admitted that he'd approached Quihuis with the bribe offer, and that after Quihuis backed out, Malachowski continued to tell Henley that Quihuis "would be giving him and Rex a not guilty verdict."

A week later Rayburn challenged Henley during a courtroom exchange that the *Register* reported "was at times heated." Rayburn also pointed out a call Darryl made to Ron Knight from prison and their comments about Tracy's light sentence. "Well, maybe not for long, you know what I'm saying?" Ron had said on the tape. Rayburn contended that it was a murder threat—Ron threatening to do away with Tracy—but what only a handful of people knew was that Ron had said this "not for long" comment the day after he learned of O'Reilly's racial remarks. "Not for long" had been Ron's reference to the new trial he felt Darryl deserved based on a racist juror and his prediction that once Tracy was convicted of perjury, she would be sentenced to more than just probation.

"Would you kill to get out of prison?" Rayburn asked Henley.

"I wouldn't kill anybody, not even you."

That line made the newspapers. It was exactly the kind of line—flippant and born of frustration—that had kept Henley off the witness stand at his trial.

Rex Henley fared no better when he took the stand two days later. Rayburn played more taped calls from MDC that proved Rex knew of the bribe within a week of the verdict. It was another resounding victory for the prosecution, who in their closing remarks would compare the Henleys' testimony to the famed Abbott and Costello skit "Who's on first?" The government's only remaining vulnerability was Quihuis's drug use, which was dismissed when Rayburn was allowed to categorize it as an "internal influence on the verdict." The U.S. Supreme Court had just ruled by a 5–4 vote that such influences could not be used to challenge a conviction. Rayburn and Eliot also cited Rule 606(b), which barred jurors from even being *asked* about such "internal influences."[2] Henley's new trial motion had crumbled. Not because the jury hadn't misbehaved but because their misbehavior hadn't been reported in time for the Henleys to benefit from it; because the jurors could not be questioned about the misbehavior; and perhaps most directly because Darryl had been involved in the bribery part of their misbehavior.

Ten years later, when asked why he didn't tell the court about Malachowski's visit the day after it happened, Darryl said: "Because the last time I cooperated with the court, I walked out of there with a bracelet on my ankle."

Judge Taylor did not like seeing Roger Cossack on his witness stand. When an attorney was sitting in that seat, it usually meant that something had gone wrong and that there was a mess in need of cleaning up. If Taylor wanted badly for Cossack to tidy things up that morning, then Cossack certainly complied. The savvy attorney denied that Henley had told him before the verdict about Malachowski's carpool deliberations with O'Reilly and Quihuis. "I would have known what to do with that if I would have heard that information," Cossack testified. It allowed Taylor to close the door on that issue rather bluntly, writing: "Darryl Henley testified he did tell his attorney about the alleged juror discussion of evidence. The attorney testified he did not. The attorney is more credible."

While Darryl's mind boiled in court, his life on 9 South had never been calmer. Rodney Anderson was off completing his USMC commitment, so Darryl's phone and food deliveries were on hold. Meanwhile, a new crop of inmates arrived. One, a thirtyish white guy from New Zealand named Shorty, had pled guilty to bank robbery back in December 1994 before Judge Taylor, and he had been a government informant ever since, something Darryl didn't realize until the day Shorty invited him to become an informant, too. When Darryl turned him down, Shorty gestured toward Rex. "If not for you, do it for him, mate."

Shorty had a point. Darryl's once jovial uncle was sinking deeper into depression. Rex was staring a decade in prison in the face, his estranged wife had moved to Texas with his daughter, and he didn't get many visitors anymore—just Darryl's mom. Rex mostly stayed in his room and tried to sleep it away. But Darryl wasn't going to turn snitch for anyone, and certainly not because some shady foreigner thought it was a good idea.

Then Shorty got a new cellmate, and Henley's life took one of its most severe turns for the worse.

Known on 9 South as "Mikey," Michael Gambino was the epitome of a Hollywood con man. He fancied himself an aspiring actor, although at age thirty and facing indictment for credit card fraud, Mikey's arrival on the movie scene seemed unlikely. Had he wanted to, he could have gotten work as a stand-in for actor Andy Garcia. Face, body, mannerisms, everything—Mikey Gambino was Garcia's clone. He claimed to be a real Gambino—a flesh-and-blood capo like the one Garcia had portrayed in *Godfather Part III*—and Mikey certainly knew how to work the system like one. He arrived at MDC carrying a secret that could sustain his criminal career for as long as he wanted. All he had to do was find the right guy to snitch on, the right cops to work with, and he'd be back on the street in no time.

It was early 1996. Rodney Anderson had returned from his military gig, and Darryl's job as the night orderly had made Anderson's food and phone deliveries easy to resume. Anderson gave Darryl nightly access to 9 South's typewriter room so Henley could make his phone calls without being disturbed or overheard. Soon Darryl began sharing his phone with Mikey Gambino, whose wit, charm, and hilarious stories had moved Darryl to trust him as much as he trusted anyone on 9 South. Capitalizing on this trust, Mikey told Darryl about a friend in the Hollywood Hills who had thirty kilos of cocaine hidden in his bedroom closet.

Mikey said that he and his friend used to use the place as a weekend party pad, so the house was empty and the sliding glass door was unlocked. If you can get somebody to run up there and steal those thirty keys, Mikey told Henley, you can either sell them on the street or turn them over to the feds. The former would bring Henley six figures in cash; the latter would almost certainly get his sentence knocked down. But Darryl didn't even honor the offer with a response. It smelled so strongly of a setup that any reaction other than walking away might have brought repercussions. So instead of a thumbs-up, Mikey got a good look at Darryl's back.

That's not to say Henley wasn't interested. And he wasn't interested in turning those thirty kilos over to the DEA, either. As Mikey watched Darryl walk out of his room, he knew Henley would be back, just like he knew everything else. He could tell Darryl wasn't the kingpin he'd been cracked up to be. He had noticed the downtrodden look on Henley's face each time he returned from a visit with his fiancée, his daughter, or his mother—the three ladies Darryl called "the Trinity." Mikey had a one-year-old daughter himself, so he knew about the changes Darryl was seeing in his little girl as she approached her first birthday—changes Alisa couldn't see as clearly because she was with Gia every day. Mikey could see those changes slicing deep into Gia's father, making the little girl's visits more depressing than uplifting. Mikey sensed that Henley and his attorneys were running out of tricks, optimism, and most important, money. And he sensed the 1996 NFL season approaching—the second straight autumn in which Darryl's projected $1.6 million salary would instead show up all zeroes. Mikey noticed the dime-sized bald spot on the side of Henley's head, and he noticed Henley's attempts to conceal it by shaving his hair closer to the crown. He could see that Darryl was under mind-bending stress, that he needed lots of money, fast, and that he would have done almost anything to get it. So Mikey wasn't surprised when Henley came back a few hours later, his jaw set, ready to talk about that house in the Hollywood Hills.

Mikey offered to have his girlfriend show one of Darryl's friends where the house was. "Call her right now," Darryl barked, thrusting his contraband cell phone at Mikey. If Mikey was trying to set him up, Darryl thought, then the female cop on the other end had better nail her role as Mikey's girlfriend. Darryl said later that he "felt like Scarface" at that moment—until Mikey plucked the phone from his hand and began dialing.

His girlfriend was named Giovanna, she wasn't a cop, and she confirmed Mikey's story about the thirty keys in the closet in the Hollywood Hills.

Darryl asked Mikey what he wanted in return.

Nothing, Mikey said. You already helped me out by keeping me on the floor. (Darryl had put in a good word for Mikey when Mikey was in danger of being moved to another unit.)

Ain't nothing free in here. What do you want?

Nothing, Mikey replied. Really.

The only thing Darryl needed now was a man on the street. He didn't know any drug contacts other than his codefendants, so he called an old friend called Junior who owed him a favor and wasn't afraid to get his hands dirty if you caught him in the right mood.

At 1 a.m. on a Saturday night, Junior picked up Giovanna at a predetermined curb on Sunset Boulevard. She guided him west on the Strip and told him to make a right onto Doheny Drive, where the glitz disappeared and the road snaked up a dark mountainside overlooking the city's carpet of lights. Parts of Doheny looked uninhabited, but its tiny offshoots to the left and right, paved with chunky asphalt and wide enough for only one car, provided access to million-dollar homes guarded by firethorn bushes that doubled as security fences. Giovanna guided Junior to a secluded house whose rear deck overlooked a ravine blanketed in darkness and ivy. She waited in the car while Junior checked the sliding glass door.

Had Junior looked behind him and to the east, he might have seen a cluster of neon matchsticks in the distance—downtown LA—where Darryl and Mikey were huddled in the typewriter room on 9 South, speaking to him by cell phone as he crept into the house.

You see it? Darryl whispered.

And there it was: a black Reebok sports bag, just like Mikey described it.

Yeah, I see it.

Leave, Darryl told Junior.

What? Junior and Mikey yelped in unison.

Don't touch that shit, Darryl said. Get out of there, drop her off, and go home. Darryl hung up.

What the fuck are you doing? Mikey gasped. That's a half a million worth of shit!

I'm not feeling this, Darryl explained curtly. Don't feel right. He walked out of the typewriter room, leaving Mikey slack-jawed and alone.

As soon as Darryl returned to his room, he called Junior.

After you drop her off, go back and get it.

"Man, I thought I was slick," Henley said years later.

It took a couple of days for the news to get back to Mikey that the cocaine had been stolen. He sat next to Darryl at lunch. You promise it wasn't you? Mikey asked.

Darryl looked at him, his eyelids dropping to half-mast. Come on, man. I told you I didn't want nothing to do with that shit.

Darryl the mark had just beaten Mikey the con man.

Or so he thought.

Junior was no drug dealer, and he was getting antsy about holding onto that Reebok bag, so Corvette Mike gave Darryl the number for a codefendant from his old cocaine case who would be happy to take that bag off Junior's hands. Within a week, this "outside man," Jimmy Washington, would give Eric Henley $60,000 in cash and a promise that there was more on the way. Eric didn't know how the money had been made, and his best guess was too troubling to consider. Darryl told him not to worry about it. And Eric always did what Darryl said.

Darryl would later call the Hollywood Hills heist "too easy." *So this is why Willie got into this back in the day*, he thought. There had been no weightlifting, no contract negotiations, no bone-crunching hits. The Hollywood Hills heist was just bang-bang-paid. Darryl felt as if he'd truly "gotten over" — beaten the system — and had thumbed his nose at his accusers in the process. *You want to say all this shit about me and make me out to be a monster? Fuck you. I'll do dirt, pay for some new lawyers, and* still *come out on top.*

It was a dangerous mind-set to have inside MDC. He'd been there a year.

By that point Darryl's parents had spent every cent of their $83,000 retirement savings on defense lawyers. Their fish store had gone belly-up, T.H. had been laid off at Lockheed, and Dot's teaching job had been eliminated. Thomas III picked up the slack, contributing thousands to his younger brother's defense, but by summer Mr. and Mrs. Henley were forced out of their home and into a hotel. By fall they were sleeping in a relative's spare room. Darryl's sinkhole of a life had drained his family dry, and the Hollywood Hills heist, while not risk-free, showed him a new way to set things right again.

The old Universal machine on 9 South was a far cry from the state-of-the-art weight room at Rams Park. Darryl was working out on that rusty apparatus with Ced McGill when Ced started whispering about "packages" and "work." If the street and law enforcement communities were in agreement on one thing, it was that Cedric McGill was one of the more creative cocaine dealers in Los Angeles history. A handsome, black thirty-six-year-old, McGill had run a sophisticated crack operation from within the Jordan Downs and Imperial Courts housing projects until his arrest in January 1996, when he and nine accomplices were brought down by the combined efforts of the FBI, LAPD, and LA County Sheriff's Department—and an informant. To lessen his sentence, Ced turned informant himself. And between sets of dips on that old Universal machine, Ced worked Darryl Henley like a master.

Eric Henley, now twenty-six, had left his management job in Texas and had been traveling between his fiancée there and his parents in California, pondering his future. Today he was sitting across from Darryl in the MDC visiting room, discussing their parents' financial woes. Then Ced walked in. Darryl waved him over and introduced him to his little brother. Ced, in turn, introduced Eric to his own brother, Marcus McGill, who had come to visit Ced that day. Except Marcus McGill wasn't Ced's brother—he was an undercover DEA investigator named Eric Miller.

When the McGill brothers adjourned to their own visiting table, Darryl asked Eric to make a few introductions for him on the outside. "Ced's brother Marcus wants to meet some people I know," Darryl said, "and all you have to do is get everybody together." Eric could not say no to someone he loved so much—someone in such obvious need—which was probably why Darryl chose him for the task. In the days ahead, Eric's nervous stammerings, caught on tape, would indicate how averse he was to getting involved in all this. But Darryl told him that this could make things right again. This would put the family back on its feet. It was the point at which friends like sportswriter Bob Keisser would later say: "I wish I could have done more. No one knew how badly things were falling apart."

Rex knew. And when he confronted Darryl about letting Eric swim with these sharks, their argument escalated into a fistfight. Darryl wore a fat lip around 9 South for a week. Still he pressed on.

On April 1, 1996, Steven Kinney met with Ced McGill, one of his more promising informants at MDC. Ced told Kinney that Darryl Henley was interested in shipping twenty-five kilos of cocaine from LA to Detroit. Kinney ordered Ced to persuade Henley to hire his "brother Marcus" for the job. Ced said he was already on it.

Soon afterward, Eric Henley introduced Marcus McGill to Jimmy Washington, the guy who had turned Darryl's Reebok bag into $60,000.[3] Marcus and Jimmy agreed that Marcus would transport the twenty-five kilos to Detroit by car, and that Jimmy would meet him there and sell the drugs for a huge profit. Eric Henley's job—making the introductions—was complete, although over the next few weeks Kinney would try to get Darryl's brother more involved. If Eric's eventual punishment was any indication, Kinney succeeded.

Shortly after 9 a.m. that Tuesday, a nervous Ron Knight drove Darryl's black Mercedes 500SL to the same IHOP where he'd met Mike Malachowski a year earlier. Ron didn't see Kinney—the cop he'd nearly come to blows with during Darryl's trial—parked across the street, secretly recording the meeting. Instead, Ron's eyes were locked on the man he was there to meet, Marcus McGill, who drove up in a dark sedan accompanied by another black man. Ron and Marcus shook hands in the parking lot. Marcus introduced himself as Ced's brother. Ron handed him half the collateral for the cocaine that Ced was fronting to Darryl: the deed for Andrew Boston's home in San Dimas.[4] Marcus drove away in the other half: Darryl's Mercedes.

The deal was a go.

Two days later, Ced told Kinney that Darryl had agreed to pay him $12,500 per kilo after Jimmy sold the kilos for $19,000 apiece in Detroit. Kinney did the math in his head: Henley was expecting about $160,000 from the deal.

It was time for Kinney to hand his case to a prosecutor. He wrote a detailed criminal complaint in which he hinted at deeper trouble lurking under the surface—trouble that would soon overshadow anything involving drugs. "[McGill] has advised me that Darryl Henley discussed with him and other inmates putting a contract out on the cheerleader," Kinney stated. "One inmate volunteered to do the hit for $100,000."

From the moment Marcus met Jimmy in Michigan to hand off the drugs, problems arose. Spooked by the idea of eavesdropping cops (the hotel where they met was the same place Jimmy had been busted in 1988), Jimmy hopped into a dark SUV and fled. He flew back to California that night. The deal was dead. Kinney's hopes of another headline-making Henley bust fizzled.

So he went back to MDC and started from scratch. When Kinney met again with Ced McGill, Ced told him that Darryl had been renting a cell phone from a prison guard for months. Darryl even let Ced call his wife with it. With the Detroit case dead—with no arrests and no drugs or cash seized—Kinney knew that this cell phone angle was all he had. Ced knew that it was his last shot at trimming his prison sentence. He told Kinney everything: *Anderson allowed Darryl to roam freely and make calls during lockdown. Darryl used his phone to try and run drugs. Darryl told other inmates about staying up all night on the phone.* Ced's story was supported, he said, by the call he'd made to his wife. Kinney subpoenaed the phone records from LA Cellular, and sure enough, there was a call to Ced's wife at 1 a.m. on April 25.

Darryl never saw Ced again. The guy vanished. It was strange but not cause for concern. It had happened before on 9 South.

Ced was settling into his new cell at the Monrovia jail—thirty miles from MDC—having just steered Kinney onto a rich and productive new path. Ced had never met Mikey Gambino, but he'd just left him in charge of helping Darryl craft his own demise.

For weeks, the U.S. Department of Justice had been looking into allegations that an MDC guard was supplying cell phones to inmates. Mikey was among the first in line to help their investigation, which is how the cell phone investigation quickly became the Darryl Henley investigation. Kinney, who had received little DEA support during his failed Detroit drug case, recalled later that "when this Gambino thing came along, it's like it was the whole group jumping in. . . . So many people were trying to put their hands on it and claim it. It's just as bad as salesmen trying to cut other's throats for the sale."

That same week, Mike Malachowski flipped. The government had added another count to his indictment, all but forcing him to plead guilty and testify on their behalf. Malachowski's only condition was that all language implicating Rex in the bribery scheme had to be removed. His exoneration of Rex was the last thing he did for the Henleys.

The meeting at which Malachowski finally folded was one of several that took place in a private room within the U.S. Attorney's Office. According to Malachowski, John Rayburn read aloud the unsigned plea agreement lying on the table between them, focusing especially on the section about Shawn O'Reilly's use of the word *nigger*. Rayburn chose that moment to inform Malachowski that if he were to be convicted of the newest count in his indictment, it could mean fifteen years in prison. If that charge were removed, however, Malachowski would probably get only eighteen months. Rayburn followed this bit of information with a question:

Did Shawn O'Reilly refer *specifically to the defendants* when he used the word *niggers*?

Malachowski looked sideways at his public defender, whom he didn't particularly trust, then at Rayburn, whom he didn't trust either. No, Mike said.

Rayburn asked Malachowski if he would testify to that fact at the next hearing.

Another glance at his attorney. Yes, Malachowski answered.

Rayburn asked if that testimony would be the truth.

Here Malachowski paused. The meaning of that word — truth — had become foggier to him during the sixteen months since jury selection began in the Henley trial. The testimony of Tracy Donaho had brought on the first clouds, and the FBI's persistent visits to his home had darkened them. Truth. Was the pact he'd just made with Rayburn the truth? Had O'Reilly been referring to someone *other* than Darryl and his codefendants when he used the word *niggers*? Or was this the loophole through which the government would escape the possibility of a second trial? For all his negative memories of this meeting, it did have the positive effect of lifting Malachowski's fog. "The truth," he said later, "was whatever the government wanted it to be."

As he sat there in the prosecutors' office, Mike thought of his three children. He thought of seeing them again as a free man when they were ten, nine, and four years old, versus seeing them at ages twenty-three, twenty-two, and sixteen.

Yeah, Mike said. It's the truth.[5]

"They don't care about the truth," Mike told his wife that night. "They just want to put Darryl away."

Mike Malachowski's plea deal was different than Tracy Donaho's. There was no "I should have known" defense, no sixty-page statement declaring his naiveté, no ex-cop father, no pricy defense lawyer. By signing it, Malachowski agreed to testify that the bribery scheme had been instigated solely by Darryl Henley and that the racial comments once attributed to Shawn O'Reilly had in fact been invented by Ron Knight and forced upon Malachowski under threat of violence.

For that to have happened, though, Knight would have also had to intimidate Bryan Quihuis into lying. Quihuis, after all, had echoed Malachowski's allegations of racism shortly after Mike first made them. As further evidence that Knight did not invent O'Reilly's racist remarks, Knight was never charged with a crime—just as he'd gone uncharged in the alleged witness tampering during the trial—and there was no investigation into Knight's alleged bullying. What really happened was simple: the government pressure Knight had warned Malachowski about a year earlier had finally achieved the result that Ron feared most.

The *Times* reported that Malachowski "sobbed" as he entered his guilty plea before Judge Taylor. Eight days would pass before Malachowski would be called to testify for the government. Everyone involved could feel the drumroll leading up to that day—the day Malachowski would have to make good on his plea deal and stick to his new story under oath. Oceans would pass beneath the bridge of Darryl Henley's life before that day arrived—a torrent of events that were directly influenced by the flipping of Mike Malachowski, whose shift in loyalty had convinced Darryl, once and for all, that he was justified in using any means necessary to win justice.

Chapter 39

It was just past midnight on May 12, 1996,
and DEA special agent Scott Eichenberger had
been stuck with the "duty agent" shift, which
meant that he had to stay up all night at the
DEA office sitting by the phone in case something happened somewhere. At about 12:30
a.m., Eichenberger received a call from a man
identifying himself as Michael Gambino, MDC
inmate. Gambino told Eichenberger that another inmate was putting together a drug deal
involving fifty kilos of cocaine and fifty kilos
of heroin. It wasn't exactly rock solid information—if prostitution was the world's oldest
profession, then calling a narc cop was the
oldest way out of the joint—but when Gambino said that the inmate's name was Darryl
Henley, Eichenberger's ears perked.

Or the events in the preceding paragraph
never happened.

They looked convincing enough on Eichenberger's DEA-6 report, but that report did not

mention that Eichenberger was the partner of DEA special agent George Eliot, the husband of prosecutor Deirdre Eliot, the person on earth most committed to quashing Henley's motion for a new trial. Ten years after Mikey Gambino made or did not make this call to Eichenberger, a number of sources close to the Henley case said that Gambino had been asked by the DEA to approach Henley and lure him into wrongdoing — to "dirty him up," as one DEA agent put it — so Henley's new trial hopes would be dashed permanently.[1] If Gambino's sudden release from prison a few days later, and Henley's eventual prison sentence were any indication, this plan was not only in place, it was a success.

In his DEA-6 report, Eichenberger relayed what Gambino allegedly told him that night: Henley had asked Gambino if his "brother in New York would be able to assist him in obtaining the heroin and cocaine [because] Henley believes that [Gambino's] brother has connections in organized crime." Mikey also told Eichenberger that a corrupt MDC guard (Anderson) had agreed to transport the drugs for Henley via commercial airline. Mikey gave Henley's cell number to Eichenberger, plus his own cell number, which had also been provided by Anderson. Mikey said he was using his phone to make this very call.

Within forty-eight hours Eichenberger reported a second contact with Mikey Gambino. Mikey informed him this time that Henley was looking for someone to supply five kilos of heroin and twenty kilos of cocaine. The quantities were smaller because Henley was short on cash, Mikey said — so short that Henley was willing to exchange weapons for the drugs.

Each call, and each DEA report, was more sinister and more damning than the one before it. When Gambino and Eichenberger touched base a third time, Mikey allegedly told the DEA agent that Henley "was in the process of making or has made arrangements for a 'hit' on the Judge and Attorney who prosecuted his case. . . . Henley said that Anderson would be the individual who would conduct the 'hit.' [Gambino] believes that Anderson is capable of performing the 'hit' because it is known that Anderson has served in the military."

When assistant U.S. attorney Marc Harris received a phone call that same day informing him that Darryl Henley had hired a prison guard to kill a judge and a prosecutor, Harris's first thought was of Rayburn, a fellow Berkeley alum who was known in the office as the man who had put Henley away. But there was too much haziness in Gambino's story to start surrounding Rayburn with security. That it had come from an incarcerated informant didn't help. So Harris had Gambino brought in to his office that afternoon for a talk.

Michael Tino Gambino — alias Michael Tarantino, alias Michael Salais, alias Michael Salas, alias Michael Schultz — was eager to help Marc Harris in any way he could. During their meeting Gambino described how he'd become friendly with Henley since arriving at MDC a few weeks earlier. Henley had confided in him, Gambino said; a trust had formed. The crucial conversation in which Darryl had mentioned murdering the judge and the prosecutor had taken place the previous night, Gambino said, when Henley told him, "I'm gonna whack the white bitch."

Plans had already been made to notify Rayburn and Judge Taylor of the threat, but only now could Harris see that Henley's alleged target wasn't Rayburn, it was Deirdre Eliot. (It would later become clear that Henley had never mentioned harming either prosecutor.) The DEA's handling of Mikey Gambino was transferred from George Eliot's investigative group to Steven Kinney's, erasing the link, real or perceived, to Deirdre Eliot.

Marc Harris had recently won a conviction against an MDC guard who was caught delivering contraband to a convicted Russian mobster. (The mobster had been informing on the guard the whole time.) So Harris knew how MDC worked — the good, the bad, and the ugly. He was not as well versed, however, in the Henley trial that Rayburn and Eliot had won a year earlier. Harris had heard something about a cheerleader being busted, but he thought it happened at LAX, not Atlanta. Until Michael Gambino entered his life, he had never needed to know more.

After ensuring that Taylor and both prosecutors were protected, Harris's next task was to have Mikey convince Henley not to hire Rodney Anderson as his hit man, but to give the job to Mikey's brother Joey. Except Joey Gambino wasn't Mikey's brother. He was a fifty-two-year-old DEA agent named Michael Bansmer, who had just been given the undercover role of a lifetime.

A member of Bansmer's investigative team would later refer to him as "intense" and "a creepy dude." Said another: "I love Mike, but a lot of people think he's crazy." Bansmer's career had spawned numerous outlandish stories. Like the time he checked out a new Glock 21 (a ferocious firearm, unapproved for street use) and announced to a fellow agent that he was headed to an ATM to make sure it worked. When the agent asked what that meant, Bansmer said he'd "stand there until some punk comes up to rob me," then he'd see how the gun performed.

Some agents were scared to work with Bansmer, yet one recalled that he "never felt safer working with anyone more than Mike." Among Bansmer's assignments had been a tour of Southeast Asia, where he and other narcoterrorism agents would drive as far into the jungle as their jeeps could take them, then climb out and hump trails in search of hidden heroin labs. When they found one, they'd deliver the required "knock-and-notice" by way of a rocket-propelled grenade through the front door. Bansmer had drunk deeply of Southeast Asian culture during his time there and had gained a better than working knowledge of the region's drug underworld. These experiences would serve him well on the Henley case, as would his uncanny physical resemblance to Mikey Gambino — a gift from the law enforcement gods.

Marc Harris began drafting the court order required to let Bansmer tap the cell phones Anderson smuggled into MDC each night. Harris knew that once the wiretap was granted, things would only get harder. Henley's cell phone had been malfunctioning lately, so Henley had asked Anderson to switch it for another one. When this new one acted up, Henley swapped with Mikey. This meant that Bansmer would not only have to determine which phone Henley was using, but he'd have to check with Harris to make sure he had legal authority to eavesdrop on it. Even then, it would be no sure thing. During the days ahead, the quality of the phones' reception would prove infuriatingly volatile for both the criminals and the crime fighters. Static would pop up at the most inopportune times, calls would end without warning, and transcribing the conversations would illuminate one of the few shortcomings on Bansmer's staff: their lack of familiarity with street slang. At the outset Bansmer and his colleagues could only hope that their "Triggerfish" audio receiver, which was aimed at 9 South from the roof of the government building next door, would hold true during those crucial moments when Henley was saying what they wanted him to say.

After Gambino's meeting with Harris, he returned to 9 South and fielded his first call from his "big brother" Joey. It was 10:30 p.m. Rodney Anderson had just given Mikey his cell phone for the night.

"Hello?"

"Mike."

"Yeah, what's up man?" Mikey said, his voice shimmering with fake brotherly love.

"Uh, is everything cool?" Bansmer asked.

"Yeah."

"We can talk?"

"Yeah."

". . . Um, is D there?"

"Yeah, you want to talk to him?"

"Does he want to talk?"

"Yeah. . . . He went to go talk to the officer [Anderson] real quick. . . . He's a good kid. He's going through a lot of shit right now, so, you know."

As they waited for Darryl, Mikey and Bansmer slipped into their respective roles, bantering about getting "the Family involved in this thing" and about their fictitious father—the don of the Gambinos.

Darryl entered. Mikey handed him the phone.

"Hello?" Darryl said. "Hello?"

"Hey, how's it going?" Joey said.

"It's all right. How you doing?"

"Yeah, good. Hey, I just wanna make sure that we're talking with the guy that's gonna call the shots, and uh . . . I understand that we can do something for you. And I just went over and made the contacts this afternoon."

"Yes sir."

"And everything's cool, but uh, can you give me an idea on the C, how many you want?"[2]

"I can move a hundred envelopes a week," Darryl said. "But you know, to start off, and so everybody's comfortable, uh, Mikey told me, you know, we can start with a dub. A twenty." (Twenty kilos.)

Joey told Darryl that if he was interested in "the cw" (China White heroin), then he was talking to the right guy. "We own the factory."

"Get the fuck out of here . . ." Darryl said. "Well, I've always moved C. I mean always. And they're just in this dire need for the cw [in Detroit]."

"Hey, I can get you all you want. Up to a hundred units a week. . . . You know, this is 100 percent [purity]. I mean—"

"Knocking 'em dead."

"It'll knock your socks off."

"That's—that was the request. If it's knocking 'em dead, it's all day long."

Problems arose, however, when they discussed quantity and price. Darryl didn't know that heroin was sold in "units" of 700 grams each—as opposed to cocaine, which was sold in kilos (1,000 grams). His inexperience on this point slowed the deal. "Oh, see, I hadn't broken it down like that," Darryl said.

"Uh huh."

Darryl handed the phone to Mikey while he ran to get a pen and pad. Deep inside the Westwood federal building, the DEA agents in the listening room winced. Henley was jotting his drug calculations inside a prison. *Was he really this green, or just stupid?*

"What's up?" Mikey said to Bansmer while Henley was out of the room.

"Yeah, it's cool," Bansmer said. "Um, I'm telling him about the cw because you didn't know this before but, uh, that's my end of the business. . . . Tell him that, y'know, I spent five years on the other side of the pond lining up all our factories over there . . ."

Mikey laughed. "Right, I hear ya."

". . . Is he coming back?"

"Yeah, he's right here, hold on."

Darryl continued to try and shove a square peg into a round hole — or in this case, a unit into a kilo — while Bansmer struggled to keep his frustration out of Joey's voice. "No, it's — let's get *real simple*, okay?" he said before explaining kilos and units again. He even tried explaining it in pounds, then he just surrendered. "Nobody sells the cw in keys," Joey said firmly. To keep his case moving, Bansmer allowed Darryl to change the way heroin had been smuggled for decades. A real supplier, of course, would have hung up instead of teaching a course on the subject. Then again, a real supplier would have never called a trafficker who was locked up and interested in just seven measly units.

Joey said his price was $125,000 per unit.

"And that's pure," Darryl said.

"That's 100 percent. I guarantee you nobody's jumped on it."[3]

Darryl asked about "the C."

"Both of them. I got all you want of both of them. . . . We're ready to roll. That's what we're in business for."

"Okay. Let me wait on the C then."

"Mm hm."

"And let me push the cw [heroin] . . ."

"Hey, there's more money in that."

"It's a lot more."

"It's a *hell* of a lot more."

Darryl needed to discuss the deal with Jimmy Washington, his man on the outside, so he asked Joey to call him back in a half hour. Joey and Mikey chatted briefly before hanging up:

"It's cool," Bansmer told Mikey.

"All right," said Mikey. "Well, I'm gonna eat some Kentucky Fried Chicken 'cause I'm hungry like a motherfucker."

Later that night, in the darkness of the typewriter room on 9 South, the light on Darryl's cell phone blinked, signaling an incoming call. It was Joey, as promised, calling him back. They set up a meeting between Joey and Jimmy Washington for 2 p.m. the next day. Darryl suggested the Marriott near the Ontario Airport. Joey switched it to the San Bernardino Hilton (across the street from a satellite DEA office). Henley described Jimmy's appearance and listened to Joey describe his own:

"You know what Mikey looks like?" Joey said.

"Yeah."

"I look about twenty years older. Just like him."

"Just like him? Hair slicked back?"

"Yeah."

"He told me that."

Finally, Joey wanted to make sure Jimmy could "talk the cw" because "it doesn't sound like you really know what you're talking about with it." As for money, Joey asked, "This is going to be COD, right? You're going to pay for it when you pick it up?"

"I didn't know that," Darryl said with a chuckle. He was flat broke, and now he was embarrassed. He'd thought Joey was going to front him the drugs.

"I mean, you can't do this kind of business on a front," Joey said.

"That's what I wanted to do the first time. I spoke to Mikey about it—"

Joey snickered. "You're talking — we're talking eight hundred grand. Nobody's gonna let go of that without holding onto something."

"Oh, I mean, I was doing that with Curly all the time. [4] So, I mean, that's why I originally hooked up with him. But. Hmm."

Henley was stuck, and Bansmer felt it. Over the next ten minutes he resuscitated the deal by saying he'd "work out the details. We can probably do something. . . . We'll work with you. . . . We'll be able to work something out. . . . Sure, we'll be able to work it out. . . . We're flexible."

When the call ended, a tape recorder clicked off inside the federal building, then clicked on again. "The time is 11:45 p.m.," a male voice said. "The preceding was an undercover telephone call between GS Bansmer and Darryl Henley. Also present was SA Steve Kinney. . . . End of tape." [5]

Deirdre Eliot was advised by the U.S. marshals not to appear at the next day's evidentiary hearing. Extra security was on hand for Taylor and Rayburn, who were the only ones aware of Henley's threats against Eliot and the judge, including, as it turned out, Henley himself, for no evidence existed or would be uncovered later that Henley had been seeking to have Taylor or Eliot killed.

Tracy was a different matter. Hard evidence from Henley's own mouth would later indicate that sometime prior to that morning's hearing he had at least mentioned killing Tracy and had discussed having Rodney Anderson obtain a rifle for that purpose. It was as foolish a plan as it was heinous, for no possible end result could have benefited Henley. First, it would have been all but impossible to have Tracy killed and escape suspicion. Surely Henley would have been the prime suspect. Even if he got away with it, killing Tracy wouldn't kill her trial testimony; it would lock it eternally into the record. Dead witnesses can't be cross-examined. So why did Henley want to do away with her?

The answer, Henley said later, was that by May 1996 he had lost confidence that Tracy would ever be questioned under oath again. Despite the hope he tried to breathe into his loved ones, Henley realized that his new trial hearings had gone abysmally, and that even if he were awarded a new trial, exposing Tracy's lies in the first one would not be a slam dunk. Henley's attempt to have Tracy killed was a sickening, cowardly, vicious choice, he admitted years later, and he expected no forgiveness for it other than from his maker.

At that moment, though, Tracy wasn't the witness Darryl was worried about. At the final and most important evidentiary hearing to resolve his new trial motion, Mike Malachowski was the person at center stage. Clad in prison fatigues, Malachowski took the stand a much different man than the Oingo Boingo fan he'd been a few weeks earlier, for the FBI's promise to him had come true: he was sitting in court with Darryl Henley, wearing the same uniform.

Jim Riddet began his questioning by asking Malachowski whether Shawn O'Reilly had ever said "that he believed all of the defendants were guilty."

"I don't believe so," Malachowski replied.

The best Riddet could do in response was show Malachowski the sworn deposition in which he'd recalled O'Reilly saying, "All the niggers are guilty."

Mike said he'd lied at the deposition.

"Did Mr. O'Reilly ever say that he thought the defendants were guilty without using the racial epithet?"

"Um, I believe that he thought they could have been guilty, but he wasn't sure."

The rest of Malachowski's testimony was full of similar evasions and contradictions. He testified that O'Reilly had used the word *nigger* during their carpool discussions and that he may have said it more than once, but when Riddet asked if "O'Reilly ever said anything to you which indicated that he was prejudiced against blacks," Malachowski answered no. Later Malachowski said he considered O'Reilly a racist. When asked how he'd reached that opinion, Mike replied, "By using the word *nigger.*"

Malachowski testified about the bribery scheme and his pre-verdict contact with Henley and Quihuis, but he never said that Henley had put him up to the bribe. The closest Malachowski came to pinning the bribe idea on Henley was his recollection that Darryl said he "needed his vote."

Quihuis also testified on this day, but federal rule 606(b) allowed him to plead the Fifth regarding his drug use during the trial. When Quihuis was done, Shawn O'Reilly took the stand and denied once again the racism charges Malachowski had retracted that morning. It was enough to defeat the "nigger" issue once and for all. Having been granted immunity by the government, however, O'Reilly made one important admission. He confessed to discussing the case with Quihuis and Malachowski during their carpool rides — a charge he had adamantly denied for more than a year.

As riveted as he was to the drama playing out before him, Darryl was also wondering what was going on in San Bernardino at that moment.

Michael Bansmer had just arrived for his meeting with Jimmy Washington at the San Bernardino Hilton, the wire in his cell phone picking up the faint sound of Sade's "Smooth Operator" playing in the hotel lobby and relaying it into the earpieces of the nine other agents — six DEA, three FBI — stationed around the property. Steven Kinney was audiotaping, videotaping, and photographing the meeting from afar.

"I was talking to D last night," Joey told Jimmy, "and he didn't know the difference between whether it was pressed or just powder. . . . We were talking price last night and I don't think he knew what he was talking about. He started talking about a deuce and a quarter. . . . He didn't know what he was talking about."

Jimmy wasn't concerned: "If you got the right product, hey, we can be king of the road." Only one thing bothered him: "We got to stop a lot of that damn communication from jail, from you to him to me . . ."

"Oh, there's no need to talk to him," Joey agreed. Talking to Henley "was like talking to the fucking wall because he didn't know what he was talking about. And he was trying to get a pencil and figure what a—he didn't know what a unit was."

The DEA lab had prepared a pinch of heroin for Bansmer. He showed it to Jimmy inside his car, "just so you know I ain't bullshittin'." By the end of the meeting Jimmy was chuckling about his good fortune, reiterating his eagerness to get started and praising Joey for being "an honorable man."

In order to have the clearest voice possible for the decisive conversations to come, he coughed a little, taking pains to stifle the sound, as it may not have sounded like a human cough and he could no longer trust his own judgment about it. Meanwhile in the adjoining room it had become completely still.

—FRANZ KAFKA, *The Metamorphosis*

Chapter 40

Saturday, May 18, 1996

It was the most critical detail of the entire investigation, and Michael Bansmer's mind worked it like a case unto itself: *How can I get Henley to hire me as his hit man?* Bansmer knew that Henley might hang up if Joey even *hinted* at murder. You don't talk about hits over the phone. Any phone. Plus, Darryl already had his hit man in Rodney Anderson. How could Bansmer offer to replace Anderson without raising Henley's suspicions?

Each of these concerns would be resolved due to Henley's naiveté, hubris, and anger, during a process that began on the night of May 18, 1996—the day after Mike Malachowski testified—when Bansmer slipped into his role as "Joey Gambino" and called Darryl's cell phone from the government building in Westwood. Joey had an offer to make, but Bansmer had to be careful about how he made it.

"How's it going?" Joey asked.

"Okay," Darryl said.

"Jimmy and I hit it off good. I like him."

"You do?"

"Yeah."

"Well, I'm, um, glad."

They hit it off so well, Joey said, that he was ready to send Rodney Anderson on a "dry run" to Detroit (a delivery of fake drugs, to test Anderson). "And if it gets there all right and nothing happens then we're cool. . . . We can turn around and put him on a real one."

"Yeah, I hear you," Darryl said. Paying for the drugs up front, though, was "gonna be hard."

"Yeah, but here's another idea." Anderson had been asking Mikey about getting "tools" for "a different kind of job," Joey said.

"Another deal?"

"Yeah."

"I don't know anything about that," Darryl said. "Now *that* bothers me."

"'Cause it's something to do with something you need done." The line was silent for five seconds.

"Oh, I got you," Darryl said. "Okay."

"Okay?"

"Yeah."

"Now you know, uh, that's right up our line of work," Joey said. "Maybe we can work something out where we wouldn't have to come up with the front on this end, if you gave that job to me. Normally we get about fifty for one of those things [a contract hit], but in this case, probably cost you about a hundred. A hundred a piece."

"Each."

"Each one. . . . But it's done right."

Another long pause.

"No trace back?" Darryl asked.

"Nothing. They won't even be able to find the pieces."

"That's what I want."

"Well, you might consider that because if you want it done right, I'm the one to do it."

"Clean."

"Clean."

More silence from Henley.

"Uh, how would you locate them?" Henley asked.

"Well, that's what you could use 'A' [Anderson] for. You give me the details."

"Details?"

"Yeah, picture, address, car, description, license plate. . . . 'A' would be better at doing something like that, and you can be sure that it'll be done right on the other end if we do it."

"Not even the pieces?"

"They won't find the pieces. It'll be like that thing in Oklahoma. . . . You want two of them, right?"

"Well, one and one. I do want to do both of them."

"Right. . . . And that way you won't have to put anything up front."

"Yeah, that'll work."

"You want to?"

"Yeah."

"Okay. All right."

". . . I'll get you a photo," Darryl said.

"Uh huh."

Their conversation turned to Anderson's trial run to Detroit. Out of the blue, Darryl snapped back to their earlier topic. "Um, no pieces?" he asked again.

"No pieces. . . . No mistakes and nobody to talk. If something did go wrong, we'll just do it again. But nobody ever gets caught on this kind of thing 'cause you ain't around when it happens."

Darryl shifted gears again, telling Bansmer about a witness who "showed up yesterday, when I was in court" but "didn't even look over at me," which had left Darryl "fucking boiling." Henley was referring to Mike Malachowski. It was the first hint that the information Mikey Gambino had given Bansmer about the murder targets was wrong. Darryl wanted *Malachowski* killed, not Judge Taylor. But the "court" reference seemed to allude to a judge, so Bansmer continued thinking that Taylor was Henley's target.

"Well, is this gonna help on your thing?" Joey asked.

"Go home."

"You'll be able to walk, huh?"

"Go right home."

"Okay, well, have [Anderson] get real good details," Joey said. "I don't like to do a sloppy job."

"Oh yeah."

Bansmer and the lead prosecutor, Marc Harris, considered arresting Henley at that point and charging him with murder-for-hire. They didn't, Harris explained later, because their information was still "dangerously incomplete." Entrapment was also an issue. Harris had made it clear that Henley was to be given every opportunity to walk away from what he and Bansmer were discussing. Harris knew that for his case to be beaten by an entrapment defense, Henley would have to show lack of intent — he'd have to prove that he'd been talked into something he initially didn't want to do. Harris felt good about where things stood in this regard. Bansmer had been the first one to raise the subject of murder, but he never had to twist Henley's arm about it, and he never would. Bansmer had made Henley so comfortable, in fact, that Henley invited him to call back that night if he needed anything else. Just after midnight, Bansmer took him up on the offer.

Sunday, May 19, 1996 — 12:20 a.m.

"Well, see, on Sunday you're gonna pay me for that other job," Joey said, reconfirming the murders on tape.

"Yeah, that's exactly right," Darryl said.

"Right. And then that can get done. And on this other thing [the heroin deal], um, we can take some time on that."

417

"Yeah, . . . I'm gonna get you one, right? The full one."

"For each hit." ($100,000 for each murder.)

"Right."

"So I'm gonna go for one hit right now," Henley said.

Henley's first motivation was money; paying Joey for one murder instead of two stood to increase his bottom line. But Bansmer didn't want Henley backtracking. He wanted him signed on for both hits. "We want to do 'em both at the same time," Joey insisted, "because if we do one then it'll be impossible to get next to the other one. See what I mean? . . . If one gets done, who knows where the other will go after something happens?"

"Oh, I got you," Darryl said.

"You'll never find him. I mean we gotta do this, uh, simultaneously. If they're connected with your case."

"Oh, one is," Henley said.

"Huh?"

"One is connected to the case."

Bansmer's assumptions had been crushed — only one of the targets has to do with his case? — but amid this confusion he saw a chance to confirm the two targets by name. On tape.

"The other one is not connected," Darryl said. "You understand what I'm saying?"

"Oh, okay, I just — I guess I was hearing, you know, maybe — you can talk on this phone?"

"Yeah, I'm fine."

"Okay, um, is this the, uh, the public, uh, official?"

"Oh," Henley said. "Okay, I got you. I'm with you now. I'm with you now."

"That's why it's costing so much. . . . Is this the judge?"

"No, that wasn't him. I do want to do him though." Henley chuckled.

"Well, that's what I thought it was," Joey said.

"But you were saying two. And I was like — but one I had actually made the plans for."

"Yeah, which one's that?"

"That was the first one. On my case."

"The prosecutor?"

"No, the cheerleader."

"Oh, the cheerleader?"

"Yeah, she's in a halfway spot."

"Mikey thought it was the prosecutor and the judge."

"No, that's a . . . straight beeline to me, isn't it? No matter how it's done."

"Yeah."

Henley asked if Anderson could help locate the judge.

"Well, you gotta ask *him*," Joey replied.

"I am. Sure. I never even took that to him," Henley said, rendering false Mikey's story about Henley hiring Anderson to kill Taylor. But it no longer mattered. Henley had just hired Joey to do it.

"I got a big old smile on my face," Darryl said. "You don't even know." Moments later he confirmed that the hit would be done "Oklahoma style, right?"

"Yeah . . . the Oklahoma way."

"I guess it couldn't be *there*, could it?"

"Where?"

"At the uh . . . just like Oklahoma." Henley was asking whether the courthouse where he'd been convicted could be detonated like the federal building in Oklahoma City.

"Oh, no no no no," Joey said. ". . . We'll do 'em in their car when they go to work in the morning. They won't get a hundred feet down the road and it'll be, uh, toasty critters."

A long pause followed.

"I like it," Darryl said.

Joey asked how Tracy traveled to and from her halfway house.

"Her mother's vehicle," Darryl said.

"And she'll be in it alone?"

"I doubt that."

"You want to do the mother, too, huh?"

Henley considered it for a few seconds, thinking back to the time he'd heard Mrs. Donaho refer to him as a nigger, thinking about how that same word had been bleached out of his trial, and now soaking in the power of talking to a man who could eliminate those he held responsible for both. "Fuck the mother," Darryl said.

Three minutes later, they were talking money. Darryl assumed that Tracy's mother would cost him an extra $100,000, bringing his total for the three murders to $300,000, but Joey said he'd throw the mom in for free. "If she's in the way, that's too bad, no?"

"Right."

Bansmer summarized things on his tape: "You want to do the judge, you want to do the cheerleader, and the prosecutor, right?"

"No, I wasn't worrying about the prosecutor," Henley said.

"Okay, you're not worried about her. . . . Yeah, you don't want to bring too much heat on you."

As for Tracy, Joey said: "There won't be any trace of it. No one will know it happened. They'll still be looking for her ten years from now."

Instead of looking for Tracy, in ten years Henley would be searching for words to explain his motives for plotting her murder. "My mind-set," Darryl recalled, "was more powerful than any motive. I was angry. Just so angry. I was fighting mad at the system, I was broke, my family was hurting. . . . Being in MDC for thirteen, fourteen months, I had changed. I was just so mad, man. And ashamed, which added to the anger."

Vengeance had joined money as his top motive. He genuinely loathed Tracy and Taylor for their roles in his demise, and now someone was offering him a $1 million heroin deal, from which they'd deduct $200,000 to take Tracy and Taylor out. That the murders were his only means of getting the heroin money mattered less the more Darryl spoke with Joey Gambino about it. In an interview later that year with the U.S. Probation Department, Henley explained that he "believed that he was actually dealing with the Gambino crime family, [so] he thought the murders of Judge Taylor and Donaho would actually be accomplished. He also felt that he would not be caught by authorities, since he knew that organized crime families believed in honor and a code of silence to never betray each other."

When Joey Gambino hung up with Henley at 12:45 a.m. and became Michael Bansmer again, he immediately contacted FBI special agent Pamela Graham, who spent the rest of that Sunday working on an affidavit which she stapled to a document from the U.S. Attorney's Office titled "Application for an Order Authorizing the Interception of Wire Communications." Later that day U.S. attorney general Janet Reno's office authorized the wiretap. Prior to that moment, Michael Bansmer and his team had only been able to record calls made to and from their landline at the Westwood listening station. Now every call involving Rodney Anderson's cell phones could be recorded. It was a huge investigative step. The agents were given thirty days to gather evidence, after which they'd have to request an extension on the wiretap. The way things were going, and as freely as Henley was talking, none of the agents thought they'd need that long.

At 4:18 p.m. that Sunday, just as the wiretap was being approved in Washington, Joey Gambino was speaking on the phone with Rodney Anderson, telling the guard that he'd be carrying two units of heroin to Detroit that night. At 10:30 p.m., Joey and Anderson met at a restaurant near the airport. As they ate, they shared stories about their military days — Anderson the Marine, Joey the Army man — which funneled into a discussion of weapons, which segued nicely toward the conversation Bansmer wanted to be picked up by the microphone hidden in his cell phone on the table. "You know the other thing that D was talking about was using you to find out some information on some people that he's interested in having us do some work on."

"Yeah, he told me about that . . ." Anderson said. "I know who he's looking for. . . . Yeah, he's always talking about, 'How we get rid of that bitch?'"

"Mm hm."

"He wants her taken off the count."[1] Anderson agreed that Joey should do the job. "You've got to have somebody know what they doing. . . . 'No body, no case.' Yeah, we talked about it, you know, we had talked about it before."

With those words, Bansmer had completed his goal of establishing a murder conspiracy: two men, Henley and Anderson, agreeing to kill someone. The flight Anderson was about to board would be Bansmer's evidence of a drug trafficking conspiracy. The government's walls weren't closing in on Henley anymore. They were pressed against him and still moving.

Monday, May 20, 1996

At 7:30 p.m. Joey called Jimmy Washington to report that Anderson had successfully moved the fake heroin to Detroit. "[The] test went perfect . . ." Joey said. "We're ready to roll with the eight [units of heroin]." They arranged a meeting so Joey could give Jimmy a new pinch of the drugs — something for his buyers to test in Detroit.

Tuesday, May 21, 1996

As he drove to deliver the pinch to Jimmy, Bansmer tested his wire: "Okay, it's on and runnin'," he told the listening agents. "Just arrived in front of the Hilton. I'm gonna be goin' in to meet Washington." Joey entered the bar and ordered a drink while a female agent kept an eye on him from across the room. Steven Kinney was listening in a dark-windowed vehicle outside.

Jimmy Washington pulled up in a Ford Explorer, entered the lobby, and exchanged pleasantries with Joey, who suggested they "go for a walk." In the back of Joey's van, Joey unzipped a bag revealing the eight packages of heroin that Anderson would deliver to Detroit the next day. Pointing out the peacock logo on the

packages — proof that the junk had come straight from Southeast
Asia — Joey said, "You're lookin' at a million dollars." He handed
Jimmy a baggie containing the pinch. "You gotta be careful because you put that shit out, this strength, out on the street, they'll
be droppin' like flies."

"That's on *them*," Jimmy said. (That's *their* problem.)

Jimmy and his pinch were scheduled to fly to Detroit that night.
Anderson and his eight bricks of heroin would follow the next day.

At 10:27 p.m. Mikey Gambino called his girlfriend, Giovanna, to
tell her he'd be coming home "next Wednesday."

"Next Wednesday?!" she squealed in surprise. "Definitely? Like
a week from tomorrow."

"Yep."

"Yay! . . . I'm so happy honey, so happy."

"Can't wait to see my kids. Fuck."

He called Bansmer a few minutes later.

"Have you been talking to D today?" Bansmer asked.

"Yeah. . . . Whatever you guys did, you guys did really well . . ."

"As far as you can tell, everyone's happy?"

"*Very.* . . . Whatever you guys did . . ."

"Okay, hang in there, okay?"

"Okay."

Bansmer hung up and tried to call Henley's cell phone, but
static intervened. So he called Mikey and told him to "walk yours
up to him." Mikey complied, bounding up the stairs and handing his phone to Henley.

Henley told Joey that Anderson had felt "very comfortable" during his trip to Detroit. Anderson had remarked that he could "do
this for years," Henley said. "And I said, 'Well, we're not going to
do this for years.'" Joey steered the conversation toward "that other
thing." Installing steel walls in his murder case, he helped Darryl
confirm that he'd asked Anderson to perform "the background"

for the hits (locating the targets) and that Darryl was going to "take care of" Anderson for his efforts (pay him). Then, the most important part:

"I need to know the two names."

"Okay."

"Can you give those to me right now?"

"Yeah, I can give them to you now."

"Yeah, what is it?"

"Um, the judge is Gary Taylor," Henley said.

"Is that the judge?"

"Yeah."

"Okay."

"He's the only—only male down there. There's three—two women and him."

Joey spoke slowly, as if writing it all down: "Okay. Gary. Taylor."

"Yeah."

"And."

"And the girl is Tracy Donaho." Henley said he could get a photo of her "very easily."

"Now, [Anderson] talked to me about some of the, y'know—he was wanting a silencer. Did he tell you that?"

"Yeah, we had talked about that earlier . . . before you got the job."

"And you still want to do the guy first, right?"

"For sure."

"Okay."

"Yeah, there might not be a whole lot of time," Darryl said. "I mean, she may have to get done the next day."

"Exactly, because uh . . . it's gonna freak them out."

"Yeah."

"And we're still gonna go with the, um, Oklahoma style for the guy and then we'll just—there won't ever be any way to trace the girl," Joey said.

"That's right. Exactly right."

It was time for Bansmer to protect himself from an entrapment defense. "I don't want you to have second thoughts," he said, "because once I say that we're gonna go on this other thing, it's gonna get done."

". . . When you get that [money] in your hands," Darryl said, "that's done now. I mean, y'know, that is a deal."

Bansmer could not have scripted it any better. Just in case the connection had been bad, or he'd hit a soft spot on the audiotape, he asked again: "Okay, so you—we got a deal right now?"

"We have a deal right now."

It was one of Henley's busiest nights on his cell phone—and also one of his last. He told the wife of a close friend that acquiring his cell phone "has been the most beneficial thing that could happen to me in here." He told her husband: "Our day in court was awesome."

"It was?"

"Helllll yeah. . . . Man, they got the jurors up there saying shit, man . . . saying that they weren't telling the truth and they were lying and, you know, they decided the case two weeks into it. One guy admitted, 'Yeah I did decide the case two weeks into it.' . . . Boy, I just wish I had my thing *up here*."

"Where, in LA?"

"Helllllllllll yeah."

Both men laughed.

On the tier below, behind a sheet of typewriter paper taped over his window, Mikey Gambino called a friend on the outside named Paul and bragged that he had just had a pizza delivered to him in prison by "this boy."

"Cool. Sounds like you're at home."

"Almost," Mikey said.

"Okay, O.J.," Paul joked.

Next, Mikey called one of his codefendants in Oakland, who complained about having to get up early the next morning for court. Mikey wished him luck.

"I need it," said his codefendant.

Knowing what he knew about the system, Mikey — aka O.J. — replied: "You don't need it dude, believe me."

Wednesday, May 22, 1996

Jimmy Washington called Darryl at 1:11 a.m. from LAX. His flight to Detroit had been delayed, but he was grateful. He wanted to slow down and discuss his concerns about the deal with his partner. First Jimmy said he didn't think the "pinch" Joey had given him would be enough for his Detroit buyers to test. And even if they liked it, they'd only be willing to pay $150,000 to $160,000 per unit, which meant that Henley was looking at a maximum profit of just $140,000.[2] And he still had to pay Anderson.

"That ain't good," Darryl said. "I mean, I don't like that at all."

When Joey and Darryl touched base at 1:50 a.m., Darryl told him he was not "overly excited about these numbers. . . . I mean, I'm gonna have to wait another week to finish the assignment."

Joey suggested they move forward "at this price. You're still gonna make out 'cause we'll turn around and they're gonna love [the heroin]. I guarantee you they're gonna love it."

Even so, Darryl could not afford to pay $200,000 for the two hits, so he told Joey to do just one. "That's all I got. . . . As opposed to my whole two."

Joey offered to do one murder on "credit . . . don't worry about that." He said "on Saturday you're gonna see some headlines."

"That quick, huh?"

"Yeah, that's what you want, right?"

"That's what I want. I have no problem . . ."

"You know, this ain't nothin' to fool around with."

"Oh yeah," Darryl said. "I mean, the decisions I make, I make." But Henley didn't want to do the second hit on credit. "I'm gonna have to wait a week to do the other one. . . . I just don't like the whole owing, y'know, the debt thing."

426

"See, the people that are gonna do the job are here now," Joey said. "So . . ."

"If they're gonna do it, then let's do it," Darryl said. "I mean, I don't have any reserves about that."

Jimmy was still at the airport, still delayed, still unsure about the whole thing. He spoke with Darryl again, trying in vain to increase their profits in a drug deal that would never happen, all the while creating a seventeen-page transcript that, once they read it in their jail cells, would plunge them into deep humiliation and even deeper legal trouble.

Darryl called Alisa at 3:09 a.m. She sounded groggy, a little sad. She carried the phone with her to check on Gia in her crib. She watched the sleeping baby's torso rise and fall in the darkness.

"How does she sleep?" Darryl asked.

"She sleeps good. . . . She only tosses and turns a little."

"I mean, is she on her stomach, her back, or —"

"Oh. She's on her stomach."

"Are her legs rocked back or what?"

"She's laying flat, like a beached whale, with her head to the side."

Moments later, Alisa asked, "Did I tell you that I bought invitations?"

"Wedding invitations?"

"Uh huh."

"Nope, you didn't tell me."

Five seconds of silence followed.

"I showed them to your mother and she was like, 'So you guys aren't gonna wait?' I said no."

Their conversation labored. Darryl seemed to clam up after the mention of marriage, possibly in humiliation for the crimes he was plotting. "I gotta go out and get this ring and stuff for you," he said finally, sounding tired and eager to hang up.

Alisa asked who he wanted to invite to the ceremony. The line crackled. Darryl didn't answer. "No one in particular?" she asked. Another wrenching silence. "Hm?"

Darryl said he had to go. There were several clicks and flashes of static.

"Hello?" Alisa said.

No one was there.

Chapter 41

Rodney Anderson slept in on Wednesday morning. He spent the afternoon shopping for new rims for his Toyota 4-Runner. Then he called in sick to work so he could catch the red-eye to Detroit that night. The profits from that business trip would have bought the most expensive rims on the market, but Anderson would not be on the plane when it took off.

His plans began to crumble at 8:45, when Jimmy called Joey from Detroit to tell him that his pinch had been tested and failed. "They can't put nothing on this," Jimmy complained.[1] "They laughing at me, man."

"No, that's bullshit," Joey said. He knew it was DEA dope—pure as the driven snow. "You shoot that up in a junkie they'll drop dead right on the spot if you give them what they normally hit."

"They *did* that," Jimmy said, "and ain't nothin' really happen."

"Yeah, well, I'll take it somewhere else. I can load it somewhere else. I can go to New York." Bansmer sounded genuinely angry. The situation had infuriated both identities inside him: Joey because his product was being questioned, Bansmer because his case was being stalled. "I mean, they're bullshittin' you, and you don't have a connect to get rid of this kind of weight, and I'm wasting my time." Bansmer hung up on Jimmy, as any mob man would have. Fuming, Bansmer met Anderson at LAX and canceled his trip to Detroit.

Thursday, May 23, 1996

When Darryl heard that the Detroit deal had crumbled, he called Mikey. It was 10:14 p.m. "Hey, I need your brother paged," Darryl said.

But Bansmer had never given Mikey his pager number. Mikey stalled: "Let me hit you back in a minute."

"I need it *now*," Darryl said.

"I don't know — I'm looking for it right now," Mikey lied.

"You should have that motherfucker memorized," Henley seethed.

Mikey said he'd call his mom right away and get the number. He made sure his phone was off before he let out a deep breath. He didn't call his mother, of course. He called the DEA office. "Um, I don't know his pager number and D asked me for the pager number and he needs to get a hold of him," Mikey told the agent who answered.

Bansmer called Mikey back within minutes. Mikey seized the chance to ask Bansmer about his release from MDC. "I was under the impression that I was supposed to be out this last week," Mikey said. "And nothing that was told to me has come true. . . . I lost out on a contract with Warner Brothers for $500,000 because I was told that I was gonna be out by this week."

"I think you'll find out that your old attorney's getting you out tomorrow," Bansmer said. "That's what I heard."

At this good news Mikey suddenly brightened and offered to go upstairs and work on Darryl. "I'm gonna talk to him and just let him know what's up," Mikey said. "Let him know that this is fuckin' bullshit, and, you know, 'You guys are putting my ass on the line for this stuff, because my brother took my word for it that this was on the up and up. And it's bullshit. The stuff was 98 percent, and this is fucking ridiculous. Now what the fuck is going on, D?' And that's just what I'm gonna say."

"Exactly," said Bansmer. "I want you to go do that right now."

Bansmer waited for Mikey to go upstairs before he called Darryl. Sensing a chance to resuscitate the Detroit deal, Bansmer lowered his price to $100,000 per unit, an un-Mafia-like discount of $25,000 from his previous price. He even offered to send "another batch" if they didn't like the first one. Meanwhile, the evidence that Darryl was engaged in interstate heroin trafficking was filling tape after tape, log sheet after log sheet.

Henley gathered more evidence against himself by calling Jimmy in Detroit. "Look, man, [Joey] is willing to do whatever he gotta do to get our business," Darryl said. "I told him, I said, 'I got motherfuckers there from Atlanta. I got motherfuckers there from Tennessee. I got motherfuckers there ready to *buy*.' . . . I just want to get the shit *sold*. . . . I gotta make some *money* out of this shit." Henley ordered Jimmy to call any potential buyers he knew and let them know the deal was back on.

Jimmy pointed out that it was 3 a.m.

Darryl didn't care. Call them anyway. "That's him right now," he said, his call waiting clicking.

It wasn't Joey, it was Mikey, calling from downstairs to warn Darryl that there was a guard in the unit—someone other than Anderson.

Henley should have heeded this warning, but instead he pressed on, cell phone wedged to his ear by the same shoulder that had tackled Jerry Rice not too many months earlier. Joey called Henley at 11:45 p.m. and together they smoothed the last wrinkles in the revived heroin deal and went over their plans for the two murders. Tracy's halfway house was in Garden Grove, Darryl said, but he was "having a little problem with the picture."

Joey asked Darryl to describe "exactly what she looks like."

"Uh, young girl. She probably looks a little rougher now. . . . She was a cheerleader."

"Mm hm. Give me a physical description on her."

"About five-six. Blonde hair. Uh, *white* white, you know, not, not like *tan* white, you know?"

"White blonde?"

"Yeah, she's a white blonde. Um, a round face."

"Round face?"

"Yeah, um . . . puffy cheeks. And kind of like, kind of like a long nose. Not a *real* long nose, but because her cheeks are—are kind of contorted." Darryl could hardly have been more descriptive, and there was not a trace of lewdness or hesitation in his voice.

"Okay, um, anything strange about her, or, you know, is she skinny, fat—"

"No, she's um, she's slender."

"Slender."

"Yeah, remember she was a cheerleader, so, you know, you should be able to tell."

"Got a good build? Good body?"

"Yeah, she's got a nice body." Again, clinically, without lewdness. "I should be able to get a picture before the weekend is over," Henley added. "I wanted to make sure that, you know, I was going to do it now, which is why . . . this right here changes me. This puts me in an awkward situation. Did you—did you want to wait a week?"

"Um, it's up to you . . ."

"I mean, I want to do it the way we said we're gonna do it. . . . Would you be more comfortable if I got you a picture first?"

"Absolutely," Joey said. Moments later: "Now what about the judge?"

"I didn't want to put [Anderson] in that. . . . No one knows about this but you, me, and Michael. . . . [Anderson] doesn't even know about the judge, y'know?"

"Oh, yeah, he does," Joey said.

"No. Not about the judge."

"Well, I was—I thought you had talked about the judge with him."

"No. I talked about the girl."

"Just about the girl?"

"Yeah."

"Because I asked him for both of the addresses."

"Did—did you say 'judge'?"

"Yeah."

"Oh, did you? . . . He didn't waver about it?"

"No."

"Because I *never* mentioned bringing—now the first person—I mean, I talked to Mikey about doing something and then he told you, and then I talked to you. . . . I was doing the girl and then the other person I was gonna do with him was the guy who ended up, you know, they ended up bringing him in [Malachowski]. . . . He's locked up now. . . . Those are the only two people I had talked to [Anderson] about."

Joey got back on track: "Yeah, so if I get a positive and my people are down there and we get that uh, first 200K, it's done."

"It's done," Darryl said.

". . . That's a deal, right?"

"I'm expecting—now that is a *deal* . . ."

"Now you're—I want to make sure. . . . You just gotta tell me that's what you want, and it's not a problem if you don't want it, but if you want it, you just tell me."

"I want it," Darryl said. These were the three words Marc Harris could stake his case on. "I want it, and I can deal with somebody saying, 'Well, I could have done this or I could have done that,' because there is absolutely no proof for none of that."

"Right. But hey, there's not gonna be any loose ends on this. . . . And again, uh, you want her to disappear and nobody ever to find her body."

"That's exactly right."

"And the judge, he'll be in so many pieces nobody'll ever be able to know what happened."

"Exactly. That's exactly what I want."

"It's still 100K each."

"That's exactly right," Darryl said.

Darryl and Joey hung up at three minutes past midnight. They would never speak again.

Friday, May 24, 1996

Within seconds of this grim, final conversation with Joey, Darryl called his parents. It was late at the Henley house, and his mother and Alisa answered the phone simultaneously. "I got it, ma," Darryl said.

When his mother hung up, Darryl let out a deep, slow breath. "God, I've been working all this crap out," he told Alisa. Her evening had been nearly as stressful. Alisa's and Darryl's relatives had spent most of the night moving her things out of the house, which was being repossessed. Darryl could hear Gia crying in the background and the sounds of his relatives still moving furniture, despite the late hour. He asked to speak to his father.

The accumulated pain of the preceding three years was far more evident in T.H.'s voice than in his son's. T.H. reported glumly that he and his wife were moving into a hotel.

"I don't want my baby in a hotel," Darryl said. He had thought the family was moving to his Aunt Valerie's house, but crashing with a relative was more shame than T.H. could take.

"I'm not going to Val's . . ." T.H. said. "We're not going over there. . . . All right, I gotta go. I'm moving. I'm packing this stuff."

"All right, let me speak to Mama."

Gia was crying in her grandmother's arms as Dorothy took the phone.

"You know we don't stay with nobody," Dot said.

An excruciating silence.

"Daddy'll be all right," she said. "Don't worry about it."

"How you gonna tell me not to worry about it?"

"I know, I know, but things gonna be all right. Things'll be all right tomorrow."

Darryl suggested they rent an apartment, "even if it had to be for six months up front. And this week, you're gonna have that."

"Oh, child," his mother moaned.

"Oh, child," said the father compassionately. . . .
"What can we do?"

—FRANZ KAFKA, *The Metamorphosis*

Chapter 42

It was 3:24 a.m. in room 657 of the Dearborn
Holiday Inn, just outside Detroit, and Jimmy
Washington was jerked from his sleep by his
ringing hotel phone. It was Darryl, calling
him from the typewriter room on 9 South,
both of them unaware that in the DEA listening station in Westwood, California, Special
Agent Louis Perez was adjusting his recording equipment. Perez would end up using
several tapes to capture the ensuing conversation, and he would need three pages to com-
pile his notes. The transcript would fill thirty-four pages, each page more damning than
the one before it.

Henley and Washington also weren't aware
that as they were speaking about heroin pu-
rity and heroin money, BOP lieutenant C. D.
Cole — the officer Mikey had warned Henley about earlier — was still walking around
on 9 South.

According to Cole's written report, the first

thing he noticed was Rodney Anderson acting "nervous and talkative." He also saw that Anderson's nightly paperwork was blank. Anderson excused himself to use the restroom, but instead walked straight to the typewriter room to tell Darryl and Mikey to lie low and stay as quiet as possible. Darryl called Mikey's roommate, Shorty. "Take that shit off the window!" Henley whispered. "Put that motherfucking phone up! Hurry up 'cause the lieutenant's walking around!" The call was so faint that Perez's only note was: *2 UM's—whispered and hung up.* [1]

Anderson returned to his desk, tugging his zipper as if he'd just used the restroom, and tried to distract Cole by reporting that an inmate named Clark had been acting strangely all night. "I thought [Anderson] didn't want me to enter the empty cell he claimed to have urinated inside of," Cole stated in his report. Cole walked over to see Inmate Clark, who told him that "nothing was wrong and he was doing great."

As Cole approached the typewriter room, Anderson raced up the stairs to try and cut him off. He was a step late. Peering into the dark, Cole spotted Mikey's white calves sticking out of his pants, glowing like flares. Cole then "became aware of another inmate. . . . I stepped in with Officer Anderson directly behind me." Anderson tried to explain the presence of Gambino and Henley by telling Cole that they were night orderlies. Mikey muttered something about "some shit going on in the unit" and pretended to square off against Darryl, as if to fight.

"I guess we gonna have to get it on," Darryl said, playing along.

Cole told the inmates to put their hands on the wall. As he patted them down, he spotted a Tupperware bowl on the floor containing "pieces of chicken or fish" and a "black cellular telephone with a black cord."

"What the fuck is that?" Anderson asked, feigning surprise.

Cole ordered Anderson not to leave his sight, then he called two more officers to the floor. One officer escorted Darryl to the third floor and searched him thoroughly. The other searched Mikey in the TV room at the opposite end of the third floor. The guards were ordered not to let Henley and Gambino communicate. Cole "told Officer Anderson to keep quiet and not say a word."

Anderson defied him, pointing to the contraband phone: "I didn't bring that motherfucker in here!"

Dawn was just beginning to strike MDC's towers when Anderson was escorted to the prison gates. His BOP identification card was confiscated, and he was ordered to go home and await further instructions.

Like Jimmy Washington, FBI agent Matt McLaughlin was asleep when his phone rang. [2] Into McLaughlin's ear poured the news that an MDC lieutenant had just stubbed his toe on the FBI's 9 South investigation, which McLaughlin had been working for weeks. When McLaughlin entered the MDC interrogation room and introduced himself to Darryl Henley as an FBI agent, Darryl still thought that all they had on him was possession of a cell phone and "outside food." He declined to talk.

Mikey Gambino was more forthcoming. He began his discussion with McLaughlin by providing his attorneys' names and phone numbers, just so there would be no question as to his role in this thing.

Mikey appeared in court later that day, where the government, "having had the opportunity to more fully investigate defendant's background," recommended he be released from prison. The judge agreed. Mikey hit the streets that afternoon, a free man.

Marc Harris couldn't take Henley down, though. Not yet. The audiotapes hadn't been transcribed, the murder evidence hadn't been vetted, and most important, no drug deal had been consummated. As tightly worded as the conspiracy laws were, Anderson and Washington could still beat the case; after all, no drugs or money had changed hands. And as incriminating as Henley's words were about the murders, his means of paying for them — drug trafficking—was not yet provable in court. The crash course Bansmer had given Henley on the drug game could be twisted into an entrapment defense by a good lawyer. Simply put, Harris didn't have an unbeatable case. The dozens of escape hatches afforded to American defendants had not all been closed. It was up to Michael Bansmer to close them.

The next morning, Bansmer settled into his seat in the listening room in Westwood and called Jimmy Washington. Jimmy told him that all his buyers had left Detroit, except one. Joey asked how many units he wanted.

"Two," Jimmy said.

Two. Bansmer's multilayered undercover Mafia ruse was about to end with a grandiose bust of—two videocassette cases of heroin. He'd be laughed out of the bullpen by his DEA peers. "All right, well, let's put *something* down," Joey groaned.

Next, Joey called Kym Taylor.

"Oh, I don't want you talking on my phone," Kym said, laughing apologetically. Unlike Jimmy, she'd heard about Henley's cell phone being taken. She described the situation as a "big mess."

"Big mess?"

"It's a mess right now. . . . They can't—they won't be calling *anybody*. Anymore."

FBI agent Matt McLaughlin was standing on Rodney Anderson's doorstep in South LA at that moment, waiting the required one hour after his knock before climbing in a window. Anderson had not followed orders and stayed home.

When the agents entered, they encountered a ringing phone that, had they answered it, would have put them on with their DEA rival Mike Bansmer, who was also trying to contact Anderson. "If this is A, give me a call," Joey said into Anderson's answering machine. "This is Joey. . . . Do it from a pay phone. Bye."

Two correctional officers arrived at Darryl's holding cell, hand-cuffed him, and led him to the elevators, where they were joined by two lieutenants and two men dressed in suits. Riding down the elevator with three echelons of prison security officers, Dar-ryl knew that something serious was afoot. Anytime the elevator dropped below the fifth floor, it wasn't a normal "move." (Inmates were housed on floors five through nine.) Henley's ride stopped abruptly on the floor known to inmates as R&D — receiving and delivery. He was given a quick tongue-raising, armpit-inspect-ing, testicle-lifting strip search, and was handed a stack of khaki clothes and a pair of Converse sneakers and told to hustle his ass up. He got dressed, then everyone got in the elevator again, head-ed down. It was obvious now that Henley was being moved to an-other prison. He asked where.

"Guam," said one of his escorts. The other five chuckled.

"Fuck you," Darryl said. In a flash their faces turned stern. Pressing his luck, Darryl told them how sorry they looked, six guys moving one, a remark that got his cuffs put back on, along with — for the first time ever — a belly chain and leg irons. When the elevator stopped at the ground floor, Darryl was passed off to two clean-cut, casually dressed young men near his own age, who he guessed correctly were U.S. marshals.

The caged pen in the marshals' Econoline van had been built to hold eight inmates, but today it would hold just one. Henley's only clue as to where he was going came after a burst of static on the marshals' walkie-talkie, when a voice announced, "Destina-tion forty-two miles."

Forty-two miles, he thought. *Terminal Island? Nah, that's for dudes who have already been sentenced.* The only thing Darryl knew was that these forty-two miles would be the longest distance he had traveled in more than a year — since he'd driven to Las Vegas dur-ing his trial. The van was headed toward Vegas now, as a matter of fact, rumbling east on the 10 Freeway, showing Henley through the bars on the windows a museum of his awful journey: the Marie Callender's where Alejandro Cuevas had been arrested; the freeway exit for his parents' house in Upland — the home he'd bought them after his rookie year, a home that was now empty and up for sale. It was a Saturday, which meant that Damien High School, just north of the freeway, was also empty. The farther east Henley went, the more uncertain he became of his destination. Even after the sprawl of suburban LA gave way to the sepia-toned scrub brush of the desert, Darryl still thought he was facing a minor contraband charge. He was more confused than angry — although he was plenty of that, too, and had been for going on three years.

Joey Gambino was on the phone with Jimmy in Detroit, acting as if everything was cool as he told him that "Curly" (cocaine) was in town.

"Oh, yeah?" Jimmy replied, eyeing a fresh drug deal.

"Yeah, he's in Detroit."

"*Is that right?*"

"Mm hm. I thought you'd like to know that."

Jimmy laughed. "Yeah."

"Yeah, he's on his way to New York, but he's held up there, so if anyone needs to talk to him — "

"How many times?"

"Uh, up to, up to fifty, I think." (I have fifty kilos.)

"For real? . . . At what?"

". . . Around fourteen." ($14,000 per kilo.)

". . . Ooooh, boy," Jimmy said excitedly. "Ooooooooooooooh, boy."

Next, Bansmer moved in on Rodney Anderson, whose preference to make his drug runs out of LAX (because he felt he could schmooze the black women who worked the screening checkpoints there) was about to be overridden by Bansmer and Harris's decision to stage his arrest at the Ontario airport. Joey told Anderson he wanted to switch airports because Anderson was becoming too well known at LAX.

Joey announced another change of plans: Anderson wouldn't have to actually board the flight. All he had to do was get his heroin-filled duffel bag past security, then hand it to a female courier at the departure gate. Anderson accepted both changes, just as he'd accepted everything else Joey ever told him. He was off to the Red Lion Inn — the site Bansmer had chosen for what would be their final rendezvous — the same Red Lion, coincidentally, where Tracy Donaho said she'd picked up her girlfriend Allison's suitcase back in July 1993. That hotel would be one of the final settings in the drama Tracy had helped to start.

When Joey asked Anderson if he'd been able to nail down Tracy's whereabouts, Anderson said he'd searched both the BOP's and U.S. marshals' computers, but both had come up empty.

Anderson didn't find anything because Tracy and her family had been warned several days earlier about the threats to her life, and her name had been taken out of the system. Bansmer had drafted a press release declaring her missing, in hopes that the ensuing newspaper stories would prove to Henley that Tracy was dead, that he was dealing with real Gambinos, and that he could continue working with Joey. It was a brilliant plan, but Bansmer would never have to use it.

Bansmer slipped into the Red Lion — into his final performance as Joey Gambino — as smoothly as the lobby's classical music seeped into his hidden microphone. Rodney Anderson, on the other hand, looked rough. His job, his military career, and his freedom were all in jeopardy, and the stress of the preceding thirty-six hours had drained him. And he still had a bag of heroin to move.

"Hey, how you doing," Joey said. "Let's sit in here."

In the lounge, Anderson said he was worried that the confiscated cell phones would be traced to him. He lifted Joey's cell phone off the table and wondered aloud whether fingerprints could be taken from its plastic shell. Of course not, Joey said, eyeing the phone in

Anderson's hand, which contained a microphone that was transmitting their conversation to a half dozen federal agents nearby.

Joey and Anderson drove to the airport separately. They walked together from the parking garage to the terminal, where Joey gave Anderson a backpack filled with eight bricks of real heroin. Anderson stuffed it in his trusty blue duffel bag and entered the airport. Joey hung back, lingering near the automatic doors. "He's approaching security right now," Bansmer whispered into his wire. "Okay, he's in." An unsettling pause filled the airwaves. "We're having a problem at the gate," Bansmer reported as he watched Anderson walking back toward him.

The meticulous Bansmer had missed a step. The airport police had been informed of the bust, but the security screeners had not, and they'd just ordered Anderson to leave his weapon with the police. Instead, Anderson removed the fanny pack containing his Smith & Wesson .40-caliber handgun and handed it to Joey Gambino. "I gotta leave my gun out," Anderson said.

"Okay, we've got the best of all worlds," Bansmer whispered into his wire as Anderson walked away. "He just gave me his gun."

Anderson was asked to put his duffel bag through the X-ray machine. Scared that they'd see the heroin bricks, he trudged back to Joey again. Joey steered him toward the men's room for a chat. When they emerged, a kindly policeman happened to walk by and ask Anderson if he needed an escort through security. To Anderson it seemed like a stroke of luck, when in fact it had been the result of a call made moments earlier by one of Bansmer's fellow agents. This helpful policeman led Anderson past the X-ray machine and toward his departure gate, the duffel bag bouncing against his hip as he walked. Moments later, Bansmer saw the glorious sight of a female undercover agent carrying Anderson's bag. Anderson had made the handoff. He was a heroin trafficker.

Joey met Anderson outside the terminal and walked him to his car. Bansmer stayed in character until the final curtain, taking an inordinately dangerous risk by handing Anderson's loaded firearm back to him. "You did a nice job," he said. "You didn't freeze in the middle of it."

"Naw, fuck, I'm cool. I'm used to pressure by now."

Joey asked Anderson again about Tracy's location. Anderson said he was having a federal employee look into it, and "if she can't do it, then I'm gonna find her. 'Cause I'm gonna call the halfway houses and ask for her."

"Uh huh," Joey said. "I'll meet you over at your car." Bansmer pretended to walk toward his own vehicle so he could get Anderson's money. "Fifteen [thousand] will do it?" he asked.

"Oh, yeah," Anderson said.

Anderson never saw the eight federal agents approaching. One second he was walking toward his car, and the next second the agents were in front of him, guns drawn, like a jump-cut in a movie. The first time Marc Harris heard the tape-recorded scream Anderson let out at that moment, he could not suppress laughter. The clunk that followed was the sound of a Smith & Wesson in a fanny pack hitting concrete.

If a soul is left in darkness, sins will be committed. The guilty one is not he who commits the sin, but he who causes the darkness.

—VICTOR HUGO

Chapter 43

Jimmy Washington was smarter than Rodney Anderson, so arresting him was easier. Undercover DEA agent Salvador Leyva did an Oscar-worthy job of impersonating "Tony," the Tijuana trucker who was driving Joey Gambino's drug shipment through Detroit. "Tony" met Jimmy at a Chili's restaurant and explained what he had. Jimmy agreed to return to Chili's that afternoon with buyers and cash.

Several DEA agents were waiting for him. Jimmy was arrested in the parking lot. Forty minutes later, one of his buyers arrived and met an identical fate. Special Agent Leyva and his colleagues found $172,000 in her trunk.

Marc Harris got a phone call before breakfast the next morning. When he hung up, he looked at his wife and said, "That's it. It's over."

Over, that is, for everyone but Darryl Henley. When Darryl finally stepped out of the marshals' van that had whisked him from MDC, he found himself outside the San Bernardino County Detention Center, or CDC, as it was known, a facility infamous among inmates for its harsh conditions and uncaring staff of sheriff's deputies. One of those deputies thrust at Henley a stack of "oranges" (county-issue orange uniforms) and a "roll" (a blanket wrapped around toiletries, writing paper, and a golf pencil), and led him to a six-by-nine cell on an otherwise empty tier. Henley's door was left open, allowing him access to the pay phones down the hall, but the lines were all dead. When he complained, he was told that he would receive no privileges whatsoever. No phone calls, no visits.

Night fell, and a desert chill settled into the concrete walls around him. Two deputies appeared and escorted Henley through a dark hallway lit only by their flashlight. A light switch was flipped, revealing a cell the size of a closet. The bunk and toilet were a step apart, the latter a reeking bowl lined with the dried excretions of previous tenants. Darryl reached to flush it, but there was no handle. The vent high over his head was the only relief.

The door closed behind him with a thud. The light went out.

All this for using a cell phone? he thought. Certainly Mikey hadn't ratted him out about what was *discussed* on that phone. Mikey would've had to capture their talks on tape to bring things to this stage. And if there was one thing Henley was sure of, it was that Joey wasn't hot. That dude was scary to talk to. "What the fuck?" Darryl said aloud. *Had the feds bugged the typewriter room?* He'd heard about jailhouse wiretaps. *Are they bugging this room?*

The *Los Angeles Times* would report a few days later that Henley faked a suicide attempt in his cell that night. A government spokesman said that Henley had been found "on the floor of his cell with a makeshift rope, fashioned out of pieces of clothing, tied around his neck as if he had tried to hang himself" from the vent. Uninjured, Henley had refused a trip to the hospital. When Darryl spoke to T. J. Simers later, he "brushed aside questions about the incident and would only say that 'at some point, everyone will know what really has happened to him.'" Years later, Henley admitted that he had tried to take his own life. The old wives' tale about one's worst crimes flashing before one's eyes when the end seems near, he said, was not an old wives' tale at all.

Henley walked into a federal courtroom three days later a beaten, deflated man. May 28, 1996, was the first time Marc Harris ever laid eyes on Henley. Although his face was fatigued, Henley's walk still showed a slight strut, revealing the side of him he'd flashed during those MDC phone calls. He still hadn't been told why he was in court, but by now he knew they'd gotten him on the "judge thing"—a hunch that was confirmed when he was handed a government document filled with every detail of Michael Bansmer's investigation, including the two contract hits Henley had approved. Henley read it silently at the defense table, and as he did so, Harris recalled later, the athlete turned as white as Harris's dress shirt. The arrogance that had sustained and misinformed Henley during the previous three years vanished from him in that moment, almost visibly, like the soul leaves the newly dead.

The next day the *Times* headline read, "Henley Accused of Plotting to Kill Judge." The stunned gasps of those who knew Darryl best were almost audible throughout Southern California and the NFL. The Darryl Henley jokes came instantly. "Gives new meaning to the term *cell* phone" was a popular one. Laypersons either shook their heads balefully at Henley's new low point, or laughed at it, or feared Henley for it, or never noticed it at all amid the continuing tremors of the O.J. earthquake. Those who did take notice could not find much tragedy in a demise fostered by what appeared to be a crippling case of stupidity. Did Henley really think he could kill his trial judge and the star witness against him and get away with it? The *Register* received an old Darryl Henley football card from a reader—a promotional item bearing the slogan "Drug Use Is Life Abuse"—with a letter to the editor calling it "ironic, prophetic, and pathetic."

447

Henley's most embarrassing crime was that he'd once again underestimated federal law enforcement, the entity that had already used phone calls to nail him — three times. Learning from his mistakes had once been among his greatest assets as an athlete. When Tom Hayes drilled into his young UCLA cornerbacks, "If you make the same mistake twice, I won't play you," Henley listened. But Henley's college days seemed like a lifetime ago. In May 1996, that once-wide-eyed freshman was sitting with federal prosecutor Marc Harris, discussing the possibility of spending the rest of his life in prison. As they spoke, Henley traced his finger through the air in an ascending line, trying to explain how he'd veered off course, before dropping it to the table like a falling airplane. "It doesn't even look like my life anymore," he said.

Henley had become everything the government said he was, and worse. One of the bitterest pills he had to swallow was the knowledge that everyone involved with the prosecution of the 1993 "Tracy case" could now say, "I told you so." Henley had been a bloodthirsty drug trafficker from day one, it now appeared, and his cries of foul play in the 1993 case could now be dismissed simply by pressing "Play" on those MDC audiotapes. After hearing them, how could anyone doubt that Tracy had been telling the truth at trial? How could anyone doubt that Henley had gone looking for a juror to bribe? That he'd bullied Mike Malachowski into helping him pull off that bribe? That he'd been a hardcore criminal in football player's clothing his whole life?

Darryl's parents learned that their son was a murder solicitor on the evening news. Their phone didn't ring like it had in 1993, when friends and family called day and night wondering what was going on, where the mistake had been made. The phone was silent now.

Mrs. Henley called Darryl's friend, sportswriter Bob Keisser of the *Long Beach Press-Telegram*, seeking help. "I've only told two other people about that call," Keisser said years later, recounting a memory he'd just as soon forget. "Things were obviously going backward for him real fast at that time. His mom called, and she basically said,

'Darryl needs help because the white people are trying to kill him.'"
Keisser paused, choked up. "I mean, what do you do?"

Keisser today chooses to harken back to better times—his chance
meetings with Mrs. Henley when she had seemed like the proudest woman on earth, his one-on-one interviews with her son, the
greatest beneficiary of her kindness. "If I wanted to go see somebody with a smile on his face and a good word, I'd see Darryl,"
Keisser recalled. "If I had a tough question to ask, I'd ask Darryl.
A lot of guys in his shoes had a limited knowledge of life outside
football. Darryl was different. He was a team leader. Other guys
looked up to him. I saw all those characteristics, and they all added up to a good person. One hundred percent of my interaction
with him was like that. . . . I can honestly say he's among the top
ten athletes I've covered over my career. And he's still there."

Eric Henley was arrested in Waco, without incident, the day after
Darryl appeared in court. In Eric's wallet, investigators found Thomas's business card from Goldman Sachs, Darryl's Shell gas card, and
Eric's ATM statement, which showed a balance of $115.03—hard-
ly the fortune of a cross-country drug trafficker. But that's exactly what Eric Henley would be considered from that day forward.

Eric was charged with felony drug conspiracy in the LA-to-De-
troit deal orchestrated by informant Ced McGill. Darryl was also
charged in that case, of course, as were Ronald Knight, Donald
Knight, Alisa Denmon, and Kym Taylor (Kym for delivering messages to and from Darryl). The only good part about Darryl's dark
cell in the San Bernardino Detention Center was that its isolation
made it impossible for him to get in any more trouble. All his life
he had been a people person, a social magnet, a trait that had certainly played a role in his downfall. But now no one was near him.
Reported the LA Daily News: "They could put Darryl Henley in
twenty-four-hour isolation in an ultra-maximum security penitentiary and he would probably still find a way to further screw [up]."
That theory would be tested soon enough.

Darryl had never thought about fleeing—not at any point during the fire and brimstone of the previous three years—but that changed in San Bernardino. *If I can just get out of here*, he thought, *they ain't never gonna see me again.* What he pondered most, though, was that his little brother was in a cell because of him.

Remembering the nervous days when Darryl had been building the doomed Detroit deal, Kym Taylor recalled Eric telling her: "I'm not comfortable with what he's asking me to do."

Kym had confronted Darryl about it. "What are you doing?" she asked. "Eric is uncomfortable."

"Tell Eric to do what I asked him to do."

"I said, 'Rethink this,'" Kym recalled.

"You don't need to worry about what I'm doing."

Kym paused and sighed. "You just didn't question him," she said.

On June 11, 1996, Darryl Henley was formally charged with participating in a murder-for-hire scheme, conspiring to traffic drugs, and bribing a prison guard. Judge Gary Taylor removed himself from all matters pertaining to Henley to avoid any appearance of bias against the man who had tried to have him killed. This meant that a new judge would rule on Darryl's motion for a new trial and, if that motion were denied, decide Henley's sentence.

Taylor was still in charge of the other four defendants, and that summer he denied their new trial motions and sentenced Busta-mante and West to twenty years in prison. Willie got seventeen and a half years. Rex got twelve and a half.

When what became known as "the judge threat" first hit the news, T. J. Simers tracked Henley down in San Bernardino and pulled into the CDC parking lot at the same instant as Darryl's family. Only relatives and preapproved friends were allowed to visit the facility's highest-profile inmate, but the Henleys helped Simers get in by signing him in as a "family friend" from out of town. Simers didn't talk much inside the visiting room that day. Mostly he watched and listened. He watched Gia Henley take some of her first steps, and listened to her happy yelps bounce off the glossy cinderblock walls as her father looked down at her with a mix of pride and humiliation. Simers wrote a story for the *Times* about that visit, titled "Not My Son." "We're talking about the U.S. government, which is all power outside of God," T.H. told Simers inside CDC. "God has assured us He is going to take care of this situation. If He doesn't, the whole family will perish.

"You hear in court how your son is the number seven dope drug lord in the world and that he's a gangster," T.H. added, "and you just know your son and that's not him. . . . Darryl was ripe. . . . He was running with the wrong people, and it snowballed."

Years later, *Press-Telegram* writer Bob Keisser recalled that he'd believed Henley's complaints about his unfair trial—"until the judge stuff. I didn't believe Darryl Henley hung with guys who were around drugs." But after the murder charges, "people who thought well of Darryl slapped themselves. What happened here? [*Register* columnist] Steve Bisheff asked me, 'Aren't you embarrassed for sticking by him?' I didn't know what to tell him. I liked Darryl. He treated me well."

Said Bisheff: "The story went from 'He made a bad mistake' to 'What *is* this guy?' . . . I remember being shocked. There's no way you could have predicted that. I covered O.J. during his Heisman season, and if you would have told me that thirty years later he'd be the major defendant in the world's biggest murder case—

"You learn in our business," Bisheff added after a pause, "you never really know these people."

Apparently, T.H.'s hometown paper didn't know these people either. The *Waco Tribune-Herald* reported that "Daryl [*sic*] Henley" had previously been "kicked out of the NFL for violations of its substance abuse policy." (Henley had never been kicked out of the NFL, and he had never violated its substance abuse policy.) [1] According to the *Register*, Henley had "offered to use money from [the heroin] transaction to pay for the killings of Taylor and [Donaho]," when in truth, that offer had come from undercover DEA agent Mike Bansmer. Henley knew that his acceptance of Joey's offer was hideous, but he at least wanted the facts straight. His attorney, however, was too shocked to process it all, much less demand corrections from the media. The murder charges were the "antithesis of who he was," Jim Riddet said years later, still moved by the shock he felt that summer. "You could have knocked me over with a feather. . . . He was so well spoken. Educated. It makes you believe in the theory of dual personality—that some people have a darker side. And I was just as astounded by how quickly he pled guilty."

Henley had decided to plead guilty to the murder and heroin charges while alone in his cell in San Bernardino, moments before a visit from his aunt Wanda. Like the rest of his family, Aunt Wanda wanted him to fight the charges with an entrapment defense. Darryl told her he was going to own up to what he'd done.

"Why?" she asked.

"Because at one point," he said, "I really wanted it to happen."

October 16, 1996—the day Darryl and Eric Henley submitted their guilty pleas—was the first time they had seen each other since the prison visits that started the whole thing back in the spring. As the proceedings began, Eric leaned toward Darryl and asked, "You sure we should do this?"

It was a good question. Eric could have won had his case gone to trial. No drugs had been transported, bought, or sold in the failed McGill deal. But standing trial was a gamble that the Henleys had learned not to take.

"I'm sure," Darryl said. [2]

Rodney Anderson was convicted of drug trafficking and murder solicitation after a five-day trial. Anderson's defense was that the only reason he had helped Henley was because Ron Knight threatened his life. The jury considered this a joke. The judge called Anderson "a complete phony" and sentenced him to thirty-four years in prison. Jimmy Washington got eleven years.

During the buildup to Henley's sentencing, Marc Harris wrote that Henley's "precise motive for these murders is not clear," which made it unanimous: three of the country's brightest young prosecutors could find no reason for the foolish, dangerous acts Henley had committed over the preceding three years. The U.S. Probation Office gleaned from its interview of Henley that he had indeed "wanted Donaho and possibly Malachowski eliminated, but . . . 'Joey' was the first person to bring up to the defendant the idea of the government official. . . . The more D. Henley thought about the 'hits,' the more real they became."

The probation report continued: "The defendant appears to be a self-centered individual who has little or no respect for human life. He even attempted to finance payment for these murders through narcotics trafficking. The defendant's continued and increasingly serious criminal behavior while incarcerated evidences his blatant disregard for the justice system and his continuing belief that he is above the law."

Years later, William Kopeny, an experienced, highly respected attorney who had assisted Henley's defense team from behind the scenes, may have pinpointed Henley's motives best. "Vanity and cool," he said. "That's the only thing I can come up with. Vanity and cool."

Epilogue

The popular Italian restaurant that Phil Trani owns in Long Beach has long been a second home to UCLA athletes and coaches. Bruins memorabilia line the dark wood walls, including a poster-size shot of 1968 Heisman winner Gary Beban, in gold and blue Technicolor, running around end, and an autographed photo of John Wooden hovering over the rows of polished scotch glasses. It is no exaggeration to say that Trani has spent most of his life in the restaurant's kitchen. Its walls have been fogged orange over the years by marinara and autographed in magic marker by seemingly every famous athlete who has ever passed through Los Angeles. James Washington's name is on there, squeezed between the signatures of gold medalists, All-Americans, and MVPS from every pro league. Trani looks at the signatures, hands on hips, and recalls nineteen-year-old Darryl Henley throwing a football in this very kitchen with

Steven Kinney at his sentencing, 2003. (Gary Thompson/*Las Vegas Review-Journal*)

his son, attending Trani family christenings, "signing autographs for every kid he passed in Pedro." He conceded that there was a big difference between that Darryl and the Darryl who was always switching phone numbers in 1993 and 1994 and asking Trani if he knew any judges who owed him a favor.

There are five photos in Trani's spartan office. The largest is an autographed shot of Henley in his Rams uniform, sprinting upfield with the ball under his arm. "Darryl was like my kid," Trani explains, looking at the photo as fathers look at sons who have been lost at war. *Phil, Thanks for being such a father-figure to me,* Henley wrote in his bubbly cursive. *I love you, Darryl Henley #20.*

The second largest photo is of a handsome man in an expensive suit—Henley's cell neighbor at Marion. *Phil: Just a quick note letting you know our friend speaks of you always. I hope this finds you well and with a clear mindset. Take care and stay strong. Your friend, John Gotti.*

Trani looks like a bit like a mobster himself. The authorities have long suspected that he has Mob ties, but the truth is that the stocky, sixtyish Italian American has more friends in the FBI than in the Mafia. This misperception, Trani says, is what has prevented him from responding to all the letters Henley has written to him from prison. "I figure if I write a letter back to him, it's going to put me on the FBI's mailing list," Trani once told a former federal agent. "I don't want that, but this kid was like a son to me. What do I do?"

"The kid's dead," the FBI man replied. "Leave it alone, Phil. He's dead."

Phil Trani cries as he tells this story.

Darryl did not meet John Gotti when he first arrived at Marion. Only after he was moved from protective custody to the regular compound was Darryl put in a cell next to the most famous Gambino of them all. That Darryl had been pinched by a fed pretending to share Gotti's Gambino blood became an inside joke between them. Gotti knew a bit about informants himself, having been done in by Sammy "The Bull" Gravano, a former confidant whose trial testimony all but secured Gotti's life sentence. Gotti assured Henley more than once: "Sammy Gravano was not my underboss. I swear on my grandkids." But Gotti's hands had been tied at trial, he said. If he'd stepped up and denied Gravano's claims,

"I woulda had to incriminate a hundred other guys." It was another of the many things Henley and Gambino had in common,
one of the shared aches they would lament together in Marion.

Darryl married Alisa there in December 1997. They were not allowed to touch during the ceremony. Instead, they exchanged their
vows through a wall of Plexiglas and passed their rings through a
sliding drawer like the ones at gas stations in bad neighborhoods.
The Marion staff was firm about allowing only two guests, so the
Henley wedding party consisted of two-year-old Gia and a female
elder from Alisa's church.

On September 26, 1997, at a ceremony at the Department of
Justice in Washington DC, John Rayburn, Deirdre Eliot, and Marc
Harris were given the Directors Award for their efforts in prosecuting Henley and his codefendants. Simultaneously, justice ad-
vocates across the country were protesting the government's ability to offer sentencing leniency and money to criminal witnesses,
arguing that if defense attorneys tried to arrange such deals, they'd
be prosecuted for bribery. The Tenth Circuit Court of Appeals
agreed with them in 1998, ruling that "testimony from a witness
who had been offered a lower sentence in exchange for the prosecution of a codefendant violated the federal bribery statute and
should not be admitted." It was an earth-shaking ruling, but it
lasted just six months before it was rejected by the entity that T.H.
Henley had once called "all power outside of God." U.S. attorneys,
the government decided, could continue offering enticements to
witnesses, while defense lawyers who did the same risked disbar-
ment and prosecution.

These are the inconsistencies that buoyed the hope of Dorothy Henley. The system was obviously corrupt and prone to error:
Can't you people see that's what happened to Darryl? Then in 2001,
the Ninth Circuit Court of Appeals reviewed Judge Taylor's decision to deny Henley's codefendants a new trial. Judge Stephen Reinhardt concluded, "The evidence pertaining to O'Reilly's alleged
racist remarks was contradictory," and "the Sixth Amendment is

violated by 'the bias or prejudice of even a single juror.' One racist juror would be enough." Reinhardt and his colleagues advised Taylor to "enter detailed findings concerning whether O'Reilly actually made racist remarks and, if so, their specific content." It was not a mandate for a new trial, but it *was* a public scolding of Taylor for his hasty dismissal of the O'Reilly/racism issue five years earlier. Instead of "detailed findings," however, Taylor and the U.S. attorneys quickly reduced the sentences of Henley's codefendants in what came off as an effort to make the new appellate ruling go away. Henley, who had been tried by the same biased jurors, would receive no such sentence reduction, having agreed to drop his new trial motion as part of his plea deal in the MDC case. And so Taylor and the prosecutors avoided a media dust-up by simply freeing Henley's codefendants. Rex Henley was released in February 2002, one year after the Ninth Circuit's ruling. Garey West got out that August, Willie McGowan in January 2003. Rafael Bustamante was released in April 2004. The grudge Bustamante had once held against Henley was long gone, for as his former attorney said, "The best thing that ever happened to him was Darryl Henley trying to bribe those jurors."

Henley's good behavior in Marion helped T. J. Simers secure an interview with him when the Rams were making their Super Bowl run in January 2000. The thirty-three-year-old who might have been the leader of the Rams' defense that season was instead locked up in the worst federal prison in the country, just a hundred miles from St. Louis, where he told Simers: "I had never heard of this place and had no idea where it was, and I get here and all they show on TV are the Rams. I remember saying to myself, 'God, now you're really punishing me.'"

Simers's interview, conducted through a phone line and a pane of Plexiglas, resulted in the most lucid piece of journalism ever produced about Henley. He had traveled to Marion with the intent of "getting Darryl to admit to the judge thing." He encountered little resistance once he got there. "Yeah, I was involved in the conspiracy to commit murder," Henley told Simers. "When it was brought up to me on the phone in jail, I said, 'How ridiculous.' But an hour later I'm entertaining the idea and then I'm on the phone listening to how it can actually be done. That whole process started on a Thursday night and ended the next Wednesday and shaped the rest of my life." He added, "The reality of it now is prison. The message—the result—has to be greater than the why. I put myself in handcuffs; I put myself in Marion by the decisions I made." Henley still insisted, however, that the 1993 case had been a sham. "Henley vigorously defended himself on the drug charges that began his troubles and still maintains he was not guilty of many of the specific things suggested by the government. But he acknowledges that he knew what was going on, and given the opportunity to stop it, he did not."

Henley told Simers several times that he didn't want to be portrayed as a crusader. That label, Henley felt, implied that he'd done everything the government said he did and that now he was seeking public forgiveness. "To me, that sounded like a confession," Henley said recently. "I don't do confessions about that [1993] case."

The only thing Darryl got out of the Ninth Circuit's opinion was an online version of it to which he could direct people interested in reading the lesser-known details about his downfall. His transfer from Marion to the slightly lower security penitentiary in Florence, Colorado—part of the complex that housed the Unabomber, Ted Kaczynski, and Ramzi Yousef, mastermind of the 1993 World Trade Center bombing—may or may not have been related to the Ninth Circuit's opinion, but Henley didn't care. Although USP Florence also served as the headquarters of the Aryan Brotherhood, compared to Marion it was "like going to heaven," Henley said. The food was a thousand times better. He began tutoring and teaching inmates in GED and pre-GED classes. He would go on to help hundreds of inmates earn the equivalent of a high school diploma. He continued to receive letters and visits from Cliff Hicks, the player he'd competed against for his first NFL starting job and the only Ram to visit him at all four of his prison stops (LA MDC, San Bernardino CDC, USP Marion, and USP Florence). Henley played shortstop in Florence's softball league, posting a highly unofficial batting average of .750. In Florence, Henley held his daughter Gia for the first time in five years.

Darryl's continued good behavior allowed him to request a transfer to California to be closer to his family. Although his transfer was granted, his destination was the diametric opposite: a new penitentiary in rural Lee County, Virginia. Henley arrived there in the fall of 2002.

He wasn't the last thing on my mind that Christmas, just number four or so on the list of stories I wanted to get to one day. I had followed his story as a college student at the University of Florida, where it arrived as just a news blip. I had forgotten much of it by December 2002, when my wife slipped John Feinstein's newest book, *The Punch*, under our Christmas tree. I'm still not sure why, but Feinstein's account of the near-fatal blow Kermit Washington struck to Rudy Tomjanovich's face during a 1977 NBA fistfight—and more important, its aftermath—inspired me to write a letter to Darryl Henley. Particularly moving was the character arc of Washington, the black NBA forward who tried desperately after nearly killing Tomjanovich to prove that he was not what that horrific moment said he was. Before the punch, Washington had often been described as a gentle giant. After it, he became The Goon Who Caved Rudy T's Face In. By 1980, Washington would be ruined in nearly every way a man can be ruined.

I dug up my thin Darryl Henley file, flipped through the newspaper stories I'd tossed in it over the years, and wrote him a letter on January 2, 2003. I sent him a copy of *The Punch*, which he read in two days. He responded on January 8:

"Mike, I've been sitting here for a couple of days now trying to figure out what it is about your letter that has me giving it so much attention. Ever since I've been locked up I have had no less than 60–75 of these requests, and most of these I don't give much attention to." Offering no guarantees, he invited me to visit him in Virginia to see if "our personalities jive."

This is probably the best place to remind readers that Darryl Henley was my primary source of information for this book. I communicated with him through letters, phone calls, and in person. During our earliest visits I told him that my aim was to write a narrative based on research and reporting, one that would not necessarily paint him in a positive light. To my surprise, after conferring with his family (most of whom understandably didn't like the idea), he agreed. He looked back on his decision eight years later and explained: "I knew that if I was happy with every word you wrote, the book wouldn't be worth the paper it was written on. It would be a failure."

Although a number of Henley's recollections were proven inaccurate by my other research, these instances were not nearly as numerous as the times his information and leads proved accurate—often in ways unflattering to him. His willingness to implicate himself in crimes both known and unknown further augmented his credibility. The "Hollywood Hills heist" of 1996 (chapter 38) is an example of an incident that was unprosecuted as of this book's first printing. (It was confirmed by confidential documents produced about it in 1996 and subsequent personal interviews.)

I agreed to the only condition Henley posed: that he be allowed to review the manuscript prior to publication to look for passages that might affect his safety in prison. Henley requested roughly a dozen changes in the manuscript on this point, nearly all of which involved his time at the Metropolitan Detention Center in Los Angeles—still a boiling cauldron of grudges, agendas, and corruption.[1] Action was taken on roughly half of Henley's requests. A few names were changed. No truths were twisted, but a few were removed. The expertise of several publishing and legal professionals was consulted to ensure that these changes were made responsibly.

A journalist would be hard pressed to find an onion more challenging to peel than a ten-year-old drug trafficking conspiracy—let alone two—which is why I'm fortunate to have come across as many legal documents, transcripts, law enforcement reports, audiotapes, and newspaper interviews as I have. My wife has often wished that she could take back *The Punch*, for the boxes holding these materials have occupied a larger space in our home than the two children we've brought into the world since I began this work. Having been produced by humans, each of these sources—including my personal interviews—is clouded to varying degrees by the self-interest of those involved. I found my personal interviews and the newspapers to be my most dependable sources—particularly the reporting in the *Los Angeles Times*, whose staff in the 1990s is due a great amount of any praise this book might receive. Journalists Davan Maharaj, Tracy Weber, Mark Platte, Michael P. Reilley, Susan Marquez-Owen, Anna Cekola, Chris Dufresne, the inimitable Thomas Bonk, and the even more inimitable T. J. Simers have my undying gratitude. Other than Henley's cooperation and my stubborn belief that this was a story worth telling, Simers's reporting during the 1990s was the most important factor in making this book possible.

My interviews with Henley's former teammates proved as vibrant as they were valuable. One of the first interviews I conducted was with James Washington, the Watts gangbanger turned Super Bowl champion turned West LA businessman and broadcaster. Near the end of our three-hour conversation, Washington lowered his head, as if searching for answers on the floor of his impressive Century City office. When he lifted his eyes, they were filled with tears. "I wasn't there to protect him," said Washington, the lead blocker on so many of Henley's pro and college punt returns. "I guess that's the biggest thing, man. I protected him for so long. I wasn't there to protect him. I wasn't there to make that block for him."

Former Ram Anthony Newman recalled a letter he received from Henley around the time of Henley's sentencing. "You know me for me," it read, "not for all this stuff. You know me for me. Keep that."

"Any black athlete can tell you that he knows a drug dealer," said Chuck Miller, Henley's UCLA teammate. "Maybe it's a cousin, a cousin's friend. . . . When you hit it big, the first thing they come at you with is, 'Loan me some money. I'll pay you back.' When I first heard about what happened with Darryl, I already had it figured it out. But the layperson just pictures him sitting at home, making $800,000 a year, thinking, 'How can I get richer? I know. I'll be a drug lord!' It didn't happen like that. And I didn't have to know any specifics about the case to realize that. I knew Darryl."

According to Louis Oliver, a former NFL safety and one of Henley's closest friends, moving drugs in the off-season was not an uncommon enticement for NFL players.

"I remember just as clear as day on the plane," Oliver said. "We were on the plane flying and [Dolphins running back] Sammie [Smith] was sitting behind me and another teammate. . . . He tapped me and my teammate and said, 'Yo man, would you guys run drugs in the off-season?' I was like, 'Run drugs? For what? Why? What sense would that make?' . . . He said, 'Because for one, we play NFL football. . . . Let's say we was making runs up to Atlanta. If five-oh [the police] stops us, all we got to do is show them our NFL card if they want to know why you're driving a Mercedes, BMW, Porsche, whatever. . . . They're not going to want to check your car, yadda yadda yadda.' I said, 'Why would you risk that when you're already making a million dollars doing what we do for seven months out of the year?' . . . He was emphatic about it: 'I'm telling you. We can get away with it. . . . It's just free money.'" Oliver laughed, then and now, at the lunacy of it.

A gifted running back who had been drafted by the Dolphins

with the ninth pick of the 1989 draft—the same draft that produced Henley and Oliver—Sammie Smith pled guilty in 1996 to two federal cocaine trafficking charges. He served five years in prison. "The only answer I can come up with is stupidity," he told the Associated Press upon his release. "I didn't need money. I was fine. . . . It was a matter of hanging around these guys. These were my friends, and I just couldn't turn my back on them. . . . We saw an easy way to make money. . . . These were the people who were still my friends, even when I was a professional player."

The sister of NFL wide receiver Sam Hurd foresaw the same dangers creeping toward her brother. "Everyone knows he has a generous heart and is not the kind of person to say no," she told the *San Antonio Express-News* in 2008, for a profile of Hurd that portrayed him as a clean-living success story. "I kind of get upset because people take advantage of him."

In January 2012 Hurd was charged with participating in a high-volume cocaine trafficking operation that spanned from Texas to Chicago.

Darryl Henley was transferred from the high-security prison in Virginia to a medium-security facility in Beaumont, Texas, in 2004, partially because of his positive disciplinary record and his service as a teacher. He was elated to be closer to his parents, who had moved back to Texas. His brothers were close by, too, having started families of their own in the state where their parents were born and raised. Gia now had the option of staying with her grandparents or one of her uncles when she flew from California to visit her dad.

FCC Beaumont Medium was where most of my visits with Henley took place. Although labeled medium-security, it's part of a Federal Corrections Complex that houses higher-security inmates, and it is the site of more physical violence than the staff there would like. A bloody Latino vs. black uprising in December 2010 left Beaumont Medium on lockdown for over a month.

In the expansive visiting room, which is set up like a school cafeteria, I have seen Henley advise younger inmates to explain prison to their children as "a factory where all the workers have to stay overnight and wear the same uniform." The truth, he explained in a whisper, is easier for kids to understand later.

During one of our conversations, Henley accidentally knocked the cap off his Aquafina water bottle, sending it skittering across the table; in a split second, he convulsed smoothly and caught it before it hit the floor. "My hands are still pretty good," he said with a sad smile.

My appetite was a running joke between us. Each time I went to the vending machines in the corner of the room (off-limits to inmates), I'd offer to get him something, but he almost always declined. I found his lack of appetite as surprising as he found my surplus of one, until the day I asked him how he could go an entire day without eating.

"Four years in Marion," he said.

During our earliest conversations, Henley would pause and warn me: "Don't believe a word of what I'm saying. There are documents and witnesses out there that tell this thing better than I ever could." His words were prescient, but one thing I struggled to corroborate over the years was his opinion of Steven Kinney, the man more responsible than anyone but Henley and his codefendants for his two convictions. I couldn't even find him. "Dude was strange," Henley told me during one of our first talks. "You can say what you want about, 'Everybody in jail thinks he's innocent,' but there was something about Kinney that was just *off*." I took it with a grain of salt. Al Capone probably said the same about Eliot Ness.

Then I learned that in 2002, just as Henley's codefendants were being released from prison, Kinney was arrested on charges of soliciting young boys for sex. He had been transferred to the DEA's Las Vegas office several years earlier and had been questioned by the police there as early as 2001 for approaching a twelve-year-old boy with a lewd offer. In January 2002 Kinney approached two brothers, ages fourteen and eleven, as they shopped for toys inside a Wal-Mart. He tossed a small rock at their feet with a note that read, "You're hot, do you want to make $20?" and indicated that he wanted to perform oral sex on them. "I'm cool/safe," the note continued. "If you want to do it, meet at the soda machine, front of store." Moments later, Kinney approached them in person and repeated his offer. The boys fled and found their mother, who found the police, who returned to find the suspect gone.

The note-wrapped pebble would be Kinney's calling card. In all, more than fifteen boys in the Las Vegas area would come forward claiming that Kinney had approached them. (None said that they'd been molested.) Before that, the only person who suspected Kinney of wrongdoing was his wife — also a DEA investigator — who had been secretly keeping an eye on her husband after he was questioned by police in 2001. Although that questioning hadn't resulted in charges, it prompted an internal DEA investigation. Mrs. Kinney told investigators that her husband asked her to get rid of the hard drive on their home computer because it contained information that could get him fired. She did as she was told, but held onto the old drive and installed a keystroke program that recorded each character Kinney typed into the new one. After discovering incriminating e-mails her husband had sent to a boy, she turned everything over to the FBI.

Kinney was arrested on March 12, 2003, his fingerprints and handwriting having linked him to one of the notes he'd tossed. The DEA fired him. He was charged with sixty-six felony counts of soliciting sex from minors. Inexplicably, he was freed on bond. Forbidden from returning to the residence he'd once shared with his wife, police found him there anyway, removing boxes through the garage. Still, the court allowed him his freedom, even after he pled guilty to fifteen of the sixty-six felony counts, plus a federal charge of coercion and enticement. He was allowed to relocate to the South and move in with his parents.

467

In May 2003 video surveillance at a Wal-Mart in Mississippi caught Kinney tossing notes to three boys. These notes were different; there was cash attached to them. Kinney lured two of the boys into a nearby restroom, but the father of one of the boys interrupted the scene and physically detained Kinney until police arrived. (Kinney tried to quell the situation by identifying himself as a DEA agent, despite having been fired several months earlier.) Three state counts of attempted molestation and one count of possessing counterfeit $20 bills (the cash tucked into the note had been fake) were added to his jacket. This time he was jailed without bond.

Kinney "appeared angry" at his sentencing, the *Las Vegas Review-Journal* reported. The disgraced agent sat and listened as his attorney, David Chesnoff, asked the court for leniency in light of Kinney having once foiled a "plot to kill a federal judge in Southern California." Chesnoff (who had represented Darryl Henley briefly in the late 1990s) called Kinney's current troubles "a very sad situation because he obviously has issues of an emotional and psychiatric nature which overpowered his good impulses." Chesnoff reiterated Kinney's claim that he'd been sexually abused as a child, and that his crimes reflected "more anger than sexual."

Assistant U.S. attorney Nancy Koppe was not moved. Responding to Chesnoff's claim that Kinney had once worn "the white hat of law enforcement," Koppe pointed out that "some of these crimes were committed while he was on DEA time." She added that Kinney "is not angry. He's sexually attracted to children."

Kinney was sentenced to four years, nine months in federal prison. His request that he be sent to a facility in Texas, so he could be close to his parents, was granted.

Darryl Henley was transferred to Texas, closer to *his* parents, two months after Kinney was. When he told his family about Kinney's conviction, Dorothy Henley responded by quoting Proverbs 19:5 by heart: "A false witness shall not be unpunished, and he that speaketh lies shall not escape."

In a 2005 letter to me, Kinney wrote: "My story, which I still can't believe, has some truth and a lot of lies by federal & state law enforcement. I allowed it to happen by playing into others' hands. I wanted to write it myself, and have started it several times, but it becomes too emotional, and I get on the wrong tract." With the exception of "& state," Darryl Henley had used identical words to describe his own downfall.

It would be unfair to theorize that Kinney's criminal acts in 2002–3 offered proof of his misconduct as a DEA agent during the Henley investigations — just as it would be unfair to retroactively declare Henley the mastermind of the "Tracy case" based on his actions inside MDC. In a series of letters written to me from prison, Kinney was surprisingly candid about Henley: "From the beginning, I felt Darryl was pulled into this by his friends and his uncle. He didn't need the money, but he knew that Willie McGowan (the real story!) gave up a sports career for the love of his sister. . . . I doubt if Darryl was ever to benefit financially. . . . I could see the whole case on Darryl being cleared by Willie McGowan sacrificing himself by owning up and testifying of Darryl's minimal involvement." Kinney described Tracy Donaho, whose trial testimony he'd helped craft, as "not as dumb as she'd have people believe. She basked in that Southern Gentleman chivalry from [Atlanta DEA agent Kevin] McLaughlin and others. I told her to cut it out with me. I'm referring to the 'Poor poor me, I was manipulated and seduced by these big dark black men.'

"I never thought she'd get as sweet a deal as she did," Kinney added. "Rayburn coached her [at trial]. I don't believe he asked her to lie about the specific elements of her involvement. But he did orchestrate the image of a seduced child taken advantage of . . . [a]nd Rayburn is close with Judge Taylor, he clerked for Taylor. Tell me a well placed eye wink couldn't work wonders. . . . I think she should have done 2-3 years in prison."

Kinney also made it clear that he had pursued Henley in hopes of getting to Suge Knight, a man he despised in a way that exceeded his role as a DEA agent. "If I'd had an arrest warrant for Suge Knight, my level of 'when do I shoot' would have been at the least legal reason, and it wouldn't be a cap gun, it would be a full load of oo buckshot from a 12 gauge."

Regarding this book, Kinney wrote: "I understand what Darryl feels, wanting his version of events to be disclosed, as he never took the stand, and held tight all the way through the sinking of the ship. I feel the same about my situation. . . . I can tell you, if I were still working there [DEA], I would not be allowed to talk to you. I'd be forced to say, Please contact our Public Affairs section in Los Angeles."

Gary Taylor retired from the federal bench in June 2005.

John Rayburn became a federal magistrate judge in 2006, and held that post for nearly three years before returning to the U.S. Attorney's Office. Repeated efforts to contact him were unsuccessful. He died in May 2012 of early onset Alzheimer's. He was fifty-two.

Deirdre Eliot was promoted to deputy chief of the U.S. Attorney's Office in Santa Ana, where she still works.

At last check, Rex Henley was running his own trucking business and living in the LA suburbs with his second wife and a growing passel of children. He credits the seven years he spent in prison as a turning point in his life. "I grew up a lot, learned a lot about myself, and met a lot of amazing people," he said.

Bryan Quihuis was sentenced to five years' probation for his role in the bribery scheme. He moved back in with his grandparents and was ordered to wear an electronic monitor on his ankle.

Michael Malachowski was released from prison in November 1997 and is currently working and raising his children.

Mikey Gambino was convicted in 2001 of felony assault on his spouse and was incarcerated for more than a year. Efforts to contact him since then have proven unsuccessful.

My initial efforts to locate Tracy Donaho were also unsuccessful. I was finally able to contact her thirdhand—through a friend of a friend—and had it relayed back to me that my request for an interview was answered with an emphatic *No*. A year or two into my work on this book, I received this e-mail: "Michael—I found on the internet your book . . . will be out soon. I am curious to know when. I am Tracy Donaho the ex-cheerleader and am anxious to see how this book reads. Thank you in advanced for you [*sic*] response. Tracy."

I responded by inviting Tracy (if it was indeed her) to help me determine how this book reads by granting me an interview. I did not receive a response. I contacted her former attorney, Stephan DeSales, who said he would relay my interview request to Tracy, then failed to return my subsequent calls and e-mails. Tracy's father politely declined an interview request when I contacted him in person at his home.

When I contacted Michael Bansmer, the retired DEA agent who had impersonated Joey Gambino, he told me that he was in the process of selling his version of the Henley-Joey story to Hollywood, and said he would have to check with his "movie people" before agreeing to speak with me. He called me the next morning and asked: "What is your agreement with Darryl Henley?" I replied that, by law, federal prisoners could not receive anything of value for telling their stories. Mr. Bansmer asked if I was a member of the Writers Guild. I told him that I had registered a couple of screenplays with the Guild a while back but was not a member. He said he had just spoken with his "friends" at the Writers Guild, and they had also told him I was not a member. Awkwardly, I thanked him for the information. "Once you dig and find the real facts," Bansmer continued, "you will see that Darryl Henley is the lowest form of life on earth." In response, I explained that what Henley really took issue with was his initial drug trafficking conviction, not Bansmer's investigation at MDC. Incredulous, Bansmer asked me what Darryl said had gone wrong with the "Tracy case." Against my better judgment, I answered: the scared daughter of a policeman testifying to keep herself out of prison, several criminal witnesses who had never met Henley doing the same, and overwhelming evidence of racial bias and drug use among the jurors. I stopped there.

"We don't live in a perfect world," Bansmer said.

These days Darryl Henley spends less energy than he used to thinking about the imperfections in his trial and the "what ifs" in his life: *What if I'd sat somewhere else at the Mount SAC Relays? What if I hadn't run into Willie that day?* He focuses more on keeping a low profile at FCC Beaumont. He rarely talks about himself with other inmates, only a few of whom know he played in the NFL, and he certainly doesn't talk with them about his deepening interest in prayer. Not long ago, when an older Beaumont inmate asked him if he kept in touch with God, Henley mumbled that he did, but he hadn't gotten much out of it yet. "What if you were God?" the inmate asked. "How would you want to be prayed to? Would you want to just hear begging all the time?" Darryl listened as the graying inmate taught him how to pray:

"First of all, you have to exalt God. Thank Him. Just thank Him. Thank Him for life, thank Him for all the good things in the world, thank Him for letting you wake up this morning. Thank Him for this sorry ass food we have to eat. Thank Him for that beautiful daughter you got. Second thing, you gotta pray for others. Pray for the kids in Ethiopia, man. Pray for all the homeless folks we can't feed in *this* country. . . . Then you gotta pray for that judge you threatened. Pray for that prosecutor—that their hearts won't be so hard. Shoot, pray for *me*. Lord knows I need it. Hard as I been trying to get back in court. And when you're done with all that, the last thing you do is pray for yourself. The very last thing. And when you do, just pray for forgiveness."

The old man rose, clapped Darryl on the shoulder, and left. The lump he left in Darryl's throat stayed there throughout his revised prayers that night and lasted until the next morning, when Darryl spotted the old man shuffling past, smiling, escorted by two correctional officers. The graying inmate had been called into court. "I need to teach you how to pray more often!" he yelled on his way out.

The government has no plans to release Darryl Henley until 2031, when he'll be sixty-five years old. He dreams of settling in Houston with the woman who has visited him more than anyone else over the years—a longtime friend who reconnected with him after he and Alisa completed what he called a "respectful divorce" in 2003.

"Shakespeare could write about it as a tragedy," said Damien athletic director Tom Carroll of Henley's downfall. "This is a tragedy because of the people involved. The family—it was such a wonderful family, and it just tore them to pieces, I know it did." Carroll paused to wipe away tears. "I don't know what to say other than God, what a terrible thing."

T. J. Simers still drops Henley's name from time to time into one of the acidic columns that have made him famous. ("I spent some time watching the San Diego Chargers practice this week. . . . I can't recall a more depressing visit since I stopped by Darryl Henley's prison cell.") Simers did not cry when reflecting on Henley. "This story isn't tragic," he said. "It's just incredibly sad. . . . Tragedy is when something bad happens to someone that's not of their own doing. Darryl got in trouble like a kid tells a lie . . . and then another lie, and things got so out of control in Darryl's case that it just swallowed him up. . . . He was a young athlete with a lot of money and things just snowballed."

Others went so far as to compare Henley to Father Damien, who lowered himself to the level of others, then watched them benefit while he suffered. (Damien died of leprosy after devoting his life to comforting an island of lepers.) John Carroll, an assistant coach at Damien who played with Darryl in the early 1980s, agreed with Simers's opinion that this isn't a tragedy. "No, a tragedy ends in death," he said. "This story isn't over yet."

Today the Beaumont inmates who do not call Henley "Teach" or

"DH" (sometimes it's hard to tell the difference) call him "Coach." He walks the sidelines of FCC Beaumont's ultracompetitive flag football league, and has coached his team to two consecutive championships. The games are played on a grass field surrounded by guard towers and scrolls of razor wire, and they attract hundreds of incarcerated spectators and wagers (postage stamps are like cash in prison), and feature elaborate game plans executed by former college players and even a few pros. (Former NFL running back Bam Morris served time at the facility shortly before Henley arrived.) The inmates begged Henley to play, but he refused, claiming that they didn't know how to play the game, and "the only thing I could accomplish out there is getting hurt." When he reluctantly agreed to coach, he learned that his new team had been called the Rams for years. One more coincidence. One more thing to laugh at.

When the Beaumont Medium Rams lost their starting quarterback to injury before a recent championship game, the thirty-eight-year-old Henley succumbed to the begging, started at quarterback, and guided his team to victory on surprisingly spry legs. It was the first time he'd played football since the more famous Rams played the Washington Redskins on Christmas Eve 1994 — the last game in LA Rams history. The joints he'd battered during his NFL career throbbed after the prison's championship game. Henley couldn't walk for two days, he said. "But it was worth it."

Acknowledgments

Yeats once wrote that a writer has a choice: "Perfection of the life or of the work." I know that both my life and my work are far from perfect in the most commonly accepted sense of the word, but I have my wife, Kelly, to thank for allowing me to spend the first ten years of our marriage tending to the latter more than the former. Typewritten words cannot convey what she meant to this process.

A close second atop the list of people responsible for this book's publication is Darryl Henley, whose brave candor and photographic memory provided countless details that proved invaluable in the researching and telling of his story. The trust he placed in me by telling me things he'd never shared with anyone inspired me to create a book that I can only hope conveys his life as compellingly as his firsthand account. I am deeply indebted to Thomas and Dorothy Henley, who in their commitment to helping me tell their son's story provided everything I asked for, including memories, photos, and documents, and plenty that I did not, namely their trust, hospitality, and grace.

My sincere gratitude also goes to Rex Henley, for inviting me into his home when he had nothing to gain by talking to me other than the freedom of delivering his truth. Darryl's older brother Thomas and his wife, Mrs. Thomas Henley III, overcame their initial reluctance enough to sit with me in a Dallas coffee shop until one in the morning—on a school night, no less. Eric Henley's warmth and his willingness to pick the scabs and show me what lay beneath them confirmed for me why this story is so important. There is a lot of hurt here—hurt I can never hope to understand. It was shared with me by brave and beautiful people.

Thanks is due to Darryl's former wife, Alisa Denmon, for mailing me Darryl's prison writings. To the late Clintell Henley: thank you for providing the missing trial transcripts. To Merina Hampton, Darryl's longtime friend and partner: thank you for grilling me, for never letting me rest, for reminding me of the sensitivity of this story and all that's at stake for those closest to it, and finally, for being an invaluable middlewoman between Darryl and me.

To Nick Ribaudo, who upon meeting me our freshman year in college and learning that I wanted to be a journalist told me bluntly, as only a future best friend can: "You'll never make it." Thanks for helping me make it, Nick. Mike Ribaudo was a wellspring of enthusiasm and inspiration during this journey, as were Louis Hagney, Mike Morrison, and Jason Bander—three of my dearest friends. Randy Vennewitz has been my most reliable advocate and sounding board since I moved to Los Angeles. George Noble's eager assistance with my research, specifically with tracking down Darryl's teammates and coaches, was invaluable. Andrew Pilger read my first ugly, awkward drafts and provided brilliant feedback. John Crosby believed in my writing when no one else did, and led me to Joel Gotler, who gave his time and advice during this book's awkward conception. Thanks to Daniel Torluemke, for his enthusiasm about and passion for this story. To Troll Sub-in, for lighting the Torch and keeping it lit. To Matt Fuerbringer, the embodiment of what a professional athlete should be: thanks for everything. Jordan Feagan provided unwavering faith in this long shot of a book since the moment I first told him about it in 2003. My agent Jill Marsal fought long and hard for this book, and for me. Thank you, Jill.

Anyone who knows me knows that my three siblings, all older, are also my heroes. Each of you, in your own way, had a profound effect on this book's creation. My in-laws, Jim and Pam Ryan, have always been there for me, even after they realized what their daughter had wrought with her life. Graphic designer Shawn Ryan helped craft the proposal that got this book published, and also made, gratis, the map at the front of this book. Special thanks to the Lodge Girls and their Boys, especially Manoj and Alexis Ali-puria, for the donation of their old laptop computer back when I didn't have money to buy one. Thanks to Tim and Patricia Ryan for their hospitality and research assistance in Las Vegas. Terry Dona-ho responded to my unannounced visit and request to dig up a sore subject (and my subsequent phone calls) with grace and patience.

The Federal Bureau of Prisons dealt with me with profession-alism and dependability, particularly the staffs at USP Lee County and at FCC Beaumont Medium. My thanks goes also to the Hermo-sa Beach Library, the Redondo Beach Public Library, the Manhat-tan Beach Public Library, the Torrance Public Library, the San Pe-dro Public Library, the Pomona Public Library, the San Bernardino Public Library, the Los Angeles Public Library system, and the Los Angeles County Public Library system. Chris Hale and Mike Sherrard were bottomless mines of insightful information, sto-ries, and support. Dozens of current and former football players donated frank and vivid recollections, spoke with me when they neither had to nor wanted to, and helped me get to know the Dar-ryl Henley of 1984–94. Kym Taylor courageously conjured dis-tant memories, good and bad, that she probably would rather have kept to herself. Thank you, Kym. Mike Collins, the world's biggest Rams fan, allowed me to watch the man described on these pages do what he did best, often under trying circumstances, by providing me with a DVD of every Rams and UCLA game I requested of him. This footage was one of my most valuable research tools.

Darryl Henley's story is a Los Angeles story. The archives of the *Los Angeles Times* were an integral part of telling it. I cannot sufficiently thank the writers and editors who worked on this story over the years. Their names are too numerous to list, but a few come readily to mind. T. J. Simers was more qualified to write this book than I, but instead he dedicated himself in the midnineties to documenting Henley's athletic and legal journey, professionally, personally, tirelessly, daily. Any writer working on a book like this would give his right arm for insights like the ones Simers provided to *Times* readers as the story was unfolding in real time. Simers repeatedly disproved his intimidating reputation by giving both his time and his knowledge whenever I asked for them. (Eric Karros put me in touch with Simers, and encouraged me onward before and after that.) Barbara Kingsley, formerly of the *Orange County Register*, wrote vividly and responsibly about the Henley trial eighteen years ago, and in our conversations made me feel as if I were sitting next to her in those wooden rows in that Santa Ana courtroom. Other writers worthy of mention include, but are certainly not limited to, Bob Keisser, Dave Strege, Chris Dufresne, Steve Bisheff, Mike Downey, Anna Cekola, Susan Marquez-Owen, John McDonald, Thomas Bonk, Tracy Weber, and Davan Maharaj. I will lift the name of Holly Kennelley, archivist at the *Inland Valley Daily Bulletin*, as an example of the hundreds of people whose names I didn't catch, people who steered me in the right direction for no other reason than human generosity. Jeff Pearlman lent advice, direction, and encouragement.

Marc Dellins, from his seat atop the watchtower of UCLA Athletics, gave me his time, his stories, his office, his files, his photos — even his photocopier. Andy and Ludina Sandoval stored a large chunk of this story in their garage for ten years. Thanks for opening it, and the rest of your home, to me.

My sincere thanks goes to the students and faculty of Damien High School, especially Steve Patten, Teresa Soltis, Scott Morrison, John Carroll, and most of all, Tom Carroll. Thanks to Julian Flores, Mary Larsen, and the rest of the faculty and students at Duarte High School. More gratitude than I can convey in this space goes to The Law Office of Ira Fierberg. My attorney Jonathan Kirsch is also the greatest man I know. My friends Jeremy Green and Jason Wormser aren't far behind.

Former federal prosecutor Marc Harris was generous with his time, his memories, and his resources; I am in his debt. Steven Kinney communicated with me bravely. Bill Kopeny and Jim Riddet cleared valuable time for me in their busy schedules. Special thanks to Charles Hack and Anthony Brooklier. To court reporter Nancy Staack: thank you for your patience and endurance. Ontario Police detective Mike Ortiz was an open book. Thanks, Mike.

Mr. and Mrs. Chuck Knox dealt patiently with my persistence. (Knox politely declined to speak with me. *Hard Knox*, by Bill Plaschke, helped me understand why, and explained the fierce loyalty within the man who stood by Henley when everyone else ran from him. Rest in peace, Coach.) Tom Maher, head football coach at Pasadena City College, didn't know me from Adam, but he let me snoop around his archives anyway.

John Feinstein, whose book *The Punch* knocked down the first domino that eventually led to this book's existence, remains one of the faces on my writers' Mount Rushmore. Thanks for inspiring me and my generation of reporters from afar, John. You, too, David Halberstam. Austin Murphy is my friend and idol. I miss Ralph Wiley. Journalist nonpareil Mark Bowden gave this strange young writer a few minutes of his time, and some much-needed advice, in a time of crisis. So did Bill Moushey.

Eric Weinberger of NFL Network in Los Angeles provided support, advice, and intermittent employment throughout my work on this project. My relationships with Brian Lockhart and all of the talented producers and production assistants at NFLN are among my most treasured. Rich Eisen and Charles Davis believed in me and made sure I knew it. If I have a son, I want him to be as kind and genuine as Fran Charles.

No one has furthered my writing career more than my trusted editor at *Sports Illustrated*, B. J. Schecter.

This book exists because its editor and shepherd, Rob Taylor of the University of Nebraska Press, is at heart a dreamer, and at work a rare and uncompromising talent. Thank you, Rob. I'm honored to have shared a bunker with the press's editorial soldiers Courtney Ochsner, Sara Springsteen, Cara Pesek, and Tish Fobben. Copy editor Elaine Otto was much more than just a copy editor.

The jurors who served during the Henley trial and spoke to me years later about it deserve to have this book dedicated to them only slightly less than my wife does.

Finally I'll thank my parents, Bob and Marilyn McKnight, for giving me life and the unconditional love that has filled each day of it.

Notes

Chapter 1

1. The winner of that award was quarterback Steve Beuerlein, who would go on to play seventeen years in the NFL.

Chapter 2

1. Henley's college teammate Troy Aikman was named Super Bowl MVP. Chris Hale, Henley's boyhood friend from Duarte, played for the losing team, the Bills.

2. Excerpt from Tracy Donaho's sixty-seven-page handwritten statement, which she completed in December 1993. Spelling and syntax appear as they appear in the original document unless otherwise noted.

Chapter 3

1. Darryl and the 1985 Alpha pledges were given the pledge-class name Sawa, a Swahili word meaning equality, chosen because less than 6 percent of UCLA's student body was African American.

Chapter 4

1. Jennifer Wilson declined to be interviewed

for this book, explaining that her daughter had once "loved Darryl and looked up to him like a father," and she did not want her to learn what had become of him. Wilson also asked that her name be changed, a request that was honored.

Chapter 5

1. The drug Irvin tested positive for was kept confidential, but he had tested positive for marijuana two summers earlier, so it was assumed at the time that it was marijuana again.

Chapter 6

1. Earl Thomas was Henley's homebuilder; he lived down the street from Henley's property in Lithonia, Georgia.

Chapter 7

1. All times local, unless noted.

2. West explained to Dabney that his current car was a rental with out-of-state plates, which might attract unwelcome attention from airport police. (It was the Chevy Lumina Darryl had rented in Atlanta.)

3. Tracy claimed throughout her statement that she believed she was carrying cash, not drugs.

4. Garey West was indicted in Memphis that same day, on unrelated federal counterfeiting charges. No one involved with the drug conspiracy knew about his indictment, including West, who wouldn't learn of it until several weeks later.

5. This call was made from the landline in the Post Chastain apartment, which had been transferred to Willie's name.

Chapter 8

1. TFA = Task Force Agent (a DEA acronym, interchangeable with TFO, Task Force Officer).

2. The car rental staff reported that these items were in the Mitsubishi upon its return.

3. Airport security was much more relaxed in 1993 than after 2001. As would be proven repeatedly during the Henley case, travelers often flew without presenting identification.

4. Telephone records indicate that Darryl left his cell phone with Willie before getting out of the car at Café Dimitri.

5. Willie had told Tracy to have a story ready in case things went wrong,

she said. (Tracy would later claim that Darryl had told her to have a story ready.)

Chapter 9

1. Wallace was convicted of stealing more than $300,000 in insurance money from the family of a deceased LAPD officer.

2. Shaw was under investigation himself at the time, the details of which remained as hidden in 2012 as in 1993.

Chapter 10

1. She meant the contents of the overnight bag she gave to Henley just before her arrest.

Chapter 11

1. During the Southern Lights trial, McLaughlin's DEA supervisor told the media that Gary Tucker was not a harmless gardening store owner but "a bum . . . a parasite . . . a master of deceit [and] a marijuana czar." McLaughlin helped the court calculate the Tuckers' sentence based on his estimate of how many plants had been grown with equipment purchased at the store. "I stopped computing at 16,000 plants," McLaughlin told the judge.

In an unrelated case, also in 1992, two nephews of Missouri governor John Ashcroft (later the U.S. attorney general) were arrested and charged with production and possession of marijuana following a raid that uncovered sixty marijuana plants—with lighting, irrigation, and security systems—in the basement of twenty-five-year-old Alex Ashcroft's house. Alex Ashcroft received three years state probation and one hundred hours of community service. He failed his first state-mandated drug test, yet no further sanctions were taken against him. Adam Ashcroft was not prosecuted.

2. A "Dooley" (or "Dually") is a pickup truck styled with two ("dual") tires on each end of the rear axle (four rear tires total).

Chapter 13

1. Manning and Dodds watched a movie that night called *American Me*, about the rise of LA's Mexican Mafia.

Chapter 14

1. Screenwriter and aspiring documentary filmmaker Laura McKinny, who recorded the infamous Fuhrman tapes, was working at the time as a tutor to UCLA student athletes. She was at UCLA when Henley was playing

football there, and although she never interacted with Henley, McKinny worked closely with James Washington, one of Henley's closest friends. In fact, it's mentioned in the Simpson evidence that Washington accompanied McKinny to one of her interviews with Fuhrman so that Washington could participate in the interview, which he did.

2. Kinney would often record the nightly news and send the tapes to his parents so they could watch their son chase Henley.

3. By comparison, the average sentences given to those convicted of sexual abuse and manslaughter were sixty-eight months and thirty months, respectively.

4. There was no evidence presented during the lengthy Henley investigation that Bustamante had conducted drug business with other professional athletes.

Chapter 16

1. It would turn out to be the first of three NBA retirements for Jordan.

2. In handing over the disk, Kellogg appeared to have violated the attorney-client privilege between Henley and Wallace. After all, Roger Cossack would argue later, the Henley disk was unrelated to the purpose of Kellogg's search. (Cossack's argument on the subject before the U.S. Supreme Court in 1984 had led to new policies about the admissibility of seized materials.) Whether the Henley disk would be admissible in court was an issue to be hashed out later, by which time Kellogg would change his allegiance and claim that Eliot had asked him to lie on the stand. Kellogg, it seemed, resented the U.S. Attorney's Office because of its prosecution of a fellow LAPD officer who had been involved in the Rodney King beating.

3. Tracy Donaho made it through the second round of tryouts for the 1993 Rams' cheerleaders before the pressure and the rumors became too much. The *Orange County Register* reported that Tracy made a tearful call to her supervisor, who told the media: "We talked to her briefly on the phone, and she said she just couldn't continue."

Chapter 17

1. Their father was Suge Knight's fraternal uncle.

Chapter 18

1. Rayburn was a senior when Thomas was in seventh grade and Darryl in sixth, so he never met either of them. He had a younger brother who played football with Thomas on the Damien varsity.

2. Rayburn said later that his clerkship under Taylor is what first "exposed him to criminal law and trials and made him realize they were the focus of his career interest." He called Taylor "a true champion among people." (In an unrelated coincidence, a DEA agent on the case had once been Willie Mc-Gowan's teammate on the Pasadena City College football team. This agent, Steve Azzam, had worked an undercover assignment in 1990 in which he had tried to buy cocaine from McGowan. When McGowan recognized the fullback-turned-fed inside the steakhouse where they met, Willie excused himself and snuck out of the restaurant.)

Chapter 19

1. Wallace, who had advised McGowan to flee to San Diego, was making a habit of obstructing justice. The previous December, federal agents had helped Gary "Little G" Dabney record a phone call to Wallace during which she coached Dabney on his upcoming grand jury appearance. "I think probably that they're going to try to ask about whether or not a white girl came to your place," Wallace told Dabney, "and I think that rather than pleading the Fifth it might be better just to say, 'I don't recall,' you know, 'There were several people that came by,' or something like that. . . . For them to even be fucking with you is really a waste of time. . . . They shouldn't even be fucking with you, period."

2. Rex had been interviewed by Kinney and McLaughlin at his home in September 1993.

3. When Rex learned that his cell was on the same floor as Bustamante's—a volatile situation considering the death threats Bustamante had made against Rex's family—Rex wondered if the government was trying to set up a fight between them. (Estranged codefendants are supposed to be kept apart.) Rex and many others believed that a good scrap between Rex and Bustamante could be redefined by the government as evidence of the Henleys' soured relationship with their drug supplier.

4. Years later McDonnell could not locate what he said was the only audiotape of that day's show.

Chapter 21

1. Winkler would be late for court at least four times during the trial. Taylor fined him after his fourth infraction.

2. Darryl was also paying Willie McGowan's two trial attorneys.

3. The Simpson trial was tried in Los Angeles Superior Court and was not subject to the jury rules of Orange County's federal court.

4. Pronounced "like kiwi fruit," he explained in court.

5. Pronounced Mal-uh-KOW-skee.

6. The names of all jurors have been changed except Malachowski, Quihuis, and O'Reilly. The biographical and demographic information of each juror has not been changed.

Chapter 22

1. The track meet was in April, not May.

2. Tracy's plane landed at 10 a.m.

3. This principle, called "inevitable discovery," was the subject of much anti-Taylor criticism in 2005, when Taylor gave privileged letters (written by a defendant to his attorney) to the prosecution in a fraud case that resulted in an eleven-year prison sentence.

Chapter 24

1. More evidence in the "who-pursued-who" argument: Tracy called Darryl's apartment thirty-five times in June, whereas, from June through November, only thirty-three calls were made to Tracy from all of the phones registered to Darryl Henley.

2. Willie McGowan recalled years later that Eric Manning had been at the TGI Friday's meeting back in April, with Darryl and Tracy, and that Manning had "charmed the pants off Tracy" and dealt with her directly in the weeks following. McGowan repeated the rumor about Tracy and Manning becoming sexually involved at some point after that meeting.

3. Hogan and Roey—the only other people present—said nothing in their trial testimony or in their thorough DEA reports about Henley asking to speak with Tracy alone.

Chapter 25

1. "Ah, the mind boggles at this continuing law school exam that's been going on," Taylor said at one point during the process. "Has anybody passed this exam?" Cossack replied. "This is the hardest exam I have ever taken."

Chapter 26

1. The number of boxes was never quantified other than with the word "several." There looked to be about six rolls in the photograph.

2. Shetelle Clifford said McLaughlin tried the same tactic. "And then also with females, [McLaughlin asked] if that would change my view," Clifford testified. "If that would change how I thought about Darryl, if I thought perhaps he cheated on me or something."

3. Jennifer had already testified that after McLaughlin left her house following one interview, he called her and said he had "left his wallet at my house and he had to come back and get it."

"Were you concerned about that?" Chaleff asked.

"Well I was wondering why he would even take his wallet out anyway. I—yeah, I was. I thought there was a purpose behind it."

Chapter 27

1. In camera = private (from the Latin: "in a chamber").

2. "They didn't say it to him," Eliot clarified, "but loud enough—he was the only one there—loud enough so that he could hear it and he believes for the specific purpose that he could hear it."

3. Although Malachowski's prior trial experience with Rayburn was the reason he was dismissed from the jury, the *LA Times* reported at least twice that Malachowski was dismissed for "work reasons." The *Times* never corrected the error (just as the *Register* never updated its copy about Tracy Donaho having spent only fifteen hours with the prosecution).

Chapter 28

1. This private meeting was about the government's allegations that a witness had been offered a bribe by the defense (allegations that were later proven meritless).

2. In the fall of 1993, in a downtown LA prison, Bustamante had tried repeatedly to speak in person with Cuevas about changing his story. The prison kept them apart, but Bustamante persuaded Cuevas to meet him at a Mormon worship service—one of the few places where estranged inmates were allowed to share the same space. "We were both Mormons for a day," Bustamante joked later. During this service, Bustamante offered Cuevas $20,000 to say that *Eric Manning* had been the cocaine supplier and that Bustamante and Cuevas had merely been Manning's debt collectors. When Cuevas declined, Bustamante called him on "the phone" (the ventilation shafts in prison) and asked, "Is your son walking yet?" followed by a demand that Cuevas "work with me." Cuevas did not respond. He was awakened one morning by two men who stabbed him in the ribs before the guards could regain control of the unit.

Chapter 29

1. Brooklier's father was LA Mob boss Dominic Brooklier. The younger Brooklier did not file tax returns between 1989 and 1996, explaining later

that "after my father died (in 1984), I did some things I am not proud of."
Like his present client, Brooklier had also had his problems with cocaine,
which may have enhanced his standing as one of the best "ugly case" defense
attorneys in LA ("ugly case" referring to matters involving drugs, sex, or
booze), and landed him in the Rolodexes of several Hollywood celebrities.

Chapter 30

1. Chaleff pointed out that his own investigator (Woolsey) had discovered these calls, not the DEA. (Tracy made the calls from her friend Wendy's house.)

Chapter 31

1. Josh described him in court as about six feet tall, black, and bald with a Fu Manchu moustache and a "medium to heavy build" (a description that matched none of the conspirators).

2. Donahue's appearance added to what was already a veritable Bruin alumni meeting. In addition to the lead defendant, Taylor, Chaleff, Cossack, Brooklier, Alexander, and Hack all held UCLA degrees. (Hack's acceptance letter to UCLA's law school in 1969 had been signed by Cossack, an associate dean at the time.)

3. Rayburn and Kinney indicated that these witnesses were frightened to come forward. The gentleman in the wheelchair could not have been called as a witness at this hearing because of the short notice.

4. It was Ron Knight, who, along with his brother Donald, was never mentioned by name during the trial despite the repeated allegations that they had tried to taint it. Years later, Kinney described his confrontation with Knight this way: "I was instructed [by Eliot] to ask [Knight] for ID. When I did so, he told me to go fuck myself. I put my hand on my gun and said I might blow his head off. 'We can go right now.' I went to the marshals about it, but they said, 'We can't make him [present identification].' . . . I was more upset with the marshals than with [Knight]."

5. Bernard Lee is Manning's brother-in-law, a prosecution witness.

Chapter 32

1. Taylor was described by another reporter as "very press conscious; he reads every [media-written] word of every case he's presiding over." He had a reputation for speaking to reporters from his bench, often to take issue with something they had written.

2. Earlier in the trial, Rayburn had mentioned "phone tolls which indeed

show several calls from Mr. Henley to Mr. Dabney's residence on 7-5-1993."
"Or at least a call from Mr. Henley's number," Taylor had corrected him.

3. This juror was replaced by a twenty-four-year-old black female medical clerk, which made the racial makeup of the deciding jury seven whites, three blacks, one Latino, and one Asian (of East Indian descent).

Chapter 33

1. Darryl would later claim that he informed Cossack that morning of Malachowski's premature carpool discussions with Quihuis and O'Reilly. Cossack would testify under oath that he was not informed of these discussions.

2. Rayburn had spent much of his closing argument disproving the alibi put forth by Bustamante's counsel—that Bustamante had loaned Henley money, not cocaine.

3. It was true. Years later, after he served more than ten years in prison, Bustamante said he had neither met nor spoken with Henley prior to Tracy's arrest.

4. Regarding "the case of a suspiciously dead three-year-old girl," Cuevas was implicated by a former girlfriend in the death of her daughter, who had been alone with Cuevas shortly before she died.

Chapter 34

1. During the legal process to follow, Malachowski would try to hide this visit to Henley's home by saying he had dropped by unannounced and was turned away by Rex.

Chapter 35

1. The pad on which Darryl had written Malachowski's phone number ten days earlier had been green.

2. Among Malachowski's other observations: he said he had heard Shawn O'Reilly say he "wanted to have sex with Miss Eliot [and] with Tracy Donaho." O'Reilly commented on their legs and see-through tops. Quihuis also "talked about having sex" with Eliot and Donaho, and "thought that Mr. Rayburn was on cocaine. . . . He said he could tell in his eyes and the way he was acting."

Chapter 36

1. In a letter dated May 15, Jackson responded: "You can be sure that my office will be following this situation closely as it unfolds."

2. The previous day, Hill had conducted the first one-on-one TV interview with Mike Tyson since Tyson's release from prison.

3. This was the same proverb Eric Henley wrote as his senior quote in the 1987 Damien yearbook.

4. A fourth juror would state during an interview for this book that he and a fifth juror heard O'Reilly refer to the defendants with racial slurs in the jury room.

Chapter 37

1. Malachowski had not been indicted at this point. His arrest was the result of a "criminal complaint"—an indictment's precursor—that alleged that Malachowski had tried to bribe a juror without officially charging him with that crime.

2. The parenthetical was Rayburn's.

3. "One day not long ago," wrote David Margolick of the *New York Times*, "a local lawyer, Jay Jaffe, approached Roger Cossack [in an LA restaurant]. 'Rog, my ratings are higher than yours,' Mr. Jaffe declared. 'Nationally, but not internationally,' Mr. Cossack replied."

4. Correctional officer.

5. Anderson later claimed that he had crossed paths with Henley before Henley's incarceration and that his brother, an LAPD officer, had once dated Angela Wallace. Darryl said he never knew Anderson prior to his incarceration.

Chapter 38

1. The quotation marks around *mandatory* were the newspaper's.

2. Quihuis had taken the stand earlier that week, but only to plead the Fifth Amendment. Years later, Henley would subscribe to the idea expressed by Harvard law professor Randall Kennedy, who, in his book *Race, Crime, and the Law*, wrote that Rule 606(b) "permits disclosure by jurors for the sake of informing or entertaining the public"—the media's questioning of jurors after the verdict, for example—"but withdraws any legal recognition to disclosures by jurors that reveal juror bias in deliberations." Kennedy continued: "[Rule 606(b)] further distort[s] an unbalanced regime that is willing to invest huge amounts of energy into sifting prospective jurors prior to trial but is unwilling to invest even relatively small amounts of energy to examine jury verdicts where there is reason to suspect their integrity."

3. "Marcus McGill" = DEA investigator Eric Miller, working in an undercover capacity. From here on, undercover investigators are referred to by their current role. For example, when Eric Miller is discussing strategy with Steven Kinney, he is Eric Miller. When he is undercover speaking to suspected criminals, he is Marcus McGill.

4. The same house at the heart of Henley's alleged improper diversion of funds during his trial.

5. John Rayburn at first agreed to be interviewed for this book, then requested that a list of questions be submitted to him beforehand. More than two years after this list of fifty-six questions was sent, and after several follow-up requests for an interview, neither Rayburn nor the U.S. Attorney's Office of Public Affairs had accepted or declined. Deirdre Eliot did not respond to the author's initial letter, nor did she return phone calls. Malachowski's public defender cited attorney-client privilege as his reason for declining to be interviewed. He did not return the author's phone calls. Through the FBI's Office of Public Affairs, the six FBI agents who worked the Henley case declined the author's written interview requests. The six DEA agents who worked the Henley case also declined to be interviewed through that agency's Office of Public Affairs.

Chapter 39

1. Eichenberger at first seemed open to being interviewed for this book, but shortly afterward, on the advice of his DEA superiors, he requested a list of questions he would be asked. Upon receiving this list, he declined the interview request and declined to confirm whether he even knew George Eliot.

2. The C = cocaine.

3. Jumped on it = mixed the drugs with filler to increase profit. Synonyms: stepped on it, hit it, whacked it.

4. Curly = cocaine.

5. GS = Group Supervisor. SA = Special Agent.

Chapter 40

1. *Taken off the count* is prison lingo meaning killed, eliminated. ("The count" refers to the daily tally of inmates.)

2. The math: Joey had agreed to front the eight units of heroin to Henley for $125,000 per unit. Jimmy's clients were willing to pay $160,000 per unit, tops; $160,000 – $125,000 = $35,000 profit per unit. Darryl and Jimmy were splitting things 50-50, which would have left Darryl with a profit of $17,500 per unit.

Chapter 41

1. "The dealers here cannot dilute this heroin any further." (Jimmy was saying that it wasn't as pure as Joey had promised.)

Chapter 42

1. UM = Unidentified Male.

2. He was no relation to DEA agent Kevin McLaughlin.

Chapter 43

1. The article also stated that Henley "was drafted in the first round in 1988" and that he was a Pro Bowl player. (Henley was drafted in 1989 and never made the Pro Bowl.)

2. Darryl had asked Marc Harris to recommend a lenient sentence for Eric in exchange for his own guilty plea. Eric would eventually be sentenced to five years in prison. He completed his sentence quietly in Texas, where he currently lives with his wife and three children.

Epilogue

1. Four guards were charged in February 2006 with smuggling cell phones and other contraband into MDC.

Source Notes

A citation consisting of only initials or a name indicates that the source was a personal interview with that party. For passages in the book that appear to need sourcing yet are not sourced, it should be assumed that (a) Darryl Henley was my only source, (b) that I interviewed the person being quoted, (c) that the sources are implied or stated within the passage itself, or (d) that the sources were granted confidentiality. The note "author's interviews" indicates either a confidential source or, more commonly, the shortening of a long list of interviewees.

Abbreviations

AUSA	assistant U.S. attorney
BQ	Bryan Quihuis
DH	Darryl Henley
EH	Eric Henley
GD	Gary Dabney
GJT	grand jury testimony
GW	Garey West
LAT	*Los Angeles Times*
MM	Mike Malachowski
NYT	*New York Times*
OCR	*Orange County Register*

38 **"To a very special person"**: Plaintiff's exhibit 69, *United States v. Rafael Bustamante, et al.*, 1995.

39 **Soon after his return to Atlanta:** DH; TT of Jennifer Wilson.

40 **Tracy was one of many women:** Phone records.

40 **Before he became embroiled:** RH; DH; Henley family; DEA-6 report, September 17, 1993; TT of Demetra Henley; RH presentence report.

41 **Hewitt asked Henley if he could play:** DH; Todd Hewitt; OCR, June 18, 1992. Accounts vary as to which Saturday the charity game was played, April 17 or April 24, 1993. The Mount SAC Relays were held April 17, 1993.

Chapter 5

43 **In July 1989:** UCLA transcript.

43 **The Rams also signed Thomas Henley:** DH; Thomas Henley III; LAT, May 23, 1989.

46 **"I want to get to the Super Bowl":** OCR, August 21, 1990.

48 **"best coach in the world":** LAT, June 21, 1995.

49 **"I hated going to the stadium":** Jeff Benedict and Don Yaeger, *Pros and Cons: The Criminals Who Play in the NFL* (New York: Warner Books, 1998).

Chapter 6

53 **On April 16, 1993:** DH; WM.

54 **Though he was nearing thirty:** Pasadena City College archives; San Bernardino County Sheriff's Department records; California DMV records; DEA-6 report, September 20, 1990; TT of Steve Azzam.

55 **Darryl and Willie were shooting the breeze:** DH; WM; TD statement; TT of TD.

57 **back in Atlanta, at Freaknik:** DH; *Atlanta Journal Constitution*, April 11, 1999; *Chicago Tribune*, April 17, 1999; *Washington Post*, April 23, 1995; GJT of GD.

60 **Tracy visited 2105 Wildflower Circle:** DH; TD statement; TT of TD, Donna Henson, and Josh Henson.

60 **Darryl later wrote a timeline:** DH memo to trial counsel, undated.

60 **a series of salary advances:** DH; TT of Jay Zygmunt; DH Rams contracts.

61 **back to the blind date:** DH; TT of Shetelle Clifford.

61 **Darryl and Jennifer flew to the Cancun Jazz Festival:** Travel records; Brea Community Hospital records; TT of Jennifer Wilson and Cancun travelers.

62 **Willie trolled behind:** *Outside the Lines,* ESPN, May 14, 2000.

62 **A kilo of cocaine sold:** TT of Brian Sullivan; interview with Brian Sullivan.

63 **After his second year at Pasadena:** WM; DH; SK; other interviews.

67 **"You know you need to call somebody":** LAT, January 22, 2000.

Chapter 7

68 **Willie McGowan and his friend Eric Manning arrived:** Airline records; Hampton Inn receipt. Information regarding flights and calls, in this and all chapters, was gleaned from travel records and phone records presented at trial.

69 **"five other unidentified black males":** DEA-6 report, August 26, 1993.

70 **Rex, who was supposed to have flown:** RH.

70 **At 7:00 a.m. sharp:** DEA-6 report, July 19, 1993; TT of TD.

70 **As Darryl waited:** DH; DEA-6 report, July 19, 1993.

71 **Gary Dabney was a former gang member:** GJT and TT of GD and Amy Thompson; TT of TD; TD statement; DEA-6 report, October 14, 1993; DEA-6 report, October 19, 1993; DEA interview of GD, December 8, 1993.

71 **He even brought Willie with him:** DH; DH undated memo to counsel; TT of Shetelle Clifford.

72 **Tracy Donaho looked so young:** GJT of Amy Thompson.

73 **"Oh, you're being paranoid":** DH.

73 **Darryl drove to the Atlanta airport:** DH; DH memo to attorneys, 1993.

74 **Darryl informed the management:** DH; DEA-6 report, August 18, 1993.

74 **Willie called the phone company:** DH; WM; DH memo to attorneys, 1993.

Chapter 8

78 **The floorboard in the back:** DEA-6 report, August 26, 1993.

78 **Darryl received a page:** DH; TD statement; TT of TD.

79 **Willie wanted to prove:** DH; TD statement; TT of TD.

79 **Darryl got out of the car:** DH; TT of TD; TD statement; WM; DEA-6 report, July 16, 1993.

81 **"Hi, I'm Darryl Henley":** TT of Agis Karakostas; DEA-6 report, August 4, 1993.

81 **The first person Henley called:** DH; TT of Chuck Knox; DEA interviews of Rod Perry and Joe Vitt, November 29, 1994.

81 **They ordered food:** DEA-6 report, August 4, 1993; TT of TD; TD statement; TT of Agis Karakostas.

81 **It was well after lunch now:** DH; TT of TD; TD statement; DEA-6 reports; TT of Agis Karakostas.

81 **The restaurant's pay phone rang:** DH; TT of Chuck Knox; DEA-6 report, October 7, 1993.

82 **At the wheel of the van:** TT of Joe Maccione; defense interview of Joe Maccione, January 21, 1995; author's interview with Joe Maccione.

83 **Tracy used a pay phone:** TD statement; TT of TD; DEA-6 report, July 16, 1993; TT of Al Hogan.

83 **"Why don't you let me know":** TT of Al Hogan.

84 **Darryl made sure once again:** DH; TD statement; TT of TD.

84 **Tracy used Darryl's cell phone:** TD statement; DH phone records.

84 **As soon as he hung up:** TT of Al Hogan.

85 **Hogan gently steered Tracy away:** DH; TT of TD; TD statement; TT of Al Hogan; DEA-6 reports.

85 **Lisa Roey was not as quick:** TT of Lisa Roey.

85 **"The color completely left her":** TT of Al Hogan.

Chapter 9

87 **Shirley Donaho, Tracy's mother:** Ontario Police Department report by Mike Ortiz, undated; author's interview with Mike Ortiz.

88 **"That's BS":** TT of TD.

89 **efforts were already under way:** TT of TD, Al Hogan, and Lisa Roey; DEA-6 reports.

90 **Shetelle finished her corrections:** DH; fax from DH to Angela Wallace; Gerry Chaleff trial notes; TT of Shetelle Clifford.

90 **Henley had no way of knowing:** Court records; LAT; author's interviews.

91 **The sight of her daughter:** TT of TD, Al Hogan, and Lisa Roey; Clayton County jail records.

92 **Tracy Ann Donaho was born:** TD statement; TT of TD; Downey Police Department records; Esperanza High School records; author's interviews.

93 **"Everything is going to be okay":** TT of Lisa Roey.

93 **Angela Wallace got there too late:** TT of TD; Clayton County jail records.

94 **in fact she had met with:** DEA-6 reports; TT of TD and Lisa Roey.

94 **Darryl snuck out:** DH; DH memo to Gerry Chaleff, undated.

95 **John Shaw showed up:** DH; LAT, August 17, 1994.

95 **He told his little brother:** DH; Henley family; GJT of Dorothy Henley and Thomas Henley III.

96 **That same magnitude:** DH; Steve Israel; Robert Bailey.

Chapter 10

98 **"We are on tape":** Audiotape and transcript of LAPD interview of TD, July 25, 1993.

99 **"Darryl, um, this is Tracy"**: Audiotape N-15 (LAPD), July 25–28, 1993.

100 **The driver's door opened:** DH; RB; GJT and TT of Denise Manning.

101 **He went straight to Chuck Knox's room:** DH.

102 **Garey West was not an easy man to find:** GW fake IDs; Montclair Police Department and court records; GJT and TT of GD; TT of Stephen Lux; GW interview; DEA-6 reports; author's interviews.

102 **The DEA had investigated:** DEA-6 reports, August 10 and 17, 1993.

104 **Woolsey gave Darryl a 9mm Glock:** DH.

104 **Henley was preparing:** *LAT*, August 1 and 3, 1993; also the *OCR* and *San Diego Union-Tribune*.

104 **His house in Brea, meanwhile:** NFL Security interview of DH, August 30, 1993.

105 **An injured shoulder:** DEA-6 reports; *OCR*, August 15, 1993.

Chapter 11

106 **the DEA conducted a search:** DEA-6 reports; TT of Kevin McLaughlin.

107 **The preseason game in Cleveland:** DH; T. J. Simers; author's interviews.

109 **Kevin McLaughlin was on a roll:** Scott Henry, "Forgotten Man," *Creative Loafing Atlanta*, December 4, 2002; author's interviews.

111 **After the game:** DH; police interviews, September 9, 1993; game program.

111 **When McLaughlin called Chaleff's cocounsel:** DH; photocopy of sample, September 1, 1993.

112 **Anthony "Q" Newman:** DH; interview with Anthony Newman and other interviews, including Todd Hewitt.

Chapter 12

115 **Until Rafael Bustamante showed up:** DH; RB; Anaheim Police Department report, September 8, 1993; TT of Alejandro Cuevas and Carrie Ellsworth; DEA interview of Alejandro Cuevas, September 25, 1993; DEA interviews of Chuck Knox.

120 **"When I started school":** "Declaration of A. Brooklier," April 1, 1994; TT of Anthony Boyce; California Highway Patrol report of RB arrest, February 24, 1991; RB.

121 **In 1991 Bustamante was pulled over:** *State of California v. Rafael Bustamante*, 1991, case #GA006923; Memorandum of Points and Authorities by AUSA, October 1993.

121 **That probation was still in effect:** DEA-6 report, October 7, 1993; RB; WM.

121 **Henley was "the bait":** Anthony Brooklier closing argument, March 17, 1995.

121 **with the whole deal gone to hell:** DEA interview of Alejandro Cuevas, September 25, 1993; TT of Alejandro Cuevas; DEA-6 report, October 5, 1993; RB.

123 **"a short, chunky black male":** *USA Today*, January 27, 2000.

Chapter 13

125 **Willie thought that Bustamante had done it:** DH; WM; RB.

125 **One witness said:** San Bernardino County Sheriff's Department. Most details about Eric Manning's murder were gleaned from the SBCSD's thick file (aka "murder book") on case #093-00157-3199-011, as well as author's interviews.

128 **Garey West was pulled over:** Texas Department of Public Safety citation R324274; DEA-6 report, May 13, 1994.

128 **the Rams restructured Henley's contract:** Ted Woolsey notes, September 1993.

128 **Woolsey would drive Henley to work:** DH; Todd Hewitt; Henley family; Ted Woolsey memoranda.

129 **Woolsey helped Darryl move:** DH; hotel records.

129 **Thomas returned home from New York City:** Thomas Henley III; GJT of Thomas Henley III.

129 **Thomas was at his parents' house:** RB; Thomas Henley III; DEA interview of Alejandro Cuevas; TT of Alejandro Cuevas; author's interviews.

130 **Ted Woolsey wrote:** DH; Todd Hewitt; Ted Woolsey notes.

Chapter 14

131 **I mean narcotics isn't full:** Transcript 9, page 12, defense exhibits, *People v. Simpson*, Los Angeles County Superior Court case #BA097211.

131 **DEA special agent Steven Kinney:** Letters from SK to author; SK criminal complaint, 1996; author's interviews.

133 **Statistics showed that DEA agents:** David McClintick, *Swordfish: A True Story of Ambition, Savagery, and Betrayal* (New York: Pantheon, 1993).

134 **Woolsey tapped the phones:** DH; Thomas Henley Jr.; SK letters; audiotapes and transcripts, September 1993.

136 **Eric Manning was eulogized:** Program from service.

138 **Darryl rode in the back:** DH.

138 **As he lined up against Darryl Henley:** Mike Sherrard interview; DH.

139 **Ted Woolsey picked Henley up:** DH.

139 **McLaughlin received the first photos:** DEA-6 report, September 20, 1993.

139 **a small battalion:** SK letters; DEA-6 report, April 29, 1994.

140 **"The war against drugs":** From the writings of Lewis Lapham, which Judge Gertner cited at a speech in Boston on January 29, 1998.

141 **"drug laws are a disaster":** *NYT*, May 14, 1993.

141 **Mandatory minimum sentencing:** Numerous published sources, including the *Washington Post*, June 24, 2006.

142 **referred to as a "drug gulag":** Numerous published sources, including the *Pittsburgh Post-Gazette*, June 17, 1999.

142 **38 percent of federal inmates:** U.S. Department of Justice, Bureau of Prisons.

142 **Darryl drove to a café:** DEA-6 report, September 26, 1993; photo lineup, September 23, 1993; Frank Durazo.

143 **Ted Woolsey found Darryl's stolen Lexus:** Ted Woolsey report, September 23, 1993.

143 **During the first six days:** Henley family.

Chapter 15

147 **Darryl's leg was gushing blood:** *LAT*, September 25, 1993; DH.

148 **Cuevas called back and set the handoff:** Based on numerous interviews and law enforcement documents, including San Bernardino County Sheriff's Department report, September 29, 1993; DEA-6 report, September 29, 1993; DEA recorded calls.

149 **Darryl Henley was in Houston:** DH.

150 **Cuevas was also surrounded by federal agents:** Audiotape and transcript of Alejandro Cuevas interview, September 25, 1993.

150 **Kinney's next move:** San Bernardino County Sheriff's Department search warrant report, September 29, 1993.

151 **Bustamante's bagman, James Saenz:** Ontario Police Department transcript, September 25, 1993.

152 **Darryl emerged into sunlight:** DH; Todd Hewitt.

153 **Bustamante turned himself in:** RB; DEA-6 report, October 2, 1993.

154 **He was in a defensive backs meeting:** DH; player and media interviews.

155 **Upon meeting Darryl:** DH; Kym Taylor.

155 **"Darryl Henley?":** Interviews with Dave Strege and Steve Bisheff of the *OCR*.

156 **"Henley has not and will not":** Tracy Weber, "Rams CB under Drug Probe," *OCR*, October 5, 1993.

156 **Karl Dorrell, who at the time:** Author's interviews.

Chapter 16

158 **The day Jordan retired:** DEA-6 reports, October 7, 1993, December 1, 1994, December 5, 1994; Todd Hewitt.

159 **"We know Darryl is a very competent":** *LAT*, October 9, 1993.

160 **Eliot's frail, blonde exterior:** Author's interviews.

162 **"I could assume":** Tape and transcript of Kevin McLaughlin interview of Denise Manning, September 22, 1993.

162 **Federal grand juries consisted of:** *Pittsburgh Post-Gazette*, December 6, 1998.

163 **a skirmish erupted:** *LAT*, October 16, 1993.

164 **Henley was shocked to find:** DH; Todd Hewitt.

164 **Henley's hypoglycemia struck:** DH; author's interviews; *OCR*, July 31, 1990; *LAT*, July 31, 1990.

165 **According to league rules:** DH; author's interviews.

166 **"two weeks of seclusion":** *RPE*, October 20, 1993.

166 **"People who know me, believe me":** *OCR*, October 19, 1993.

166 **Then he read in the paper:** DH; Anthony Newman; author's interviews.

Chapter 17

168 **Some friends Henley did not need:** DH; author's interviews.

169 **rumors were swirling:** Randall Sullivan, "Unsolved Mystery of Notorious B.I.G.," *Rolling Stone*, December 15, 2005; *LAT*, July 27, 1997, January 22, 1998. These sources were also used for Suge Knight and Death Row Records passages in chapter 36.

170 **Death Row Inner City Out Reach:** DH; author's interviews.

170 **Knight was a man of contradictions:** *LAT*, May 15, 1995.

171 **One day Suge asked Darryl:** DH. Jimmy Iovine and Ron Brown did not respond to numerous interview requests.

172 **his parents and two brothers testified:** Transcripts, August 1993; Thomas Henley III.

175 **they had recovered a vacuum bag from the Brea home:** Deirdre Eliot letter, November 3, 1994.

175 **they ended up in Las Vegas:** DH; author's interviews.

176 **Ron had been a starting linebacker:** DH; *LAT*.

Chapter 18

182 **he could lean forward and whisper:** DH; interview with Brian Sullivan.

182 **he "begged Darryl" to cooperate:** SK letters.

183 **"Tangled Web of Drugs and Death":** *OCR*, December 3, 1993.

183 **Donaho hired herself a defense attorney:** TT of TD; *OCR*, December 7 and 21, 1993.

184 **Taylor was precisely the kind of judge:** U.S. district court bio, 1990–91; *LAT*, August 4, 1990, June 30, 1995.

185 **Rayburn had once been Taylor's clerk:** John Rayburn bio by San Bernardino County Bar Association, 2008; author's interviews.

186 **"portrayed as Pablo Escobar":** Interview with Jerome Stanley.

187 **"world knows where Darryl is sleeping":** Ted Woolsey memo, December 5, 1993.

188 **"garden spot of Nixonia":** *LAT*, April 27, 1994.

Chapter 19

189 **The sun was out:** DH; author's interviews.

190 **Chaleff had been in the running:** Toobin, *Run of His Life*.

191 **Constantine had taken over:** *U.S. News & World Report*, June 5, 1995; author's interviews.

191 **Because of his bond agreement:** DH.

191 **He was returning home:** DH; WM.

192 **he had made a duplicate of it:** DEA report, April 22, 1994; SK letter.

192 **"We would have let you go":** DH; WM. SK denied saying this.

192 **Rex Henley had also left LA:** RH; DEA-6 report, June 30, 1994.

193 **When he finally arrived:** RH; RB.

194 **Rex's new defense attorney:** DH; RH; Jim Riddet.

195 **"I have to have that trial":** *LAT*, August 17, 1994.

195 **The *LA Times* published:** *LAT*, August 6, 1994; also *OCR*, August 7, 1994.

195 **"I don't know about the safety":** *RPE*, August 5, 1994.

195 **Most of the Rams:** Interview with T. J. Rubley.

196 **Live on the air:** DH; Joe McDonnell.

196 **"I find it hard to believe":** *LAT*, August 29, 1994.

197 **"I was terrified":** *LAT*, August 17, 1994.

Chapter 20

198 **Henley was hemorrhaging money:** DH.

199 **"added element of tension on this team":** *OCR*, September 11, 1994.

199 **"Shoot, he can play":** *OCR*, September 11, 1994.

199 **"The Commissioner decided":** *OCR*, September 11, 1994.

199 **"Nice to have you back to battle":** DH.

200 **"They beat the Dodgers":** *NYT*, December 22, 1994.

201 **"coming to work smiling":** Robert Bailey.

202 **Kym Taylor had her doubts:** Kym Taylor; DH.

202 **Washington was determined:** James Washington; Tom Carroll.

203 **Except when the Rams:** Author's interviews.

204 **The doctors told him:** *OCR*, November 24, 1994.

204 **"We are not just losing":** *LAT*, November 28, 1994.

205 **When the team returned:** DEA-6 reports, December 1 and 5, 1994.

206 **"We just lost":** *RPE*, December 12, 1994.

206 **"We're not dead":** *LAT*, December 19, 1994.

206 **the team gathered solemnly:** *OCR*, December 25, 1994; *LAT*, December 25, 1994; Todd Hewitt.

208 **"traditional bail bondsman":** *OCR* and *RPE*, September 22, 1994.

208 **Henley granted an interview:** *OCR*, December 29, 1994.

Chapter 21

210 **It rained hard that January:** Observations on the mannerisms and moods of those present in the courtroom were obtained via newspaper accounts and/or author's interviews.

210 **He kept a bucket:** *Orange County Business Journal*, February 16, 1998.

210 **predicted to last three weeks:** AUSA memo, January 13, 1995.

211 **One of seven children:** John Rayburn bio by San Bernardino County Bar Association, 2008.

212 **Woolsey tracked down:** Ted Woolsey memos, January 10, 21, and 22, 1995.

213 **"Your case is full of holes":** Ted Woolsey memo, January 24, 1995.

213 **McLaughlin was "not happy":** Ted Woolsey memo, January 24, 1995; TT of Shetelle Clifford.

214 **McLaughlin and his partner staked out:** DEA-6 report, January 17, 1995; TT of Shetelle Clifford; DH.

215 **"impossible to convict O.J.":** *Washington Times*, June 3, 2004.

215 **LA's neighbor to the south:** *OCR*, February 26, 2001, January 21, 2003, March 20, 2003; Eric Schlosser, *Fast Food Nation: The Dark Side of the All-American Meal* (Boston: Houghton Mifflin, 2001); orangecounty.net.

218 **"Blacks rallied around O.J.":** Randall Kennedy, *Race, Crime, and the Law* (New York: Pantheon, 1997).

218 **Carroll, Damien's longtime athletic director:** Author's interviews.

219 **At 6:20 a.m.:** Upland Fire Department report, January 23, 1995; author's interviews.

219 **These were only theories:** SK letters.

220 **"Here were four African American defendants":** Charles Hack interviews.

221 **Shawn O'Reilly was one guy:** Shawn O'Reilly juror questionnaire; voir dire; FBI reports; Ninth Circuit Court of Appeals opinion, February 7, 2001; author's interviews.

221 **Twenty-five-year-old Bryan Quihuis:** Several FBI reports, September 1996.

221 **Mike Malachowski, twenty-four:** FBI interview of BQ, May 24, 1995; author's interviews.

221 **Malachowski made the cut, along with:** Juror questionnaires.

Chapter 22

223 **Darryl arrived early:** DH; *OCR*, January 28, 1995. An early example of Barbara Kingsley's clear, crisp reporting throughout the trial.

227 **"I wanted to testify":** *LAT*, March 23, 1995.

229 **Tracy said she didn't know who he was:** TT of TD.

230 **"Knox winked":** *OCR*, February 1, 1995.

230 **David Lang had defied these orders:** DH; Dorothy Henley.

230 **Miller went to dinner with Henley:** DH; interview with Chuck Miller.

230 **Ronald and Donald Knight sat together:** Trial transcripts; DH; RH; transcript of in camera hearing, February 10, 1995.

231 **Darryl's mom was ordered:** Dorothy Henley; DH.

232 **The jurors, who had gotten to know:** Author's interviews.

232 **Richards hit it off:** Interview with Edmund Richards.

232 **The other jurors felt uncomfortable:** Author's interviews.

233 **Quihuis sliced deli meat:** MM; Jerry Mulligan interview of BQ, April 20, 1995.

233 **O'Reilly was an unlikely recruit:** Shawn O'Reilly testimony, May 17, 1996; MM DEA and FBI reports; BQ FBI and defense investigator reports; author's interviews.

Chapter 23

234 **Tracy Donaho entered the courtroom:** DH; WM; author's interviews.

234 **"There was a feeling":** Interview with Susan Marquez-Owen.

235 **The defense attorneys scribbled:** DH; *OCR*, February 2, 1995.

236 **"a well-amplified voice":** *OCR*, February 2, 1995.

237 **"wonder if they were refreshing her memory":** Author's interview.

237 **"I thought she enjoyed it":** DH; author's interviews.

Chapter 24

244 **"a recorded message of rap music":** TT of Lisa Roey.

248 **"I knew what was going on"**: RH.

252 **"it wasn't for Darryl"**: Mike Ortiz and Roy Kaiser interview of TD, July 25, 1993.

254 **"We all agreed"**: *LAT*, March 29, 1995.

254 **"bringing [Tracy] to tears"**: *OCR*, February 3, 1995.

256 **"while Donaho could remember"**: *OCR*, February 4, 1995.

Chapter 25

258 **"She wasn't charged"**: Interview with Jim Riddet.

258 **"the innocent one in all this"**: DEA interview of Denise Manning, September 22, 1993.

261 **Wearing a peach-colored suit**: *LAT*, February 9, 1995.

262 **"Do you think Tracy's"**: Author's interviews; MM deposition, April 11, 1995; Jerry Mulligan interview of BQ, April 20, 1995; Jerry Mulligan interview of MM, April 24, 1995; FBI interviews of MM and BQ; MM testimony, May 17, 1996; Shawn O'Reilly declaration, May 1996; Shawn O'Reilly testimony, May 17, 1996.

264 **Darryl wrote a note**: Actual note, with handwriting that is unmistakably DH's and Gerry Chaleff's.

265 **"avoided looking at Henley"**: *OCR*, February 2, 1995.

Chapter 26

268 **During an exchange**: *LAT*, February 11, 1995.

Chapter 27

272 **Judge Taylor always adjourned at 1 p.m.**: Trial transcript, March 10, 1995.

272 **The matter at hand was serious**: Transcript of in camera hearing, February 10, 1995.

275 **Henley was unanimously regarded**: Transcript, March 10, 1995; *OCR*, January 28, 1995; author's interviews.

275 **Mike Malachowski lived at the edge**: FBI report, February 10, 1995.

279 **dying to be a part of it**: MM; author's interviews.

279 **During jury selection**: Trial transcript, January 17, 1995.

Chapter 28

281 **The Santa Ana winds**: *LAT* (Ventura ed.), March 12, 1995.

282 **they had given Gary Dabney $3,000**: GD letter, December 28, 1993; Deirdre Eliot letter, December 29, 1994; GJT of GD; TT of GD; GD photo; DEA-6 report, October 14, 1993; author's interviews.

285 **the cost of the Simpson trial:** LAT.

289 **Cuevas had lost his job:** TT of Alejandro Cuevas.

290 **But Bustamante's clout didn't matter:** RB; TT of Alejandro Cuevas; letter from AUSA, February 21, 1995; author's interviews.

290 **"A government witness testified":** LAT, February 24, 1995.

Chapter 29

292 **Tracy wrote six pages:** Photocopy of TD's notes.

293 **Denise Manning's testimony:** DEA interview of Denise Manning, September 22, 1993; GJT and TT of Denise Manning.

295 **"this angry widow":** Charles Hack.

Chapter 30

298 **It was Steven Kinney's job to testify:** SK letters.

303 **"Thomas was quiet":** Ted Woolsey memo, March 5, 1995.

Chapter 31

305 **The most powerful witnesses:** DH; Charles Hack; Donna Henson.

307 **"Sweet," he said:** Josh Henson.

308 **he had tacked Alisa's ultrasound:** DH; Kym Taylor.

308 **his Irvine-based law firm:** LAT, January 24, 1995.

308 **he was also a longtime friend:** Trial transcript, March 9, 1995; author's interviews.

308 **His sense of humor:** TT of Bill Hanley; author's interviews; LAT, June 18, 1996.

310 **Taylor called Henley and his attorneys:** Dorothy Henley; Andrew Boston; DH; FBI report, July 24, 1995; LA County Recorder's documents, March 3, 1995; cashier's check, March 3, 1995; note secured by deed of trust, March 2, 1995; court transcripts.

Chapter 32

318 **"pissed off" and "very cross":** Barbara Kingsley.

319 **the party held in his honor:** DH; author's interviews.

320 **"Did I know what was going on?":** LAT, January 22, 2000.

320 **To Darryl's horror:** Trial transcripts; author's interviews.

321 **At least one juror believed:** Author's interviews.

Chapter 33

322 **The whole thing started:** Exactly what happened between DH, MM, and BQ remained as difficult to discern after the millennium as it had been

for FBI investigators to discern in 1995–96. This part of the narrative reflects my best effort to mine threads of truth from numerous accounts of those eight days in March 1995.

322 **It was Monday night:** DH; MM; RH; Jerry Mulligan interview of MM, April 24, 1995; FBI interviews of MM; DH testimony, January 18, 1996; MM testimony, May 17, 1996; Jerry Mulligan interview of Debbie Dudek, April 20, 1995; GJT of Debbie Dudek, May 1995; author's interviews.

327 **Hanley advised Darryl:** Author's interviews (including Dorothy Henley, who was present for the second comment, which could only have been made in connection with the first).

327 **preceded by one from T. J. Simers:** Interview with T. J. Simers; *LAT*, March 23, 1995.

328 **Darryl found Roger Cossack:** DH; Roger Cossack testimony, March 12, 1996; defense memo, January 22, 1996; *LAT*, May 1, 1995; author's interviews.

329 **Chaleff had worked relentlessly:** DH; trial transcript; author's interviews.

334 **Mike had been busy:** Jerry Mulligan interview of BQ, April 20, 1995; author's interviews.

Chapter 34

337 **On the last day of the trial:** Author's interviews.

337 **Darryl was standing in his driveway:** DH; interviews with Donna Henson, Robert Jackson, and others.

339 **His pager went off:** DH; MM; author's interviews; Jerry Mulligan interview of BQ, April 20, 1995; FBI interview of BQ, May 24, 1995.

342 **The jurors elected:** Author's interviews, except where noted in the narrative.

344 **Darryl invited Mike and his wife:** MM; DH; DH testimony, January 18, 1996; author's interviews; FBI interview of Shaunti Malachowski, September 22, 1995; GJT of Carolyn Malachowski; MM testimony, May 17, 1996.

345 **"I have not thought about it":** *LAT*, March 23, 1995.

345 **"Go ahead," said the clerk:** Interview with Bob Bolton. Bolton said that this was not intended to predict the length of deliberations.

346 **Bryan wanted it to be over:** MM and BQ phone conversation, April 17, 1995.

348 **Sometime over the weekend:** DH. WM did not remember this call.

349 **"I don't believe":** *OCR*, March 29, 1995.

350 **Darryl "bowed his head":** *LAT*, March 29, 1995.

351 **A similar perspective was offered:** sk letters.

352 **in pursuit of the Henley jurors:** *LAT* and *OCR*, March 29, 1995; author's interviews.

Chapter 35

353 **Constructed in the late 1980s:** *LAT*, January 3, 1989, August 29, 2003.

354 **Rex Henley was placed among:** Deirdre Eliot letter to MDC, December 11, 1995; RH; RB; DH.

356 **Within a week, Darryl would terminate:** DH; Roger Cossack letter to Gary Taylor, May 1, 1995.

356 **"He did not expect it":** *LAT*, June 18, 1996.

357 **Worried about a government setup:** DH; MM.

358 **Bill Hanley, the Orange County lawyer:** Jim Riddet notes; Joint Excerpt of Record of Consolidated Appeals, Vol. 4; Jim Riddet memo, January 22, 1996.

359 **The consensus was that:** Defense memo, March 7, 1996.

360 **They knew Mike Malachowski lived far away:** MM; Ron Knight; Alisa Denmon; author's interviews; Jim Riddet notes regarding call with Ron Knight, April 8, 1995.

360 **one of Judge Taylor's closest colleagues:** Gary Taylor court bio, 1990–91.

361 **"I guess everything went all good":** MDC transcript of recorded calls.

Chapter 36

363 **Private eye Jerry Mulligan reported:** Quotes from Jerry Mulligan's interviews of BQ, MM, and Debbie Dudek were taken from transcripts of those interviews.

365 **"there may have been some problems":** Bob Bolton phone conversation with BQ, April 26, 1995.

365 **Taylor entered the room:** FBI interviews of Bob Bolton and Abigail Roth, June 6, 1995.

367 **As soon as he hung up:** FBI report, April 28, 1995; MM.

368 **The next day T. J. Simers drove:** *LAT*, May 1, 1995.

368 **That there had been racism present:** John McDonald.

369 **"Forget Rex, forget Willie":** RH.

369 **The FBI picked up its pace:** FBI report, May 24, 1995.

370 **On May 25 the local CBS TV:** Courtesy KCBS-2 and KCAL-9 Los Angeles.

371 **Ron Knight had been scheduled:** "Status Report re GJ Investigation," June 14, 1995.

371 **After her grand jury testimony:** Author's interviews; *LAT*, June 18, 1996.

Chapter 37

375 **And Darryl spent more time:** DH; RH.

376 **Malachowski broke down crying:** Jim Riddet declaration, January 3, 1996.

377 **"truthfully testify to the court":** Transcript of in camera hearing, October 20, 1995.

377 **The next day the government asked:** OCR, October 19, 1995.

377 **"If I tell you the truth":** FBI report, October 2, 1995.

378 **"O.J. got off":** James Washington.

378 **The week of the Simpson verdict:** LAT, October 11, 1995; *San Francisco Chronicle*, August 2, 1995.

378 **"human sound bites":** LAT, September 28, 1995.

378 **"hitting the lottery":** LAT, October 11, 1995.

378 **a taste of the surreal:** LAT, December 11, 1995.

384 **Henley's financial walls:** Notice of Trustee's Sale, November 6, 1995.

385 **Cuevas was never charged:** TT of Paula Juarez; Brief Appellant in Consolidated Appeals, April 2, 1998.

Chapter 38

387 **Clad in a green windbreaker:** LAT, January 19, 1996.

388 **it was near capacity:** LAT, January 24 and 28, 1996; OCR, January 24, 1996.

389 **"he was now telling the truth":** FBI report, February 26, 1996.

389 **"was at times heated":** OCR, March 6, 1996.

390 **another resounding victory:** AUSA Opposition to Motion for New Trial, August 1, 1996.

390 **Rule 606(b):** Supplemental Memo in Support of Motion for New Trial, June 17, 1996.

395 **By that point Darryl's parents:** LAT, June 18, 1996.

396 **Cedric McGill was one of the more creative:** U.S. district court case #96-CR-11-1; LAT, January 11, 1996; author's interviews; SK letters.

396 **Darryl asked Eric to make a few introductions:** DH; EH; DEA reports; EH presentence report.

397 **On April 1, 1996:** SK criminal complaint, April 26, 1996; EH presentence report.

397 **Shortly after 9 a.m.:** DEA-6 reports; SK criminal complaint, April 26, 1996.

398 **"[McGill] has advised me":** SK criminal complaint, April 26, 1996.

398 **With the Detroit case dead:** DEA-6 reports, May 2 and 7, 1996.

399 **"when this Gambino thing came along":** sk letters.

399 **The meeting at which Malachowski:** mm testimony, May 17, 1996; undated ausa memo; author's interviews.

400 **"The truth," he said later:** mm.

401 **Malachowski "sobbed":** *LAT*, May 10, 1996.

Chapter 39

402 **At about 12:30 a.m.:** dea-6 report, May 14, 1996.

404 **During their meeting:** dea-6 report, May 17, 1996; Marc Harris; Marc Harris notes, undated.

404 **The dea's handling:** dea-6 reports, May 14 and 17, 1996; sk letters.

404 **Marc Harris had recently won:** *LAT*, March 16, 1996, May 30, 1997; author's interviews.

405 **A member of Bansmer's investigative team:** Author's interviews.

410 **Deirdre Eliot was advised:** Deirdre Eliot letter to defense, July 16, 1996.

Chapter 40

417 **their information was still "dangerously incomplete":** Marc Harris affidavit, May 1996.

Chapter 41

429 **Rodney Anderson slept in:** fbi report, May 24, 1996; recorded calls.

430 **Bansmer had never given Mikey his pager number:** mdc transcript. These are my suppositions as to Michael Gambino's thought process, based on his inflections and an understanding of the two speakers gained by my interviews.

Chapter 42

436 **According to Cole's written report:** C. D. Cole mdc memo, May 24, 1996.

438 **Mikey appeared in court:** Government brief modifying Michael Gambino bail conditions, May 24, 1996.

Chapter 43

445 **Jimmy Washington was smarter:** dea-6 reports, May 28 and 30, 1996; sk letters.

446 **Henley faked a suicide attempt:** *LAT*, June 5, 1996.

447 **The Darryl Henley jokes came instantly:** *LAT*, August 31, 1996, October 15, 1996; *ocr*, June 6, 1996.

448 **"I've only told two other people":** Bob Keisser.

449 **"They could put Darryl Henley":** *LA Daily News,* June 1, 1996.

450 **"I'm not comfortable":** Kym Taylor.

451 **"We're talking about the U.S. government":** *LAT,* June 18, 1996.

451 **"The story went from":** Steve Bisheff.

451 **Apparently, T.H.'s hometown paper:** *Waco Tribune-Herald,* June 2, 1996.

452 **"antithesis of who he was":** Jim Riddet.

453 **"precise motive for these murders":** Marc Harris brief, October 8, 1996.

453 **"wanted Donaho and possibly Malachowski":** DH presentence report, October 1996.

453 **"Vanity and cool":** William Kopeny.

Epilogue

457 **Darryl did not meet John Gotti:** DH; T. J. Simers; *LAT,* January 22, 2000; Benedict and Yeager, *Pros and Cons.*

458 **The Tenth Circuit Court of Appeals agreed:** *PBS Frontline,* "Snitch," January 1999.

459 **Henley's good behavior:** DH; T. J. Simers; *LAT,* January 22, 2000.

465 **"The only answer":** *Washington Post,* June 17, 1996.

466 **Kinney was arrested:** *Las Vegas Review-Journal,* March 14 and 16, 2002, April 9, 2002, June 14, 2002, July 17, 2002, March 26, 2003, May 29, 2003, July 11, 2003, January 6, 2005; Associated Press, June 13, 2003, July 10, 2003; *Las Vegas Sun,* July 10, 2003; U.S. Attorney's Office Las Vegas; KRNV-TV Reno; SK letters.

Notes

484 **Kinney would often record:** SK letters.

484 **Kellogg would change his allegiance:** *LAT,* July 26, 1994; *OCR,* July 26, 1994.

486 **More evidence in the "who-pursued-who" argument:** TD and DH phone bills; author's interviews.

487 **Brooklier's father was LA Mob boss:** Interview with Anthony Brooklier, *Los Angeles* magazine, May 2000; *LAT,* September 17, 1989.

488 **Years later, Kinney described:** SK letters; DH. Ron Knight declined comment.

490 **"One day not long ago":** *NYT,* November 4, 1994.